Black Pearls of Wisdom

David Walker, Maria Stewart, Frederick Douglass, Henry Highland Garnet, Harriet Tubman, John M. Langston, John Brown, Abraham Lincoln, Sojourner Truth, Martin R. Delany, Benjamin "Pap" Singleton, Alexander Crummell, Anna J. Cooper, Booker T. Washington, Henry McNeal Turner, Moses Fleetwood Walker, W. E. B. Du Bois, Carter G. Woodson, A. Philip Randolph, Marcus Garvey, Ida B. Wells-Barnett, Mary McLeod Bethune, Father Divine, Charles Hamilton Houston, Adam Clayton Powell, Jr., Paul Robeson, Fannie Lou Hamer, Lyndon Baines Johnson, Martin Luther King, Jr., Malcolm X, Stokely Carmichael, Huey P. Newton, Angela Davis, Jesse Jackson, Barack Obama

Black Pearls of Wisdom

Voicing the African-American Journey for Freedom, Empowerment, and the Future

Edited by

Donald Spivey

CAROLINA ACADEMIC PRESS

Durham, North Carolina

Library of Congress Cataloging-in-Publication Data

Black pearls of wisdom : voicing the African-American journey for freedom, empowerment, and the future / edited by Donald Spivey.
     pages cm
  ISBN 978-1-61163-483-9 (alk. paper)
  1. African Americans--Social conditions--Sources. 2. African Ameri-
cans--History--Sources. I. Spivey, Donald.

  E185.86.B528 2014
  305.896'073--dc23

                              2013035434

CAROLINA ACADEMIC PRESS
700 Kent Street
Durham, North Carolina 27701
Telephone (919) 489-7486
Fax (919) 493-5668
www.cap-press.com

Printed in the United States of America

Contents

Preface

Martin Luther King, Jr. asked a profound question years ago that is just as important to us today: "Where do we go from here?" Today's America is plagued with the burden of racism, sexism, classism, and other isms too numerous to mention. We have in America, and indeed in the world, an economy that has left the overwhelmingly vast majority of the people drowning in a sea of unfairness, inequity, and exploitation that speaks pointedly to an order that places profits above humanity and materialistic gain above the rights, privileges, wellness, security, and decency of life of the majority. But the solution or solutions are in "the past before us." There is much to be learned from the wisdom of the elders, and today's African Americans, American society in general, and much of the world would do well to heed the messages that the thirty-five visionary leaders assembled here bequeathed us.

We better heed them for we are going backward not forward. In an America where the middle class moves each day closer to complete annihilation, black America as usual is the bellwether to the storm. It is no exaggeration to state that black Americans and the so-called African-American communities are today at their lowest ebb since the end of Reconstruction and the heydays of Jim Crow and the color line. The unemployment rate of blacks in some urban communities now tops fifty percent and there is no end in sight. The future of African-American males finds that at least three in ten will either spend time in prison or have some serious run-in with the legal system. The overall educational level of black America continues to be problematic with the highest percentage of black folk failing to finish high school since the early 1960s. Our major cities are decaying relics of what they once were. And no group finds itself more downtrodden and hopeless than black Americans. African Americans and all Americans should be asking themselves: Where do we go from here? What do we do now? How do I help myself? Is there any solution to the problems we as a people face?

History is foundation and context. It is also the roadmap, the beacon that offers understanding and direction. "What is past is prologue" is an apt phrase often cited. The voices of wisdom and solutions have been with us dating back over a hundred years. The readers are urged to imbibe the warnings, insights, and courses of action of the great minds assembled in this collection. Their insights are surprisingly timeless and invaluable. We would all do well to listen and learn from the rich tapestry of opinions and analyses offered. Whether trying to figure out how the system works or what plan to embrace and implement to circumvent today's multifaceted barriers to personal and group advancement, the elders speak and we should listen to what they have to say. They speak of freedom, social justice, and solutions to the American dilemma that range from overcoming slavery to achieving equality, from black separatism and African repatriation to building power bases and gaining economic independence, from working within the system to armed resistance against it.

White America always fares better than black, and that has never changed. But even white America is suffering under the unbridled yoke of a vicious capitalism gone wild.

Hence, blacks, browns, whites, and all groups, men and women, can benefit from a reading of the words of wisdom and guidance from the prominent historical voices brought together in this anthology, black America in particular. These powerful and thought-provoking essays, these words of wisdom from some of the greatest minds in African-American history, challenge and inspire.

Each pearl of wisdom begins with a brief background to the speaker and the document selected. Several questions are posed for the reader to consider. In each case, the reader is encouraged to interpret, contemplate, extrapolate, and to think through, on one's own terms, the ideas expressed with an eye to the past, the present, and the future. As Mary McLeod Bethune often said, "Knowledge Is Power."

Copyright Acknowledgments

David Walker, "The Wretchedness in Consequence of Ignorance," in *David Walker's Appeal to the Coloured Citizens of the World, but in particular, and very expressly, to those of the United States of America* (Boston, MA: David Walker, 1830, 3rd Edition)

Maria Stewart, "The African Masonic Hall Speech" (delivered in Boston, MA; Hartford, CT: Maria Stewart, 1833)

Frederick Douglass, "The Hypocrisy of American Slavery" (delivered in Rochester, NY; Frederick Douglass, 4 July 1852)

Henry Highland Garnet, *The Past and The Present Condition, and The Destiny of The Colored Race* (Troy, NY: Female Benevolent Society, 1848), 14–22

Harriet Tubman, "An Hour with Harriet Tubman" [interview conducted by James B. Clarke] in William Easton, *Christophe: A Tragedy in Prose of Imperial Haiti* (Los Angeles, CA: Gafton Publishing Co., 1911)

John M. Langston, "Speech to the Anti-Slavery Society, New York City, in 1855," in John M. Langston, *From the Virginia Plantation to the National Capitol: An Autobiography* (Hartford, CT: American Publishing Company, 1894)

John Brown, "Address to the Court" (Charles Town, VA: 1859)

Abraham Lincoln, "Annual Message to Congress" *Congressional Record* (Washington, DC: 1 December 1862)

Sojourner Truth, "Ain't I A Woman" (Akron, Ohio: National Suffragette Conference, 1851)

Martin R. Delany, "Practical Utility of Colored People of the Present Day as Members of Society" in *The Condition, Elevation, Emigration, and Destiny of the Colored People of the United States* (Philadelphia, PA: Martin R. Delany, 1852)

Walter L. Fleming, "'Pap' Singleton, the Moses of the Colored Exodus," *American Journal of Sociology* 15, No. 1 (July 1909), 61–82. Grateful copyright acknowledgement is given to the University of Chicago Press for permission to reprint.

Alexander Crummell, *The Relations and Duties of Free Colored Men in America to Africa: A Letter to Charles B. Dunbar* (Hartford, CT: Press of Case, Lockwood and Co., 1861)

Black Pearls of Wisdom

I

One of the most powerful spokespersons who early in the nineteenth century urged blacks to stand up and to fight for their freedom and for justice and equality was David Walker (1785–1830). The readers will hopefully find Walker's nineteenth-century clarion call, "The Wretchedness in Consequence of Ignorance," both enlightening and challenging. Black men in particular will want to take to heart Walker's abhorrence of complacency. Consider what Walker has to say about the importance of knowing one's history, especially the role of ancient Africa. Proceeding from that context, he calls to question black manhood and the need to stand tall in the face of adversity against the race. Walker prods you to rethink the role of Christianity and how religion was used in an effort of social control of African Americans. What do you think? What is the relevance of his analysis to today's African-American struggle?

"Our Wretchedness in Consequence of Ignorance"

David Walker

Ignorance, my brethren, is a mist, low down into the very dark and almost impenetrable abyss in which, our fathers for many centuries have been plunged. The Christians, and enlightened of Europe, and some of Asia, seeing the ignorance and consequent degradation of our fathers, instead of trying to enlighten them, by teaching them that religion and light with which God had blessed them, they have plunged them into wretchedness ten thousand times more intolerable, than if they had left them entirely to the Lord, and to add to their miseries, deep down into which they have plunged them tell them, that they are an inferior and distinct race of beings, which they will be glad enough to recall and swallow by and by. Fortune and misfortune, two inseparable companions, lay rolled up in the wheel of events, which have from the creation of the world, and will continue to take place among men until God shall dash worlds together.

When we take a retrospective view of the arts and sciences—the wise legislators—the Pyramids, and other magnificent buildings—the turning of the channel of the river Nile, by the sons of Africa or of Ham, among whom learning originated, and was carried thence into Greece, where it was improved upon and refined. Thence among the Romans, and all over the then enlightened parts of the world, and it has been enlightening the dark and benighted minds of men from then, down to this day. I say, when I view retrospectively, the renown of that once mighty people, the children of our great progenitor I am indeed cheered. Yea further, when I view that mighty son of Africa, Hannibal, one of the greatest generals of antiquity, who defeated and cut off so many thousands of the white Romans or murderers, and who carried his victorious arms, to the very gate of Rome, and I give it as my candid opinion, that had Carthage been well united and had given him good support, he would have carried that cruel and barbarous city by storm. But they were dis-united, as the coloured people are now, in the United States of America, the reason our natural enemies are enabled to keep their feet on our throats.

Beloved brethren—here let me tell you, and believe it, that the Lord our God, as true as he sits on his throne in heaven, and as true as our Savior died to redeem the world, will give you a Hannibal, and when the Lord shall have raised him up, and given him to you for your possession, O my suffering brethren! Remember the divisions and consequent sufferings of Carthage and of Hayti. Read the history particularly of Hayti, and see how they were butchered by the whites, and do you take warning. The person whom God shall give you, give him your support and let him go his length, and behold in him the salvation of your God. God will indeed, deliver you through him from your deplorable and wretched condition under the Christians of America. I charge you this day before my God to lay no obstacle in his way, but let him go.

The whites want slaves, and want us for their slaves, but some of them will curse the day they ever saw us. As true as the sun ever shown in its meridian splendor, my colour will root some of them out of the very face of the earth. They shall have enough of making slaves of, and butchering, and murdering us in the manner which they have. No doubt some may say that I write with a bad spirit, and that I being a black, wish these things to occur. Whether I write with a bad or a good spirit, I say if these things do not occur in their proper time, it is because the world in which we live does not exist, and we are deceived with regard to its existence.—It is immaterial however to me, who believe, or who refuse—though I should like to see the whites repent peradventure God may have mercy on them, some however, have gone so far that their cup must be filled.

But what need have I to refer to antiquity, when Hayti, the glory of the blacks and terror of tyrants, is enough to convince the most avaricious and stupid of wretches— which is at this time, and I am sorry to say it, plagued with that scourge of nations, the Catholic religion; but I hope and pray God that she may yet rid herself of it, and adopt in its stead the Protestant faith; also, I hope that she may keep peace within her borders and be united, keeping a strict look out for tyrants, for if they get the least chance to injure her, they will avail themselves of it, as true as the Lord lives in heaven. But one thing which gives me joy is, that they are men who would be cut off to a man, before they would yield to the combined forces of the whole world—in fact, if the whole world was combined against them, it could not do anything with them, unless the Lord delivers them up.

Ignorance and treachery one against the other—a groveling servile and abject submission to the lash of tyrants, we see plainly, my brethren, are not the natural elements of the blacks, as the Americans try to make us believe; but these are misfortunes which God has suffered our fathers to be enveloped in for many ages, no doubt in consequence of their disobedience to their Maker, and which do, indeed, reign at this time among us, almost to the destruction of all other principles: for I must truly say, that ignorance, the mother of treachery and deceit, gnaws into our very vitals. Ignorance, as it now exists among us, produces a state of things, Oh my Lord! too horrible to present to the world. Any man who is curious to see the full force of ignorance developed among the coloured people of the United States of America, has only to go into the southern and western states of this confederacy, where, if he is not a tyrant, but has the feelings of a human being, who can feel for a fellow creature, he may see enough to make his very heart bleed! He may see there, a son take his mother, who bore almost the pains of death to give him birth, and by the command of a tyrant, strip her as naked as she came into the world, and apply the cow-hide to her, until she falls a victim to death in the road! He may see a husband take his dear wife, not infrequently in a pregnant state, and perhaps far advanced, and beat her for an unmerciful wretch, until his infant falls a lifeless lump at her feet!

Can the Americans escape God Almighty? If they do, can he be to us a God of Justice? God is just, and I know it—for he has convinced me to my satisfaction—I cannot doubt him. My observer may see fathers beating their sons, mothers their daughters, and children their parents, all to pacify the passions of unrelenting tyrants. He may also, see them telling news and lies, making mischief one upon another. These are some of the productions of ignorance, which he will see practiced among my dear brethren, who are held in unjust slavery and wretchedness, by avaricious and unmerciful tyrants, to whom, and their hellish deeds, I would suffer my life to be taken before I would submit. And when my curious observer comes to take notice of those who are said to be free, (which assertion I deny) and who are making some frivolous pretentions to common sense, he will see that branch of ignorance among the slaves assuming a more cunning and deceitful course of procedure.—He may see some of my brethren in league with tyrants, selling their own brethren into hell upon earth, not dissimilar to the exhibitions in Africa, but in a more secret, servile and abject manner. Oh Heaven! I am full!!! I can hardly move my pen!!! and as I expect some will try to put me to death, to strike terror into others, and to obliterate from their minds the notion of freedom, so as to keep my brethren the more secure in wretchedness, where they will be permitted to stay but a short time (whether tyrants believe it or not)—I shall give the world a development of facts, which are already witnessed in the courts of heaven. My observer may see some of those ignorant and treacherous creatures (coloured people) sneaking about in the large cities, endeavoring to find out all strange coloured people, where they work and where they reside, asking them questions, and trying to ascertain whether they are runaways or not, telling them, at the same time, that they always have been, are, and always will be, friends to their brethren; and, perhaps, that they themselves are absconders, and a thousand such treacherous lies to get the better information of the more ignorant!!! There have been and are at this day in Boston, New-York, Philadelphia, and Baltimore, coloured men, who are in league with tyrants, and who receive a great portion of their daily bread, of the moneys which they acquire from the blood and tears of their more miserable brethren, whom they scandalously delivered into the hands of our natural enemies!

To show the force of degraded ignorance and deceit among us some farther, I will give here an extract from a paragraph, which may be found in the Columbian Centinel of this city, for September 9, 1829, on the first page of which, the curious may find an article, headed

"Affray And Murder." Portsmouth, (Ohio) Aug. 22, 1829.

A most shocking outrage was committed in Kentucky, about eight miles from this place, on 14th inst. A Negro driver, by the name of Gordon, who had purchased in Maryland about sixty Negroes, was taking them, assisted by an associate named Allen, and the wagoner who conveyed the baggage, to the Mississippi. The men were hand-cuffed and chained together, in the usual manner for driving those poor wretches, while the women and children were suffered to proceed without encumbrance. It appears that, by means of a file the Negroes, unobserved, had succeeded in separating the iron which bound their hands, in such a way as to be able to throw them off at any moment. About 8 o'clock in the morning, while proceeding on the state road leading from Greenup to Vanceburg, two of them dropped their shackles and commenced a fight, when the wagoner (Petit) rushed in with his whip to compel them to desist. At this moment, every negro was found to be perfectly at liberty; and one of them seizing a club, gave Petit a violent blow on the head, and laid him dead at his feet; and Allen, who came to his assistance, met a similar fate, from the contents of a pistol fired by another of the gang. Gordon was then attacked, seized and held by one of the negroes, whilst another fired twice at him with a pistol, the ball of which each time grazed his head, but not proving effectual, he was beaten with clubs, and left for dead. They then commenced pillaging the wagon, and with an axe split open the trunk of Gordon, and rifled it of the money, about $2,400. Sixteen of the negroes then took to the woods; Gordon, in the mean time, not being materially injured, was enabled, by the assistance of one of the women, to mount his horse and flee; pursued, however, by one of the gang on another horse, with a drawn pistol; fortunately he escaped with his life barely, arriving at a plantation, as the negro came in sight; who then turned about and retreated.

The neighborhood was immediately rallied, and a hot pursuit given—which, we understand, has resulted in the capture of the whole gang and the recovery of the greatest part of the money. Seven of the negro men and one woman, it is said were engaged in the murders, and will be brought to trial at the next courts in Greenupsburg.

Here my brethren, I want you to notice particularly in the above article, the ignorant and deceitful actions of this coloured woman. I beg you to view it candidly, as for eternity!!!! Here a notorious wretch, with two other confederates had sixty of them in a gang, driving them like brutes—the men all in chains and hand-cuffs, and by the help of God they got their chains and hand-cuffs thrown off, and caught two of the wretches and put them to death, and beat the other until they thought he was dead, and left him for dead; however, he deceived them, and rising from the ground, this servile woman helped him upon his horse, and he made his escape.

Brethren, what do you think of this? Was it the natural fine feelings of this woman, to save such a wretch alive? I know that the blacks, take them half enlightened and ignorant, are more humane and merciful than the most enlightened and refined European that can be found in all the earth. Let no one say that I assert this because I am prejudiced on the side of my colour, and against the whites or Europeans. For what I write, I do it candidly, for my God and the good of both parties: Natural observations have taught me these things; there is a solemn awe in the hearts of the blacks, as it respects murdering men: which is the reason the whites take the advantage of us. Whereas the whites, (though they are great cowards) where they have the advantage, or think that there are any prospects of getting it, they murder all before them, in order to subject men to wretchedness and degradation under them. This is the natural result of pride and avarice. But I declare, the actions of this black woman are really insupportable. For my own part, I cannot think it was anything but servile deceit, combined with the most gross ignorance: for we must remember that humanity, kindness and the fear of the Lord, does not consist in protecting devils.

Here is a set of wretches, who had SIXTY of them in a gang, driving them around the country like brutes, to dig up gold and silver for them, (which they will get enough of yet.) Should the lives of such creatures be spared? Are God and Mammon in league? What has the Lord to do with a gang of desperate wretches, who go sneaking about the country like robbers—light upon his people wherever they can get a chance, binding them with chains and hand-cuffs, beat and murder them as they would rattle-snakes? Are they not the Lord's enemies? Ought they not to be destroyed? Any person who will save such wretches from destruction, is fighting against the Lord, and will receive his just recompense. The black men acted like blockheads. Why did they not make sure of the wretch? He would have made sure of them, if he could. It is just the way with black men—eight white men can frighten fifty of them; whereas, if you can only get courage into the blacks, I do declare it, that one good black man can put to death six white men; and I give it as a fact, let twelve black men get well armed for battle, and they will kill and put to flight fifty whites. The reason is, the blacks, once you get them started, they glory in death. The whites have had us under them for more than three centuries, murdering, and treating us like brutes; and, as Mr. Jefferson wisely said, they have never found us out—they do not know, indeed, that there is an unconquerable disposition in the breasts of the blacks, which, when it is fully awakened and put in motion, will be subdued, only with the destruction of the animal existence. Get the blacks started, and if you do not have a gang of tigers and lions to deal with, I am a deceiver of the blacks and of the whites.

How sixty of them could let that wretch escape unskilled, I cannot conceive—they will have to suffer as much for the two whom, they secured, as if they had put one hundred to death: if you commence, make sure work—do not trifle, for they will not trifle with you—they want us for their slaves, and think nothing of murdering us in order to subject us to that wretched condition—therefore, if there is an attempt made by us, kill or be killed. Now, I ask you, had you not rather be killed than to be a slave to a tyrant, who takes the life of your mother, wife, and dear little children? Look upon your mother, wife and children, and answer God Almighty; and believe this, that it is no more harm for you to kill a man, who is trying to kill you, than it is for you to take a drink of water when thirsty; in fact, the man who will stand still and let another murder him, is worse than an infidel, and, if he has common sense, ought not to be pitied.

The actions of this deceitful and ignorant coloured woman, in saving the life of a desperate wretch, whose avaricious and cruel object was to drive her, and her companions in miseries, through the country like cattle, to make his fortune on their carcasses, are but too much like that of thousands of our brethren in these states: if anything is whispered by one, which has any allusion to the melioration of their dreadful condition, they run and tell tyrants, that they may be enabled to keep them the longer in wretchedness and miseries. Oh! coloured people of these United States, I ask you, in the name of that God who made us, have we, in consequence of oppression, nearly lost the spirit of man, and, in no very trifling degree, adopted that of brutes? Do you answer, no?—I ask you, then, what set of men can you point me to, in all the world, who are so abjectly employed by their oppressors, as we are by our natural enemies?

How can, Oh! how can those enemies but say that we and our children are not of the human family, but were made by our Creator to be an inheritance to them and theirs forever? How can the slaveholders but say that they can bribe the best coloured person in the country, to sell his brethren for a trifling sum of money, and take that atrocity to confirm them in their avaricious opinion, that we were made to be slaves to them and their children? How could Mr. Jefferson but say.

> I advance it therefore as a suspicion only, that the blacks, whether originally a distinct race, or made distinct by time and circumstances, are *inferior* to the whites in the endowments both of body and mind?

"It," says he, "is not against experience to suppose, that different species of the same genius, or varieties of the same species, may possess different qualifications."

[Here, my brethren, listen to him.]

> Will not a lover of natural history, then, one who views the gradations in all the races of *animals* with the eye of philosophy, excuse an effort to keep those in the department of *man* as *distinct* as nature has formed them?"

I hope you will try to find out the meaning of this verse—its widest sense and all its bearings: whether you do or not, remember the whites do. This very verse, brethren, having emanated from Mr. Jefferson, a much greater philosopher the world never afforded, has in truth injured us more, and has been as great a barrier to our emancipation as anything that has ever been advanced against us. I hope you will not let it pass unnoticed. He goes on further, and says:

> This unfortunate difference of colour, and perhaps of faculty, is a powerful obstacle to the emancipation of these people. Many of their advocates, while they wish to vindicate the liberty of human nature are anxious also to preserve its dignity and beauty. Some of these, embarrassed by the question, 'What further is to be done with them?' join themselves in opposition with those who are actuated by sordid avarice only.

Now I ask you candidly, my suffering brethren in time, who are candidates for the eternal worlds, how could Mr. Jefferson but have given the world these remarks respecting us, when we are so submissive to them, and so much servile deceit prevail among ourselves—when we so meanly submit to their murderous lashes, to which neither the Indians nor any other people under Heaven would submit? No, they would die to a man, before they would suffer such things from men who are no better than themselves, and perhaps not so good. Yes, how can our friends but be embarrassed, as Mr. Jefferson says, by the question, "What further is to be done with these people?" For while they are working for our emancipation, we are, by our treachery, wickedness and deceit, working against ourselves and our children—helping ours, and the enemies of God, to keep us and our dear little children in their infernal chains of slavery!!! Indeed, our friends cannot but relapse and join themselves with those who are actuated by sordid avarice only!!!!

For my own part, I am glad Mr. Jefferson has advanced his positions for your sake; for you will either have to contradict or confirm him by your own actions, and not by what our friends have said or done for us; for those things are other men's labours, and do not satisfy the Americans, who are waiting for us to prove to them ourselves, that we are MEN, before they will be willing to admit the fact; for I pledge you my sacred word of honour, that Mr. Jefferson's remarks respecting us, have sunk deep into the hearts of millions of the whites, and never will be removed this side of eternity.—For how can they, when we are confirming him every day, by our groveling submissions and treachery? I aver, that when I look over these United States of America, and the world, and see the ignorant deceptions and consequent wretchedness of my brethren, I am brought of times solemnly to a stand, and in the midst of my reflections I exclaim to my God, "Lord didst thou make us to be slaves to our brethren, the whites?" But when I reflect that God is just, and that millions of my wretched brethren would meet death with glory—yea, more, would plunge into the very mouths of cannons and be torn into particles as minute as the atoms which compose the elements of the earth, in preference to a mean submission to the lash of tyrants, I am with streaming eyes, compelled to shrink back into nothingness before my Maker, and exclaim again, thy will be done, O Lord God Almighty.

Men of colour, who are also of sense, for you particularly is my appeal designed. Our more ignorant brethren are not able to penetrate its value. I call upon you therefore to cast your eyes upon the wretchedness of your brethren, and to do your utmost to enlighten them—go to work and enlighten your brethren!—Let the Lord see you doing what you can to rescue them and yourselves from degradation. Do any of you say that you and your family are free and happy, and what have you to do with the wretched slaves and other people? So can I say, for I enjoy as much freedom as any of you, if I am not quite as well off as the best of you. Look into our freedom and happiness, and see of what kind they are composed!! They are of the very lowest kind—they are the very dregs!—they are the most servile and abject kind, that ever a people was in possession of! If any of you wish to know how free you are, let one of you start and go through the southern and western States of this country, and unless you travel as a slave to a white man (a servant is a slave to the man whom he serves) or have your free papers, (which if you are not careful they will get from you) if they do not take you up and put you in jail, and if you cannot give good evidence of your freedom, sell you into eternal slavery, I am not a living man: or any man of colour, immaterial who he is, or where he came from, if he is not the fourth from the negro race!! (as we are called) the white Christians of America will serve him the same they will sink him into wretchedness and degradation for ever while he lives. And yet some of you have the hardihood to say that you are free and happy! May God have mercy on your freedom and happiness!!

I met a coloured man in the street a short time since, with a string of boots on his shoulders; we fell into conversation, and in course of which, I said to him, what a miserable set of people we are! He asked, why?—Said I, we are so subjected under the whites, that we cannot obtain the comforts of life, but by cleaning their boots and shoes, old clothes, waiting on them, shaving them &c. Said he, (with the boots on his shoulders) "I am completely happy!!! I never want to live any better or happier than when I can get a plenty of boots and shoes to clean!!!" Oh! how can those who are actuated by avarice only, but think, that our Creator made us to be an inheritance to them forever, when they see that our greatest glory is centered in such mean and low objects? Understand me, brethren, I do not mean to speak against the occupations by which we acquire enough and sometimes scarcely that, to render ourselves and families comfortable through life. I am subjected to the same inconvenience, as you all. — My objections are, to our glorying and being happy in such low employments; for if we are men, we ought to be thankful to the Lord for the past, and for the future. Be looking forward with thankful hearts to higher attainments than wielding the razor and cleaning boots and shoes. The man whose aspirations are not above, and even below these, is indeed, ignorant and wretched enough.

I advance it therefore to you, not as a problematical, but as an unshaken and forever immoveable fact, that your full glory and happiness, as well as all other coloured people under Heaven, shall never be fully consummated, but with the entire emancipation of your enslaved brethren all over the world. You may therefore, go to work and do what you can to rescue, or join in with tyrants to oppress them and yourselves, until the Lord shall come upon you all like a thief in the night. For I believe it is the will of the Lord that our greatest happiness shall consist in working for the salvation of our whole body. When this is accomplished a burst of glory will shine upon you, which will indeed astonish you and the world. Do any of you say this never will be done? I assure you that God will accomplish it—if nothing else will answer, he will hurl tyrants and devils into atoms and make way for his people. But O my brethren! I say unto you again, you must go to work and prepare the way of the Lord.

There is a great work for you to do, as trifling as some of you may think of it. You have to prove to the Americans and the world, that we are MEN, and not brutes, as we have been represented, and by millions treated. Remember, to let the aim of your labours among your brethren, and particularly the youths, be the dissemination of education and religion.

Never mind what the ignorant ones among us may say, many of whom when you speak to them for their good, and try to enlighten their minds, laugh at you, and perhaps tell you plump to your face, that they want no instruction from you or any other Niger, and all such aggravating language. Now if you are a man of understanding and sound sense, I conjure you in the name of the Lord, and of all that is good, to impute their actions to ignorance, and wink at their follies, and do your very best to get around them some way or other, for remember they are your brethren; and I declare to you that it is for your interests to teach and enlighten them. It is lamentable, that many of our children go to school, from four until they are eight or ten, and sometimes fifteen years of age, and leave school knowing but a little more about the grammar of their language than a horse does about handling a musket—and not a few of them are really so ignorant, that they are unable to answer a person correctly, general questions in geography, and to hear them read, would only be to disgust a man who has a taste for reading; which, to do well, as trifling as it may appear to some, (to the ignorant in particular) is a great part of learning.

Some few of them, may make out to scribble tolerably well, over a half sheet of paper, which I believe has hitherto been a powerful obstacle in our way, to keep us from acquiring knowledge. An ignorant father, who knows no more than what nature has taught him, together with what little he acquires by the senses of hearing and seeing, finding his son able to write a neat hand, sets it down for granted that he has as good learning as anybody; the young, ignorant grump, hearing his father or mother, who perhaps may be ten times more ignorant, in point of literature, than himself, extolling his learning, struts about, in the full assurance, that his attainments in literature are sufficient to take him through the world, when, in fact, he has scarcely any learning at all!

I promiscuously fell in conversation once, with an elderly coloured man on the topics of education, and of the great prevalence of ignorance among us: Said he, "I know that our people are very ignorant but my son has a good education: I spent a great deal of money on his education: he can write as well as any white man, and I assure you that no one can fool him," &c. Said I, what else can your son do, besides writing a good hand? Can he post a set of books in a mercantile manner? Can he write a neat piece of composition in prose or in verse? To these interrogations he answered in the negative. Said I, did your son learn, while he was at school, the width and depth of English Grammar? To which he also replied in the negative, telling me his son did not learn those things. Your son, said I, then, has hardly any learning at all—he is almost as ignorant, and more so, than many of those who never went to school one day in all their lives. My friend got a little put out, and so walking off, said that his son could write as well as any white man. Most of the coloured people, when they speak of the education of one among us who can write a neat hand, and who perhaps knows nothing but to scribble and puff pretty fair on a small scrap of paper, immaterial whether his words are grammatical, or spelt correctly, or not; if it only looks beautiful, they say he has as good an education as any white man—he can write as well as any white man, &c. The poor, ignorant creature, hearing, this, he is ashamed, forever after, to let any person see him humbling himself to another for knowledge but going about trying to deceive those who are more ignorant than himself, he at last falls an ignorant victim to death in wretchedness.

I pray that the Lord may undeceive my ignorant brethren, and permit them to throw away pretensions, and seek after the substance of learning. I would crawl on my hands and knees through mud and mire, to the feet of a learned man, where I would sit and humbly supplicate him to instill into me, that which neither devils nor tyrants could remove, only with my life—for colored people to acquire learning in this country, makes tyrants quake and tremble on their sandy foundation. Why, what is the matter? Why, they know that their infernal deeds of cruelty will be made known to the world. Do you suppose one man of good sense and learning would submit himself, his father, mother, wife and children, to be slaves to a wretched man like himself, who, instead of compensating him for his labours, chains, hand-cuffs and beats him and family almost to death, leaving life enough in them, however, to work for, and call him master? No! No! He would cut his devilish throat from ear to ear, and well do slave-holders know it. The bare name of educating the coloured people, scares our cruel oppressors almost to death. But if they do not have enough to be frightened for yet, it will be, because they can always keep us ignorant, and because God approbates their cruelties, with which they have been for centuries murdering us. The whites shall have enough of the blacks, yet, as true as God sits on his throne in Heaven.

Some of our brethren are so very full of learning, that you cannot mention any thing to them which they do not know better than yourself!!—nothing is strange to them!!—

they knew every thing years ago!—if anything should be mentioned in company where they are, immaterial how important it is respecting us or the world, if they had not divulged it; they make light of it, and affect to have known it long before it was mentioned and try to make all in the room, or wherever you may be, believe that your conversation is nothing!!—not worth hearing! All this is the result of ignorance and ill-breeding; for a man of good-breeding, sense and penetration, if he had heard a subject told twenty times over, and should happen to be in company where one should commence telling it again, he would wait with patience on its narrator, and see if he would tell it as it was told in his presence before—paying the most strict attention to what is said, to see if any more light will be thrown on the subject: for all men are not gifted alike in telling, or even hearing the most simple narration. These ignorant, vicious, and wretched men, contribute almost as much injury to our body as tyrants themselves, by doing so much for the promotion of ignorance amongst us; for they, making such pretensions to knowledge, such of our youth as are seeking after knowledge, and can get access to them, take them as criterions to go by, who will lead them into a channel, where, unless the Lord blesses them with the privilege of seeing their folly, they will be irretrievably lost forever, while in time!!!

I must close this article by relating the very heart-rending fact, that I have examined school-boys and young men of colour in different parts of the country, in the most simple parts of Murray's English Grammar, and not more than one in thirty was able to give a correct answer to my interrogations. If anyone contradicts me, let him step out of his door into the streets of Boston, New-York, Philadelphia, or Baltimore, (no use to mention any other, for the Christians are too charitable further south or west!)—I say, let him who disputes me, step out of his door into the streets of either of those four cities, and promiscuously collect one hundred school-boys, or young men of colour, who have been to school, and who are considered by the coloured people to have received an excellent education, because, perhaps, some of them can write a good hand, but who, notwithstanding their neat writing, may be almost as ignorant, in comparison, as a horse.—And, I say it, he will hardly find (in this enlightened day, and in the midst of this charitable people) five in one hundred, who, are able to correct the false grammar of their language.—The cause of this almost universal ignorance among us, I appeal to our schoolmasters to declare.

Here is a fact, which I this very minute take from the mouth of a young coloured man, who has been to school in this state (Massachusetts) nearly nine years, and who knows grammar this day, nearly as well as he did the day he first entered the school-house, under a white master. This young man says: "My master would never allow me to study grammar." I asked him, why? "The school committee," said he "forbid the coloured children learning grammar"—they would not allow any but the white children "to study grammar." It is a notorious fact, that the major part of the white Americans, have, ever since we have been among them, tried to keep us ignorant, and make us believe that God made us and our children to be slaves to them and theirs. Oh! my God, have mercy on Christian Americans!!!

[1830]

II

Another outstanding firebrand of the early nineteenth century was Maria Stewart (1803–1879), the pioneering black woman abolitionist who spoke throughout the North championing freedom for all and equality for women. She was the first black woman to gain national recognition as an abolitionist and suffragette. Her bravery should never be understated. For a black woman to be traveling unescorted to various cities and towns and speaking forcefully for an end to slavery and the elevation of women was dangerous business. Nevertheless, Maria Stewart persisted. She was a visionary beyond her times. Her address at the Boston African Masonic Hall in 1833 tells much about her commitment to the cause and willingness to stand tall for the moral principles she believed in. Stewart's views of African repatriation are also clear from a reading of that speech. Her pleas for black folk to fight for their rights and to oppose sexism are equally expressed. What message do you take away from her spirited words? Do the words make you reflect on the present situation for people of color, especially African-American men and women?

"The African Masonic Hall Speech in Boston"

Maria Stewart

African rights and liberty is a subject that ought to fire the breast of every free man of color in these United States, and excite in his bosom a lively, deep, decided and heartfelt interest. When I cast my eyes on the long list of illustrious names that are enrolled on the bright annals of fame among the whites, I turn my eyes within, and ask my thoughts, "Where are the names of our illustrious ones?" It must certainly have been for the want of energy on the part of the free people of color, that they have been long willing to bear the yoke of oppression. It must have been the want of ambition and force that has given the whites occasion to say, that our natural abilities are not as good, and our capacities by nature inferior to theirs. They boldly assert, that, did we possess a natural independence of soul, and feel a love for liberty within our breasts, some one of our sable race, long before this, would have testified it, notwithstanding the disadvantages under which we labor. We have made ourselves appear altogether unqualified to speak in our own defense, and are therefore looked upon as objects of pity and commiseration. We have been imposed upon, insulted and derided on every side; and now, if we complain, it is considered as the height of impertinence. We have suffered ourselves to be considered as Bastards, cowards, mean, faint-hearted wretches; and on this account, (not because of our complexion) many despise us, and would gladly spurn us from their presence.

These things have fired my soul with a holy indignation, and compelled me thus to come forward; and endeavor to turn their attention to knowledge and improvement; for knowledge is power. I would ask, is it blindness of mind, or a stupidity of soul, or the want of education, that has caused our men who are 60 to 70 years of age, never to let their voices be heard, or nor their hands be raised in behalf of their color? Or has it been for the fear of offering the whites? If it has, O ye fearful ones, throw of your fearfulness, and come forth in the name of the Lord, and in the strength of the God of Justice, and make yourselves useful and active members in society; for they admire a noble and patriotic spirit in others; and should they not admire it in us? If you are men, convince them that you possess the spirit of men; and as your day, so shall your strength be. Have the sons of Africa no souls? feel they no ambitious desires? shall the chains of ignorance forever confine them? shall the insipid appellation of "clever negroes," or "good creatures," any longer content them? Where can we find among ourselves the man of science, or a philosopher, or an able statesman, or a counsellor at law? Show me our fearless and brave, our noble and gallant ones. Where are our lecturers on natural history, and our critics in useful knowledge? There may be a few such men among us, but they are rare. It is true, our fathers bled and died in the revolutionary war, and others fought bravely under the command of Jackson, in defense of liberty. But where is the man that has distinguished himself in these modern days by acting wholly in the defense of African rights and liberty? There was one, although he sleeps, his memory lives.

I am sensible that there are many highly intelligent gentlemen of color in those United States, in the force of whose arguments, doubtless, I should discover my inferiority; but if they are blest with wit and talent, friends and fortune, why have they not made themselves men of eminence, by striving to take all the reproach that is cast upon the people of color, and in endeavoring to alleviate the woes of their brethren in bondage? Talk, without effort, is nothing; you are abundantly capable, gentlemen, of making yourselves men of distinction; and this gross neglect, on your part, causes my blood to boil within me. Here is the grand cause which hinders the rise and progress of the people of color. It is their want of laudable ambition and requisite courage.

Individuals have been distinguished according to their genius and talents, ever since the first formation of man, and will continue to be while the world stands. The different grades rise to honor and respectability as their merits may deserve. History informs us that we sprung from one of the most learned nations of the whole earth; from the seat, if not the parent of science; yes, poor, despised Africa was once the resort of sages and legislators of other nations, was esteemed the school for learning, and the most illustrious men in Greece flocked thither for instruction. But it was our gross sins and abominations that provoked the Almighty to frown thus heavily upon us, and give our glory unto others. Sin and prodigality have caused the downfall of nations, kings and emperors; and were it not that God in wrath remembers mercy; we might indeed despair; but a promise is left us; "Ethiopia shall again stretch forth her hands unto God."

But it is of no use for us to boast that we sprung from this learned and enlightened nation, for this day a thick mist of moral gloom hangs over millions of our race. Our condition as a people has been low for hundreds of years, and it will continue to be so, unless, by true piety and virtue, we strive to regain that which we have lost. White Americans, by their prudence, economy and exertions, have sprung up and become one of the most flourishing nations in the world, distinguished for their knowledge of the arts and sciences, for their polite literature. While our minds are vacant, and starving for want of knowledge, theirs are filled to overflowing. Most of our color have been taught to stand in fear of the white man, from their earliest infancy, to work as soon as they could walk, and call "master," before they scarce could lisp the name of mother. Continual fear and laborious servitude have in some degree lessened in us that natural force and energy which belong to man; or else, in defiance of opposition, our men, before this, would have nobly and boldly contended for their rights. But give the man of color an equal opportunity with the white from the cradle to manhood, and from manhood to the grave, and you would discover the dignified statesman, the man of science, and the philosopher. But there is no such opportunity for the sons of Africa, and I fear that our powerful ones are fully determined that there never shall be. For bid, ye Powers on high, that it should any longer be said that our men possess no force. O ye sons of Africa, when will your voices be heard in our legislative halls, in defiance of your enemies, contending for equal rights and liberty? How can you, when you reflect from what you have fallen, refrain from crying mightily unto God, to turn away from us the fierceness of his anger, and remember our transgressions against us no more forever. But a God of infinite purity will not regard the prayers of those who hold religion in one hand, and prejudice, sin and pollution in the other; he will not regard the prayers of self-righteousness and hypocrisy. Is it possible, I exclaim, that for the want of knowledge, we have labored for hundreds of years to support others, and been content to receive what they chose to give us in return? Cast your eyes about, look as far as you can see; all, all is owned by the lordly white, except here and there a lowly dwelling which the man of color, midst deprivations, fraud and opposition, has been scarce able to procure. Like King Solomon, who put neither nail nor hammer to the temple, yet received the praise; so also have the white Americans gained themselves a name, like the names of the great men that are in the earth, while in reality we have been their principal foundation and support. We have pursued the shadow, they have obtained the substance; we have performed the labor they have received the profits; we have planted the vines, they have eaten the fruits of them.

I would implore our men, and especially our rising youth, to flee from the gambling board and the dance-hall; for we are poor, and have no money to throw away. I do not consider dancing as criminal in itself, but it is astonishing to me that our young men are so blind to their own interest and the future welfare of their children, as to spend their hard earnings for this frivolous amusement; for it has been carried on among us to such an unbecoming extent, that it has became absolutely disgusting. "Faithful are the wounds of a friend, but the kisses of an enemy are deceitful." Had those men among us, who have had an opportunity, turned their attention as assiduously to mental and moral improvement as they have to gambling and dancing, I might have remained quietly at home, and they stood contending in my place. These polite accomplishments will never enroll your names on the bright annals of fame, who admire the belle void of intellectual knowledge, or applaud the dandy that talks largely on politics, without striving to assist his fellow in the revolution, when the nerves and muscles of every other man forced him into the field of action. You have a right to rejoice, and to let your hearts cheer you in the days of your youth; yet remember that for all these things, God will bring you into judgment. Then, O ye sons of Africa, turn your mind from these perishable objects, and contend for the cause of God and the rights of man. Form yourselves into temperance societies. There are temperate men among you; then why will you any longer neglect to strive, by your example, to suppress vice in all its abhorrent forms? You have been told repeatedly of the glorious results arising from temperance, and can you bear to see the whites arising in honor and respectability, without endeavoring to grasp after that honor and respectability also?

But I forbear. Let our money, instead of being thrown away as heretofore, be appropriated for schools and seminaries of learning for our children and youth. We ought to follow the example of the whites in this respect. Nothing would raise our respectability, add to our peace and happiness, and reflect so much honor upon us, as to be ourselves the promoters of temperance, and the supporters, as far as we are able, of useful and scientific knowledge. The rays of light and knowledge have been hid from our view; we have been taught to consider ourselves as scarce superior to the brute creation; and have performed the most laborious part of American drudgery. Had we as a people received, one half the early advantages the whites have received, I would defy the government of these United States to deprive us any longer of our rights.

I am informed that the agent of the Colonization Society has recently formed an association of young men, for the purpose of influencing those of us to go to Liberia who may feel disposed. The colonizationists are blind to their own interest, for should the nations of the earth make war with America, they would find their forces much weakened by our absence; or should we remain here, can our "brave soldiers," and "fellow-citizens," as they were termed in time of calamity, condescend to defend the rights of the whites, and be again deprived of their own, or sent to Liberia in return? Or, if the colonizationists are real friends to Africa, let them expend the money which they collect, in erecting a college to educate her injured sons in this land of gospel light and liberty; for it would be most thankfully received on our part, and convince us of the truth of their professions, and save time, expense and anxiety. Let them place before us noble objects, worthy of pursuit, and see if we prove ourselves to be those unambitious negroes they term us. But ah! methinks their hearts are so frozen towards us, they had rather their money should be sunk in the ocean than to administer it to our relief; and I fear, if they dared, like Pharaoh, king of Egypt, they would order every male child among us to be drowned. But the most high God is still as able to subdue the lofty pride of these white Americans, as He was the heart of that ancient rebel. They say, though we are looked upon as things, yet we sprang from a scientific people. Had our men the requisite force and energy, they would soon convince them by their efforts both in public and private, that they were men, or things in the shape of men. Well may the colonizationists laugh us to scorn for our negligence; well may they cry, "Shame to the sons of Africa." As the burden of the Israelites was too great for Moses to bear, so also is our burden too great for Moses to bear, so also is our burden too great for our noble advocate to bear. You must feel interested, my brethren, in what he undertakes, and hold up his hands by your good works, or in spite of himself, his soul will become discouraged, and his heart will die within him; for he has, as it were, the strong bulls of Bashan to contend with.

It is of no use for us to wait any longer for a generation of well educated men to arise. We have slumbered and slept too long already; the day is far spent; the night of death approaches; and you have sound sense and good judgement sufficient to begin with, if you feel disposed to make a right use of it. Let every man of color throughout the United States, who possesses the spirit and principles of a man, sign a petition to Congress, to abolish slavery in the District of Columbia, and grant you the rights and privileges of common free citizens; for if you had had faith as a grain of mustard seed, long before this the mountains of prejudice might have been removed. We are all sensible that the Anti-Slavery Society has taken hold of the arm of our whole population, in order to raise them out of the mire. Now all we have to do is, by a spirit of virtuous ambition to strive to raise ourselves; and I am happy to have it in my power thus publicly to say, that the colored inhabitants of this city, in some respects, are beginning to improve. Had the free people of color in these United States nobly and boldly contended for their rights, and showed a natural genius and talent, although not so brilliant as some; had they help up, encouraged and patronized each other, nothing could have hindered us from being a thriving and flourishing people. There has been a fault among us. The reason why our distinguished men have not made themselves more influential is, because they fear that the strong current of opposition through which they must pass, would cause their downfall and prove their overthrew. And what gives rise to this opposition? Envy. And what has it amounted to? Nothing. And who are the cause of it? Our whited sepulchers, who want to be great, and don't know how; who love to be called of men Rabbi, Rabbi, who put on false sanctity, and humble themselves to their brethren, for the sake of acquiring the highest place in the synagogue, and the uppermost seats at the feast. You, dearly beloved, who are the genuine followers of our Lord Jesus Christ, the salt of the earth and the light of the world, are not so culpable. As I told you, in the very first of my writing, I tell you again, I am but as a drop in the bucket—as one particle of the small dust of the earth. God will surely raise up those among us who will plead the cause of virtue, and the pure principles of morality, more eloquently than I am able to do.

It appears to me that America has become like the great city of Babylon, for she has boasted in her heart,—I sit a queen, and am no widow, and shall see no sorrow! She is indeed a seller of slaves and the souls of men; she has made the Africans drunk with the wine of her fornication; she has put them completely beneath her feet, and she means to keep them there; her right hand supports the reins of government, and her left hand the wheel of power, and she is determined not to let go her grasp. But many powerful sons and daughters of Africa will shortly arise, who will put down vice and immorality among us, and declare by Him that sitteth upon the throne, that they will have their rights; and if refused, I am afraid they will spread horror and devastation around. I believe that the oppression of injured Africa has come up before the Majesty of Heaven; and when our cries shall have reached the ears of the Most High, it will be a tremendous day for the people of this land; for strong is the arm of the Lord God Almighty.

Life has almost lost its charms for me; death has lost its sting and the grave its terrors; and at times I have a strong desire to depart and dwell with Christ, which is far better. Let me entreat my white brethren to awake and save our sons from dissipation, and our daughters from ruin. Lend the hand of assistance to feeble merit, plead the cause of virtue among our sable race; so shall our curses upon you be turned into blessings; and though you should endeavor to drive us from these shores, still we will cling to you the more firmly; nor will we attempt to rise above you: we will presume to be called your equals only.

The unfriendly whites first drove the native American from his much loved home. Then they stole our fathers from their peaceful and quiet dwellings, and brought them hither, and made bond-men and bond-women of them and their little ones; they have obliged our brethren to labor, kept them in utter ignorance, nourished them in vice, and raised them in degradation; and now that we have enriched their soil, and filled their coffers, they say that we are not capable of becoming like white men, and that we never can rise to respectability in this country. They would drive us to a strange land. But before I go, the bayonet shall pierce me through. African rights and liberty is a subject that ought to fire the breast of every free man of color in these United States, and excite in his bosom a lively, deep, decided and heart-felt interest.

[1833]

III

It was Frederick Douglass (1818–1895) who became the most prominent African-American leader of the nineteenth century. In "The Hypocrisy of American Slavery" Douglass identifies the contradictions inherent in American society that must be addressed and corrected if the country is to live up to its great founding principles and to advance as a nation. The American journey for people of African descent began in chains, not in a coming to America in hopes of fulfilling the American dream. Americans, black and white, in reading Douglass's remarks would do well to ask whether a nation built on the institution of slavery was flawed to such an extent that even the Civil War might not be able to bring permanent resolution. Just as importantly, the readers might wish to take note of Douglass's questioning of the different America for blacks as compared to that of whites. He was, of course, speaking at a time when slavery still existed. But does Douglass's admonition to the nation about its future resonate today in terms of the different American experiences that shaped black America as compared to white America? Is that difference of the American experience the necessary starting point for any assessment of the black condition in America then and now? Have the stultifying effects of four hundred years of enslavement been eradicated?

"The Hypocrisy of American Slavery"

Frederick Douglass

Fellow citizens, pardon me, and allow me to ask, why am I called upon to speak here today? What have I or those I represent to do with your national independence? Are the great principles of political freedom and of natural justice, embodied in that Declaration of Independence, extended to us? And am I, therefore, called upon to bring our humble offering to the national altar, and to confess the benefits, and express devout gratitude for the blessings resulting from your independence to us?

Would to God, both for your sakes and ours, that an affirmative answer could be truthfully returned to these questions. Then would my task be light, and my burden easy and delightful. For who is there so cold that a nation's sympathy could not warm him? Who so obdurate and dead to the claims of gratitude, that would not thankfully acknowledge such priceless benefits? Who so stolid and selfish that would not give his voice to swell the hallelujahs of a nation's jubilee, when the chains of servitude had been torn from his limbs? I am not that man. In a case like that, the dumb might eloquently speak, and the "lame man leap as an hart."

But such is not the state of the case. I say it with a sad sense of disparity between us. I am not included within the pale of this glorious anniversary! Your high independence only reveals the immeasurable distance between us. The blessings in which you this day rejoice are not enjoyed in common. The rich inheritance of justice, liberty, prosperity, and independence bequeathed by your fathers is shared by you, not by me. The sunlight that brought life and healing to you has brought stripes and death to me. This Fourth of July is yours, not mine. You may rejoice, I must mourn. To drag a man in fetters into the grand illuminated temple of liberty, and call upon him to join you in joyous anthems, were inhuman mockery and sacrilegious irony. Do you mean, citizens, to mock me, by asking me to speak today? If so, there is a parallel to your conduct. And let me warn you, that it is dangerous to copy the example of a nation (Babylon) whose crimes, towering up to heaven, were thrown down by the breath of the Almighty, burying that nation in irrecoverable ruin.

Fellow citizens, above your national, tumultuous joy, I hear the mournful wail of millions, whose chains, heavy and grievous yesterday, are today rendered more intolerable by the jubilant shouts that reach them. If I do forget, if I do not remember those bleeding children of sorrow this day, "may my right hand forget her cunning, and may my tongue cleave to the roof of my mouth!"

To forget them, to pass lightly over their wrongs and to chime in with the popular theme would be treason most scandalous and shocking, and would make me a reproach before God and the world.

My subject, then, fellow citizens, is "American Slavery." I shall see this day and its popular characteristics from the slave's point of view. Standing here, identified with the American bondman, making his wrongs mine, I do not hesitate to declare, with all my soul, that the character and conduct of this nation never looked blacker to me than on this Fourth of July.

Whether we turn to the declarations of the past, or to the professions of the present, the conduct of the nation seems equally hideous and revolting. America is false to the past, false to the present, and solemnly binds herself to be false to the future. Standing with God and the crushed and bleeding slave on this occasion, I will, in the name of humanity, which is outraged, in the name of liberty, which is fettered, in the name of the Constitution and the Bible, which are disregarded and trampled upon, dare to call in question and to denounce, with all the emphasis I can command, everything that serves to perpetuate slavery—the great sin and shame of America! "I will not equivocate—I will not excuse." I will use the severest language I can command, and yet not one word shall escape me that any man, whose judgment is not blinded by prejudice, or who is not at heart a slave-holder, shall not confess to be right and just.

But I fancy I hear some of my audience say it is just in this circumstance that you and your brother Abolitionists fail to make a favorable impression on the public mind. Would you argue more and denounce less, would you persuade more and rebuke less, your cause would be much more likely to succeed. But, I submit, where all is plain there is nothing to be argued. What point in the anti-slavery creed would you have me argue? On what branch of the subject do the people of this country need light? Must I undertake to prove that the slave is a man? That point is conceded already. Nobody doubts it. The slave-holders themselves acknowledge it in the enactment of laws for their government. They acknowledge it when they punish disobedience on the part of the slave. There are seventy-two crimes in the State of Virginia, which, if committed by a black man (no matter how ignorant he be), subject him to the punishment of death; while only two of these same crimes will subject a white man to like punishment.

What is this but the acknowledgment that the slave is a moral, intellectual, and responsible being? The manhood of the slave is conceded. It is admitted in the fact that Southern statute books are covered with enactments, forbidding, under severe fines and penalties, the teaching of the slave to read and write. When you can point to any such laws in reference to the beasts of the field, then I may consent to argue the manhood of the slave. When the dogs in your streets, when the fowls of the air, when the cattle on your hills, when the fish of the sea, and the reptiles that crawl, shall be unable to distinguish the slave from a brute, then I will argue with you that the slave is a man!

For the present it is enough to affirm the equal manhood of the Negro race. Is it not astonishing that, while we are plowing, planting, and reaping, using all kinds of mechanical tools, erecting houses, constructing bridges, building ships, working in metals of brass, iron, copper, silver, and gold; that while we are reading, writing, and ciphering, acting as clerks, merchants, and secretaries, having among us lawyers, doctors, ministers, poets, authors, editors, orators, and teachers; that we are engaged in all the enterprises common to other men—digging gold in California, capturing the whale in the Pacific, feeding sheep and cattle on the hillside, living, moving, acting, thinking, planning, living in families as husbands, wives, and children, and above all, confessing and worshipping the Christian God, and looking hopefully for life and immortality beyond the grave—we are called upon to prove that we are men?

Would you have me argue that man is entitled to liberty? That he is the rightful owner of his own body? You have already declared it. Must I argue the wrongfulness of slavery? Is that a question for republicans? Is it to be settled by the rules of logic and argumentation, as a matter beset with great difficulty, involving a doubtful application of the principle of justice, hard to understand? How should I look today in the presence of Americans, dividing and subdividing a discourse, to show that men have a natural right to freedom, speaking of it relatively and positively, negatively and affirmatively? To do so would be to make myself ridiculous, and to offer an insult to your understanding. There is not a man beneath the canopy of heaven who does not know that slavery is wrong for him.

What! Am I to argue that it is wrong to make men brutes, to rob them of their liberty, to work them without wages, to keep them ignorant of their relations to their fellow men, to beat them with sticks, to flay their flesh with the lash, to load their limbs with irons, to hunt them with dogs, to sell them at auction, to sunder their families, to knock out their teeth, to burn their flesh, to starve them into obedience and submission to their masters? Must I argue that a system thus marked with blood and stained with pollution is wrong? No—I will not. I have better employment for my time and strength than such arguments would imply.

What, then, remains to be argued? Is it that slavery is not divine; that God did not establish it; that our doctors of divinity are mistaken? There is blasphemy in the thought. That which is inhuman cannot be divine. Who can reason on such a proposition? They that can, may—I cannot. The time for such argument is past.

At a time like this, scorching irony, not convincing argument, is needed. Oh! had I the ability, and could I reach the nation's ear, I would today pour out a fiery stream of biting ridicule, blasting reproach, withering sarcasm, and stern rebuke. For it is not light that is needed, but fire; it is not the gentle shower, but thunder. We need the storm, the whirlwind, and the earthquake. The feeling of the nation must be quickened; the conscience of the nation must be roused; the propriety of the nation must be startled; the hypocrisy of the nation must be exposed; and its crimes against God and man must be denounced.

What to the American slave is your Fourth of July? I answer, a day that reveals to him more than all other days of the year, the gross injustice and cruelty to which he is the constant victim. To him your celebration is a sham; your boasted liberty an unholy license; your national greatness, swelling vanity; your sounds of rejoicing are empty and heartless; your shouts of liberty and equality, hollow mock; your prayers and hymns, your sermons and thanksgivings, with all your religious parade and solemnity, are to him mere bombast, fraud, deception, impiety, and hypocrisy—a thin veil to cover up crimes which would disgrace a nation of savages. There is not a nation of the earth guilty of practices more shocking and bloody than are the people of these United States at this very hour.

Go search where you will, roam through all the monarchies and despotisms of the Old World, travel through South America, search out every abuse and when you have found the last, lay your facts by the side of the everyday practices of this nation, and you will say with me that, for revolting barbarity and shameless hypocrisy, America reigns without a rival.

[4 July 1852]

IV

A voice at the same time as that of Douglass, but far more radical, was that of Henry Highland Garnet (1815–1882), an abolitionist, Presbyterian minister, powerful speaker, and militant Black Nationalist. Garnet delivered what would be termed his most radical and memorable speech at the Negro National Convention in Buffalo, New York, in 1843. The speech, "Address to the Slaves of the United States," was a blistering indictment of the peculiar institution in which he advanced the notion that the enslaved should rise up and gain their freedom by any means necessary, including violence. Many though Garnet's speech "an advocating of rebellion." Indeed, it was. It drew the wrath of most abolitionists, including Frederick Douglass, who were committed to moral suasion as the way to end the dreaded institution. Garnet was impatient with the progress being made to abolish slavery and contended that whites might achieve abolition but it was up to blacks to free themselves. Garnet traveled to England, Scotland, and Jamaica, as a supporter and spokesperson for the foreign anti-slavery society, and for his own African civilization society. In 1848 he spoke in detail about "The Past and Present Condition, and the Destiny of the Negro Race," an excerpt from which is provided here. Was Garnet correct in his advocacy and his warnings about the future if the black race did not assert itself? The following year Garnet would become a dedicated proponent of African repatriation and the immigration of black folk to Liberia and other parts of the African continent and West Indies. He had become convinced that black separatism was the only way for blacks to proceed to assure their own future given what he saw as the depths of racism and the color line in America. He died in 1882 in Liberia. His words and ideas live on.

"The Past and The Present Condition, and The Destiny, of The Colored Race"

Henry Highland Garnet

Briefly, and imperfectly have I noticed the former condition of the colored race. Let us turn for a moment to survey our present state. The woeful volume of our history as it now lies open to the world, is written with tears and bound in blood. As I trace it my eyes ache and my heart is filled with grief. No other people have suffered so much, and none have been more innocent. If I might apostrophize, that bleeding country I would say, O Africa! thou has bled, freely bled, at every pore! Thy sorrow has been mocked, and thy grief has not been heeded. Thy children are scattered over the whole earth, and the great nations have been enriched by them. The wild beasts of thy forests are treated with more mercy than they. The Lybian lion and the fierce tiger are caged to gratify the curiosity of men, and the keeper's hands are not laid heavily upon them. But thy children are tortured, taunted, and hurried out of life by unprecedented cruelty. Brave men formed in the divinest mould, are bartered, sold and mortgaged. Stripped of every sacred right, they are scourged if they affirm that they belong to God. Women sustaining the dear relation of mothers, are yoked with the horned cattle to till the soil, and their heart strings are torn to pieces by cruel separations from their children. Our sisters ever manifesting the purest kindness, whether in the wilderness of their fatherland, or amid the sorrows of the middle passage, or in crowded cities, are unprotected from the lusts of tyrants. They have a regard for virtue, and they possess a sense of honor, but there is no respect paid to these jewels of noble character. Driven into unwilling concubinage, their offspring are sold by their Anglo Saxon fathers. To them the marriage institution is but a name, for their despoilers break down the hymeneal alter and scatter its sacred ashes on the winds.

Our young men are brutalized in intellect, and their manly energies are chilled by the frosts of slavery. Sometimes they are called to witness the agonies of the mothers who bore them writing under the lash, and as if to fill up to overflowing the already full cup of demonism, they are sometimes compelled to apply the lash with their own hands. Hell itself cannot overmatch a deed like this,—and dark damnation shudders as it sinks into its bosom, and seeks to hide itself from the indignant eye of God.

> "They till oppression's soil where men,
> For liberty have bled,
> And the eagle wing of freedom waves,
> In mockery overhead.
> The earth is filled with the triumph shouts
> Of men who have burst their chains,
> But theirs the heaviest of them all
> Still lay on their burning veins.
>
> In the tyrants halls there are luxury,
> And wealth, and mental light,
> But the very book cited Christian law,
> Is hidden from their sight.
> In the tyrants halls there are wine, and mirth,
> And songs for the newly free,
> But their own low cabins are desolate,
> Of all but misery."

Spain, who gave the first impulse and royal sanction to the slave trade, still clings to her idolatry. It rests as a plague spot upon the faces of her people. A case lately ordered before the United States Supreme Court, by one of her subjects, and favored by President Van Buren, secured one of the most important decisions ever given in this Nation. I allude to the case of the Amistad, whose whole cargo of souls were emancipated on the high seas, by the heroism of the chieftain Joseph Cinque. He arose in the strength of his manhood, and slew the captain, and imprisoned the crew, as they were pursuing their course from Havana to Matanzas. Being unacquainted with navigation, he commanded the seamen to steer towards the sun rise, knowing that his native country was in the East. But the sky becoming cloudy, the traders directed the vessel towards the, American coast, expecting to find favor and assistance from their fellow bandits and brother pirates in this country. But in this they were mistaken, for justice triumphed. When the woe freighted bark neared our coast, and Cinque saw the star-spangled banner floating in the breeze, it was then that the hero addressed his despairing comrades, while a triumphant smile played upon his face, and said, "Brothers, we would have conquered, but the sun was against us." A sentence more heroic was never uttered by an untutored savage.

It may be asked, why did he despair when he saw the flag of our country? Here is the answer, and be not surprised at it. Because he had seen it waving protectively from the masts of slavers, when freedom owned him as her child, and when he breathed her spirit on his native hills.

The slave trade is carried on briskly in the beautiful island of Cuba. A few years ago, I witnessed the landing of a cargo of slaves, fresh from the coast of Africa, in the port of Havana, in the presence of the Governor, and under the shadow of the Moro Castle, one of the strongest fortifications of the world.

Recently, a great sacrifice has been made in that Island to the Spirit of despotism, in the death of the Patriot and Poet, Placido. Freedom mourns over his early tomb. The waves of the Atlantic, of whose vastness and sublimity he had sung, chanted his dirge as the tyrants hid him in the grave! Placido was a mulatto, a true Poet, and of course a Patriot. His noble soul was moved with pity as he saw his fellow men in chains. Born to feel, and to act, he made a bold attempt to effect a revolution, and failing in it, he fell a martyr to his principles.

On the day previous to his death, he wrote the following lines, of which Coolridge or Montgomery would not have been ashamed. They present a blaze of poetic fire, intense and sublime:—

"O Liberty! I wait for thee,
To break this chain, and dungeon bar
I hear thy voice calling me,
Deep in the frozen North, afar,
With voice like God's, and vision like a star.

Long cradled in the mountain wind,
Thy mates, the eagle and the storm
Arise; and from thy brow unbind
The wreath that gives its starry form,
And smite the strength, that would thy strength deform.

Yet Liberty! thy dawning light,
Obscured by dungeon bars, shall cast
A splendor on the breaking night,
And tyrants flying thick and fast,
Shall tremble at thy gaze, and stand aghast."

The next day they led Placido forth to execution, and from the mouths of bristling musketry a shower of lead was poured upon his quivering heart. That heart stood still,—and a truer, braver one, never beat in the breast of a mortal man!

The Brazilian Government holds three millions of the colored race in slavery. The United States have about the same number. The Spanish Colonies have one million.

But it is proper to turn the other side of the picture, and I rejoice that there is another side. Nine hundred thousand of these people are enjoying their freedom in the British West India Isles. There are six hundred thousand free people in the United States, while in Hayti we have an independent population of nearly a million. Possessing a land of unsurpassed fertility, they have but to turn their attention manfully to Agricultural pursuits and it will shine forth the brightest Isle that slumbers in the arms of old ocean.

In regard to the enslavement of our race, this Country presents as mournful a picture as any other beneath the sun, but still it is not hopelessly enshrouded in darkness. The good institutions of the land are well adapted to the development of the mind. So far as the oppressed shall make their own way towards them, and shall escape the influence of those that are evil, so far shall they succeed in throwing off their bitter thralldom, and in wrenching the scourge from the hands of tyranny.

Slavery has done much to ruin us, and we ourselves have done some things which effect the same. Perhaps the evils of which I am about to speak arise from slavery, and are the things without which the system cannot exist. But nevertheless we must contribute largely towards their overthrow. If it is in our power to destroy these evils, and we do not, then much of our own blood will be found on us.

We are divided by party feuds, and are torn in pieces by dissensions. Some men have prostituted good talents, for the base purpose of kindling the fires of discord. Some who officiated in the temples said to be dedicated to God, are idolaters to sectarianism. And some too would draw a line of blood distinction, and would form factions upon the shallow basis of complexion. But I am glad to know that the number of this class is small, and small as it is, I pray that we may soon be able to write a cipher in its place. Let there be no strife between us, for we are brethren, and we must rise or fall together. How unprofitable it is for us to spend our golden moments in long and solemn debate upon the questions whether we shall be called "Africans," "Colored Americans," or "Africo Americans," or "Blacks." The question should be, my friends, shall we arise and act like men, and cast off this terrible yoke? Many are too apt to follow after shams, and to neglect that which is solid. Thousands are often expended for an hour's display of utter emptiness, which ought to be laid aside to increase our wealth, and for the acquirement of knowledge, and for the promotion of education. Societies, called benevolent, frequently squander more money for the purchase of banners and badges, and in feasting, than they use in acts of charity. What are regalia and other trappings worth, if they signify nothing but sham and parade? In 1846, $5000 were paid by the oppressed Colored people at the Temperance Celebration held in Poughkeepsie, N. Y., and yet we do not adequately support a single Newspaper in the United States.

The first of August meeting, held in Canandaigua, in 1847, cost the same class not less than $10,000; and yet we do not find a hundred of our young men and women in our high-schools and colleges. The gorgeous pageant of the Odd Fellows in October

1847, drew from the pockets of the people at a very moderate calculation, the sum of $8000, while many of their offspring who ought to be drinking at the fountain of learning, are mourning by the turbid and cold waters of servile employments. The FREE AND ACCEPTED MASONS can boast nothing over other fraternities in regard to unnecessary expenditures. The Masons have led off in this course of wastefulness, and a majority of the other institutions are but children of the great ORIGINAL, and they resemble their parent more or less. Let no one say that I seek the destruction of these Institutions. I desire rather to remove the unfruitful branches of the trees, that it may be ascertained whether their trunks are capable of bearing good fruit. If they can produce good, if there is life in the stock, let them remain that they may be beautified by the dresser's hands. But if the roots are corrupt, and their branches cast a deadly shade, let them be cut down, for why should they cumber the ground?

May God grant, that we may betake ourselves to greater wisdom and frugality. I know that the oppressed above all other people need holidays, and pastimes, but in no case should we bid adieu to our common sense. Let all be careful, lest in this age of ribbon, velvet and gold lace revival, that we do not fall into fanaticism. Fanatics sometimes have strange visions, and it would be strange, "passing strange," should any considerable portion of a whole race imagine themselves in a world of, ribbons, painted sticks, and vanity without measure.

We ought to have our monster meetings, but we should assemble with the same spirit, that animated the Irish people, when they were led by that giant of freedom Daniel O'Connell, which should be, to use his own words, to "agitate, and agitate, and agitate until the chains of the three million's are broken." A half penny's worth of green ribbon and a sprig of shamrock signified to the Irishman more than all the gaudy trappings of a Grand Master, or a Prince of Jerusalem. These little things represented a grand principle to the minds of the unconquerable sons of Erin. The principles of progress in the ways of truth, and resistence to tyranny should be the bases of all our public demonstrations, and numerical representations.

We should have likewise, days of bitter bread, and tabernacle in the wilderness, in which to remember our grief-worn brothers and sisters. They are now pleading with million tongues against those who have dispoiled them. They cry from gory fields—from pestilential rice swamps—from cane breaks, and forests—from plantations of cotton and tabacco—from the dark holds of slave ships, and from countless acres where the sugar cane, nods to the sighing winds. They lift up their voices from all the land over which the flag of our country floats. From the banks of our silver streams, and broad rivers, from our valleys and sloping hills, and mountain tops!

The silence that reigns in the region where the pale nations of the earth slumber, is solemn, and awful. But what think ye, when you are told that every rood of land in this Union is the grave of a murdered man, and their epitaphs are written upon the monuments of the nation's wealth. Ye destroyers of my people draw near, and read the mournful inscription; aye! read it, until it is daguerotyped on your souls. "You have slain us all the day long—you have had no mercy." Legions of haggard ghosts stalk through the land. Behold! see, they come. Oh what myriads! Hark! hear their broken bones as they clatter together! With deep unearthly voices they cry "We come, we come! for vengeance we come! Tremble, guilty nation, for the God of Justice lives and reigns."

The screaming of the eagle as he darts through lightning and storm is unheard because of these voices. The tocsin of the sabbath, and the solemn organ are mocked by them. They drown the preacher's voice, and produce discord in the sacred choirs. Sworn senators and perjured demagogues, as they officiate around the alter of Moloch in the national capitol, they hear the wailings of the victims of base born democracy, and they are ill at ease in their unexampled hypocrisy. The father of waters, may roar in his progress to the ocean—the Niagara may thunder, but these voices from the living and the dead, rise above them all.

Such, ladies and gentlemen, are the outlines of the picture of the Colored Race throughout the world. Behind us and on either side are waste places, and deserts, but before us are green spots and living springs.

[1848]

V

In reading this interview, you are invited to think about the great contributions of the most courageous black abolitionist in history. Harriet Tubman (1820–1913) carried on a never-ending struggle for justice, equality, and empowerment. The "Moses of her people" who, in her capacity as the most heralded conductor on the Underground Railroad, made countless trips into the slave South and spirited hundreds of her enslaved brothers and sisters to freedom in the North, Tubman did not leave a written record or a body of noted speeches. There was an "autobiography" of sorts but it was not really authentic. She was a person of deeds more than words. In "An Hour with Harriet Tubman," we are afforded a close approximation of her own voice on a host of subjects through this one-hour interview with a non-white activist. Even in Tubman's last years, her actions spoke volumes about her commitment to the advancement of her people, her belief in equality of women and the necessity of the vote, and her life of example and continued service. Tubman was determined to rise above the weight of repression and injustice. Readers are urged to take note of the life of commitment to inspiring her people. Does she continue to inspire? Is a life of public service something we need to see more of today?

"An Hour with Harriet Tubman"

Harriet Tubman

[Interviewed by James Clarke]

Harriet Tubman, the Moses of the Negro bondsmen of the South, counsellor and associate of John Brown, scout and spy and nurse in the Union Army, is quietly rounding out a long and useful life in the Home for aged colored people which she founded and which bears her name.

Like most Americans who have had to choose their own surnames, Harriet must also fix the date of her birth. But this was so long ago that she cannot, like Booker T. Washington and others who were born in slavery, dispense with day and month and claim one of two years. If she did, it would probably be 1811 or 1812, for before the enactment of the Fugitive Slave Law, she had already become an experienced and intrepid conductor of the Underground Railroad.

"I remember," she said, "once after I had brought some colored people from the South, I went up to Peterboro to the Big House. Gerrit Smith's son, Greene, was going hunting with his tutor and some other boys. I had no shoes. It was a Saturday afternoon.

and—would you believe it?—those boys went right off to the village and got me a pair of shoes so I could go with them."

In those days Harriet was equally skilled with the gun or the hoe, in the laundry or the kitchen. Until recently she possessed enough of her old-time energy to keep house and entertain her friends—the old and sick and homeless—in the little cottage by the road, just outside of Auburn, N. Y., which she purchased from Secretary Seward. Her failing strength has obliged her to share with four or five old women the modest home that she had established on the adjoining land. But, in spite of her advanced age, she is not ready to be *oslerized*. On the day of my visit she had without assistance gone down stairs to breakfast, and I saw her eat a dinner that would tax the stomach of a gourmand. A friend had sent her a spring chicken and had the pleasure of seeing it placed before her with rice and pie and cheese and other good things. "Never mind me," Aunt Harriet replied to the friend's remark that the conversation was interfering with the dinner, "I'll eat all you give me, but I want you to have some of this chicken first." And when the lady protested that she was not hungry, but would taste the rice, Aunt Harriet extended her hospitable invitation to another visitor to share her favorite viand. She resented the suggestion that someone should feed her. She only wanted the nurse to cut the chicken and place the tray on her lap.

Although her face is furrowed and her hand has lost its one-time vigor, Harriet Tubman's mind is astonishingly fresh and active. She not only remembers things that happened when most people's grandmothers were little girls; she has the newspapers read to her and she follows with great interest the important events of the day. Hearing of the coronation of King George V, she requested Miss Anne F. Miller, the granddaughter of Gerrit Smith, to send her congratulations to the king, whose grandmother, the late Queen Victoria, sent a medal and a letter to the old Negro woman who had brought so many of her people to the free soil of Canada.

No such medal or letter is mentioned in the biography of Harriet Tubman, so Miss Miller visited her to obtain further information about this mark of appreciation from the "Great White Mother," as Queen Victoria was affectionately called by her black subjects in Africa. Aunt Harriet said: "It was when the queen had been on the throne sixty years, she sent me the medal. It was a silver medal, about the size of a dollar. It showed the queen and her family. The letter said, 'I read your book to Her Majesty, and she was pleased with it. She sends you this medal.' She also invited me to come over for her birthday party, but I didn't know enough to go. The letter was worn to a shadow, so many people read it. It got lost, somehow or other. Then I gave the medal to my brother's daughter to keep."

I afterward found, on inquiring at the home of her niece, that Aunt Harriet had made no mistake in describing the medal. It is of silver and bears the likenesses of Queen Victoria, her son, grandson and great grandson, the present Prince of Wales. Such medals were circulated throughout the British Empire in commemoration of the Diamond Jubilee of Queen Victoria in 1897, but there can be no doubt that the queen personally directed one to be sent to Harriet Tubman, whose "book" had been read to her. This explains why this token from the greatest white woman of the nineteenth century is not mentioned in the biography of the greatest black woman, for the book of Harriet Tubman, by Mrs. S. H. Bradford, closes with the Civil War.

Satisfied that her honored friend had reasonable ground to congratulate the grand-son of Queen Victoria on his coronation, Miss Miller assured Aunt Harriet that she would send a letter to the King of England, but that she would ask me to write it for, as a British subject from the West Indies, I might be more familiar with the proper form of address. And Aunt Harriet immediately replied, "I know where he came from as soon as I heard him speak."

Aunt Harriet's ready wit is one of her most pleasing qualities. Wishing to make her an honorary member of the Geneva Political Equality Club, Miss Miller said, "I re-member seeing you years ago at a suffrage convention in Rochester."

"Yes," the old woman affirmed, "I belonged to Miss Sus'n B. Antony's 'sociation."

"I should like to enroll you as a life member of our Geneva Club. Our motto is Lin-coln's declaration: 'I go for all sharing the privileges of the government who assist in bear-ing its burdens, by no means excluding women.' You certainly have assisted in bearing the burden. Do you really believe that women should vote?"

Aunt Harriet paused a moment as if surprised at this question, then quietly replied, "I suffered enough to believe it."

When Miss Miller asked her full name she answered in solemnly measured tones, "Harriet Tubman Davis."

"Shall I write it with or without Mrs.?"

"Any way you like, jus' so you git der Tubman," the old woman responded.

Aunt Harriet proved by this answer that she is a good suffragette and an indepen-dent, self-assertive woman. Tubman, not Davis, was the name of the woman who raided southern plantations and led away slaves, often at the point of the gun, to freedom at the North. Tubman was the name of the woman who nursed the wounded negro sol-diers, who broke through the Confederate lines bearing messages to Shaw and Hunter and Gilmore, never hesitating to risk her life in the cause of human freedom and in the service of her country. This woman does not wish the name under which she did her great work to be obscured or forgotten.

One of the exploits in which Harriet Tubman took part during the Civil War was the bringing of eight hundred slaves to the headquarters of the Federal army at Beau-fort, S. C. These people had been unwilling to leave the plantations, for they mistrusted the Yankee strangers even more than they feared their southern masters. The Federal commander, wishing to cut off the supplies of the Confederates, sent an expedition up the Combahee River to sack the plantations in that region. The expedition was com-manded by Colonel Montgomery, and Harriet, with a few colored soldiers, was sent to round up the slaves. When the colonel saw this motley throng of frightened black Is-raelites, he told their Moses to give them a "word of consolation." And with all the emotional fervor of her African nature the centenarian Amazon sang the words that reassured and consoled her bewildered followers:

"Come along, come along, and don't be fool',

Uncle Sam rich enough to sen' us all to school;

Come along, come along don't be alarm',

Uncle Sam rich enough to give us all a farm."

At the refrain "come along," Aunt Harriet waved her withered arm with an imperious gesture. After nearly fifty years it had not lost its appeal. To illustrate the effect of her song upon the slaves who first heard it, the African Joan clapped her hands and thumped her feet upon the floor. And the old woman's wrinkles shared the pleasant memory of this splendid achievement as she smiled and said, "I done it dat time, but I don't t'ink I coulda done it ag'in."

Harriet Tubman has long been waiting for Uncle Sam to fulfill the promises which she made to her followers. As her own book-knowledge was acquired wholly out of school and consists of passages from the Bible which have been read and expounded in her hearing, she has not been able to hasten the educational, millenium of black Uncle Sam. But she has anticipated the free farm by giving up her own property to provide a home, small and ill-equipped as it is, for the aged and infirm of her race. Her life has been one long "word of consolation" and inspiration to her people. Her song is wellnigh ended. But when her voice is forever stilled, her soul, like the soul of him whom she calls her dearest friend, will yet be "marching on." For Harriet Tubman's soul—the spirit of progress, the determination to rise above the weight of oppression and injustice and breathe the free air of opportunity—is deeply rooted in the people for whom she has lived and worked.

[1911]

VI

John M. Langston (1829–1894), although not well known today, was one of the most prominent African Americans of the nineteenth century, an attorney, educator, politician, and activist. Born of free blacks, he was educated at Oberlin College, served as president of the Ohio Anti-Slavery Society, advised Senator Charles Sumner in the drafting of the Civil Rights Act of 1875 (and was the last African American elected to Congress from the South until 1972). Langston was the first dean of the Howard University Law School, became President of Virginia State University, and American Ambassador to Haiti. He was, in short, one of the most accomplished blacks in American history. The African Americans who in 1889 settled the all-black town of Langston, Oklahoma, named their beloved enclave after him. An excerpt included here from *The Autobiography of John M. Langston* is to entice the readers not only to relive a bit of Langston's vast experience, but to take to heart the wisdom of his words and deeds that he bequeathed to us. This was a speech he made early in his career, and brought his name and intellect to the attention of established leaders of the abolition movement. How do his words resonate with you?

"Speech to the Anti-Slavery Society"

John M. Langston

MR. PRESIDENT, LADIES AND GENTLEMEN:

Some great man has remarked that a nation may lose its liberty in a day, and be a century in finding it out. Does our own nation afford illustration of this statement? There is not, within the length and breadth of this entire country, from Maine to Georgia, from the Atlantic to the Pacific Oceans, a solitary man or woman who is in the possession of his or her full share of civil, religious and political liberty. This is a startling announcement perhaps, made in the heart and center of a country loud in its boasts of its free institutions, its democratic organizations, its equality, its justice and its liberality. We have been in the habit of boasting of our Declaration of Independence, of our Federal Constitution, of the Ordinance of 1787, and various enactments in favor of popular liberty for so long, that we verily believe that we are a free people; and yet I am forced to declare, looking the truth directly in the face and seeing the power of American slavery, that there is not within the bosom of this entire country, a solitary man or woman who can say "I have my full share of liberty." Let the president of this society clothe himself with the panoply of the Constitution of the United States, the Declaration of Independence and the Word of God, and stand up in the presence of the people of South Carolina and say, "I believe in the sentiments contained in the Constitution of my country, in the Declaration of Independence and in the Word of God, respecting the rights of man," and where will be his legal protection? Massachusetts will sit quietly by and see him outraged; the president of the United States will not dare to interfere for his protection; he will be at the mercy of the tyrant slaveholders. Why? Because slavery is the great lord of this country, and there is no power in this nation today strong enough to withstand it.

It would afford me great pleasure, Mr. President, to dwell upon the achievements already gained by the anti-slavery movement. I know that they have been great and glorious; I know that this movement has taught the American people who the slave is, and what his rights are—that he is a man and entitled to all the rights of a man; I know that the attention of the public has been called to the consideration of the colored people, and the attention of the colored people themselves has been awakened to their own condition, so that with longing expectations they begin to say in the language of the poet:—

> "O tell me not that I am blessed,
> Nor hide my glory in my lot,
> That plebeian freemen are oppressed
> With wants and woes that you are not.
> Go let a cage, with grates of gold,
> And pearly roof, the eagle hold;
> Let dainty viands be his fare,
> And give the captive tend'rest care;
> But say, in luxury's limits pent,
> Find you the king of birds content?
> No; oft he'll sound the startling shriek,
> And dash those grates with angry beak.
> Precarious freedom's far more dear
> Than all the prison's pampering cheer;
> He longs to seek his eyrie seat—
> Some cliff on Ocean's lonely shore,
> Whose old bare top the tempests beat,
> And round whose base the billows roar;
> When, clashed by gales, they yawn like graves.
> He longs for joy to skim those waves,
> Or rise through tempest-shrouded air
> All thick and dark with wild winds swelling,
> To brave the lightning's lurid glare,
> And talk with thunders in their dwelling."

As the mountain eagle hates the cage; loathes confinement and longs to be free; so the colored man hates chains, loathes his enslavement and longs to shoulder the responsibilities of dignified life. He longs to stand in the Church, in the State, a man; he longs to stand up a man upon the great theater of existence, everywhere a man; for verily he is a man, and may well adopt the sentiment of the Roman Terrence when he said, "Homo sum, atque humani nihil a me alienum puto"—I am a man, and there is nothing of humanity as I think, estranged to me! Yes, the anti-slavery movement has done this — and it has done more. It has revolutionized to a great degree, the theology and religion of this country. It has taught the American people that the Bible is not on the side of American slavery. No, it cannot be. It was written in characters of light across the gateway of the old Mosaic system, "He that stealeth a man and selleth him, or if he be found in his hand, he shall surely be put to death." That is the only place in the Scriptures where the matter of chattel slavery is mentioned, and the declaration of the Almighty through Moses is: "He that stealeth a man and selleth him, or if he be found in his hand, he shall surely be put to death."

Theodore Weld was right when he said — "The spirit of slavery never takes refuge in the Bible of its own accord. The horns of the altar are its last resort. It seizes them if at all, only in desperation, rushing from the terror of the avenger's arm. Like other unclean spirits it hateth the light, neither cometh to the light lest its deeds should be reproved. Goaded to madness in its conflicts with common sense and natural justice, denied all quarter and hunted from every covert, it breaks at last into the sacred enclosure and courses up and down the Bible, seeking rest and finding none. The Law of Love streaming from every page, flashes around it an omnipresent anguish and despair. It shrinks from the hated light, and howls under the consuming touch, as the demoniacs recoiled from the Son of God and shrieked, 'Torment us not.' At last it slinks away among the shadows of the Mosaic system, and thinks to burrow out of sight among its types and symbols. Vain is its hope! Its asylum is its sepulcher, its city of refuge, the city of destruction. It rushes from light into the sun; from heat into devouring flame; and from the voice of God into the thickest of his thunders."

Yes, the anti-slavery movement has taught the American people this, and more than this. It has taught them that no political party established on the basis of ignoring the question of slavery, can live and breathe in the North. Where is the Whig party?

> "Gone glimmering through the dream of things that were,
> A school-boy's tale, the wonder of an hour!"

The anti-slavery movement has dug its grave deep; it has buried it and is writing for its epitaph, "It was, but is no more." With Daniel Webster the Whig party breathed its last breath.

And where is the Democratic party? It is in power, but all over it is written — *Mene, mene, tekel upharsin.* Weighed in the balances and found wanting!

I would like to dwell on these results of the anti-slavery movement, but I want to make good before this audience my proposition, that there is not within the length and breadth of this land, a solitary freeman. The American people may be divided into four classes; the slaves, the slaveholders and the non-slaveholding whites, and the free people of color.

I need not undertake to show to this audience that the American slave is deprived of his rights. He has none. He has a body, but it is not his own; he has all intellect, but he cannot think for himself; he has sensibility, but he must feel for another. He can own nothing, all belongs to his master.

Then as to the slaveholder himself, we have all come to think that he has all rights; that he is wholly independent, in no wise the subject of regulation made even in the interest of slavery itself. Not so; for a slaveholder cannot sit on the bench or stand at the bar, in the forum or in the pulpit, and utter a solitary sentiment that could be construed as tending to create insubordination among the free people of color anti insurrection among the slaves. Look at the press in the Southern States; it is muzzled and dare not speak out a sentiment in favor of freedom. Let but a sentiment tending toward abolition escape and what is the consequence? Behold the *Parkvile Luminary*, broken to atoms, and the people of that portion of Missouri avowing that that paper never uttered their sentiments or represented their views, and giving thanks to God Almighty that they have had the mob spirit strong enough to destroy that press. Is not this evidence sufficient to show that even slaveholders themselves, are not in possession of their full share of civil, religious and political liberty? If not, consult the statute books of Louisiana and other southern and slaveholding States, burdened with acts forbidding the expression of any sentiment or opinion, tending to the disturbance of their slaves and slaveholding interests.

As to the great mass of the white people at the North, have they their rights. I recollect, when the anti-slavery people held a convention at Cleveland, in 1850, the question came up whether they should hold their next national convention in the city of Washington. The strong political anti-slavery men of the country were there. There were present, Chase and Lewis of Ohio; Cassius M. Clay of Kentucky; Lewis Tappan of New York, and a great many other strong men of the party, and yet when this question came up, how was it decided? Slavery existed in the District of Columbia! And the convention voted that they would not hold the next national meeting at Washington. And what was the reason given? Because the people of that city might use violence! Had the people their full share of liberty, would they have been afraid to go to the capital of the country, and there utter their sentiments on the subject of slavery or any other topic?

But to make the fact more apparent, some two years afterwards, the great National Woman's Rights Convention was held in the same city; and there the very same question came up, whether they should hold their next meeting at Washington or Pittsburg. How was it decided? As the question was about being put, Lucy Stone came forward and said, "I am opposed to going to the city of Washington. They buy and sell women there, and they might outrage us." So the convention voted to hold the next meeting at Pittsburg. Were they in the possession of their full share of liberty? Think of it; our mothers, our wives and our sisters of the North, dare not go to the capital of the country, to hold a Meeting to discuss the question of the rights of their own sex. And yet the Constitution declares that the "citizens of each State shall be entitled to all the rights and immunities of citizens in the several States."

I now wish to speak of another class, and more at length—of that class which I have the honor to represent—the free people of color. What is our condition in respect to civil, religious and political liberty? In the State in which I live, (Ohio), they do not enjoy the elective franchise, and why? It is owing to the indirect influence of American slavery. Slavery in Kentucky, the adjoining State, says to the people of Ohio, you must not allow colored people to vote and be elected to office, because our slaves will hear of it and become restless, and directly we shall have an insurrection and our throats will be cut. And so the people of Ohio say to the colored people, that they cannot allow them the privilege of voting, notwithstanding the colored people pay taxes like others, and in the face of the acknowledged principle that taxation and representation should always go together. And I understand that in the State of New York, the colored man is only allowed the elective franchise through a property qualification, which amounts to nothing short of an insult; for it is not the colored man that votes, but the two hundred and fifty dollars that he may possess. It is not his manhood but his money that is represented. But that is the Yankee idea — the dollar and the cent! In the State of Ohio, the colored man has not the privilege of sending his child to the ordinary common schools, certainly not to those provided for white scholars. Nor is he placed even in the penitentiary on a fair equal footing. If a colored man knocks a white man down, perhaps in defence of his rights, he is sent to the penitentiary; and when he gets there, there is no discrimination made between him and the worst white criminal; but when he marches out to take his meal, he is made to march behind the white criminal, and you may see the prisoners marching, horse thieves in front, colored people behind.

All the prejudice against color that you see in the United States is the fruit of slavery, and is a most effectual barrier to the exercise and enjoyment of the rights of the colored man. In the State of Illinois, they have a law something like this: that if any colored man comes there with the intent to make it his residence, he shall be taken up and fined ten dollars for the first offence; and if he is unable to pay for it, he is put up and sold, and the proceeds of the sale are to go, first towards paving the costs that may accrue in the case, and the residue towards the support and maintenance of a charity fund for the benefit of the *poor whites* of that State. That is a part of the legislation of the State that Stephen A. Douglas has the honor to represent. The public sentiment that is growing up in this country, however, will soon, I hope, be the death of Douglas, and of that sort of legislation.

In the light, therefore, of all the facts, can there be any question that there is no full enjoyment of freedom to anyone in this country? Could John Quincy Adams come forth from his mausoleum, shrouded in his grave clothes, and in the name of the sovereignty of Massachusetts stand up in Charleston and protest against the imprisonment of the citizens of Massachusetts as a violation of their constitutional rights, do you think the people of South Carolina would submit to it? Do you think the reverence due to his name and character, or even the habiliments of the grave about him, would protect him from insult and outrage? So far are the people of this country lost to all sense of shame, that many would laugh at such an outrage.

American slavery has corrupted the whole mass of American society. Its influence has pervaded every crevice and cranny of it. But, Mr. President, I am glad to know that a great change is coming on, and that the American people are beginning to feel that the question of slavery is not one which affects the colored people alone. I am glad to know that they are beginning to feel that it is a National question, in which every man and woman is more or less interested. And when the people of the North shall rise and put on their strength, powerful though slavery is and well-nigh omnipotent, it shall die.

It is only for the people to will it, and it is done. But while the Church and the political parties continue to sustain it; while the people bow down at its bloody feet to worship it, it will live and breathe, active and invincible. Now the question comes home to us, and it is a practical question, in the language of Mr. Phillips, Shall liberty die in this country? Has God Almighty scooped out the Mississippi Valley for its grave? Has

He lifted up the Rocky Mountains for its monument? Has He set Niagara to hymn its requiem? Sir, I hope not. I hope that the Mississippi Valley is to be its cradle; that the Rocky Mountains are to be the stony tablets upon which shall be written its glorious triumphs; and that Niagara has been set not to hymn the death dirge but the triumphal song of our freedom! But, my friends, the question is with us, shall the Declaration of American Independence stand? Shall the Constitution of the United States, if it is anti-slavery, stand? Shall our free institutions triumph, and our country become the asylum of the oppressed of all climes? Shall our government become, in the language of ex-Senator Allen, "a democracy which asks nothing but what it concedes, and concedes nothing but what it demands, destructive of despotism, it is the sole conservator of Liberty, Labor and Property?" May God help the right!

[9 May 1855]

VII

Words from the one white person still most heralded in African-American history are included here. John Brown (1800–1859) to this very day stands as a paramount martyr in the fight against slavery and one of the most determined moral crusaders for black freedom and equality. Brown asked the seminal question: Was America truly a Christian nation? John Brown challenged the nation to abide by the tenants of the Bible. He forfeited his life for the furtherance of his belief in the equality of human beings regardless of race. If his vision and sacrifice have meaning, the readers should take to heart what Brown had to say in his "Address to the Court" during his trial after the failed revolt at Harper's Ferry. He stands tall in his commitment to free the slaves, but even beyond that, the readers are invited to ponder Brown's insistence that what he did would not have been condemned had he led an action in the service of the rich and powerful rather than the downtrodden. What do you think? In your opinion, were his actions necessary? Were they justified? Does violence have a place in resolving issues? Who rules America?

"Address to the Virginia Court"

John Brown

I have, may it please the court, a few words to say.

In the first place, I deny everything but what I have all along admitted,—the design on my part to free slaves. I intended certainly to have made a clean thing of that matter, as I did last winter, when I went into Missouri and took slaves without the snapping of a gun on either side, moved them through the country, and finally left them in Canada. I designed to do the same thing again, on a larger scale. That was all I intended. I never did intend murder, or treason, or the destruction of property, or to excite or incite slaves to rebellion, or to make insurrection.

I have another objection; and that is, it is unjust that I should suffer such a penalty. Had I interfered in the manner which I admit, and which I admit has been fairly proved (for I admire the truthfulness and candor of the greater portion of the witnesses who have testified in this case),—had I so interfered in behalf of the rich, the powerful, the intelligent, the so-called great, or in behalf of any of their friends—either father, mother, sister, wife, or children, or any of that class—and suffered and sacrificed what I have in this interference, it would have been all right; and every man in this court would have deemed it an act worthy of reward rather than punishment.

The court acknowledges, as I suppose, the validity of the law of God. I see a book kissed here which I suppose to be the Bible, or at least the New Testament. That teaches me that all things whatsoever I would that men should do to me, I should do even so to them. It teaches me further to "remember them that are in bonds, as bound with them." I endeavored to act up to that instruction. I say, I am too young to understand that God is any respecter of persons. I believe that to have interfered as I have done—as I have always freely admitted I have done—in behalf of His despised poor, was not wrong, but right. Now if it is deemed necessary that I should forfeit my life for the furtherance of the ends of justice, and mingle my blood further with the blood of my children and with the blood of millions in this slave country whose rights are disregarded by wicked, cruel, and unjust enactments.—I submit; so let it be done!

Let me say one word further.

I feel entirely satisfied with the treatment I have received on my trial. Considering all the circumstances, it has been more generous than I expected. I feel no consciousness of my guilt. I have stated from the first what was my intention, and what was not. I never had any design against the life of any person, nor any disposition to commit treason, or excite slaves to rebel, or make any general insurrection. I never encouraged any man to do so, but always discouraged any idea of any kind.

Let me say also, a word in regard to the statements made by some to those connected with me. I hear it has been said by some of them that I have induced them to join me. But the contrary is true. I do not say this to injure them, but as regretting their weakness. There is not one of them but joined me of his own accord, and the greater part of them at their own expense. A number of them I never saw, and never had a word of conversation with, till the day they came to me; and that was for the purpose I have stated.

Now I have done.

[2 November 1859, Charles Town, Virginia]

VIII

Abraham Lincoln (1809–1865), the Sixteenth President of the United States and the most revered White in African-American history, after John Brown, continues to spark debate, controversy, and disagreement among historians and lay persons. Was Lincoln's primary commitment to preserving the Union or to ending slavery, or was it to both simultaneously? What would be the future for the emancipated blacks? Did Lincoln envision them as equal members of society or as displaced Africans who should be returned to their motherland when the Civil War was over? There is arguably no better or clearer statement of Lincoln's thinking about the future for blacks once they were emancipated than in his "Annual Message to Congress, December 1, 1862." The readers are urged to pay special attention to what Lincoln has to say about the possibility of compensating former slave masters for their slaves and how emancipation will help bring the war more quickly to an end. Is Lincoln in favor of equality for blacks? If so, why does he advocate African repatriation or colonization for the blacks? Did freedom for the blacks, as Lincoln thought it would, benefit white as well as black workers? Finally, what do you think of Lincoln's contention that by "giving freedom to the slaves, we assure freedom to the free"? What does this have to say about the present situation of African Americans? As Lincoln liked to say, "We cannot escape history."

"Annual Message to Congress"

Abraham Lincoln

Fellow-citizens of the Senate and House of Representatives:

Since your last annual assembling another year of health and bountiful harvests has passed. And while it has not pleased the Almighty to bless us with a return of peace, we can but press on, guided by the best light He gives us, trusting that in His own good time, and wise way, all will yet be well.

The correspondence touching foreign affairs which has taken place during the last year is herewith submitted, in virtual compliance with a request to that effect, made by the House of Representatives near the close of the last session of Congress.

If the condition of our relations with other nations is less gratifying than it has usually been at former periods, it is certainly more satisfactory than a nation so unhappily distracted as we are might reasonably have apprehended. In the month of June last there were some grounds to expect that the maritime Powers which, at the beginning of our domestic difficulties, so unwisely and unnecessarily, as we think, recognized the insurgents as a belligerent, would soon recede from that position, which has proved only less injurious to themselves than to our own country. But the temporary reverses which afterwards befell the national arms, and which were exaggerated by our own disloyal citizens abroad, have hitherto delayed that act of simple justice.

The civil war, which has so radically changed for the moment the occupations and habits of the American people, has necessarily disturbed the social condition, and affected very deeply the prosperity of the nations with which we have carried on a commerce that has been steadily increasing throughout a period of half a century. It has, at the same time, excited political ambitions and apprehensions which have produced a profound agitation throughout the civilized world. In this unusual agitation we have forborne from taking part in any controversy between foreign states, and between parties or factions in such states. We have attempted no propagandism, and acknowledged no revolution. But we have left to every nation the exclusive conduct and management of its own affairs. Our struggle has been, of course, contemplated by foreign nations with reference less to its own merits, than to its supposed and often exaggerated effects and consequences resulting to those nations themselves. Nevertheless, complaint on the part of this government, even if it were just, would certainly be unwise.

The treaty with Great Britain for the suppression of the slave trade has been put into operation with a good prospect of complete success. It is an occasion of special pleasure to acknowledge that the execution of it on the part of her Majesty's government has been marked with a jealous respect for the authority of the United States, and the rights of their moral and loyal citizens.

The convention with Hanover for the abolition of the stade dues has been carried into full effect, under the act of Congress or that purpose.

A blockade of three thousand miles of sea-coast could not be established, and vigorously enforced, in a season of great commercial activity like the present, without committing occasional mistakes, and inflicting unintentional injuries upon foreign nations and their subjects.

A civil war occurring in a country where foreigners reside and carry on trade under treaty stipulations, is necessarily fruitful of complaints of the violation of neutral rights. All such collisions end to excite misapprehensions, and possibly to produce mutual reclamations between nations which have a common interest in preserving peace and friendship. In clear cases of these kinds I have, so far as possible, heard and redressed complaints which lave been presented by friendly powers. There is still, however, a large and an augmenting number of doubtful cases upon which the government is unable to agree with the governments whose protection is demanded by the claimants. There are, moreover, many cases in which the United States, or their citizens, suffer wrongs from the naval or military authorities of foreign nations, which the governments of those states are not at once prepared to redress. I have proposed to some of the foreign states, thus interested, mutual conventions to examine and adjust such complaints. This proposition has been made especially to Great Britain, to France, to Spain, and to Prussia. In each case it has been kindly received, but has not yet been formally adopted.

I deem it my duty to recommend an appropriation in behalf of the owners of the Norwegian bark Admiral P. Tordenskiold which vessel was, in May, 1861, prevented by the commander of the blockading force off Charleston from leaving that port with cargo, notwithstanding a similar privilege had, shortly before been granted to an English vessel. I have directed the Secretary of State to cause the papers in the case to be communicated to the proper committees.

Applications have been made to me by many free Americans of African descent to favor their emigration, with a view to such colonization as was contemplated in recent acts of Congress. Other parties, at home and abroad — some from interested motives, others upon patriotic considerations, and still others influenced by philanthropic sentiments — have suggested similar measures; while, on the other hand, several of the Spanish-American republics have protested against the sending of such colonies to their respective territories. Under these circumstances, I have declined to move any such colony to any state, without first obtaining the consent of its government, with an agreement on its part to receive and protect such emigrants in all the rights of freemen; and I have, at the same time, offered to the several states situated within the tropics, or having colonies there, to negotiate with them, subject to the advice and consent of the Senate, to favor the voluntary emigration of persons of that class to their respective territories, upon conditions which shall be equal, just, and humane. Liberia and Hayti are, as yet, the only countries to which colonists of African descent from here, could go with certainty of being received and adopted as citizens; and I regret to say such persons, contemplating colonization do not seem so willing to migrate to those countries as to some others, nor so willing as I think their interest demands. I believe, however, opinion among them, in this respect, is improving; and that ere long, there will be an augmented and considerable migration to both these countries, from the United States.

The new commercial treaty between the United States and the Sultan of Turkey has been carried into execution.

A commercial and consular treaty has been negotiated, subject to the Senate's consent, with Liberia; and a similar negotiation is now pending with the republic of Hayti. A considerable improvement of our national commerce is expected to result from these measures.

Our relations with Great Britain, France, Spain, Portugal, Russia, Prussia, Denmark, Sweden, Austria, the Netherlands, Italy, Rome, and the other European states, remain undisturbed. Very favorable relations also continue to be maintained with Turkey, Morocco, China and Japan.

During the last year there has not only been no change of our previous relations with the independent states of our own continent, but, more friendly sentiments than have heretofore existed are believed to be entertained by these neighbors, whose safety and progress are so intimately connected with our own. This statement especially applies to Mexico, Nicaragua, Costa Rica, Honduras, Peru, and Chile.

The commission under the convention with the republic of New Granada closed its session, without having audited and passed upon all the claims which were submitted to it. A proposition is pending to revive the convention, that it may be able to do more complete justice. The joint commission between the United States and the republic of Costa Rica has completed its labors and submitted its report.

I have favored the project for connecting the United States with Europe by an Atlantic telegraph, and a similar project to extend the telegraph from San Francisco, to connect by a Pacific telegraph with the line which is being extended across the Russian empire.

The Territories of the United States, with unimportant exceptions, have remained undisturbed by the civil war, and they are exhibiting such evidence of prosperity as justifies an expectation that some of them will soon be in a condition to be organized as States, and be constitutionally admitted into the federal Union.

The immense mineral resources of some of those Territories ought to be developed as rapidly as possible. Every step in that direction would have a tendency to improve the revenues of the government, and diminish the burdens of the people. It is worthy of your serious consideration whether some extraordinary measures to promote that end cannot be adopted. The means which suggests itself as most likely to be effective is a scientific exploration of the mineral regions in those Territories, with a view to the publication of its results at home and in foreign countries—results which cannot fail to be auspicious.

The condition of the finances will claim your most diligent consideration. The vast expenditures incident to the military and naval operations required for the suppression of the rebellion, have hitherto been met with a promptitude, and certainty, unusual in similar circumstances, and the public credit has been fully maintained. The continuance of the war, however, and the increased disbursements made necessary by the augmented forces now in the field, demand your best reflections as to the best modes of providing the necessary revenue, without injury to business and with the least possible burdens upon labor.

The suspension of specie payments by the banks, soon after the commencement of your last session, made large issue of United States notes unavoidable. In no other way could the payment of the troops, and the satisfaction of other just demands, be so economically, or so well provided for. The judicious legislation of Congress, securing the receivability of these notes for loans and internal duties, and making them a legal tender for other debts, has made them an universal currency; and has satisfied, partially at least, and for the time, the long felt want of an uniform circulating medium, saving thereby to the people immense sums in discounts and exchanges.

A return to specie payments, however, at the earliest period compatible with due regard to all interests concerned, should ever be kept in view. Fluctuations in the value of currency are always injurious, and to reduce these fluctuations to the lowest possible point will always be a leading purpose in wise legislation. Convertibility, prompt and certain convertibility, into coin is generally acknowledged to be the best and surest safeguard against them; and it is extremely doubtful whether a circulation of United States notes, payable in coin, and sufficiently large for the wants of the people, can be permanently, usefully and safely maintained.

Is there, then, any other mode in which the necessary provision for the public wants can be made, and the great advantages of a safe and uniform currency secured?

I know of none which promises so certain results, and is, at the same time, so unobjectionable, as the organization of banking associations, under a general act of Congress, well guarded in its provisions. To such associations the government might furnish circulating notes, on the security of United States bonds deposited in the treasury. These notes, prepared under the supervision of proper officers, being uniform in appearance and security, and convertible always into coin, would at once protect labor against the evils of a vicious currency, and facilitate commerce by cheap and safe exchanges.

A moderate reservation from the interest on the bonds would compensate the United States for the preparation and distribution of the notes and a general supervision of the system, and would lighten the burden of that part of the public debt employed as securities. The public credit, moreover, would be greatly improved, and the negotiation of new loans greatly facilitated by the steady market demand for government bonds which the adoption of the proposed system would create.

It is an additional recommendation of the measure, of considerable weight, in my judgment, that it would reconcile, as far as possible, all existing interests, by the opportunity offered to existing institutions to reorganize under the act, substituting only the secured uniform national circulation for the local and various circulation, secured and unsecured, now issued by them.

The receipts into the treasury from all sources, including loans and balance from the preceding year, for the fiscal year ending on the 30th June, 1862, were $583,885,247.06, of which sum $49,056,397.62 were derived from customs; $1,795,331.73 from the direct tax; from public lands, $152,203.77; from miscellaneous sources, $931,787.64; from loans in all forms, $529,692,460.50. The remainder, $2,257,065.80, was the balance from last year.

The disbursements during the same period were for congressional, executive, and judicial purposes, $5,939,009.29; for foreign intercourse, $1,339,710.35; for miscellaneous expenses, including the mints, loans, post office deficiencies, collection of revenue, and other like charges, $14,129,771.50; for expenses under the Interior Department, $3,102,985.52; under the War Department, $394,368,407.36; under the Navy Department, $42,674,569.69; for interest on public debt, $13,190,324.45; and for payment of public debt, including reimbursement of temporary loan, and redemptions, $96,096,922.09; making an aggregate of $570,841,700.25, and leaving a balance in the treasury on the first day of July, 1862, of $13,043,546.81.

It should be observed that the sum of $96,096,922.09, expended for reimbursements and redemption of public debt, being included also in the loans made, may be properly deducted, both from receipts and expenditures, leaving the actual receipts for the year $487,788,324.97; and the expenditures, $474,744,778.16.

Other information on the subject of the finances will be found in the report of the Secretary of the Treasury, to whose statements and views I invite your most candid and considerate attention.

The reports of the Secretaries of War, and of the Navy, are herewith transmitted. These reports, though lengthy, are scarcely more than brief abstracts of the very numerous and extensive transactions and operations conducted through those departments. Nor could I give a summary of them here, upon any principle, which would admit of its being much shorter than the reports themselves. I therefore content myself with laying the reports before you, and asking your attention to them.

It gives me pleasure to report a decided improvement in the financial condition of the Post Office Department, as compared with several preceding years. The receipts for the fiscal year 1861 amounted to $8,349,296.40, which embraced the revenue from all the States of the Union for three quarters of that year. Notwithstanding the cessation of revenue from the so-called seceded States during the last fiscal year, the increase of the correspondence of the loyal States has been sufficient to produce a revenue during the same year of $8,299,820.90, being only $50,000 less than was derived from all the States of the Union during the previous year. The expenditures show a still more favorable result. The amount expended in 1861 was $13,606,759.11. For the last year the amount has been reduced to $11,125,364.13, showing a decrease of about $2,481,000 in the expenditures as compared with the preceding year and about $3,750,000 as compared with the fiscal year 1860. The deficiency in the department for the previous year was $4,551,966.98. For the last fiscal year it was reduced to $2,112,814.57. These favorable results are in part owing to the cessation of mail service in the insurrectionary States, and in part to a careful review of all expenditures in that department in the interest of economy. The efficiency of the postal service, it is believed, has also been much improved. The Postmaster General has also opened a correspondence, through the Department of State, with foreign governments, proposing a convention of postal representatives for the purpose of simplifying the rates of foreign postage, and to expedite the foreign mails. This proposition, equally important to our adopted citizens, and to the commercial interests of this country, has been favorably entertained, and agreed to, by all the governments from whom replies have been received.

I ask the attention of Congress to the suggestions of the Postmaster General in his report respecting the further legislation required, in his opinion, for the benefit of the postal service.

The Secretary of the Interior reports as follows in regard to the public lands:

"The public lands have ceased to be a source of revenue. From the 1st July, 1861, to the 30th September, 1862, the entire cash receipts from the sale of lands were $137,476.26—a sum much less than the expenses of our land system during the same period. The homestead law, which will take effect on the 1st of January next, offers such inducements to settlers, that sales for cash cannot be expected, to an extent sufficient to meet the expenses of the General Land Office, and the cost of surveying and bringing the land into market."

The discrepancy between the sum here stated as arising from the sales of the public lands, and the sum derived from the same source as reported from the Treasury Department, arises, as I understand, from the fact that the periods of time, though apparently, were not really, coincident at the beginning point—the Treasury report including a considerable sum now, which had previously been reported from the Interior—sufficiently large to greatly overreach the sum derived from the three months now reported upon by the Interior, and not by the Treasury.

The Indian tribes upon our frontiers have, during the past year, manifested a spirit of insubordination, and, at several points, have engaged in open hostilities against the white settlements in their vicinity. The tribes occupying the Indian country south of Kansas renounced their allegiance to the United States, and entered into treaties with the insurgents. Those who remained loyal to the United States were driven from the country. The chief of the Cherokees has visited this city for the purpose of restoring the former relations of the tribe with the United States. He alleges that they were constrained, by superior force, to enter into treaties with the insurgents, and that the United States neglected to furnish the protection which their treaty stipulations required.

In the month of August last the Sioux Indians, in Minnesota, attacked the settlements in their vicinity with extreme ferocity, killing, indiscriminately, men, women, and children. This attack was wholly unexpected, and, therefore, no means of defence had been provided. It is estimated that not less than eight hundred persons were killed by the Indians, and a large amount of property was destroyed. How this outbreak was induced is not definitely known, and suspicions, which may be unjust, need not to be stated. Information was received by the Indian bureau, from different sources, about the time hostilities were commenced, that a simultaneous attack was to be made upon the white settlements by all the tribes between the Mississippi River and the Rocky Mountains. The State of Minnesota has suffered great injury from this Indian war. A large portion of her territory has been depopulated, and a severe loss has been sustained by the destruction of property. The people of that State manifest much anxiety for the removal of the tribes beyond the limits of the State as a guarantee against future hostilities. The Commissioner of Indian Affairs will furnish full details. I submit for your especial consideration whether our Indian system shall not be remodelled. Many wise and good men have impressed me with the belief that this can be profitably done.

I submit a statement of the proceedings of commissioners, which shows the progress that has been made in the enterprise of constructing the Pacific railroad. And this suggests the earliest completion of this road, and also the favorable action of Congress upon the projects now pending before them for enlarging the capacities of the great canals in New York and Illinois, as being of vital and rapidly increasing importance to the whole nation, and especially to the vast interior region hereinafter to be noticed at some greater length. I propose having prepared and laid before you at an early day some interesting and valuable statistical information upon this subject. The military and commercial importance of enlarging the Illinois and Michigan canal, and improving the Illinois River, is presented in the report of Colonel Webster to the Secretary of War, and now transmitted to Congress. I respectfully ask attention to it.

To carry out the provisions of the act of Congress of the 15th of May last, I have caused the Department of Agriculture of the United States to be organized.

The commissioner informs me that within the period of a few months this department has established an extensive system of correspondence and exchanges, both at home and abroad, which promises to effect highly beneficial results in the development of a correct knowledge of recent improvements in agriculture, in the introduction of new products, and in the collection of the agricultural statistics of the different States.

Also, that it will soon be prepared to distribute largely seeds, cereals, plants and cuttings, and has already published, and liberally diffused, much valuable information in anticipation of a more elaborate report, which will in due time be furnished, embracing some valuable tests in chemical science now in progress in the laboratory.

The creation of this department was for the more immediate benefit of a large class of our most valuable citizens; and I trust that the liberal basis upon which it has been organized will not only meet your approbation, but that it will realize, at no distant day, all the fondest anticipations of its most sanguine friends, and become the fruitful source of advantage to all our people.

On the twenty-second day of September last a proclamation was issued by the Executive, a copy of which is herewith submitted.

In accordance with the purpose expressed in the second paragraph of that paper, I now respectfully recall your attention to what may be called "compensated emancipation."

A nation may be said to consist of its territory, its people, and its laws. The territory is the only part which is of certain durability. "One generation passeth away, and another generation cometh, but the earth abideth forever." It is of the first importance to duly consider, and estimate, this ever-enduring part. That portion of the earth's surface which is owned and inhabited by the people of the United States is well adapted to be the home of one national family; and it is not well adapted for two, or more. Its vast extent, and its variety of climate and productions, are of advantage, in this age, for one people, whatever they might have been in former ages. Steam, telegraphs, and intelligence have brought these to be an advantageous combination for one united people.

In the inaugural address I briefly pointed out the total inadequacy of disunion, as a remedy for the differences between the people of the two sections. I did so in language which I cannot improve, and which, therefore, I beg to repeat:

"One section of our country believes slavery is right, and ought to be extended, while the other believes it is wrong, and ought not to be extended. This is the only substantial dispute. The fugitive slave clause of the Constitution, and the law for the suppression of the foreign slave trade, are each as well enforced, perhaps, as any law can ever be in a community where the moral sense of the people imperfectly supports the law itself. The great body of the people abide by the dry legal obligation in both cases, and a few break over in each. This, I think, cannot be perfectly cured; and it would be worse in both cases after the separation of the sections, than before. The foreign slave trade, now imperfectly suppressed, would be ultimately revived without restriction in one section; while fugitive slaves, now only partially surrendered, would not be surrendered at all by the other.

"Physically speaking, we cannot separate. We cannot remove our respective sections from each other, nor build an impassable wall between them. A husband and wife may be divorced, and go out of the presence, and beyond the reach of each other; but the different parts of our country cannot do this. They cannot but remain face to face; and intercourse, either amicable or hostile, must continue between them. Is it possible, then, to make that intercourse more advantageous, or more satisfactory, after separation than before? Can aliens make treaties, easier than friends can make laws? Can treaties be more faithfully enforced between aliens, than laws can among friends? Suppose you go to war, you cannot fight always; and when, after much loss on both sides, and no gain on either, you cease fighting, the identical old questions, as to terms of intercourse, are again upon you."

There is no line, straight or crooked, suitable for a national boundary, upon which to divide. Trace through, from east to west, upon the line between the free and slave country, and we shall find a little more than one-third of its length are rivers, easy to be crossed, and populated, or soon to be populated, thickly upon both sides; while nearly all its remaining length are merely surveyor's lines, over which people may walk back and forth without any consciousness of their presence. No part of this line can be made any more difficult to pass, by writing it down on paper, or parchment, as a national boundary. The fact of separation, if it comes, gives up, on the part of the seceding section, the fugitive slave clause, along with all other constitutional obligations upon the section seceded from, while I should expect no treaty stipulation would be ever made to take its place.

But there is another difficulty. The great interior region, bounded east by the Alleghanies, north by the British dominions, west by the Rocky Mountains, and south by the line along which the culture of corn and cotton meets, and which includes part of Virginia, part of Tennessee, all of Kentucky, Ohio, Indiana, Michigan, Wisconsin, Illinois, Missouri, Kansas, Iowa, Minnesota, and the Territories of Dakota, Nebraska, and part of Colorado, already has above ten millions of people, and will have fifty millions within fifty years, if not prevented by any political folk or mistake. It contains more than one third of the country owned by the United States—certainly more than one million of square miles. Once half as populous as Massachusetts already is, it would have more than seventy-five millions of people. A glance at the map shows that, territorially speaking, it is the great body of the republic. The other parts are but marginal borders to it, the magnificent region sloping west from the Rocky Mountains to the Pacific, being the deepest and also the richest in undeveloped resources. In the production of provisions, grains, grasses, and all which proceed from them, this great interior region is naturally one of the most important in the world. Ascertain from the statistics the small proportion of the region which has, as yet, been brought into cultivation, and also the large and rapidly increasing amount of its products, and we shall be overwhelmed with the magnitude of the prospect presented. And yet this region has no sea-coast, touches no ocean anywhere. As part of one nation, its people now find, and may forever find, their way to Europe by New York, to South America and Africa by New Orleans, and to Asia by San Francisco. But separate our common country into two nations, as designed by the present rebellion, and every man of this great interior region is thereby cut off from some one or more of these outlets, not, perhaps, by a physical barrier, but by embarrassing and onerous trade regulations.

And this is true, wherever a dividing or boundary line may be fixed. Place it between the now free and slave country, or place it south of Kentucky, or north of Ohio, and still the truth remains, that none south of it, can trade to any port or place north of it, and none north of it, can trade to any port or place south of it, except upon terms dictated by a government foreign to them. These outlets, east, west, and south, are indispensable to the well-being of the people inhabiting, and to inhabit, this vast interior region. Which of the three may be the best, is no proper question. All are better than either, and all, of right, belong to that people, and to their successors forever. True to themselves, they will not ask where a line of separation shall be, but will vow, rather, that there shall be no such line. Nor are the marginal regions less interested in these communications to, and through them, to the great outside world. They, too, and each of them, must have access to this Egypt of the West, without paying toll at the crossing of any national boundary.

Our national strife springs not from our permanent part; not from the land we inhabit; not from our national homestead. There is no possible severing of this, but would multiply, and not mitigate, evils among us. In all its adaptations and aptitudes, it demands union, and abhors separation. In fact, it would, ere long, force reunion, however much of blood and treasure the separation might have cost.

Our strife pertains to ourselves—to the passing generations of men; and it can, without convulsion, be hushed forever with the passing of one generation.

In this view, I recommend the adoption of the following resolution and articles amendatory to the Constitution of the United States:

"Resolved by the Senate and House of Representatives of the United States of America in Congress assembled, (two-thirds of both Houses concurring), That the following articles be proposed to the legislatures (or conventions) of the several States as amendments to the Constitution of the United States, all or any of which articles when ratified by three fourths of the said legislatures (or conventions) to be valid as part or parts of the said Constitution, viz:

"Article—.

"Every State, wherein slavery now exists, which shall abolish the same therein, at any time, or times, before the first day of January, in the year of our Lord one thousand and nine hundred, shall receive compensation from the United States, as follows, to wit:

"The President of the United States shall deliver to every such State, bonds of the United States, bearing interest at the rate of _____ percent, per annum, to an amount equal to the aggregate sum of _____ for each slave shown to have been therein, by the eighth census of the United States, said bonds to be delivered to such State by installments, or in one parcel, at the completion of the abolishment, accordingly as the same shall have been gradual, or at one time, within such State; and interest shall begin to run upon any such bond, only from the proper time of its delivery as aforesaid. Any State having received bonds as aforesaid, and afterwards reintroducing or tolerating slavery therein, shall refund to the United States the bonds so received, or the value thereof, and all interest paid thereon.

"Article —.

"All slaves who shall have enjoyed actual freedom by the chances of the war, at any time before the end of the rebellion, shall be forever free; but all owners of such, who shall not have been disloyal, shall be compensated for them, at the same rates as is provided for States adopting abolishment of slavery, but in such way, that no slave shall be twice accounted for.

"Article —.

"Congress may appropriate money, and otherwise provide, for colonizing free colored persons, with their own consent, at any place or places without the United States."

I beg indulgence to discuss these proposed articles at some length. Without slavery the rebellion could never have existed: without slavery it could not continue.

Among the friends of the Union there is great diversity of sentiment, and of policy, in regard to slavery, and the African race amongst us. Some would perpetuate slavery; some would abolish it suddenly, and without compensation; some would abolish it gradually, and with compensation; some would remove the freed people from us, and some would retain them with us; and there are yet other minor diversities. Because of these diversities, we waste much strength in struggles among ourselves. By mutual concession we should harmonize, and act together. This would be compromise; but it would be compromise among the friends, and not with the enemies of the Union. These articles are intended to embody a plan of such mutual concessions. If the plan shall be adopted, it is assumed that emancipation will follow, at least, in several of the States.

As to the first article, the main points are: first, the emancipation; secondly, the length of time for consummating it—thirty-seven years; and thirdly, the compensation.

The emancipation will be unsatisfactory to the advocates of perpetual slavery; but the length of time should greatly mitigate heir dissatisfaction. The time spares both races from the evils of sudden derangement—in fact, from the necessity of any derangement—while most of those whose habitual course of thought will be disturbed by the measure will have passed away before its consummation. They will never see it. Another class will hail the prospect of emancipation, but will deprecate the length of time. They will feel that it gives too little to the now living slaves. But it really gives them much. It saves them from the vagrant destitution which must largely attend immediate emancipation in localities where their numbers are very great; and it gives the inspiring assurance that their posterity shall be free forever. The plan leaves to each State, choosing to act under it, to abolish slavery now, or at the end of the century, or at any intermediate time, or by degrees, extending over the whole or any part of the period; and it obliges no two States to proceed alike. It also provides for compensation, and generally the mode of making it. This, it would seem, must further mitigate the dissatisfaction of those who favor perpetual slavery, and especially of those who are to receive the compensation. Doubtless some of those who are to pay, and not to receive will object. Yet the measure is both just and economical. In a certain sense the liberation of slaves is the destruction of property—property acquired by descent, or by purchase, the same as any other property. It is no less true for laving been often said, that the people of the South are not more responsible for the original introduction of this property, than are the people of the North; and when it is remembered how unhesitatingly we all use cotton and sugar, and share the profits of leafing in them, it may not be quite safe to say, that the South has been more responsible than the North for its continuance. If then, for a common object, this property is to be sacrificed is it not just that it be done at a common charge?

And if, with less money, or money more easily paid, we can preserve the benefits of the Union by this means, than we can by the war alone, is it not also economical to do it? Let us consider it then. Let us ascertain the sum we have expended in the war since compensated emancipation was proposed last March, and consider whether, if that measure had been promptly accepted by even some of the slave States, the same sum would not have done more to close the war, than has been otherwise done. If so the measure would save money, and in that view, would be a prudent and economical measure. Certainly it is not so easy to pay something as it is to pay nothing; but it is easier to pay a large sum than it is to pay a larger one. And it is easier to pay any sum when we are able, than it is to pay it before we are able. The war requires large sums, and requires them at once. The aggregate sum necessary for compensated emancipation, of course, would be large. But it would require no ready cash; nor the bonds even, any faster than the emancipation progresses. This might not, and probably would not, close before the end of the thirty-seven years. At that time we shall probably have a hundred millions of people to share the burden, instead of thirty-one millions, as now. And not only so, but the increase of our population may be expected to continue for a long time after that period, as rapidly as before, because our territory will not have become full. I do not state this inconsiderately. At the same ratio of increase which we have maintained, on an average, from our first national census, in 1790, until that of 1860, we should, in 1900, have a population of 103,208,415. And why may we not continue that ratio far beyond that period? Our abundant room—our broad national homestead—is our ample resource. Were our territory as limited as are the British Isles, very certainly our population could not expand as stated. Instead of receiving the foreign born, as now, we should be compelled to send part of the native born away. But such is not our condition. We have two millions nine hundred and sixty-three thousand square miles. Europe has three millions and eight hundred thousand, with a population averaging seventy-three and one-third persons to the square mile. Why may not our country, at some time, average as many? Is it less fertile? Has it more waste surface, by mountains, rivers, lakes, deserts, or other causes? Is it inferior to Europe in any natural advantage? If, then, we are, at some time, to be as populous as Europe, how soon? As to when this may be, we can judge by the past and the present; as to when it will be, if ever, depends much on whether we maintain the Union. Several of our States are already above the average of Europe—seventy three and a third of the square mile. Massachusetts has 157; Rhode Island, 133; Connecticut, 99; New York and New Jersey, each, 80. Also two other great States, Pennsylvania and Ohio, are not far below, the former having 63, and the latter 59. The States already above the European average, except New York, have increased in as rapid a ratio, since passing that point, as ever before; while no one of them is equal to some other parts of our country in natural capacity for sustaining a dense population.

Taking the nation in the aggregate, and we find its population and ratio of increase, for the several decennial periods, to be as follows:

1790	3,929,827	
1800	5,305,937	35.02 per cent. ratio of increase.
1810	7,239,814	36.45 " " " "
1820	9,638,131	33.13 " " " "
1830	12,866,020	33.49 " " " "
1840	17,069,453	32.67 " " " "
1850	23,191,876	35.87 " " " "
1860	31,443,790	35.58 " " " "

This shows an average decennial increase of 34.60 per cent, a population through the seventy years from our first, to our last census yet taken. It is seen that the ratio of increase, at no one of these seven periods, is either two per cent, below, or two per cent, above, the average; thus showing how inflexible, and, consequently, how reliable, the law of increase, in our case, is. Assuming that it will continue, gives the following results:—

1870	42,323,341
1880	56,967,216
1890	76,677,872
1900	103,208,415
1910	138,918,526
1920	186,984,335
1930	251,680,914

These figures show that our country may be as populous as Europe now is, at some point between 1920 and 1930—say about 1925—our territory, at seventy-three and a third persons to the square mile, being of capacity to contain 217,186,000.

And we will reach this, too, if we do not ourselves relinquish the chance, by the folly and evils of disunion, or by long and exhausting war springing from the only great element of national discord among us. While it cannot be foreseen exactly how much one huge example of secession, breeding lesser ones indefinitely, would retard population, civilization, and prosperity, no one can doubt that the extent of it would be very great and injurious.

The proposed emancipation would shorten the war, perpetuate peace, insure this increase of population, and proportionately the wealth of the country. With these, we should pay all the emancipation would cost, together with our other debt easier than we should pay our other debt, without it. If we had allowed our old national debt to run at six per cent per annum, simple interest, from the end of our revolutionary struggle until today, without paying anything on either principal or interest, each man of us would owe less upon that debt now, than each owed upon it then; and this because our increase of men, through the whole period, has been greater than six per cent— has run faster than the interest upon the debt. Thus, time alone relieves a debtor nation, so long as its population increases faster than unpaid interest accumulates on its debt.

This fact would be no excuse for delaying payment of what is justly due; but it shows the great importance of time in this connexion—the great advantage of a policy by which we shall not have to pay until we number a hundred millions, what, by a different policy, we would have to pay now, when we number but thirty one millions. In a word, it shows that a dollar will be much harder to pay for the war, than will be a dollar for emancipation on the proposed plan. And then the latter will cost no blood, no precious life. It will be a saving of both.

As to the second article, I think it would be impracticable to return to bondage the class of persons therein contemplated. Some of them, doubtless, in the property sense, belong to loyal owners; and hence, provision is made in this article for compensating such.

The third article relates to the future of the freed people. It does not oblige, but merely authorizes, Congress to aid in colonizing such as may consent. This ought not to be regarded as objectionable, on the one hand, or on the other, in so much as it comes of nothing, unless by the mutual consent of the people to be deported, and the American voters, through their representatives in Congress.

I cannot make it better known than it already is, that I strongly favor colonization. And yet I wish to say there is an objection urged against free colored persons remaining in the country, which is largely imaginary, if not sometimes malicious.

It is insisted that their presence would injure, and displace white labor and white laborers. If there ever could be a proper time for mere catch arguments, that time surely is not now. In times like the present, men should utter nothing for which they would not willingly be responsible through time and in eternity. Is it true, then, that colored people can displace any more white labor, by being free, than by remaining slaves? If they stay in heir old places, they jostle no white laborers; if they leave their old places, they leave them open to white laborers. Logically, here is neither more nor less of it. Emancipation, even without deportation, would probably enhance the wages of white labor, and, very surely, would not reduce them. Thus, the customary amount of labor would still have to be performed; the freed people would surely not do more than their old proportion of it, and very probably, for a time, would do less, leaving an increased part to white laborers, bringing their labor into greater demand, and, consequently, enhancing the wages of it. With deportation, even to a limited extent, enhanced wages to white labor is mathmatically certain. Labor is like any other commodity in the market — increase the demand for it, and you increase the price of it. Reduce the supply of black labor, by colonizing the black laborer out of the country, and, by precisely so much, you increase the demand for, and wages of, white labor.

But it is dreaded that the freed people will swarm forth, and cover the whole land? Are they not already in the land? Will liberation make them any more numerous? Equally distributed among the whites of the whole country, and there would be but one colored to seven whites. Could the one, in any way, greatly disturb the seven? There are many communities now, having more than one free colored person, to seven whites; and this, without any apparent consciousness of evil from it. The District of Columbia, and the States of Maryland and Delaware, are all in this condition. The district has more than one free colored to six whites; and yet, in its frequent petitions to Congress, I believe it has never presented the presence of free colored persons as one of its grievances. But why should emancipation south, send the freed people north? People, of any color, seldom run, unless there be something to run from. Heretofore colored people, to some extent, have fled north from bondage; and now, perhaps, from both bondage and destitution. But if gradual emancipation and deportation be adopted, they will have neither to flee from. Their old masters will give them wages at least until new laborers can be procured; and the freed men, in turn, will gladly give their labor for the wages, till new homes can be found for them, in congenial climes, and with people of their own blood and race. This proposition can be trusted on the mutual interests involved. And, in any event, cannot the north decide for itself, whether to receive them?

Again, as practice proves more than theory, in any case, has there been any irruption of colored people northward, because of the abolishment of slavery in this District last spring?

What I have said of the proportion of free colored persons to the whites, in the District, is from the census of 1860, having no reference to persons called contrabands, nor to those made free by the act of Congress abolishing slavery here.

The plan consisting of these articles is recommended, not but that a restoration of the national authority would be accepted without its adoption.

Nor will the war, nor proceedings under the proclamation of September 22, 1862, be stayed because of the recommendation of this plan. Its timely adoption, I doubt not, would bring restoration and thereby stay both.

And, notwithstanding this plan, the recommendation that Congress provide by law for compensating any State which may adopt emancipation, before this plan shall have been acted upon, hereby earnestly renewed. Such would be only an advance part of the plan, and the same arguments apply to both.

This plan is recommended as a means, not in exclusion of, but additional to, all others for restoring and preserving the national authority throughout the Union. The subject is presented exclusively in its economical aspect. The plan would, I am confident, secure peace more speedily, and maintain it more permanently, than can be done by force alone; while all it would cost, considering amounts, and manner of payment, and times of payment, would be easier paid than will, be the additional cost of the war, if we rely solely upon force. It is much—very much—that it would cost no blood at all.

The plan is proposed as permanent constitutional law. It cannot become such without the concurrence of, first, two-thirds of Congress, and, afterwards, three-fourths of the States. The requisite three-fourths of the States will necessarily include seven of the Slave States. Their concurrence, if obtained, will give assurance of their severally adopting emancipation, at no very distant day, upon the new constitutional terms. This assurance would end the struggle now, and save the Union forever.

I do not forget the gravity which should characterize a paper addressed to the Congress of the nation by the Chief Magistrate of the nation. Nor do I forget that some of you are my seniors, nor that many of you have more experience than I, in the conduct of public affairs. Yet I trust that in view of the great responsibility resting upon me, you will perceive no want of respect yourselves, in any undue earnestness I may seem to display.

Is it doubted, then, that the plan I propose, if adopted, would shorten the war, and thus lessen its expenditure of money and of blood? Is it doubted that it would restore the national authority and national prosperity, and perpetuate both indefinitely? Is it doubted that we here—Congress and Executive—can secure its adoption? Will not the good people respond to a united and earnest appeal from us? Can we, can they, by any other means, so certainly, or so speedily, assure these vital objects? We can succeed only by concert. It is not "can any of us imagine better?" but, "can we all do better?" Object whatsoever is possible, still the question recurs, "can we do better?" The dogmas of the quiet past, are inadequate to the stormy present. The occasion is piled high with difficulty, and we must rise with the occasion. As our case is new, so we must think anew, and act anew. We must disenthrall ourselves, and then we shall save our country.

Fellow-citizens, we cannot escape history. We of this Congress and this administration, will be remembered in spite of ourselves. No personal significance, or insignificance, can spare one or another of us. The fiery trial through which we pass, will light us down, in honor or dishonor, to the latest generation. We say we are for the Union. The world will not forget that we say this. We know how to save the Union. The world knows we do know how to save it. We—even we here—hold the power, and bear the responsibility. In giving freedom to the slave, we assure freedom to the free—honorable alike in what we give, and what we preserve. We shall nobly save, or meanly lose, the last best hope of earth. Other means may succeed; this could not fail. The way is plain, peaceful, generous, just—a way which, if followed, the world will forever applaud, and God must forever bless.

[1 December 1862]

—

IX

No voice ran with keener assertion in the struggle for freedom and advancement of the race and for gender equality than that of Sojourner Truth (c 1797–1883). A pioneer abolitionist and fighter for women's rights, Sojourner Truth, although unlettered, was an articulate and powerful spokesperson for freedom, equality, and empowerment. The most noted of her speeches, "Ain't I A Woman," she delivered in Ohio in 1851 at a national suffragette meeting. She spoke truth to power without hesitation. Courageous and feisty in the best sense of the word, Truth spoke in a passionate voice to men as well as to women. Her speech is not long, but poignant and powerful. Her words have stood the test of time. The readers might well benefit by asking: Is Sojourner Truth speaking to me? What do I take away from her words of wisdom? Are there obstacles today that need to be approached with the same vigor and determination as she exemplified?

"Ain't I A Woman?"

Sojourner Truth

Well, children, where there is so much racket there must be something out of kilter. I think that 'twixt the negroes of the South and the women at the North, all talking about rights, the white men will be in a fix pretty soon. But what's all this here talking about?

That man over there says that women need to be helped into carriages, and lifted over ditches, and to have the best place everywhere. Nobody ever helps me into carriages, or over mud-puddles, or gives me any best place! And ain't I a woman? Look at me! Look at my arm! I have ploughed and planted, and gathered into barns, and no man could head me! And ain't I a woman? I could work as much and eat as much as a man—when I could get it—and bear the lash as well! And ain't I a woman? I have borne thirteen children, and seen most all sold off to slavery, and when I cried out with my mother's grief, none but Jesus heard me! And ain't I a woman?

Then they talk about this thing in the head; what's this they call it? [member of audience whispers, "intellect"] That's it, honey. What's that got to do with women's rights or negroes' rights? If my cup won't hold but a pint, and yours holds a quart, wouldn't you be mean not to let me have my little half measure full?

Then that little man in black there, he says women can't have as much rights as men, 'cause Christ wasn't a woman! Where did your Christ come from? Where did your Christ come from? From God and a woman! Man had nothing to do with Him.

If the first woman God ever made was strong enough to turn the world upside down all alone, these women together ought to be able to turn it back, and get it right side up again! And now they is asking to do it, the men better let them.

Obliged to you for hearing me, and now old Sojourner ain't got nothing more to say.

[1851]

X

Timeless direction was offered by Martin R. Delany (1812–1885), abolitionist, physician, writer, and advocate of African repatriation. Delany was an African American of many firsts. He was a member of the first class of African Americans to attend Harvard Medical School, the highest ranking black officer in the Civil War when he attained the rank of major, and one of the first of the noted Black Nationalists, writing diligently of the African continent and the future for it and its people of the Diaspora. Delany's efficacy of African repatriation is often cited, but he told too of the business successes of blacks in the United States and their ability to achieve despite the odds. He offers the readers strong historical examples of black entrepreneurship and calls on the race to continue this momentum. In "Practical Utility of Colored People of the Present Day as Members of Society," Delaney presents an economic vision and, citing examples, an action agenda for African Americans. Today's readers may well find Delany's words as practical today as they were back then. Are they? What do you think?

"Practical Utility of Colored People of the Present Day as Members of Society— Business Men and Mechanics"

Martin R. Delany

In calling attention to the practical utility of colored people of the present day, we shall not be general in our observations, but simply, direct attention to a few particular instances, in which colored persons have been responsibly engaged in extensive business, or occupying useful positions, thus contributing to the general welfare of community at large, filling their places in society as men and women.

It will studiously be borne in mind, that our sole object in giving these cases publicity, is to refute the objections urged against us, that we are not useful members of society. That we are consumers and non-producers—that we contribute nothing to the general progress of man. No people who have enjoyed no greater opportunity for improvement, could possibly have made greater progress in the same length of time than have done the colored people of the present day.

A people laboring under many disadvantages, may not be expected to present at once, especially before they have become entirely untrammeled, evidence of entire equality with more highly favored people.

When Mr. Jefferson, the great American Statesman and philosopher, was questioned by an English gentleman, on the subject of American greatness, and referred to their literature as an evidence of inferiority to the more highly favored and long-existing European nations; Mr. Jefferson's reply was—"When the United States have existed as long as a nation, as Greece before she produced her Homer and Socrates; Rome, before she produced her Virgil, Horace, and Cicero; and England, before she produced her Pope, Dryden, and Bacon"; then he might consider the comparison a just one. And all we shall ask, is not to wait so long as this, not to wait until we become a nation at all, so far as the United States are concerned, but only to unfetter our brethren, and give us, the freemen, an equal chance for emulation, and we will admit any comparison you may please to make in a quarter of a century after.

For a number of years, the late James Forten, of Philadelphia, was the proprietor of one of the principal sail manufactories, constantly employing a large number of men, black and white, supplying a large number of masters and owners of vessels, with full rigging for their crafts.

On the failure of an extensive house, T. & Co., in that city, during the pressure which followed a removal of the deposits of the United States Treasury in 1837, Mr. Forten lost by that firm, nine thousand dollars. Being himself in good circumstances at the time, hearing of the failure of old constant patrons, he called at the house; one of the proprietors, Mr. T., on his entering the warehouse door, came forward, taking him by the hand observed, "Ah! Mr. Forten, it is useless to call on us—we are gone—we can do nothing!" at which Mr. Forten remarked, "Sir, I hope you think better of me than to suppose me capable of calling on a friend to torture him in adversity! I came, sir, to express my regret at your misfortune, and if possible, to cheer you by words of encouragement. If your liabilities were all in my hands, you should never be under the necessity of closing business." Mr. Forten exchanged paper and signatures with some of the first business men in Philadelphia, and raised and educated a large and respectable family of sons and daughters, leaving an excellent widow.

Joseph Cassey, recently deceased, was the "architect of his own fortune," and by industry and application to business, became a money broker in the city of Philadelphia; who becoming indisposed from a chronic affection, was obliged to retire from business for many years previous to his death. Had Mr. Cassey been favored with health, he doubtless would have become a very wealthy man. His name and paper was good in any house in the city, and there was no banker of moderate capital, of more benefit to the business community than was Joseph Cassey. He also left a young and promising family of five sons, one daughter, a most excellent widow, and a fortune of seventy-five thousand dollars, clear of all encumbrance.

Stephen Smith, of the firm of Smith and Whipper, is a remarkable man in many respects, and decidedly the most wealthy colored man in the United States. Mr. Smith commenced business after he was thirty years of age, without the advantages of a good business education, but by application, qualified himself for the arduous duties of his vocation. For many years, he has been known as the principal lumber merchant in Columbia, Lancaster Co., Pa., and for several years past associated with W. Whipper, a gentleman of great force of character, talents, and business qualifications, Mr. Smith residing in Philadelphia. Smith and Whipper, are very extensive business men, and very valuable members of the community, both of Lancaster and Philadelphia counties. By the judicious investment of their capital, they keep in constant employment a large number of persons; purchasing many rafts at a time, and many thousand bushels of coal. It is not only the laborer in "drawing boards," and the coal hauler and heaver, that are here benefitted by their capital, but the original owners of the lumber and coal purchased by them, and the large number of boatmen and raftsmen employed in bringing these commodities to market.

In the winter of 1849, these gentlemen had in store, several thousand bushels of coal, two million two hundred and fifty thousand feet of lumber; twenty-two of the finest merchantmen cars running on the railway from Philadelphia to Baltimore; nine thousand dollars' worth of stock in the Columbia Bridge; eighteen thousand dollars in stock in the Columbia Bank; and besides this, Mr. Smith was then the reputed owner of fifty-two good brick houses of various dimensions in the city of Philadelphia, besides several in the city of Lancaster, and the town of Columbia. Mr. Smith's paper, or the paper of the firm, is good for any amount wherever they are known; and we have known gentlemen to present the paper of some of the best men in the city, which was cashed by him at sight. The principal active business attended to by Mr. S. in person, is that of buying good negotiable and other paper, and speculating in real estate. The business of the firm is attended to by Mr. Whipper, who is a relative. Take Smith and Whipper from Lancaster and Philadelphia counties, and the business community will experience a hiatus in its connexion, that may not be easily filled.

Samuel T. Wilcox, of Cincinnati, Ohio, also stands conspicuously among the most respectable business men of the day. Being yet a young man, just scanning forty, he is one among the extraordinary men of the times.

Born, like the most of colored men in this country, in obscurity, of poor parents, raised without the assistance of a father, and to a commonplace business, without the advantages of schools, by his own perseverance, he qualified himself to the extent that gave him an inclination to traffic, which he did for several years on the Mississippi and Ohio rivers, investing his gains in real estate, until he acquired a considerable property. For the purpose of extending his usefulness, and at the same time pursuing a vocation more in accordance with his own desires, a few years since, he embarked in the wholesale and retail Family Grocery business, and now has the best general assortment and most extensive business house of the kind, in the city of Cincinnati. The establishment is really beautiful, having the appearance more of an apothecary store, than a Grocery House. Mr. Wilcox has a Pickling and Preserving establishment besides, separate from his business house, owning a great deal of first class real estate. There is no man in the community in which he lives, that turns money to a greater advantage than Mr. Wilcox, and none by whom the community is more benefited for the amount of capital invested. He makes constant and heavy bills in eastern houses, and there are doubtless now many merchants in New York, Boston, and Baltimore cities, who have been dealing with S.T. Wilcox, and never until the reading of this notice of him, knew that he was a colored man. He has never yet been east after his goods, but pursuing a policy which he has adopted, orders them; but if deceived in an article, never deals with the same house again. He always gets a good article. The paper of Mr. Wilcox, is good for any amount.

Henry Boyd, is also a man of great energy of character, the proprietor of an extensive Bedstead manufactory, with a large capital invested, giving constant employment to eighteen or twenty-five men, black and white. Some of the finest and handsomest articles of the bedstead in the city, are at the establishment of Mr. Boyd. He fills orders from all parts of the West and South, his orders from the South being very heavy. He is the patentee, or holds the right of the Patent Bedsteads, and like Mr. Wilcox, there are hundreds who deal with Mr. Boyd at a distance, who do not know that he is a colored man. Mr. Boyd is a useful member of society, and Cincinnati would not, if she could, be without him. He fills a place that every man is not capable of supplying, of whatever quarter of the globe his forefathers may have been denizens.

Messrs. Knight and Bell of the same place, Cincinnati, Ohio, are very successful and excellent mechanics. In the spring of 1851, (one year ago) they put in their "sealed proposal" for the plastering of the public buildings of the county of Hamilton—almshouse, &c.—and got the contract, which required ten thousand dollars' security. The work was finished in fine artistic style, in which a large number of mechanics and laborers were employed, while at the same time, they were carrying on many other contracts of less extent, in the city—the public buildings being some four miles out. They are men of stern integrity, and highly respected in the community.

David Jenkins of Columbus, Ohio, a good mechanic, painter, glazier, and paperhanger by trade, also received by contract, the painting, glazing, and papering of some of the public buildings of the State, in autumn 1847. He is much respected in the capital city of his state, being extensively patronised, having on contract, the great "Neill House," and many of the largest gentlemen's residences in the city and neighborhood, to keep in finish. Mr. Jenkins is a very useful man and member of society.

John C. Bowers, for many years, has been the proprietor of a fashionable merchant tailor house, who has associated with him in business, his brother Thomas Bowers, said to be one of the best, if not the very best, mercers in the city. His style of cutting and fitting, is preferred by the first business men, and other gentlemen of Philadelphia, in whom their patrons principally consist.

Mr. Cordovell, for more than twenty-five years, was the leading mercer and tailor, reporter and originator of fashions in the city of New Orleans, Louisiana. The reported fashions of Cordovell, are said to have frequently become the leading fashions of Paris; and the writer was informed, by Mr. B., a leading merchant tailor in a populous city, that many of the eastern American reports were nothing more than a copy, in some cases modified, of those of Cordovell. Mr. Cordovell, has for the last four or five years, been residing in France, living on a handsome fortune, the fruits of his genius; and though "retired from business," it is said, that he still invents fashions for the Parisian reporters, which yields him annually a large income.

William H. Riley, of Philadelphia, has been for years, one of the leading fashionable gentlemen's boot-makers. Riley's style and cut of boots, taking the preeminence in the estimation of a great many of the most fashionable, and business men in the city. Mr. Riley is much of a gentleman, and has acquired considerable means.

James Prosser, Sen., of Philadelphia, has long been the popular proprietor of a fashionable restaurant in the city. The name of James Prosser, among the merchants of Philadelphia, is inseparable with their daily hours of recreation, and pleasure. Mr. Prosser, is withal, a most gentlemanly man, and has the happy faculty of treating his customers in such a manner, that those who call once, will be sure to call at his place again. His name and paper is good among the business men of the city.

Henry Minton also is the proprietor of a fashionable restaurant and resort of business men and gentlemen of the city. The tables of Mr. Henry Minton are continually laden with the most choice offerings to epicures, and the saloon during certain hours of the day, presents the appearance of a bee hive, such is the stir, din, and buz, among the throng of Chesnut street gentlemen, who flock in there to pay tribute at the shrine of bountifulness. Mr. Minton has acquired a notoriety, even in that proud city, which makes his house one of the most popular resorts.

Mr. Hill, of Chillicothe, Ohio, was for years, the leading tanner and currier in that section of country, buying up the hides of the surrounding country, and giving employment to large numbers of men. Mr. Hill kept in constant employment, a white clerk, who once a year took down, as was then the custom, one or more flatboats loaded with leather and other domestic produce, by which he realised large profits, accumulating a great deal of wealth. By endorsement, failure, and other mistransactions, Mr. Hill became reduced in circumstances, and died in Pittsburgh, Pennsylvania, in 1845. He gave his children a liberal business education.

Benjamin Richards, Sen., of Pittsburgh, Pennsylvania, forty years ago, was one of the leading business men of the place. Being a butcher by trade, he carried on the business extensively, employing a white clerk, and held a heavy contract with the United States, supplying the various military posts with provisions. Mr. Richards possessed a large property in real estate, and was at one time reputed very wealthy, he and the late general O'H. being considered the most wealthy individuals of the place,—Mr. Richards taking the precedence; the estate of general O'H. now being estimated at seven millions of dollars. Mr. Richards has been known, to buy up a drove of cattle at one time. By mismanagement, he lost his estate, upon which many gentlemen are now living at ease in the city.

William H. Topp, of Albany, N.Y., has for several years been one of the leading merchant tailors of the city. Starting in the world without aid, he educated and qualified himself for business; and now has orders from all parts of the state, the city of New York not excepted, for "Topp's style of clothing." Mr. Topp stands high in his community as a business man, and a useful and upright member of society. His paper or endorsement is good at any time.

Henry Scott & Co., of New York city, have for many years been engaged extensively in the pickling business, keeping constantly in warehouse, a very heavy stock of articles in their line. He, like the most of others, had no assistance at the commencement, but by manly determination and perseverance, raised himself to what he is. His business is principally confined to supplying vessels with articles and provisions in his line of business, which in this great metropolis is very great. There have doubtless been many a purser, who cashed and filed in his office the bill of Henry Scott, without ever dreaming of his being a colored man. Mr. Scott is extensively known in the great City, and respected as an upright, prompt, energetic business man, and highly esteemed by all who know him.

Mr. Hutson, for years, kept in New York, an intelligence office. At his demise, he was succeeded by Philip A. Bell, who continues to keep one of the leading offices in the city. Mr. Bell is an excellent business man, talented, prompt, shrewd, and full of tact. And what seems to be a trait of character, only to be found associated with talent, Mr. Bell is highly sensitive, and very eccentric. A warm, good hearted man, he has not only enlisted the friendship of all his patrons, but also endeared himself to the multitude of persons who continually throng his office seeking situations. One of his usual expressions to the young women and men in addressing himself to them is, "My child"—this is kind, and philanthropic, and has a tendency to make himself liked. His business is very extensive, being sought from all parts of the city, by the first people of the community. It is said to be not unusual, for the peasantry of Liverpool, to speak of Mr. Bell, as a benefactor of the emigrant domestics. Mr. Bell is extensively known in the business community—none more so—and highly esteemed as a valuable citizen.

Thomas Downing, for thirty years, in the city of New York, has been proprietor of one of the leading restaurants. His establishment situated in the midst of the Wall street bankers, the business has always been of a leading and profitable character. Mr. Downing has commanded great influence, and much means, and it is said of him that he has made "three fortunes." Benevolent, kind, and liberal minded, his head was always willing, his heart ready, and his hands open to "give." Mr. Downing is still very popular, doing a most excellent business, and highly respected throughout New York. Indeed, you scarcely hear any other establishment of the kind spoken of than Downing's.

Henry M. Collins, of the City of Pittsburg, stands among the men of note; and we could not complete this list of usefulness, without the name of Mr. Collins. Raised a poor boy, thrown upon the uncertainties of chance, without example of precept, save such as the public at large presents; Mr. Collins quit his former vocation of a riverman, and without means, except one hundred and fifty dollars, and no assistance from any quarter, commenced speculating in real estate. And though only rising forty, has done more to improve the Sixth Ward of Pittsburg, than any other individual, save one, Captain W., who built on Company capital. Mr. Collins was the first person who commenced erecting an improved style of buildings; indeed, there was little else than old trees in that quarter of the city when Mr. Collins began. He continued to build, and dispose of handsome dwellings, until a different class of citizens entirely, was attracted to that quarter of the town, among them, one of the oldest and most respectable and wealthy citizens, an ex-Alderman. After this, the wealthy citizens turned their attention to the District; and now, it is one of the most fashionable quarters of the City, and bids fair to become, the preferred part for family residences. Mr. Collins' advice and counsel was solicited by some of the first lawyers, and land speculators, in matters of real estate. He has left or contemplates leaving Pittsburg, in April, for California, where he intends entering extensively into land speculation, and doubtless, with the superior advantages of this place, if his success is but half what it was in the former, but a few years will find him counted among the wealthy. Mr. Collins is a highly valuable man in any community in which he may live, and he leaves Pittsburg much to the regret of the leading citizens. Without capital, he had established such a reputation, that his name and paper were good in some of the first Banking houses.

Owen A. Barrett of Pittsburg, Pa., is the original proprietor of "B.A. Fahnestock's Celebrated Vermifuge." Mr. Fahnestock raised Mr. Barrett from childhood, instructing him in all the science of practical pharmacy, continuing him in his employment after manhood, when Mr. Barrett discovered the "sovereign remedy" for *lumbricalii*, and as an act of gratitude to his benefactor, he communicated it to him, but not until he had fully tested its efficacy. The proprietor of the house, finding the remedy good, secured his patent, or copy right, or whatever is secured, and never in the history of remedies in the United States, has any equaled, at least in sale, this of "B.A. Fahnestock's Vermifuge." Mr. Fahnestock, like a gentleman and Christian, has kept Mr. Barrett in his extensive House, compounding this and other medicines, for sixteen or eighteen years.

In 1840 it was estimated, that of this article alone, the concern had realized eighty-five thousand dollars. Doubtless, this is true, and certainly proves Mr. Barrett to be of benefit, not only in his community, but like many others we have mentioned, to the country and the world.

Lewis Hayden, of Boston, is well deserving a place among the examples of character here given. But eight years ago, having emerged from bondage, he raised by his efforts, as an act of gratitude and duty, six hundred and fifty dollars, the amount demanded by mutual agreement, by the authorities in Kentucky, as a ransom for Calvin Fairbanks, then in the State Prison, at Frankfort, accused for assisting him in effecting his escape. In 1848, he went to Boston, and having made acquaintance, and gained confidence with several business men, Mr. Hayden opened a fashionable Clothing House in Cambridge street, where he has within the last year, enlarged his establishment, being patronized by some of the most respectable citizens of that wealthy Metropolis. Mr. Hayden has made considerable progress, considering his disadvantages, in his educational improvements. He has great energy of character, and extensive information. Lewis Hayden by perseverance, may yet become a very wealthy man. He is generally esteemed by the Boston people—all seeming to know him.

George T. Downing, a gentleman of education and fine business attainments, is proprietor of one of the principal Public houses and places of resort, at Newport, Rhode Island, during the watering Season. This fashionable establishment is spoken of as among the best conducted places in the country—the Proprietor among the most gentlemanly.

Edward V. Clark, is among the most deserving and active business men in New York, and but a few years are required, to place Mr. Clark in point of business importance, among the first men in the city. His stock consists of Jewelry and Silver Wares, and consequently, are always valuable, requiring a heavy capital to keep up business. His name and paper, has a respectable credit, even among the urbane denizens of Wall street.

John Julius and Lady, were for several years, the Proprietors of Concert Hall, a *Caffé*, then the most fashionable resort for ladies and gentlemen in Pittsburg. Mr. and Mrs. Julius, held Assemblies and Balls, attended by the first people of the city—being himself a fine violinist and dancing master, he superintended the music and dancing. When General William Henry Harrison in 1840, then the President elect of the United States, visited that city, his levee to and reception of the Ladies were held at Concert Hall, under the superintendence of Monsieur John and Madame Edna Julius, the colored host and hostess. No House was ever better conducted than under their fostering care, and excellent management, and the citizens all much regretted their retirement from the establishment.

In Penyan, Western New York, Messrs. William Platt and Joseph C. Cassey, are said to be the leading Lumber Merchants of the place. Situated in the midst of a great improving country, their business extends, and increases in importance every year. The latter gentleman was raised to the business by Smith and Whipper, the great Lumber Merchants of Columbia, Pa., where he was principal Book-Keeper for several years. Mr. Cassey has the credit of being one of the best Accountants, and Business Men in the United States of his age. Doubtless, a few years' perseverance, and strict application to business, will find them ranked among the most influential men of their neighborhood.

Anthony Weston, of Charleston, South Carolina, has acquired an independent fortune, by his mechanical ingenuity, and skillful workmanship. About the year 1831, William Thomas Catto, mentioned in another place, commenced an improvement on a Thrashing Machine, when on taking sick, Mr. Weston improved on it, to the extent of thrashing a thousand bushels a day. This Thrashing Mill, was commenced by a Yankee, by the name of Emmons, who failing to succeed, Mr. Catto, then a Millwright— since a Minister—improved it to the extent of thrashing five hundred bushels a day; when Mr. Weston, took it in hand, and brought it to the perfection stated, for the use of Col. Benjamin Franklin Hunt, a distinguished lawyer of Charleston, upon whose plantation, the machine was built, and to whom it belonged. Anthony Weston, is the greatest Millwright in the South, being extensively employed far and near, and by Southern people, thought the best in the United States.

Dereef and Howard, are very extensive Wood-Factors, keeping a large number of men employed, a regular Clerk and Book-Keeper, supplying the citizens, steamers, vessels, and factories of Charleston with fuel. In this business a very heavy capital is invested: besides which, they are the owners and proprietors of several vessels trading on the coast. They are men of great business habits, and command a great deal of respect and influence in the city of Charleston.

There is nothing more common in the city of New Orleans, than Colored Clerks, Salesmen and Business men. In many stores on Chartier, Camp and other business streets, there may always be seen colored men and women, as salesmen, and saleswomen, behind the counter. Several of the largest Cotton-Press houses, have colored Clerks in them; and on the arrival of steamers at the Levees, among the first to board them, and take down the Manifestos to make their transfers, are colored Clerks. In 1839-40, one of the most respectable Brokers and Bankers of the City, was a black gentleman.

Mr. William Goodrich of York, Pennsylvania, has considerable interest in the branch of the Baltimore Railroad, from Lancaster. In 1849, he had a warehouse in York, and owned ten first-rate merchandise cars on the Road, doing a fine business. His son, Glenalvon G. Goodrich, a young man of good education, is a good artist, and proprietor of a Daguerreo-type Gallery.

Certainly, there need be no further proofs required, at least in this department, to show the claims and practical utility of colored people as citizen members of society. We have shown, that in proportion to their numbers, they vie and compare favorably in point of means and possessions, with the class of citizens who from chance of superior advantages, have studiously contrived to oppress and deprive them of equal rights and privileges, in common with themselves.

[1852]

XI

No one heeded the call to action nor professed it personally in a more active and determined manner than did Benjamin "Pap" Singleton (1809–1892). He was a firebrand and a doer. Born into slavery, Singleton successfully escaped in 1846 and found his way to the North. He spent many years in Detroit, Michigan, working for the abolitionist cause and became an advocate and example of black self-assertion. Singleton concluded that the black people in America would never rise to greatness under the heels of a hostile white South. He was likewise doubtful that the North was much better in the long run. He urged blacks to separate themselves from whites, find their own land, and develop their own self-sustained communities. He contemplated African repatriation but saw the possibilities of black nation building in America as a more realistic possibility. His was a clarion call to Black Nationalism in the strongest sense: "a nation within but without white America." Pap Singleton was at the heart of what became known as the Kansas Fever Exodus of 1879 as thousands of blacks ventured to the new territories of the West in hope of establishing their own black towns. The results were places like Nicodemus, Kansas; Boley, Oklahoma; Langston, Oklahoma; and Taft, California, among others. Included here are statements by Pap Singleton for readers to imbibe. Was his cry for Black Nationalism and nation building a course of action that blacks should have taken? What about now? We have little in the way of a comprehensive text by Pap Singleton in which he expresses his views in his own words. Walter Fleming's article, presented here, has some of the best extensive quotes of Pap Singleton that, taken as a whole, provide a sampling that is informative of the philosophy and actions of the leading *Black Exoduster.*

"'Pap' Singleton, the Moses of the Colored Exodus"

Walter L. Fleming

During an investigation of that movement of negros from the South to Kansas in 1879–80, known as the "Colored Exodus," the writer of this sketch was impressed by the importance of the activity and influence of one man, an ignorant negro, who in himself seemed to embody the longings and the strivings of the bewildered negro race. His name was Benjamin Singleton, but on account of his advanced age and kindly disposition most people called him "Pap;" he himself later added and insisted upon the title, "The Moses of the Colored Exodus." He was born a slave in 1809 at Nashville, in middle Tennessee, and was by occupation a carpenter and cabinet maker. Evidently he was of a restless disposition, and probably his master considered him "trifling," for "Pap" asserted that although he was "sold a dozen times or more" to the Gulf States, yet he always ran away and came back to Tennessee. Finally he decided to strike for Canada and freedom, and after failing in three attempts he made his way over the "Underground Railway" to Ontario, opposite Detroit. Soon afterward he came back to Detroit where he worked, he says, until 1865 as a "scavenger," and also kept a "secret boardinghouse for fugitive slaves."

Singleton was not of imposing appearance. From newspaper descriptions of him written during the 70's we learn that he was a slender man, below medium height, a light mulatto with long, wavy iron-gray hair, gray mustache, and thin chin whiskers. His square jaw showed strength of character; he had "full quick eyes and a general expression of honesty, courage, and modesty." He could not read. With all his later prominence Singleton remained frank, simple, and unspoiled.

"After freedom cried out," Pap was not content to remain in the North and soon went back to his old home in Tennessee to work at his trade. His experience in the North had opened his eyes to the economic weaknesses and dangers of his race, and soon he began to complain that the blacks were profiting little by freedom. They had personal liberty but no homes, and they were often hungry, he says, and were frequently cheated. He then began his "mission," as he called it, urging the blacks to save their earnings and buy homes and little plots of land as a first step toward achieving industrial independence. His later career showed that he had little confidence in political measures as a means of elevating the race and it was always difficult for political agitators to get endorsement from him. His ideas and plans were chiefly about industrial matters and much of the criticism he received from his race was like that later directed at Booker T. Washington. He declared in 1868 when he began his "mission" that his people were being exploited for the benefit of the carpetbaggers, whose promises were always broken:

After the war [he said] my race willingly slipped a noose over their necks and knuckled to a bigger boss than the old ex-one.... By and by the fifteenth amendment came along and the carpetbaggers, and our poor people thought they was goin' to have Canaan right off. But I knowed better.... I said to 'em "Hy'ar you is a-potter'n' round in politics and tryin' to git in offices that aint fit, and you can't see that these white tramps from the North is simply usin' you for to line their pockets and when they git through they'll drop you and the rebels will come into power and then whar'll you be?"

For several years Singleton had but slight success in making converts to his plan of salvation for the blacks. But after the dream of "40 acres and a mule" had failed to materialize and after the negros in Tennessee began to see that they were going to get few rewards from the politicians, they were willing to listen to other than political prophets, and Singleton at last found his opportunity. It was in 1869, he says, that he succeeded in inducing some negros "to get it into their minds" that they ought to quit renting and farming on the credit system and endeavor to secure homes of their own. In order to direct their efforts he and others organized and incorporated at Nashville the Tennessee Real Estate and Homestead Association. The professed object of the organization was to assist Tennessee negros to buy small tracts of farm land, or houses and lots in the towns to which so many negros flocked after the war. All colored people were invited to join. Local societies were organized and incorporated under such names as the Edgefield Real Estate Association, in Davidson County, and these held frequent meetings in the negro churches and secret-society halls; committees were appointed by them to look out for land that was for sale, circulars of advice were scattered among the blacks, and speeches were made at the meetings by Singleton and others in regard to the economic situation of the negro race. Numbers of the whites favored the movement and gave assistance and encouragement to Singleton, while others opposed it. On the whole it was not successful in Tennessee. The real cause of failure was the inability of the negros to purchase land at the high prices asked. The whites, hoping for better times, were still holding their lands at something like ante-bellum prices, notwithstanding the fact that the net income was yearly lessening. The only cheap lands were the worn-out lands, "where peas would not sprout."

The conviction grew upon Singleton that the negros must be segregated from the whites. Whether they were friendly or unfriendly, he felt that they should be separated for the good of the blacks. In the South, after the failure to acquire land, the situation of the race was, he thought, precarious. He had no confidence in the new ruling class of whites that came after the carpetbaggers; they were not as friendly to the negros as was the old master class which had been put out of politics after 1865; there was danger of helpless, hopeless serfdom. "Conditions might get better," said Pap, "a hundred years from now when all the present generation's dead and gone, but not afore, sir, not afore, an' what's agoin' to be a hundred years from now aint much account to us in this present o' de Lord." The only remedy, he decided, was for the blacks to quit the South and go to a new country where they would not have to compete with whites. "I had studied it all out," he said, "and it was clar as day to me. I dunno how it come to me; but I spec it was God's doin's. Anyhow I knowed my people couldn't live thar.... .The whites had the lands and the sense an' the blacks had nothin' but their freedom, an' it was jest like a dream to them."

Singleton now turned his thoughts to Kansas as the most promising place for the settlement of home-seeking blacks. There were several reasons for this choice. In the first place, the history of Kansas appealed powerfully to the negros. Besides, railroad-building in Missouri, Arkansas, and Kansas had attracted numbers of Tennessee negros as laborers and these sent back reports of the fine western lands open to settlement. Beginning with 1869 a few negros went to Kansas each year to open small farms on the fertile prairies. In 1871, after finding that lands in Tennessee were too high priced for the blacks to purchase, Singleton's Real Estate and Homestead Association turned its attention to Kansas. An "exploring committee" was sent to "spy out" the land! A favorable report was made and a slight migration followed. In 1872 another committee sent to Kansas reported that negros would do better to stay in Tennessee. Singleton then went himself to Kansas in 1873 as representative of the Tennessee Real Estate and Homestead Association, of which he was president. He was favorably impressed with the country and, returning to Nashville, he took three hundred blacks to the public lands in Cherokee County in the southeastern part of Kansas and there founded "Singleton Colony." Prospects seemed good and Singleton went back to Tennessee to get more emigrants. For this purpose the organization of the Tennessee Real Estate Association was continued.

From this time to 1879 Singleton was actively engaged in developing negro sentiment in Tennessee and Kentucky in favor of emigration or "exodus" to Kansas. The whites approved his policy, he says, aided him in various ways, told him that it "was better than politics," sat in his meetings, and in the Tennessee newspapers they published his notices and wrote up the movement for him. Every year with a few negros he went to Kansas. Always upon his return he distributed circulars about "Sunny Kansas." He spent $600 for circulars, he says. All his life Singleton well understood the value of advertising. His literature was given to preachers going into the interior districts, to porters on the railroads, and to employees on the steamboats to be scattered among the negros farther south. But not until 1876 was there much response to these efforts. In that year the local organizations in Tennessee were active, and Singleton and Columbus Johnson, another shrewd Nashville negro, went to Kansas and looked up more good locations for settlements on the public lands. An arrangement was made by which Johnson was to stay in Topeka and from there direct the newly arriving blacks to the various colonies. A. D. DeFrantz, a Nashville barber, another lieutenant of Singleton's, assisted in working up the parties in Tennessee. Singleton had headquarters in Nashville, but traveled back and forth conducting immigrants to Topeka. The steamers from Nashville granted a special rate of $10 to Topeka.

There was more enthusiasm now at the meetings in Tennessee. At all of them Pap delivered addresses asking his people to stand together, to "consolidate the race," and to arouse themselves to their duty to the race. Most of these gatherings were called "investigating meetings"—to investigate conditions in Tennessee and Kansas by listening to the reports of the officials who had been there. Now was the time to go, the leaders urged, or as Pap in highflown language said, "Place and time have met and kissed each other." The leaders of this migration saw to it that a certain selection of the emigrants was made. None who were entirely without means were advised to go; "no political negros" were wanted, for "they would want to pilfer and rob the cents before they got to the dollars;" "it was the muscle of the arm, the men that worked that we wanted;" it was "root hog or die." One of the circulars entitled, News from Kansas, declared that there was "abundant room for all good citizens, but no room for loafers in Kansas."

For educated negros, Singleton had a profound and bitter contempt, perhaps because they generally opposed his movement. Most of the negros in the North who were well situated wanted no more of their race to come; they feared that a negro migration to the North would make uncertain the position of those already there. For obvious reasons the negro politicians opposed it. Singleton asked his people not to believe in those who would keep the blacks in the South for selfish reasons.

The colored race he said is ignorant and altogether too simple, and invests too much confidence in Professor Tom Cat, or some of the imported slippery chaps from Washington, Oberlin, Chicago, or scores of places whence are sent intriguing reverends, deputy doorkeepers, military darkeys or teachers, to go often around the corrals and see that not an appearance of a hole exists through which the captives within can escape or even see through.

The "exodus" songs possess considerable interest and afford an insight into the feelings of the black people. At the meetings held to stimulate interest in the "exodus," as Singleton called it, it was the custom to sing songs composed for such occasions. Pamphlet copies of these, poorly printed by negro printers, were sold by Singleton at ten cents each. The money received helped to pay expenses. One of these songs was called "The Land That Gives Birth to Freedom." Some of the verses were as follows:

1. We have held meetings to ourselves to see if we can't plan some way to live. (Repeat.)

Chorus—Marching along, yes, we are marching along,

To Kansas City we are bound. (Repeat.)

2. We have Mr. Singleton for our president. He will go on before us and lead us through. (Repeat.)

4. For Tennessee is a hard slavery state, and we find no friends in that country. (Repeat.)

6. We want peaceful homes and quiet firesides, no one to disturb us or turn us out. (Repeat.)

As soon as a party was enrolled Singleton would advertise that on a certain date the "Tennessee Real Estate and Homestead Association" would leave "for the Southwest in pursuit of homes." At the meetings before departure and at the start another "exodus" song was sung. This was called "Extending Our Voices to Heaven." Some lines were:

1. We are on our rapid march to Kansas, the land that gives birth to freedom. May God Almighty bless you all.

Chorus — Farewell, dear friends, farewell.

2. Many dear mothers are sleeping in the tomb of clay, have spent all their days in slavery in old Tennessee.

4. It seems to me that the year of jubilee has come; surely this is the time that is spoken of in history.

These songs indicate clearly the feelings of the negros who were going on the new "Exodus from the land of Egypt." Another song sung on the way and after arrival, was altogether hopeful:

"In the midst of earth's dominion Christ has promised us a kingdom

Not left to other nations

And we've surely gained the day."

Three colonies were founded by Singleton, Johnson, and DeFrantz, and to these most of the negros who went to Kansas in 1876–78 were conducted. Dunlap Colony was in the Neosho Valley in Morris and Lyon counties; Singleton Colony in Cherokee County in the southeastern corner of the state, and Nicodemus Colony in the northwestern part of the state in Graham County. Singleton Colony, already referred to as having been settled in 1874, was soonest in good condition. Here, by 1878 the negros had paid for 1,000 acres of land, good cabins had been erected, cows and pigs were common, and shade trees and fruit trees were growing. The climate here was better suited to the negro than that of the other colonies. Dunlap Colony, also founded in 1874, grew slowly and was in good condition in 1878. In that year there were at Dunlap 200 negro families, two churches and a school, and the settlers had purchased 7,500 acres of government land. In all the colonies the negros took up homesteads on government land or bought railroad and university lands on long credit at low prices.

Nicodemus, the third colony and later the largest, was in less prosperous condition in 1878. Prominent Topeka negros were promoting this colony, and in 1877 it was being "boomed" as a negro paradise. It was, the promoters claimed, "the largest colored colony in the United States." A town company was incorporated and a fee of five dollars entitled one to membership in the company and to a town lot. Churches were to be built by the company, and no saloons were tolerated. The promoters invited "our colored friends to come and join us in this beautiful Promised Land." But a migration of negros reached Nicodemus in the fall of 1877 too late to make crops that year, and in consequence there was considerable suffering during the following winter. Most of the early settlers of Nicodemus were from Kentucky. They had a song all their own called "Nicodemus." The allusion is obscure, though it may be said that some ignorant negros believed that the biblical character (Nicodemus) was "Nigger Demus," that is, a negro. The first verse and the chorus were:

"Nicodemus was a slave of African birth,
And was bought for a bag full of gold.
He was reckoned a part of the salt of the earth,
But he died years ago, very old.

Chorus—Good time coming, good time coming.

Long, long time on the way;
Run and tell Elijah to hurry up Pomp
To meet us under the cottonwood tree,
In the Great Solomon Valley,
At the first break of day."

The year 1878 marks the close of the second period of Singleton's activity as a "Moses of the negro race." By the end of the year he had brought to Kansas, so he claimed, 7,432 negros. Nearly all of these were doing fairly well—certainly as well as could have been expected during a period of readjustment, and better than they would have done in Tennessee, because they worked harder and were more frugal. In addition to the colonies named above, there were many negros about the larger towns; "Tennessee Town," the negro suburb of Topeka, was growing; a few had settled in Crawford County in southeastern Kansas, just above Cherokee; and numbers had stopped on the way, at Kansas City, St. Louis, and other Missouri towns.

In the early spring of 1879 began what the entire country soon knew as the "negro exodus" from the Egypt of the southern states to the Kansas Canaan. The remote but fundamental causes of the movement lay in the disturbed conditions in the South—social, economic, and political. The credit and crop-lien system which had been substituted for the slave-labor system had worked badly; the "40 acres and a mule" delusion, the Freedmen's Bank failure, and educational disappointments had discouraged the race; the negro-republican governments in the South had all fallen, and now the blacks declared that legal protection was often denied them; the failure within ten years of all the plans for the immediate elevation of the blacks to the position of the whites had left the entire race restless and anxious for a change. The circulars sent out by Singleton had penetrated into all parts of the black South, and far and wide had spread exaggerated reports of his work. Speculators in western lands, agents for railroads and steamboat companies that were anxious for passenger traffic, negro preachers and white and black politicians, now out of jobs, took advantage of the uneasy feeling and stirred up the blacks of the far South to go to "Sunny Kansas."

As a result there began in February, 1879, a heavy migration from the black districts bordering on the Mississippi River, which continued, with some interruptions, for two years. It was a surprise to the white South and even more of a surprise to Kansas. Pap Singleton, perhaps the immediate cause of the exodus, was for a while lost sight of in the excitement that arose in Kansas when the first boatloads of unexpected negros arrived. The exodus from the lower South overshadowed the smaller one from Tennessee and Kentucky. However, Pap worked on as usual, carrying people from Tennessee to Dunlap, Nicodemus, and Singleton colonies. Circulars were sent among the Mississippi and Louisiana "exodusters" to herald the virtues of the several negro colonies. The name of Singleton is attached to all of them and he always signs himself as "Father of the Exodus," or "Moses of the Colored Exodus."

Not all of the negros from Mississippi, Arkansas, and Louisiana went directly to Kansas. Many of them stopped in St. Louis and waited to hear about conditions in Kansas before going farther. Others stopped because their funds gave out. But the whites and blacks of St. Louis were anxious to speed the "exodusters" on their way, and formed several aid societies to assist them to go farther west. One of these, "The Colored Men's Land Association of St. Louis," sent Singleton and DeFrantz as "land inspectors" to search out other suitable places for the settlement of "exodusters" in the western states. All the colonizing societies had Singleton on their lists of officials, as president, "founder," or "father of the exodus." His fame had a cash value to them.

Most of the immigrants were destitute, and the whites of Kansas were forced to organize the "Kansas Freedmen's Relief Association" in order to save some of the needy blacks from starvation. Pap was now brought forward by them as an authority on exodus conditions, and for several years he was considered the leading negro of Kansas. At first he was inclined to glory in the movement as a result of his efforts and to say little about causes. However, the "exodus" soon became an issue in Kansas and national politics, and Singleton found that the past treatment of the negros in the South rather than his own ideas of their future in the Northwest was what northern people, especially the radicals, wanted to know about. So for the first time he raises the familiar "southern outrage" issue, and describes the South as a horrible place where murder, outrage, theft, etc., were common crimes by whites against the negros. The Southern people were, he said, like "a muddy-faced bellowing bull," and "Democratic threats were as thunder in a colored man's ear," and in consequence the negros were "exodusting." However, he never went into particulars, and always preferred to talk about "consolidating the race" in a new country.

Singleton's activity sometimes embarrassed the relief association. He published frequent appeals in Kansas and eastern newspapers asking that aid be sent to the Kansas Freedmen's Relief Association, not only for the relief of the refugees in Kansas, but also for the purpose of assisting more negros from Egypt to Canaan. But the whites of Kansas wanted no more; the Democrats were accusing the Republicans of stirring up the migration for political purposes, that is, to lessen the southern representation in Congress and to make Kansas safely Republican; and the relief association was trying to close up its work. Hence the numerous appeals for assistance signed by Singleton, DeFrantz, and other negros, were embarrassing, because it seemed that they were acting under authority. The association on the contrary was doing all in its power to check the migration. The "exodus" was not well supported by public opinion in Kansas even among the blacks. The whites and resident blacks of Kansas helped the "exodusters" much, but they wanted no more of them; the laboring-class of whites threatened violence if more negros should come.

This larger "exodus," like Singleton's original one, met opposition from the leading negros like Fred Douglass, Pinchback, and Bruce, who objected to any scheme of moving masses of negros into the North. Against these race leaders Singleton spoke with considerable feeling. "They had good luck," he said, "and now are listening to false prophets; they have boosted up and got their heads a whirlin', and now they think they must judge things from where they stand, when the fact is the possum is lower down the tree—down nigh to the roots;" they either "saw darkly" or were playing into the hands of the southern planters who feared a scarcity of labor. To those who objected that negros without means should not come to Kansas he replied that "it is because they are poor that they want to get away. If they had plenty they wouldn't want to come. It's to better their condition that they are thinking of. That's what white men go to new countries for, isn't it? Who was the homestead law made for if it was not for poor men?"

However, Pap was finally made to see that popular opinion in Kansas was not in favor of encouraging further migration of "paupers," and through the influence of the whites he was brought to the point where he used his influence to discourage the exodus movement. But unwillingly did he come to this. In May, 1879, he had denounced in advance a meeting of the National negro Convention soon to be held at Nashville for the purpose of considering the causes of the exodus and the condition of the blacks. He feared that the negros like Douglass and Pinchback would control the convention and try to keep the blacks in the South. He wanted the Kansas negro Convention, which was to be held about the same time, to inform southern negros about Kansas and assist them to get there. Soon, however, in order to relieve and reassure Kansas, he planned to divert the immigration to the states farther west, but only a few went to Nebraska and Colorado. His next plan, suggested by the whites, was to turn the migration to the states north of the Ohio. He visited Illinois and Indiana to investigate conditions, but received little encouragement. He then began to play upon the fear of the whites in those states about a possible "exodus," declaring that the "exodus was working," but that if the North would force the South to treat the negros well, let them vote, sell land to them, etc., they would stay in the South.

The migration began to decrease in the summer of 1879 and Singleton busied himself in looking after the negros in the colonies, and in the relief work. About 200 Tennessee negros went to his colonies in 1879, besides those from the lower South. When the exodus began afresh in the spring of 1880, the Kansas newspapers very willingly published statements from Singleton advising prospective "exodusters" either to stay at home or to scatter out into other northern states, for, as all maintained, Kansas had her share, there was no employment for more, and no more aid could be given to them. The southern newspapers gave wide circulation to this advice, for the planters wanted to keep the negro labor, and soon the exodus was checked. After this, Singleton moderated his activity as an organizer of immigration to the North and West. The scattering of circulars was stopped and he now always advised that none come north unless with enough money to last one year.

In 1880 we hear Singleton and others complaining that certain funds raised by the relief societies for the needy "exodusters" had been turned over to a negro school. This, they protested, was not right; the money should be divided among those for whom it was raised—the "exodusters"—and not given to a school. Singleton cared little for schools and disliked educated negros, for, as a matter of fact, the educated blacks then best known to the race had not been good examples of the benefits of education.

Singleton was called before the exodus committee of the U. S. Senate in 1880 and in his testimony explained at length his plans and methods. After describing the "real estate" companies, his Kansas colonies, and his method of advertising, he spoke of the causes of the movement which, in his opinion, were mainly social and economic: the negro was helpless in the South, which was "all out of joint;" the only way "to bring the South to her senses" was for the negros to leave in large numbers, and thus force a reorganization of industry and a bettering of the condition of the laborers who remained in the South. He scored a point on the Democratic majority of the committee when he pointed out the fact that they had selected their witnesses from a class of negros who were prosperous and who knew little of the conditions surrounding the average black. As to himself, he declared "the blood of a white man runs through my veins"—hence he could understand both races. "I am the father of the exodus.... .the whole cause of the Kansas migration," he boasted and looked upon the attempt of the Democrats to place responsibility for the movement upon Kansas Republicans as a scheme to defraud him of due credit.

When in the fall of 1880 Singleton went to Illinois and Indiana he had a double mission: to see if there was room for "exodusters," and to deliver Republican speeches in favor of Garfield. As to the first he received no encouragement, but he delivered several speeches on conditions in the South and notified Illinois and Indiana that unless conditions were bettered and a Republican president elected a great migration across the Ohio might be expected. In November after the Republican victory, Singleton declared that to him was due the credit for making Indiana safe for Garfield. He explained it by saying that after he learned that the Democrats feared colonization of negros by the Republicans, he had gone to their leaders and told them that "unless they allowed the state to go Republican he would import 250,000 negros into the state." They were so impressed, he says, that several thousand failed to vote, and thus the state was saved to the Republicans. In spite of the vivid imagination shown by these incidents, they indicate that Pap had learned that neither Republican nor Democrat in the North would welcome an exodus of negros.

After the exodus ceased the negros who had come to Kansas felt that they needed race organization and a settled policy in order to enable them to do their best. Almost at once they had become of importance as voters and as laborers. So in January, 1881, Singleton called and presided over a colored convention in Topeka, which considered means of bettering the condition of the race. A result of this meeting was the organization on March 4, 1881, in "Tennessee Town," Topeka, of the "Colored United Links," Singleton being the "founder and president." The objects were to "consolidate the race as a band of brethren," and to "harmonize together," to keep the race out of labor disputes, to care for the sick and the destitute, and to provide for training the children in trades from which they were now excluded by the jealousy of the white laborers. "In unity there is strength," and "United we stand, divided we fall" were the favorite mottoes on the circulars sent out to advertise the "United Links." Local orders of the "Links" were formed in each Kansas town that had a negro population, and for several years an annual convention was held at Topeka. The first convention in 1881 showed a body of fairly prosperous negros. At the conventions the opening song was always "John Brown's Body."

For various reasons some of the negros, especially the ex-politicians from Louisiana and Mississippi, were dissatisfied with the "lily white" policy of the white Republicans, and their restlessness invited, an attempt by the "Greenbackers" to capture the organization of the "Links." Singleton himself began to talk as an "independent," and declared that the Kansas Democrats had treated the negros as well as the Republicans had. The "Links" and the "Greenbackers" had meetings on the same day at Topeka, and had a joint barbecue, but no fusion was effected. However for several years the Republicans were not certain of the entire negro vote. The "Links" flourished for some years and in 1887 Pap declared that the body had done much good in uniting the race and that the "hand of the Lord must of been upon him" when he organized that society.

The "exodusters" soon met opposition in labor matters. The migration caused a lowering of wages and the poorer whites became incensed against the blacks in the parts of the state where the "exodusters" were more numerous. One of the professed objects of the "United Links" was to avoid trouble by trying to regulate wages. The negros were willing to work for less than white laborers, and on this account white employers and white laborers were divided in their opinion as to what the negros should do. The latter were inclined to take the advice of the employers. There was complaint that negro youths were not admitted to the trades.

The matters that came up in the public meetings of the negros showed that social and political agitators were attempting to use the race to further their own ends. Some rather noisy ones complained that the whites of Kansas kept them apart, treated them as a separate people, refused to accommodate them in hotels, etc. About the earliest and loudest complaint was that of J. M. Langston, who was refused admission to an ice-cream parlor in 1881. This was disappointing conduct from the white people of Kansas, the state of John Brown. The Mississippi and Louisiana ex-politicians, of whom there were many, began to talk about a proper division of offices. The Kansas whites were willing that the blacks should vote, but nominated none of them for office. The blacks were divided on the question as to whether an organization should be maintained for the purpose of bargaining with the Democratic and Republican parties for the disposal of the negro vote. Singleton cared little about these questions except as indicating the attitude of the whites toward his race. However, though a Republican always, he favored bargaining with both political parties, not so much for office, but to secure consideration for the race.

Under such circumstances, more and more did Kansas prove disappointing to "the father of the exodus." Too many of those who came insisted on staying about the towns and living as they had lived in the South; lands and homes were as far off as ever; competition with the whites was keener than in the South; the whites were distinctly business-like in their treatment of the blacks, and some were unfriendly; little sentiment was allowed to interfere in relations between races, and most threatening of all, thousands of European immigrants were coming every year to the prairie lands of Kansas and thus decreasing the opportunities of the blacks.

So Singleton looked about for another "Promised Land." Remembering Canada as a haven for runaway slaves, he suggested an exodus to that place. The British government, he believed, would assist the blacks. It was objected that Canada was too cold.

He then suggested Liberia, began to preach a new exodus, and in September, 1883, issued an address to the blacks of the South declaring that since they had refused to come to Kansas in sufficient numbers to accomplish good results, the best that they could now do was to go to Canada under the protection of the British government or go to Liberia where they could have a government of their own. He advised them to leave the South at once, and said that in North Carolina, South Carolina, and Georgia 27,000 blacks had enrolled and were ready to go. There was no hope he thought, for political and economic independence in the South, and conditions were but little better in the North.

Some person who objected to Canada and also to Liberia proposed Cyprus as a substitute and wrote a long description of it for a St. Louis newspaper. He stated that England no doubt would willingly grant the negros permission to settle there. Singleton had not the slightest idea as to where and what Cyprus was but eagerly accepted the suggestion and for about two years tried to work up a migration to that place. He was, in his disappointed old age, more credulous and visionary. Finally he started to Cyprus to investigate and went as far as St. Louis where he stopped, probably because of lack of funds.

Pap was now about seventy-five years old and somewhat feeble, but he kept up his "mission." He could with difficulty speak above a hoarse whisper and was accompanied by a smooth-tongued preacher, who did most of the talking and drew his income from the results of Singleton's popularity. Singleton declared that the blacks were unable to compete with the whites, and must make "a fresh start where the color line is not too rigid;" there was no hope for final success in America, for here "there can't be no transmogrification of the races;" foreigners had many advantages over negros and were welcomed; but not even by his friends was the negro wanted, and foreign immigration "would shortly prove the uprooting of our race."

After the Cyprus disappointment Singleton was again attracted by the Liberian or Ethiopian movement which was being agitated in the lower South by Bishop Turner and other southern negros. In furtherance of this movement in January, 1885, Singleton organized the "United Transatlantic Society" for the "great and grand purpose of migration to Africa." All over the South the negros were thinking of "Ethiopia" as a refuge that might soon be needed. The election of Cleveland in 1884 had caused uneasy feelings among the southern blacks, in spite of the fact that he had sent personal messages to them to assure them that slavery was not to be re-established. Some waves of this uneasiness reached the Kansas negros and many of them enrolled in the United Transatlantic Society. According to the official papers of the society the movement was the result of the conviction that the relations between whites and blacks would continue to be unsatisfactory and that negros could not expect to reach "perfect manhood" in America; for it was clear that ex-slaves would never be accorded important positions in political or social life, and that fewer and fewer opportunities would be open to them. The negro could not accept such a condition; therefore, the only solution was "a national existence" apart from the whites. The society evidently intended to deal with foreign powers, for in the constitution there is a curious clause providing that "No persons shall hold any communications with any foreign power.... without the authority of this organization.... and the Father of this organization, Benjamin (alias) Pap Singleton, if he be alive and sane."

Singleton, in his addresses and proclamations as "father" of the United Transatlantic Society, went to the root of the trouble. The negros must be a separate "nation," he said; in no other way can they survive. They had been able to secure no stronghold in America, for after emancipation "we were turned loose like so many cattle with nothing to live on," and all efforts at economic independence had failed. Now the "scum of foreign powers emigrate to America and put their feet on our necks;" and they could live and work where a negro would starve. This was shown by conditions in Kansas, he said, where "three thousand women and children once fully engaged in washing and ironing are now forced into idleness and hundreds of them into base prostitution through the steam laundries and Chinamen;" the races were bound to be separate from the cradle to the grave, and "prejudice will follow you to the days of your offspring twenty generations ahead of this." For these reasons he advocated colonization in Africa, though he acknowledged that the average "exoduster" who had stayed in Kansas was doing fairly well. The United Transatlantic Society had considerable strength for several years; it held regular meetings and always passed resolutions in favor of negro "national existence" in Liberia, but it sent out no organized body of emigrants. Possibly individuals from Kansas joined the parties from the South that went, but they were few. For better or for worse the movement for a "national existence" failed.

The last years of Pap's life were not spent in obscurity as might have been expected. He was ignorant, he had no property, no home, no family, and it was suspected that smart rascals made use of him in his old age to get money from the generous blacks. But he himself was always popular with both races. In all the mass of material relating to Pap and his schemes there is no hint that he was not just what he professed to be; no doubt is manifested of his honesty and sincerity. Wherever he went the negros welcomed him as the "father of the exodus." All his savings he spent on his schemes, and by 1881, in his seventy-third year, he was in want. So he proceeded to announce through the Topeka newspapers that he would accept donations if sent to a certain warehouse. The Topeka Commonwealth endorsed his character and motives; and the donations received kept him from want for a time.

A year later the blacks at Topeka planned a birthday party for the old man. The celebration was to be held in a park and five cents admission fee charged. Pap at once announced that all who desired to assist him entertain his friends on his birthday might send donations—"anything in the way of eatables," he said, "will be kindly received." He invited the higher government officials at Washington to attend his party, and some of them sent polite regrets which he had printed in the local newspapers. He made out a programme and put the Kansas notables—governor, mayors, preachers—down for speeches. They did not come, but the party was a success. One hundred guns were fired at sunrise and a hundred more at sunset; "John Brown's Body" was sung, everybody had a good time, and Pap made $50 clear. The next year a barbecue on his birthday netted him $274.25. In 1884 the negros of St. Louis gave him a celebration, and so it was until he died at Topeka in 1892 at the age of eighty-three. At all of his celebrations Singleton gloried in his title of "father (or Moses) of the exodus," and as the years passed his achievements were greatly magnified by himself and others. For instance, the St. Louis and Topeka newspapers in the late 80's declared that Singleton brought 82,000 negros out of the South; this was about ten times the actual number.

It is usually asserted that the "exodus" failed. But did it really fail? Most of the negros were discouraged and returned to the South. The weak ones who remained in Kansas went to the wall, the stronger ones who remained did well, as negros usually do when in small numbers surrounded by whites and incited by white example, competition, and public opinion to exertions not known in the "black belt." Kansas, too, was on a business basis; the "black belt" was not so and could not be; the industrious negro in the "black belt" would be "eaten up" by visiting friends and relations, while in Kansas he might hope to enjoy more of the fruits of his labor. The negros certainly had to work harder in Kansas, but that was what they needed, and some succeeded because they had to work who would have been loafers in Mississippi. Then, too, on the race question a radical state became moderate; the change, if correctly illustrated by newspaper comment, was ludicrously sudden. Could Singleton and others have succeeded in bringing a large portion of the blacks to the North and thus have somewhat equalized conditions and nationalized the negro problem, it might have had some far-reaching good effects, political, social, and economic; it certainly would have relieved the "southern situation." Meanwhile, one fact was again proven by the Kansas experiment—individual negros could succeed under severe conditions, even though the mass might fail.

XII

Another towering black intellect of the late nineteenth century who left us a rich body of insights into the challenges facing African Americans both at that time and into the future was Alexander Crummell (1819–1898). A protégé of Pan-Africanist pioneer Henry Highland Garnet, Crummell placed Africa as the centerpiece of his vision for a viable black race. Alexander Crummell was an Episcopal priest who repatriated from America to Liberia and lived there for twenty years. He was at heart a Christian missionary who wanted the best for his fellow native Africans as well as for America's black population, the race that he embraced wholeheartedly. In "The Relations and Duties of Free Colored Men in America to Africa," Crummell articulates his hopes for the improvement of the race and for the best way to proceed. In reading his words, one is struck by his commitment to repatriation, to elevating the condition of the black race in America and in Africa, the condition of black labor in America, and the opportunities that abound for people of African descent by working for the advancement of the mother continent. Crummell also has some important insights about the condition of the black family and the direction that needs to be taken to assure its progress. His Pan-Africanist thinking influenced future generations of black leaders which included W. E. B. Du Bois and Marcus Garvey, among others. Do his positive words and vision for Africa and the Diaspora continue to have meaning and to inspire?

"The Relations and Duties of Free Colored Men in America to Africa"

Alexander Crummell

First, I am to speak with reference to the temporal, and material interests of adventurous, enterprising and aspiring men in the United States of America. I wish to bring before such persons reasons why they should feel interest in Africa. These reasons are not, I am free to confess, directly and distinctively philanthropic: although I do, indeed, aim at human well-being through their force and influence. But I appeal now more especially to the hopes, desires, ambition, and aspirations of such men. I am referring to that sentiment of self-regard which prompts to noble exertions for support and superiority. I am aiming at that principle of SELF LOVE which spurs men on to self-advantage and self-aggrandizement; a principle which, in its normal state and in its due degree, to use the words of BUTLER, "is as just and morally good as any affection whatever." In tine, I address myself to all that class of sentiments in the human heart which creates a thirst for wealth, position, honor, and power. I desire the auxiliary aid of this class of persons, and this class of motives, for it is such influences and agencies which are calculated to advance the material growth of Africa. She needs skill, enterprise, energy, worldly talent, to raise her; and those applied here to her needs and circumstances, will prove the handmaid of Religion, and will serve the great purposes of civilization and enlightenment through all her borders.

There seems to me to be a natural call upon the children of Africa in foreign lands, to come and participate in the opening treasures of the land of their fathers. Though these treasures are the manifest gift of God to the negro race, yet that race reaps but the most partial measure of their good and advantage. It has always been thus in the past, and now as the resources of Africa are being more and more developed, the extent of our interest therein is becoming more and more diminutive. The slave-trade is interdicted throughout Christendom; the chief powers of earth have put a lien upon the system of slavery; interest and research in Africa have reached a state of intensity; mystery has been banished from some of her most secret quarters; sunlight, after ages of darkness, has burst in upon the charmed, regions of her wealth and value; and yet the negro, on his native soil, is but "a hewer of wood and drawer of water;" and the sons of Africa in foreign lands, inane and blinded, suffer the adventurous foreigner, with greed and glut, to jostle him aside, and to seize, with skill and effect, upon their own rightful inheritance.

For three centuries and upwards, the civilized nations of the earth have been engaged in African commerce. Traffic on the coast of Africa anticipated the discoveries of Columbus. From Africa the purest gold got its characteristic three hundred years ago. From Africa dyes of the greatest value have been carried to the great manufacturing marts of the world. From Africa palm oil is exported by thousands of tons; and now as the observant eye of commerce is becoming more and more fastened upon this continent, grain, gums, oils of diverse kinds, valuable woods, copper and other ore, are being borne from the soil to meet the clamorous demands of distant marts.

The chief item of commerce in this continent has been, the "slave trade." The coast of Africa has been more noted for this than for anything else. Ever since 1600, the civilized nations of the earth have been transporting in deadly holds, in poisonous and pestilential cabins, in "perfidious barks," millions of our race to foreign lands. This trade is now almost universally regarded as criminal; but in the light of commercial prudence and pecuniary advantage, the slave trade was as great a piece of folly as it was a crime; for almost beneath their eyes, yea, doubtless, often immediately in their sight, were lying treasures, rivaling far the market value of the flesh and blood they had been so eager to crowd beneath their hatches.

Africa is as rich in resources as India is; not as yet as valuable in products, because she is more unenlightened, and has a less skilful population. But so far as it respects mineral and vegetable capacity, there seems to me but little, if any doubt that Africa more than rivals the most productive lands on the globe.

Let me set before you, though briefly, some of the valuable articles of West African trade. I must remind you, however, of three things; first, that the soil, the rocks, and the flora of Africa have not had the advantage of scientific scrutiny, and as a consequence but little is known as yet of her real worth and wealth in these respects. Second, that West African trade is only in a nascent state — that it comes from but a slight fringe of the coast, while the rich interior yields, as yet, but a reluctant hold upon the vast and various treasures it possesses. And third, that such is the mysterious secrecy

American and English houses retain and enjoin upon this subject, that even approximation to the facts of the case is remote and distant.

The following Table is an attempt to classify, valuable products and articles of present trade. Nearly every article mentioned has come under my own personal inspection; the exceptions are not over a dozen and a half.... .

I can not dismiss these Tables without a few remarks relative to some few prominent items they enumerate; I mean the PALM NUT and OIL, COTTON, INDIAN CORN, and SUGAR CANE.

PALM OIL. — This article, more than any other West African product, shows the rapidity with which legitimate commerce has sprung up on the coast of Africa. A few years ago palm oil was an insignificant item in the coast trade. Now it is an article which commands whole fleets of sailing vessels, seeks the auxiliary aid of steamers, and effects most powerfully the commerce of England, France, and the United States.

I copy several items pertaining to this export from a report of a former acquaintance and correspondent, the late Mr. Consul Campbell, of Lagos. The report, as will be seen, includes several other items besides palm oil, and it refers exclusively to LAGOS.... .

I have no reliable information of the amount of oil exported at the present; but I do not think I shall be far from the point of accuracy, if I put it down at 60,000 tons, which, at the probable value of £45 per ton, equals £2,700,000.

COTTON. — Next to palm oil, cotton is now commanding more attention than any other article. The interesting fact with regard to this staple is that it excites as much interest in Africa as it does in England and America. There are few things in the history of trade more important, more interesting, morally as well as commercially, than the impetus which has recently been given to the growth of cotton.

In 185–, Mr. Consul Campbell made a statement of the probable amount of cotton exported from West Africa. I have to rely upon my memory for the items of that statement; and, if I mistake not, he stated that the people of Abbeokuta exported nigh 200,000 country cloths annually. These cloths are purchased for transportation to Brazil, where there are thousands of African slaves who still dress in the same style as when at their homes. He supposed that full 200,000 country cloths were manufactured for home use, which would make the probable number manufactured in Africa, 400,000. And he calculated 2&1/2 lbs. as the average weight of each country cloth;—and 100,000 x 2&1/2 = 1,000,000 lbs. of cotton manufactured by the natives of interior Africa, in one locality, that is Yoruba. Doubtless as much more is allowed to grow and run to waste, unused.

Now these facts, to a partial extent, were well known in Liberia, for our merchants are accustomed to purchasing "country cloths," as they are called, and selling them to foreign traders; but Consul Campbell's statements far exceed any realities we have ever thought of, and show that interior Africa is as great a field for the production of cotton, as America or India.

SUGAR CANE. — To what extent West Africa is to become a sugar-producing country it is difficult to conjecture. Many, doubtless, have grave doubts whether this will ever be the case for my own part I have no misgivings upon the point, that is, its capability of becoming a great sugar-producing country. The natives grow it in all the country about Cape Palmas, and frequently bring cane to the American settlements for sale. With some small encouragement, and a little stimulus, it could easily be made a staple here. My opinions have been strengthened by some observations made in a recent missionary tour. I found cane but little inferior to that grown on the St. Paul's river, growing in nearly all the towns and villages through which I passed, forty, fifty, and sixty miles in the interior. On inquiry, I learned that it is grown by the natives in the interior, two hundred miles back. Dr. Livingstone, in his journal, states a like fact concerning the natives in South Africa.

What a germ have we here for systematic labor, plodding industry, the proper direction of the acquisition principle, and thereby, of civilization and Christianity, if only a company of right-minded men were settled on the Cavalla, prepared for the production of sugar, willing to stimulate national energy, and at the same time to uplift and enlighten the heathen!

MAIZE. — What is the case respecting sugar, cane equally pertains to corn. It is grown plenteously and extensively in West Africa. On the Cavalla river it is planted with rice, and I am told that in the gathering season hundreds of bushels of corn are left by the natives untouched in their fields. In some cases American colonists have gone and gathered quantities of it without any payment. Here, then, with an enterprising settlement, corn could be obtained, as an export. The natives, if encouraged, might easily be made vast and extensive corn-growers. This has already taken place on the Gold Coast. Several cargoes of corn were exported thence in 1859, to England.

As with the palm oil, so with maize, sugar-cane, and cotton; civilized men could, with but little difficulty, increase the cultivation of these articles among the natives, and ship them to traders to their own advantage. And this process is the great secret of West African trade; the foreign merchant, by his goods, excites the cupidity of the simple native who at Fernandapo brings him barwood; at St. Paul Loando, beeswax; at Congo, copal and gutta percha; at Accra, maize; at Cababar, black ebony wood; at Bonny and Lagos, palm oil; at Bassa, (Liberia,) camwood; at Lagos, cotton; at Tantamquerry and Gambra, ground nuts and pepper; at Sierra Leone, nearly all kinds of African produce; at Elmina, Cape Coast, Accra, and Bassam, gold. By this multiform traffic, yet, be it remembered, in its infancy, and capable of being increased a thousand-fold, millions of dollars are being made, every year, on the coast of Africa.

Now all this flows into the coffers of white men. I mean nothing invidious by this. I state a fact, and am utterly unconscious of any unworthy or ungenerous feeling, in stating it. "The earth is the Lord's, and the fullness thereof;" and this "fullness" he has given to man, irrespective of race or color. The main condition of the obtainment of it is intelligence, forecast, skill, and enterprise. If the black man—the black man, I mean, civilized and enlightened, has lying before him a golden heritage, and fails to seize upon and to appropriate it; Providence, none the less, intends it to be seized upon, and wills it to be used. And if the white man, with a keen eye, a cunning hand, and a wise practicalness, is enabled to appropriate it with skill and effect, it is his; God gives it to him; and he has a right to seek and to search for a multiplication of it; and when he secures it, a right to the use of it,—responsible, however, both to God and man for the use of right means to the ends he has before him, and for the moral features of his traffic.

But while conceding that the white man has, in the main, fairly won the present trade of Africa; I can not but lament over non-participation therein for the larger advantages of it, go to Europe and America, and help to swell the broad stream of their wealth, luxury, and refinement. And how deep and broad and mighty is that stream, as shown by two facts: 1st, That England, France, and the United States, expend annually more than a million and a half of dollars for the protection of trade on this coast. And 2d, That the coast swarms with white men, using all possible means and contrivances to open trade into the interior. To this one single end, an immense amount of capital is spent by great mercantile houses, in England, France, and America. One single house in Liverpool, employs such a fleet of trading vessels, that it is necessitated to keep a resident physician at the mouth of one of our great rivers for the benefit of their captains and sailors. "A single merchant now living, in the course of three or four years has spent more than $100,000 in exploring the rivers and creeks of Western Africa, merely to ascertain the extent of her commercial relations." While I am writing these pages, I receive the information that one of the great Liverpool houses, has just sent out a small steamer to the Brights, to collect the oil for their trading vessels. Simultaneously with this intelligence, I am advised that a number of agents are employed by English capitalists to visit the towns from Lagos to Abbeokuta, and to leave with their chiefs, small bags of cotton seed for the growth of cotton. And but a few months ago we hailed in our roads a little fairy craft—the "Sunbeam," steamer sent out by "Laird and Company" for the Niger trade; and since then, I have heard of two of her trips, four hundred miles up that mighty river, bringing thence valuable cargoes from the factories which are now established three hundred miles up upon its banks.

And now perhaps you ask,—"How shall the children of Africa, sojourning in foreign lands, avail themselves of the treasures of this continent?" I answer briefly,—"In the same way white men do." They have pointed out the way; let us follow in the same track and in the use of the like [legitimate] agencies by which trade is facilitated and money is made by them.

Perhaps this is too general; let me therefore attempt something more specific and distinctive.

FIRST, then, I remark that if individuals are unable to enter upon a trading system, they can form associations. If one has not sufficient capital, four or six united can make a good beginning. If a few persons can not make the venture, then a company can be formed. It was in this way the first attempts at trading were made by the Dutch and the English, both in India and Africa. A few men associated themselves together, and sent out their agent or agents, and started a factory. And from such humble beginnings, in the 17th century, has arisen that magnificent Indian Empire, which has helped to swell the vast wealth, and the cumbrous capital of England, from whose arena have come forth such splendid and colossal characters, as Cleve, and Wellington, and Metcalf, and the Laurences, and Havelock; and which has furnished the church of Christ a field on which to display the Apostolic virtues and the primitive self-sacrifice of Middleton, and Heber, and Wilson, of Henry Martyn, of Fox and Ragland.

Without doubt God designs as great things as these for Africa, and among the means and agencies He will employ, commercial enterprise is most certainly one. To this end however, high souls and lofty resolves are necessary, as in any other vocation of life. Of course the timid, the over-cautious, the fearful; men in whose constitution FAITH is a needed quality, are not fitted for this service. If ever the epoch of negro civilization is brought about in Africa; whatever external influences may he brought to bear upon this end, whatever foreign agencies and aids, black men themselves are without doubt to he the chief instruments. But they are to be men of force and energy; men who will not suffer themselves to be outrivaled in enterprise and vigor; men who are prepared for pains, and want and suffering; men of such invincible courage that the spirit can not be tamed by transient failures, incidental misadventure, or even glaring miscalculations; men who can exaggerate the feeblest resources into potent agencies and fruitful capital. Moreover these men are to have strong moral proclivities, equal to the deep penetration and the unyielding tenacity of their minds. No greater curse could be entailed upon Africa than the sudden appearance upon her shores, of a mighty host of heartless black buccaneers [for such indeed they would prove themselves;] — men sharpened up by letters and training; filled with feverish greed; with hearts utterly alien from moral good and human well-being; and only regarding Africa as a convenient goldfield from which to extract emolument and treasure to carry off to foreign quarters.

Such men would only reproduce the worst evils of the last three sad centuries of Africa's history; and quickly and inevitably so soil their character, that the just imputation would be fastened upon them of that malignant lie which has recently been spread abroad through Europe and America against us; that is, of complicity with the slave trade.

Happily for Africa, most the yearnings of her sons towards her are gentle, humane and generous. When the commercial one shall show itself, it will not differ, I feel assured, from all the others her children have showed. God grant that it may soon burst from many warm and ardent and energetic hearts, for the rescue of a continent!

SECOND. I proceed to show that the whole coast offers facilities for adventurous traders. There are few, if any localities but where they can set up their factories and commence business. If there are exceptions they are rare; and even then, not really such, but cases where at some previous time the natives have been so basely and knavishly treated, that they themselves have learned to practice the same upon some hapless, unsuspecting captain and his crew. As a general thing, however, native African chiefs court and invite the residence of a trader in their neighborhood; will give him protection; and will strive to secure his permanent stay. On our Liberian coast we see the proof of this in the many factories in existence at divers points. I have myself seen mere boys, — young Englishmen not of age, — who have come out to this country seeking their fortunes, living on the coast in native towns, without any civilized companionship, and carrying on a thriving trade. The chiefs have an interest in these men, and therefore make their residence safe and comfortable. The traders' presence and barter give the King or head-man importance, increase his wealth, augment his influence in the neighborhood, swell the population of his town, and thus make it the center or capital of the surrounding region. But even if it were not thus, the security of traders is insured by the felt power of the three great nations of the civilized world. Such, and so great is the naval force of England, France, and America, on this coast, that the coast may be regarded as protected. The native chiefs, for many hundred miles, have been taught to fear the destructive instruments of war they carry with them, and now a days but seldom give occasion for their use.

But aside from all this, I may remark here, 1st, that of all rude and uncivilized men, the native African is the mildest and most gentle; and 2nd, that no people in the world are so given to trade and barter as the negroes of the western coast of Africa.

THIRDLY. Let me refer to the means and facilities colored men have for an entrance upon African commerce. And 1st, I would point out the large amount of capital which is lying in their hands dead and unproductive. There is, as you are doubtless aware, no small amount of wealth possessed by the free colored population of the United States, both North and South. Notwithstanding the multitudinous difficulties which beset them in the pathway of improvement, our brethren have shown capacity, perseverance, oftentimes thrift and acquisitiveness. As a consequence they are, all over the Union, owners of houses, farms, homesteads, and divers other kinds of property; and stored away in safe quarters, they have large amounts of gold and silver; deep down in large stockings, in the corners of old chests, in dark and undiscoverable nook and crannies; besides larger sums invested in banks, and locked up in the safes of city savings banks.

I have no statistics by me of the population and property of the colored people of Cincinnati, but 1 am told that their wealth exceeds that of the same class, in any other city in the American Union — that is, according to their numbers. Nashville, Tenn., Charleston, S. C., St. Louis, Mo., Mobile and New Orleans, stand in nearly the same category. Baltimore holds a respectable position. In the "Weekly Anglo-African," (September, 1850,) I find that the current property of the colored population in Philadelphia is put down at $231,481. Doubtless their personal real estate must be worth millions. And the same must be true of New York city.

The greater portion of their wealth, however, is unproductive. As a people we have been victimized in a pecuniary point of view, as well as morally and politically; and as a consequence there is an almost universal dread of entrusting out monies in the hands of capitalists, and trading companies, and stock; though in the great cities large sums are put in savings banks. There are few, however, who have the courage to take shares in railroad and similar companies, and in many places it could not be done.

There is one most pregnant fact that will serve to show, somewhat, their monetary ability. "THE AFRICAN METHODIST EPISCOPAL CHURCH" is one of the denominations of the United States. It has its own organization; its own bishops; its conferences, its organ, or magazine; and these entirely intersect — absolutely disconnected with all the white denominations of America. This religious body is spread out in hamlet, village, town and city, all through the eastern, northern, western, and (partly) the southern States. But the point to which I desire to direct your attention is the fact that they have built and now own some 800 church edifices, mostly brick; and in the large cities, such as New York, Philadelphia and Baltimore, they are large, imposing, capacious, and will seat mime two or three thousand people. The free black people of the United States built these churches; the funds were gathered from their small and large congregations; and in some cases they have been known to collect, that is, in Philadelphia and Baltimore, at one collection, over $1,000. The aggregate value of their property can not be less than $5,000,000.

Now this, you will notice, is an exhibit of the corporate monied power of but one class or our brethren. I have said nothing about the Episcopal churches, of the Presbyterians, of the Baptists, nor of the divers sections of the Methodists. But this will suffice. You can easily see from the above, that there must be a large amount of pecuniary means in the hands of the free colored population of the American States.

2nd. I turn now to another of their facilities for engaging in African commerce. I refer to Navigation. And here I might rest the case upon the fact that money will purchase vessels, and command seamen and navigators. But you already have both. Turn for a moment to New Bedford, Mass. It is now some twenty years since I visited that important seaport. Though but a boy, I kept my eyes open, especially upon the condition of our race there; and I retain still a vivid remembrance of the signs of industry and thrift among them, of the evidences of their unusual wealth, and of their large interest in shipping. I had the names of several parties mentioned to me who were owners of whale craft, and I made the acquaintance of some of them. Among these I remember well some youthful descendants of Paul Cuffe. The same state of things I apprehend exists, though perhaps in a much less degree, in some places in Connecticut; on the Hudson, that is, at Albany and Newburgh, in the State of New York; on the Potomac; at St. Louis, on the Mississippi, and on Red River. There are scores, if not hundreds of colored men who own schooners, and other small craft in those localities; pilots and engineers, captains and seamen, who, if once moved with a generous impulse to redeem the land of their fathers, could, in a brief time, form a vast commercial marine, equal to all the necessities of such a glorious project.

Let me dwell for a moment upon the suggestion, that is, the facilities for securing seamen, in large numbers, I apprehend, can easily be obtained. Even in the United States their numbers are legion; and we may proudly say that in activity, dutifulness and skill, they are equal to any sailors on the globe. Nor would there be any great lack of the needed class just above the grade of sailors, that is, a class who would join intelligence and knowledge to practicalness. What a number of men, trained to a late boyhood in the colored schools, do we not know who have sailed for years out of New York as "stewards" in the "liners"! How many of these are there not, who both at school and by experience, have attained a real scientific acquaintance with navigation. And how many of them, had they been white men, would long ere this, have risen to the posts of mates and captains! How many of such could you and I point out, who were our school-mates, in the old "free school" in Mulberry street!

Here, then, you have the material and the designated agency for an almost, boundless commercial staff, for the purposes of trade in West Africa. The facts I have adduced can, not, I think, be disputed. And on the condition that this machinery is brought into operation, the influences and results are easily anticipated. It must follow, as a necessity, that the trade and commerce of Africa shall fall into the hands of black men. At an early day whole fleets of vessels, manned and officered by black men from the United States and Liberia, would outrival all the other agencies which are now being used for grasping West African commerce. Large and important houses would spring into existence among you, all through the states. Wealth would flow into your coffers, and affluence would soon exhibit itself amid all your associations. The reproach of penury and the consciousness of impotency in all your relations would rapidly depart. And as a people you would soon be able to make yourselves a felt element of society in all the relations of life, on the soil where you were born.

These are some of the material influences which would result from this movement. The moral and philanthropic results would be equally if not more notable. The kings and tradesmen of Africa, having the demonstration of negro capacity before them, would hail the presence of their black kinsmen from America, and would be stimulated to a generous emulation. To the farthest interior, leagues and combinations would be formed with the men of commerce, and thus civilization, enlightenment and Christianity would be carried to every state, and town, and village of interior Africa. The galling remembrances of the slave trade on the coast, and of slavery in America, would quicken the blood and the brain of both parties; and every wretch of a slave trader who might visit the coast, would have to atone for his temerity by submitting to the rigid code framed for piracy. And when this disturbing and destructive hindrance to African progress was once put down, noble cities, vast agricultural establishments, the seeds of universities, and ground-work of church organizations, would spring up all along the banks, and up the valley of the Niger.

There is one certain commercial result—to return to my subject—that would surely grow out of this movement; I mean the flow of large amounts of capital from the monied men of America, that is, if black men showed skill, energy and practicability. Philanthropy would come forward with largess for colored men, thus developing the resources of Africa. Religion would open a large and generous hand in order to hasten the redemption of a continent, alien from Christ and His church. And capital would hasten forward, not only for its wonted reduplication, but also to exemplify the vitality and fruitfulness which it always scatters from golden hands in its open pathway. And when you consider the fact of kinship, on our part, with Africa, the less liability to fever, the incentive to gain, the magnificent objects before us, and the magnificent field on which to develop them, and the probable early power of intelligent black men to penetrate, scathless, any neighborhood where they might reside, you can see the likelihood of an early repossession of Africa, in trade, commerce, and moral power, by her now scattered children, in distant lands.

For the carrying out such a plan you have, I repeat myself, you have almost, if not quite, all the needed means and agencies, even now, at hand. You have, all through the states, men who can at once furnish the capital for the commencement of such a venture. You know I am not one to exaggerate the wealth of colored men. In such matters I prefer fact to conjecture; for certainly among us on this subject, imagination has too often proved "a forward and delusive faculty." Yet I do know of some of our brethren in the States who have become monied men,—not millionaires indeed, but men worth their thousands. Some of these men are more prominent individuals than others, and as their names are not unfrequently mentioned in such a connection as this, it may not seem invidious in a like mention on these pages. Some of these persons are acquaintances—a few, old friends of former years, but the most are personally unknown to me. There are Rev. Stephen Smith, William Whipper, Esq., of Philadelphia; Messrs. Knight Smith, of Chicago, Ill.; Messrs. Cook & Moxly, of Buffalo, N.Y.; Youngs & Wilcox, of Cincinnati, &c., &c.

It is possible that in a few instances earnest prejudice against everything African may cause displeasure at this designation. Any one can see that I have intended nothing discourteous; and it should be remembered that commercial enterprise in Africa has no necessary connection with emigration, or colonization. How great so ever the diversities of opinion upon these points, on this platform Douglass and Delany can stand beside the foremost citizens and merchants of Liberia. Hence those men whose feelings are the most averse to anything like colonization, can not object to the promotion of trade and the acquisition of wealth. Indeed, I have no doubt that there are thousands who would be glad of a safe investment in anything wherein there is probability of advantage. Moreover the fretted mind of our brethren needs distraction from grief and the causes of grief. Just now, when darkness shrouds their Southern heavens, what could be more opportune, what more desirable than such a movement. The danger is that thousands of them, in their sorrows, may sit down, hopeless, careless, and " — Nurse despair and feed the dreadful appetite of death."

Your leading men should strive to occupy the vacant minds of their despairing brethren by the healthful stimulant of duty and enterprise.

[1861]

XIII

Anna J. Cooper (c 1858–1964) was a towering intellect who gave voice particularly to African-American women in an era that largely failed to acknowledge the capacity of women and especially the capacity of black women. Cooper lived a long and productive life of 105 years. Her book, *A Voice from the South: By A Black Woman of the South*, was published in 1892. It indeed gave voice to the struggle of women and black women in particular. The work would serve as the basis for her dissertation as she went on to receive a PhD from the Sorbonne in Paris, France, in 1925, making her one of the first African-American women of the United States to obtain the doctorate. She would teach for many years at the famous M-Street School in Washington, DC, a landmark institution for educating young blacks. She continued to speak out as a perceptive voice for African-American education and advancement. She also had a world view and appreciation of the larger African Diaspora and its people. Cooper was one of the few women who spoke at the 1900 Pan-African Conference in London. In the excerpt from her book presented here, "Womanhood: A Vital Element in the Regeneration and Progress of A Race," the reader is given to rethink the visionary ideas of one of black America's greatest intellectuals, past or present. Do you find her words profound? Does she articulate a roadmap that was helpful for the advancement of women then and of value for the advancement of black women today?

"Womanhood: A Vital Element in the Regeneration and Progress of A Race"

Anna J. Cooper

The two sources from which, perhaps, modern civilization has derived its noble and ennobling ideal of woman are Christianity and the Feudal System.

In Oriental countries woman has been uniformly devoted to a life of ignorance, infamy, and complete stagnation. The Chinese shoe of to-day does not more entirely dwarf, cramp, and destroy her physical powers, than have the customs, laws, and social instincts, which from remotest ages have governed our Sister of the East, enervated and blighted her mental and moral life.

Mahomet makes no account of woman whatever in his polity. The Koran, which, unlike our Bible, was a product and not a growth, tried to address itself to the needs of Arabian civilization as Mahomet with his circumscribed powers saw them. The Arab was a nomad. Home to him meant his present camping place. That deity who, according to our western ideals, makes and sanctifies the home, was to him a transient bauble to be toyed with so long as it gave pleasure and then to be thrown aside for a new one. As a personality, an individual soul, capable of eternal growth and unlimited development, and destined to mould and shape the civilization of the future to an incalculable extent, Mahomet did not know woman. There was no hereafter, no paradise for her. The heaven of the Mussulman is peopled and made gladsome not by the departed wife, or sister, or mother, but by houri—a figment of Mahomet's brain, partaking of the ethereal qualities of angels, yet imbued with all the vices and inanity of Oriental women. The harem here, and—"dust to dust" hereafter, this was the hope, the inspiration, the summum bonum of the Eastern woman's life! With what result on the life of the nation, the "Unspeakable Turk," the "sick man" of modern Europe can to-day exemplify.

Says a certain writer: "The private life of the Turk is vilest of the vile, unprogressive, unambitious, and inconceivably low." And yet Turkey is not without her great men. She has produced most brilliant minds; men skilled in all the intricacies of diplomacy and statesmanship; men whose intellects could grapple with the deep problems of empire and manipulate the subtle agencies which check-mate kings. But these minds were not the normal outgrowth of a healthy trunk. They seemed rather ephemeral excrescencies which shoot far out with all the vigor and promise, apparently, of strong branches; but soon alas fall into decay and ugliness because there is no soundness in the root, no life-giving sap, permeating, strengthening and perpetuating the whole. There is a worm at the core! The homelife is impure! and when we look for fruit, like apples of Sodom, it crumbles within our grasp into dust and ashes.

It is pleasing to turn from this effete and immobile civilization to a society still fresh and vigorous, whose seed is in itself, and whose very name is synonymous with all that is progressive, elevating and inspiring, viz., the European bud and the American flower of modern civilization.

And here let me say parenthetically that our satisfaction in American institutions rests not on the fruition we now enjoy, but springs rather from the possibilities and promise that are inherent in the system, though as yet, perhaps, far in the future.

"Happiness," says Madame de Stael, "consists not in perfections attained, but in a sense of progress, the result of our own endeavor under conspiring circumstances toward a goal which continually advances and broadens and deepens till it is swallowed up in the Infinite." Such conditions in embryo are all that we claim for the land of the West. We have not yet reached our ideal in American civilization. The pessimists even declare that we are not marching in that direction. But there can be no doubt that here in America is the arena in which the next triumph of civilization is to be won; and here too we find promise abundant and possibilities infinite.

Now let us see on what basis this hope for our country primarily and fundamentally rests. Can any one doubt that it is chiefly on the homelife and on the influence of good women in those homes? Says Macaulay: "You may judge a nation's rank in the scale of civilization from the way they treat their women." And Emerson, "I have thought that a sufficient measure of civilization is the influence of good women." Now this high regard for woman, this germ of a prolific idea which in our own day is bearing such rich and varied fruit, was ingrafted into European civilization, we have said, from two sources, the Christian Church and the Feudal System. For although the Feudal System can in no sense be said to have originated the idea, yet there can be no doubt that the habits of life and modes of thought to which Feudalism gave rise, materially fostered and developed it; for they gave us chivalry, than which no institution has more sensibly magnified and elevated woman's position in society.

Tacitus dwells on the tender regard for woman entertained by these rugged barbarians before they left their northern homes to overrun Europe. Old Norse legends too, and primitive poems, all breathe the same spirit of love of home and veneration for the pure and noble influence there presiding—the wife, the sister, the mother.

And when later on we see the settled life of the Middle Ages "oozing out," as M. Guizot expresses it, from the plundering and pillaging life of barbarism and crystallizing into the Feudal System, the tiger of the field is brought once more within the charmed circle of the goddesses of his castle, and his imagination weaves around them a halo whose reflection possibly has not yet altogether vanished.

It is true the spirit of Christianity had not yet put the seal of catholicity on this sentiment. Chivalry, according to Bascom, was but the toning down and softening of a rough and lawless period. It gave a roseate glow to a bitter winter's day. Those who looked out from castle windows revelled in its "amethyst tints." But God's poor, the weak, the unlovely, the commonplace were still freezing and starving none the less, in unpitied, unrelieved loneliness.

Respect for woman, the much lauded chivalry of the Middle Ages, meant what I fear it still means to some men in our own day—respect for the elect few among whom they expect to consort.

The idea of the radical amelioration of womankind, reverence for woman as woman regardless of rank, wealth, or culture, was to come from that rich and bounteous fountain from which flow all our liberal and universal ideas—the Gospel of Jesus Christ.

And yet the Christian Church at the time of which we have been speaking would seem to have been doing even less to protect and elevate woman than the little done by secular society. The Church as an organization committed a double offense against woman in the Middle Ages. Making of marriage a sacrament and at the same time insisting on the celibacy of the clergy and other religious orders, she gave an inferior if not an impure character to the marriage relation, especially fitted to reflect discredit on woman. Would this were all or the worst! but the Church by the licentiousness of its chosen servants invaded the household and established too often as vicious connections those relations which it forbade to assume openly and in good faith. "Thus," to use the words of our authority, "the religious corps became as numerous, as searching, and as unclean as the frogs of Egypt, which penetrated into all quarters, into the ovens and kneading troughs, leaving their filthy trail wherever they went." Says Chaucer with characteristic satire, speaking of the Friars:

'Women may now go safely up and doun,

In every bush, and under every tree,

Ther is non other incubus but he,

And he ne will don hem no dishonour.'

Henry, Bishop of Liege, could unblushingly boast the birth of twenty-two children in fourteen years.

It may help us under some of the perplexities which beset our way in "the one Catholic and Apostolic Church" to-day, to recall some of the corruptions and incongruities against which the Bride of Christ has had to struggle in her past history and in spite of which she has kept, through many vicissitudes, the faith once delivered to the saints.

Individuals, organizations, whole sections of the Church militant may outrage the Christ whom they profess, may ruthlessly trample under foot both the spirit and the letter of his precepts, yet not till we hear the voices audibly saying "Come let us depart hence," shall we cease to believe and cling to the promise, "*I am with you to the end of the world.*"

"Yet saints their watch are keeping,

The cry goes up 'How long!'

And soon the night of weeping

Shall be the morn of song."

However much then the facts of any particular period of history may seem to deny it, I for one do not doubt that the source of the vitalizing principle of woman's development and amelioration is the Christian Church, so far as that church is coincident with Christianity.

Christ gave ideals not formulæ. The Gospel is a germ requiring millennia for its growth and ripening. It needs and at the same time helps to form around itself a soil enriched in civilization, and perfected in culture and insight without which the embryo can neither be unfolded or comprehended. With all the strides our civilization has made from the first to the nineteenth century, we can boast not an idea, not a principle of action, not a progressive social force but was already mutely foreshadowed, or directly enjoined in that simple tale of a meek and lowly life. The quiet face of the Nazarene is ever seen a little way ahead, never too far to come down to and touch the life of the lowest in days the darkest, yet ever leading onward, still onward, the tottering childish feet of our strangely boastful civilization.

By laying down for woman the same code of morality, the same standard of purity, as for man; by refusing to countenance the shameless and equally guilty monsters who were gloating over her fall,—graciously stooping in all the majesty of his own spotlessness to wipe away the filth and grime of her guilty past and bid her go in peace and sin no more; and again in the moments of his own careworn and footsore dejection, turning trustfully and lovingly, away from the heartless snubbing and sneers, away from the cruel malignity of mobs and prelates in the dusty marts of Jerusalem to the ready sympathy, loving appreciation and unfaltering friendship of that quiet home at Bethany; and even at the last, by his dying bequest to the disciple whom he loved, signifying the protection and tender regard to be extended to that sorrowing mother and ever afterward to the sex she represented;—throughout his life and in his death he has given to men a rule and guide for the estimation of woman as an equal, as a helper, as a friend, and as a sacred charge to be sheltered and cared for with a brother's love and sympathy, lessons which nineteen centuries' gigantic strides in knowledge, arts, and sciences, in social and ethical principles have not been able to probe to their depth or to exhaust in practice.

It seems not too much to say then of the vitalizing, regenerating, and progressive influence of womanhood on the civilization of today, that, while it was foreshadowed among Germanic nations in the far away dawn of their history as a narrow, sickly and stunted growth, it yet owes its catholicity and power, the deepening of its roots and broadening of its branches to Christianity.

The union of these two forces, the Barbaric and the Christian, was not long delayed after the Fall of the Empire. The Church, which fell with Rome, finding herself in danger of being swallowed up by barbarism, with characteristic vigor and fertility of resources, addressed herself immediately to the task of conquering her conquerers. The means chosen does credit to her power of penetration and adaptability, as well as to her profound, unerring, all-compassing diplomacy; and makes us even now wonder if aught human can successfully and ultimately withstand her far-seeing designs and brilliant policy, or gainsay her well-earned claim to the word Catholic.

She saw the barbarian, little more developed than a wild beast. She forbore to antagonize and mystify his warlike nature by a full blaze of the heartsearching and humanizing tenets of her great Head. She said little of the rule "If thy brother smite thee on one cheek, turn to him the other also;" but thought it sufficient for the needs of those times, to establish the so-called "Truce of God" under which men were bound to abstain from butchering one another for three days of each week and on Church festivals. In other words, she respected their individuality: non-resistance pure and simple being for them an utter impossibility, she contented herself with less radical measures calculated to lead up finally to the full measure of the benevolence of Christ.

Next she took advantage of the barbarian's sensuous love of gaudy display and put all her magnificent garments on. She could not capture him by physical force, she would dazzle him by gorgeous spectacles. It is said that Romanism gained more in pomp and ritual during this trying period of the Dark Ages than throughout all her former history.

The result was she carried her point. Once more Rome laid her ambitious hand on the temporal power, and allied with Charlemagne, aspired to rule the world through a civilization dominated by Christianity and permeated by the traditions and instincts of those sturdy barbarians.

Here was the confluence of the two streams we have been tracing, which, united now, stretch before us as a broad majestic river. In regard to woman it was the meeting of two noble and ennobling forces, two kindred ideas the resultant of which, we doubt not, is destined to be a potent force in the betterment of the world.

Now after our appeal to history comparing nations destitute of this force and so destitute also of the principle of progress, with other nations among whom the influence of woman is prominent coupled with a brisk, progressive, satisfying civilization,—if in addition we find this strong presumptive evidence corroborated by reason and experience, we may conclude that these two equally varying concomitants are linked as cause and effect; in other words, that the position of woman in society determines the vital elements of its regeneration and progress.

Now that this is so on a priori grounds all must admit. And this not because woman is better or stronger or wiser than man, but from the nature of the case, because it is she who must first form the man by directing the earliest impulses of his character.

Byron and Wordsworth were both geniuses and would have stamped themselves on the thought of their age under any circumstances; and yet we find the one a savor of life unto life, the other of death unto death. "Byron, like a rocket, shot his way upward with scorn and repulsion, flamed out in wild, explosive, brilliant excesses and disappeared in darkness made all the more palpable."

Wordsworth lent of his gifts to reinforce that "power in the Universe which makes for righteousness" by taking the harp handed him from Heaven and using it to swell the strains of angelic choirs. Two locomotives equally mighty stand facing opposite tracks; the one to rush headlong to destruction with all its precious freight, the other to toil grandly and gloriously up the steep embattlements to Heaven and to God. Who—who can say what a world of consequences hung on the first placing and starting of these enormous forces!

Woman, Mother,—your responsibility is one that might make angels tremble and fear to take hold! To trifle with it, to ignore or misuse it, is to treat lightly the most sacred and solemn trust ever confided by God to human kind. The training of children is a task on which an infinity of weal or woe depends. Who does not covet it? Yet who does not stand awe-struck before its momentous issues! It is a matter of small moment, it seems to me, whether that lovely girl in whose accomplishments you take such pride and delight, can enter the gay and crowded salon with the ease and elegance of this or that French or English gentlewoman, compared with the decision as to whether her individuality is going to reinforce the good or the evil elements of the world. The lace and the diamonds, the dance and the theater, gain a new significance when scanned in their bearings on such issues. Their influence on the individual personality, and through her on the society and civilization which she vitalizes and inspires—all this and more must be weighed in the balance before the jury can return a just and intelligent verdict as to the innocence or banefulness of these apparently simple amusements.

Now the fact of woman's influence on society being granted, what are its practical bearings on the work which brought together this conference of colored clergy and laymen in Washington? "We come not here to talk." Life is too busy, too pregnant with meaning and far reaching consequences to allow you to come this far for mere intellectual entertainment.

The vital agency of womanhood in the regeneration and progress of a race, as a general question, is conceded almost before it is fairly stated. I confess one of the difficulties for me in the subject assigned lay in its obviousness. The plea is taken away by the opposite attorney's granting the whole question.

"Woman's influence on social progress"—who in Christendom doubts or questions it? One may as well be called on to prove that the sun is the source of light and heat and energy to this many-sided little world.

Nor, on the other hand, could it have been intended that I should apply the position when taken and proven, to the needs and responsibilities of the women of our race in the South. For is it not written, "Cursed is he that cometh after the king?" and has not the King already preceded me in "The Black Woman of the South"?

They have had both Moses and the Prophets in Dr. Crummell and if they hear not him, neither would they be persuaded though one came up from the South.

I would beg, however, with the Doctor's permission, to add my plea for the Colored Girls of the South:—that large, bright, promising fatally beautiful class that stand shivering like a delicate plantlet before the fury of tempestuous elements, so full of promise and possibilities, yet so sure of destruction; often without a father to whom they dare apply the loving term, often without a stronger brother to espouse their cause and defend their honor with his life's blood; in the midst of pitfalls and snares, waylaid by the lower classes of white men, with no shelter, no protection nearer than the great blue vault above, which half conceals and half reveals the one Care-Taker they know so little of. Oh, save them, help them, shield, train, develop, teach, inspire them! Snatch them, in God's name, as brands from the burning! There is material in them well worth your while, the hope in germ of a staunch, helpful, regenerating womanhood on which, primarily, rests the foundation stones of our future as a race.

It is absurd to quote statistics showing the Negro's bank account and rent rolls, to point to the hundreds of newspapers edited by colored men and lists of lawyers, doctors, professors, D. D's, LL D's, etc., etc., etc., while the source from which the life-blood of the race is to flow is subject to taint and corruption in the enemy's camp.

True progress is never made by spasms. Real progress is growth. It must begin in the seed. Then, "first the blade, then the ear, after that the full corn in the ear." There is something to encourage and inspire us in the advancement of individuals since their emancipation from slavery. It at least proves that there is nothing irretrievably wrong in the shape of the black man's skull, and that under given circumstances his development, downward or upward, will be similar to that of other average human beings.

But there is no time to be wasted in mere felicitation. That the Negro has his niche in the infinite purposes of the Eternal, no one who has studied the history of the last fifty years in America will deny. That much depends on his own right comprehension of his responsibility and rising to the demands of the hour, it will be good for him to see; and how best to use his present so that the structure of the future shall be stronger and higher and brighter and nobler and holier than that of the past, is a question to be decided each day by every one of us.

The race is just twenty-one years removed from the conception and experience of a chattel, just at the age of ruddy manhood. It is well enough to pause a moment for retrospection, introspection, and prospection. We look back, not to become inflated with conceit because of the depths from which we have arisen, but that we may learn wisdom from experience. We look within that we may gather together once more our forces, and, by improved and more practical methods, address ourselves to the tasks before us. We look forward with hope and trust that the same God whose guiding hand led our fathers through and out of the gall and bitterness of oppression, will still lead and direct their children, to the honor of His name, and for their ultimate salvation.

But this survey of the failures or achievements of the past, the difficulties and embarrassments of the present, and the mingled hopes and fears for the future, must not degenerate into mere dreaming nor consume the time which belongs to the practical and effective handling of the crucial questions of the hour; and there can be no issue more vital and momentous than this of the womanhood of the race.

Here is the vulnerable point, not in the heel, but at the heart of the young Achilles; and here must the defenses be strengthened and the watch redoubled.

We are the heirs of a past which was not our fathers' moulding. "Every man the arbiter of his own destiny" was not true for the American Negro of the past: and it is no fault of his that he finds himself to-day the inheritor of a manhood and womanhood impoverished and debased by two centuries and more of compression and degradation.

But weaknesses and malformations, which to-day are attributable to a vicious schoolmaster and a pernicious system, will a century hence be rightly regarded as proofs of innate corruptness and radical incurability.

Now the fundamental agency under God in the regeneration, the re-training of the race, as well as the ground work and starting point of its progress upward, must be the black woman.

With all the wrongs and neglects of her past, with all the weakness, the debasement, the moral thralldom of her present, the black woman of to-day stands mute and wondering at the Herculean task devolving around her. But the cycles wait for her. No other hand can move the lever. She must be loosed from her bands and set to work.

Our meager and superficial results from past efforts prove their futility; and every attempt to elevate the Negro, whether undertaken by himself or through the philanthropy of others, cannot but prove abortive unless so directed as to utilize the indispensable agency of an elevated and trained womanhood.

A race cannot be purified from without. Preachers and teachers are helps, and stimulants and conditions as necessary as the gracious rain and sunshine are to plant growth. But what are rain and dew and sunshine and cloud if there be no life in the plant germ? We must go to the root and see that it is sound and healthy and vigorous; and not deceive ourselves with waxen flowers and painted leaves of mock chlorophyll.

We too often mistake individuals' honor for race development and so are ready to substitute pretty accomplishments for sound sense and earnest purpose.

A stream cannot rise higher than its source. The atmosphere of homes is no rarer and purer and sweeter than are the mothers in those homes. A race is but a total of families. The nation is the aggregate of its homes. As the whole is sum of all its parts, so the character of the parts will determine the characteristics of the whole. These are all axioms and so evident that it seems gratuitous to remark it; and yet, unless I am greatly mistaken, most of the unsatisfaction from our past results arises from just such a radical and palpable error, as much almost on our own part as on that of our benevolent white friends.

The Negro is constitutionally hopeful and proverbially irrepressible; and naturally stands in danger of being dazzled by the shimmer and tinsel of superficials. We often mistake foliage for fruit and overestimate or wrongly estimate brilliant results.

The late Martin R. Delany, who was an unadulterated black man, used to say when honors of state fell upon him, that when he entered the council of kings the black race entered with him; meaning, I suppose, that there was no discounting his race identity and attributing his achievements to some admixture of Saxon blood. But our present record of eminent men, when placed beside the actual status of the race in America to-day, proves that no man can represent the race. Whatever the attainments of the individual may be, unless his home has moved on pari passu, he can never be regarded as identical with or representative of the whole.

Not by pointing to sun-bathed mountain tops do we prove that Phoebus warms the valleys. We must point to homes, average homes, homes of the rank and file of horny handed toiling men and women of the South (where the masses are) lighted and cheered by the good, the beautiful, and the true,—then and not till then will the whole plateau be lifted into the sunlight.

Only the BLACK WOMAN can say "when and where I enter, in the quiet, undisputed dignity of my womanhood, without violence and without suing or special patronage, then and there the whole Negro race enters with me." Is it not evident then that as individual workers for this race we must address ourselves with no half-hearted zeal to this feature of our mission. The need is felt and must be recognized by all. There is a call for workers, for missionaries, for men and women with the double consecration of a fundamental love of humanity and a desire for its melioration through the Gospel; but superadded to this we demand an intelligent and sympathetic comprehension of the interests and special needs of the Negro.

I see not why there should not be an organized effort for the protection and elevation of our girls such as the White Cross League in England. English women are strengthened and protected by more than twelve centuries of Christian influences, freedom and civilization; English girls are dispirited and crushed down by no such all-levelling prejudice as that supercilious caste spirit in America which cynically assumes "A Negro woman cannot be a lady." English womanhood is beset by no such snares and traps as betray the unprotected, untrained colored girl of the South, whose only crime and dire destruction often is her unconscious and marvelous beauty. Surely then if English indignation is aroused and English manhood thrilled under the leadership of a Bishop of the English church to build up bulwarks around their wronged sisters, Negro sentiment cannot remain callous and Negro effort nerveless in view of the imminent peril of the mothers of the next generation. "I am my Sister's keeper!" should be the hearty response of every man and woman of the race, and this conviction should purify and exalt the narrow, selfish and petty personal aims of life into a noble and sacred purpose.

We need men who can let their interest and gallantry extend outside the circle of their aesthetic appreciation; men who can be a father, a brother, a friend to every weak, struggling unshielded girl. We need women who are so sure of their own social footing that they need not fear leaning to lend a hand to a fallen or falling sister. We need men and women who do not exhaust their genius splitting hairs on aristocratic distinctions and thanking God they are not as others; but earnest, unselfish souls, who can go into the highways and byways, lifting up and leading, advising and encouraging with the truly catholic benevolence of the Gospel of Christ.

As Church workers we must confess our path of duty is less obvious; or rather our ability to adapt our machinery to our conception of the peculiar exigencies of this work as taught by experience and our own consciousness of the needs of the Negro, is as yet not demonstrable. Flexibility and aggressiveness are not such strong characteristics of the Church to-day as in the Dark Ages.

As a Mission field for the Church the Southern Negro is in some aspects most promising; in others, perplexing. Aliens neither in language and customs, nor in associations and sympathies, naturally of deeply rooted religious instincts and taking most readily and kindly to the worship and teachings of the Church, surely the task of proselytizing the American Negro is infinitely less formidable than that which confronted the Church in the Barbarians of Europe. Besides, this people already look to the Church as the hope of their race. Thinking colored men almost uniformly admit that the Protestant Episcopal Church with its quiet, chaste dignity and decorous solemnity, its instructive and elevating ritual, its bright chanting and joyous hymning, is eminently fitted to correct the peculiar faults of worship—the rank exuberance and often ludicrous demonstrativeness of their people. Yet, strange to say, the Church, claiming to be missionary and Catholic, urging that schism is sin and denominationalism inexcusable, has made in all these years almost no inroads upon this semi-civilized religionism.

Harvests from this over ripe field of home missions have been gathered in by Methodists, Baptists, and not least by Congregationalists, who were unknown to the Freedmen before their emancipation.

Our clergy numbers less than two dozen priests of Negro blood and we have hardly more than one self-supporting colored congregation in the entire Southland. While the organization known as the A. M. E. Church has 14,063 ministers, itinerant and local, 4,069 self-supporting churches, 4,2754,275 Sunday-schools, with property valued at $7,772,284, raising yearly for church purposes $1,427,000.

Stranger and more significant than all, the leading men of this race (I do not mean demagogues and politicians, but men of intellect, heart, and race devotion, men to whom the elevation of their people means more than personal ambition and sordid gain—and the men of that stamp have not all died yet) the Christian workers for the race, of younger and more cultured growth, are noticeably drifting into sectarian churches, many of them declaring all the time that they acknowledge the historic claims of the Church, believe her apostolicity, and would experience greater personal comfort, spiritual and intellectual, in her revered communion. It is a fact which any one may verify for himself, that representative colored men, professing that in their heart of hearts they are Episcopalians, are actually working in Methodist and Baptist pulpits; while the ranks of the Episcopal clergy are left to be filled largely by men who certainly suggest the propriety of a "perpetual Diaconate" if they cannot be said to have created the necessity for it.

Now where is the trouble? Something must be wrong. What is it?

A certain Southern Bishop of our Church reviewing the situation, whether in Godly anxiety or in "Gothic antipathy" I know not, deprecates the fact that the colored people do not seem drawn to the Episcopal Church, and comes to the sage conclusion that the Church is not adapted to the rude untutored minds of the Freedmen, and that they may be left to go to the Methodists and Baptists whither their racial proclivities undeniably tend. How the good Bishop can agree that all-foreseeing Wisdom, and Catholic Love would have framed his Church as typified in his seamless garment and unbroken body, and yet not leave it broad enough and deep enough and loving enough to seek and save and hold seven millions of God's poor, I cannot see.

But the doctors while discussing their scientifically conclusive diagnosis of the disease, will perhaps not think it presumptuous in the patient if he dares to suggest where at least the pain is. If this be allowed, a Black woman of the South would beg to point out two possible oversights in this southern work which may indicate in part both a cause and a remedy for some failure. The first is not calculating for the Black man's personality; not having respect, if I may so express it, to his manhood or deferring at all to his conceptions of the needs of his people. When colored persons have been employed it was too often as machines or as manikins. There has been no disposition, generally, to get the black man's ideal or to let his individuality work by its own gravity, as it were. A conference of earnest Christian men have met at regular intervals for some years past to discuss the best methods of promoting the welfare and development of colored people in this country. Yet, strange as it may seem, they have never invited a colored man or even intimated that one would be welcome to take part in their deliberations. Their remedial contrivances are purely theoretical or empirical, therefore, and the whole machinery devoid of soul.

The second important oversight in my judgment is closely allied to this and probably grows out of it, and that is not developing Negro womanhood as an essential fundamental for the elevation of the race, and utilizing this agency in extending the work of the Church.

Of the first I have possibly already presumed to say too much since it does not strictly come within the province of my subject. However, Macaulay somewhere criticises the Church of England as not knowing how to use fanatics, and declares that had Ignatius Loyola been in the Anglican instead of the Roman communion, the Jesuits would have been schismatics instead of Catholics; and if the religious awakenings of the Wesleys had been in Rome, she would have shaven their heads, tied ropes around their waists, and sent them out under her own banner and blessing. Whether this be true or not, there is certainly a vast amount of force potential for Negro evangelization rendered latent, or worse, antagonistic by the halting, uncertain, I had almost said, trimming policy of the Church in the South. This may sound both presumptuous and ungrateful. It is mortifying, I know, to benevolent wisdom, after having spent itself in the execution of well conned theories for the ideal development of a particular work, to hear perhaps the weakest and humblest element of that work asking "what doest thou?"

Yet so it will be in life. The "thus far and no farther" pattern cannot be fitted to any growth in God's kingdom. The universal law of development is "onward and upward." It is God-given and inviolable. From the unfolding of the germ in the acorn to reach the sturdy oak, to the growth of a human soul into the full knowledge and likeness of its Creator, the breadth and scope of the movement in each and all are too grand, too mysterious, too like God himself, to be encompassed and locked down in human molds.

After all the Southern slave owners were right: either the very alphabet of intellectual growth must be forbidden and the Negro dealt with absolutely as a chattel having neither rights nor sensibilities; or else the clamps and irons of mental and moral, as well as civil compression must be driven asunder and the truly enfranchised soul led to the entrance of that boundless vista through which it is to toil upwards to its beckoning God as the buried seed germ, to meet the sun.

A perpetual colored diaconate, carefully and kindly superintended by the white clergy; congregations of shiny faced peasants with their clean white aprons and sunbonnets catechised at regular intervals and taught to recite the creed, the Lord's prayer and the ten commandments—duty towards God and duty towards neighbor, surely such well tended sheep ought to be grateful to their shepherds and content in that station of life to which it pleased God to call them. True, like the old professor lecturing to his solitary student, we make no provision here for irregularities. "Questions must be kept till after class," or dispensed with altogether. That some do ask questions and insist on answers, in class too, must be both impertinent and annoying. Let not our spiritual pastors and masters however be grieved at such self-assertion as merely signifies we have a destiny to fulfill and as men and women we must be about our Father's business.

It is a mistake to suppose that the Negro is prejudiced against a white ministry. Naturally there is not a more kindly and implicit follower of a white man's guidance than the average colored peasant. What would to others be an ordinary act of friendly or pastoral interest he would be more inclined to regard gratefully as a condescension. And he never forgets such kindness. Could the Negro be brought near to his white priest or bishop, he is not suspicious. He is not only willing but often longs to unburden his soul to this intelligent guide. There are no reservations when he is convinced that you are his friend. It is a saddening satire on American history and manners that it takes something to convince him.

That our people are not "drawn" to a Church whose chief dignitaries they see only in the chancel, and whom they reverence as they would a painting or an angel, whose life never comes down to and touches theirs with the inspiration of an objective reality, may be "perplexing" truly (American caste and American Christianity both being facts) but it need not be surprising. There must be something of human nature in it, the same as that which brought about that "the Word was made flesh and dwelt among us" that He might "draw" us towards God.

Men are not "drawn" by abstractions. Only sympathy and love can draw, and until our Church in America realizes this and provides a clergy that can come in touch with our life and have a fellow feeling for our woes, without being imbedded and frozen up in their "Gothic antipathies," the good bishops are likely to continue "perplexed" by the sparsity of colored Episcopalians.

A colored priest of my acquaintance recently related to me, with tears in his eyes, how his reverend Father in God, the Bishop who had ordained him, had met him on the cars on his way to the diocesan convention and warned him, not unkindly, not to take a seat in the body of the convention with the white clergy. To avoid disturbance of their godly placidity he would of cource please sit back and somewhat apart. I do not imagine that that clergyman had very much heart for the Christly (!) deliberations of that convention.

To return, however, it is not on this broader view of Church work, which I mentioned as a primary cause of its halting progress with the colored people, that I am to speak. My proper theme is the second oversight of which in my judgment our Christian propagandists have been guilty: or, the necessity of church training, protecting and uplifting our colored womanhood as indispensable to the evangelization of the race.

Apelles did not disdain even that criticism of his lofty art which came from an uncouth cobbler; and may I not hope that the writer's oneness with her subject both in feeling and in being may palliate undue obtrusiveness of opinions here. That the race cannot be effectually lifted up till its women are truly elevated we take as proven. It is not for us to dwell on the needs, the neglects, and the ways of succor, pertaining to the black woman of the South. The ground has been ably discussed and an admirable and practical plan proposed by the oldest Negro priest in America, advising and urging that special organizations such as Church Sisterhoods and industrial schools be devised to meet her pressing needs in the Southland. That some such movements are vital to the life of this people and the extension of the Church among them, is not hard to see. Yet the pamphlet fell still-born from the press. So far as I am informed the Church has made no motion towards carrying out Dr. Crummell's suggestion.

The denomination which comes next our own in opposing the proverbial emotionalism of Negro worship in the South, and which in consequence like ours receives the cold shoulder from the old heads, resting as we do under the charge of not "having religion" and not believing in conversion—the Congregationalists—have quietly gone to work on the young, have established industrial and training schools, and now almost every community in the South is yearly enriched by a fresh infusion of vigorous young hearts, cultivated heads, and helpful hands that have been trained at Fisk, at Hampton, in Atlanta University, and in Tuskegee, Alabama.

These young people are missionaries actual or virtual both here and in Africa. They have learned to love the methods and doctrines of the Church which trained and educated them; and so Congregationalism surely and steadily progresses.

Need I compare these well known facts with results shown by the Church in the same field and during the same or even a longer time.

The institution of the Church in the South to which she mainly looks for the training of her colored clergy and for the help of the "Black Woman" and "Colored Girl" of the South, has graduated since the year 1868, when the school was founded, five young women; and while yearly numerous young men have been kept and trained for the ministry by the charities of the Church, the number of indigent females who have here been supported, sheltered and trained, is phenomenally small. Indeed, to my mind, the attitude of the Church toward this feature of her work, is as if the solution of the problem of Negro missions depended solely on sending a quota of deacons and priests into the field, girls being a sort of tertium quid whose development may be promoted if they can pay their way and fall in with the plans mapped out for the training of the other sex.

Now I would ask in all earnestness, does not this force potential deserve by education and stimulus to be made dynamic? Is it not a solemn duty incumbent on all colored churchmen to make it so? Will not the aid of the Church be given to prepare our girls in head, heart, and hand for the duties and responsibilities that await the intelligent wife, the Christian mother, the earnest, virtuous, helpful woman, at once both the lever and the fulcrum for uplifting the race.

As Negroes and churchmen we cannot be indifferent to these questions. They touch us most vitally on both sides. We believe in the Holy Catholic Church. We believe that however gigantic and apparently remote the consummation, the Church will go on conquering and to conquer till the kingdoms of this world, not excepting the black man and the black woman of the South, shall have become the kingdoms of the Lord and of his Christ.

That past work in this direction has been unsatisfactory we must admit. That without a change of policy results in the future will be as meagre, we greatly fear. Our life as a race is at stake. The dearest interests of our hearts are in the scales. We must either break away from dear old landmarks and plunge out in any line and every line that enables us to meet the pressing need of our people, or we must ask the Church to allow and help us, untrammelled by the prejudices and theories of individuals, to work aggressively under her direction as we alone can, with God's help, for the salvation of our people.

The time is ripe for action. Self-seeking and ambition must be laid on the altar. The battle is one of sacrifice and hardship, but our duty is plain. We have been recipients of missionary bounty in some sort for twenty-one years. Not even the senseless vegetable is content to be a mere reservoir. Receiving without giving is an anomaly in nature. Nature's cells are all little workshops for manufacturing sunbeams, the product to be given out to earth's inhabitants in warmth, energy, thought, action. Inanimate creation always pays back an equivalent.

Now, How much owest thou my Lord? Will his account be overdrawn if he call for singleness of purpose and self-sacrificing labor for your brethren? Having passed through your drill school, will you refuse a general's commission even if it entail responsibility, risk and anxiety, with possibly some adverse criticism? Is it too much to ask you to step forward and direct the work for your race along those lines which you know to be of first and vital importance?

Will you allow these words of Ralph Waldo Emerson? "In ordinary," says he, "we have a snappish criticism which watches and contradicts the opposite party. We want the will which advances and dictates [acts]. Nature has made up her mind that what cannot defend itself, shall not be defended. Complaining never so loud and with never so much reason, is of no use. What cannot stand must fall; and the measure of our sincerity and therefore of the respect of men is the amount of health and wealth we will hazard in the defense of our right."

[First given before the convocation of black clergy of the Episcopal Church in Washington, DC, in 1886; reprinted in her book 1892]

XIV

The Great Accommodator, as some called Booker T. Washington (1856–1915), spoke in a quiet and often disarming voice. Washington, who came to fame as the founder of Tuskegee Institute in 1881, would become the most prominent race leader of the late nineteenth and early twentieth centuries. His notoriety skyrocketed after his 1895 Atlanta Exposition Address. In that speech he talked about mutual cooperation between the races on all matters economic, but accepted the separation of the races on all matters social. His metaphor of the hand working together, but separated like the fingers on that hand in referring to economic and race relations in the South, became one of the most discussed phrases in African-American history during his lifetime and afterwards. The Atlanta Exposition Address is presented here for your perusal, analysis, and discussion. Was Booker T. Washington correct in his understanding of the racial and economic divide in America? What do you think of his prescribed course of action? How do his words resonate with the current economic situation of black folk in America? These are just some questions to get you going in your discussion of his message, the times, and the relevance of his prognosis for the future.

"Address to the Atlanta Exposition"

Booker T. Washington

Mr. President and Gentlemen of the Board of Directors and Citizens.

One-third of the population of the South is of the Negro race. No enterprise seeking the material, civil, or moral welfare of this section can disregard this element of our population and reach the highest success. I but convey to you, Mr. President and Directors the sentiment of the masses of my race when I say that in no way have the value and manhood of the American Negro been more fittingly and generously recognized than by the managers of this magnificent Exposition at every stage of its progress. It is a recognition that will do more to cement the friendship of the two races than any occurrence since the dawn of our freedom.

Not only this, but the opportunity here afforded will awaken among us a new era of industrial progress. Ignorant and inexperienced, it is not strange that in the first years of our new life we began at the top instead of at the bottom; that a seat in Congress or the state legislature was more sought than real estate or industrial skill; that the political convention or stump speaking had more attractions than starting a dairy farm or truck garden.

A ship lost at sea for many days suddenly sighted a friendly vessel. From the mast of the unfortunate vessel was seen a signal, "water, water; we die of thirst!" The answer from the friendly vessel at once came back, "cast down your bucket where you are." A second time the signal, "Water, water; send us water!" ran up from the distressed vessel, and was answered, "Cast down your bucket where you are." The captain of the distressed vessel, at last heeding the injunction, cast down his bucket, and it came up full of fresh, sparkling water from the mouth of the Amazon River. To those of my race who depend on bettering their condition in a foreign land or who underestimate the importance of cultivating friendly relations with the Southern white man, who is their next-door neighbour, I would say: "Cast down your bucket where you are"—cast it down in making friends in ever manly way of the people of all races by whom we are surrounded.

Cast it down in agriculture, mechanics, in commerce, in domestic service, and in the professions. And in this connection it is well to bear in mind that whatever other sins the South may be called to bear, when it comes to business, pure and simple, it is in the South that the Negro is given a man's chance in the commercial world, and in nothing is this Exposition more eloquent than in emphasizing this chance. Our greatest danger is that in the great leap from slavery to freedom we may overlook the fact that the masses of us are to live by the productions of our hands, and fail to keep in mind that we shall prosper in proportion as we learn to dignify and glorify common life; shall prosper in proportion as we learn to draw the line between the superficial and the substantial, the ornamental gewgaws of life and the useful. No race can prosper till it learns that there is as much dignity in tilling a field as in writing a poem. It is at the bottom of life we must begin, and not at the top. Nor should we permit our grievances to overshadow our opportunities.

To those of the white race who look to the incoming of those of foreign birth and strange tongue and habits for the prosperity of the South, were I permitted I would repeat what I say to my own race, "Cast down your bucket where you are." Cast it down among the eight millions of Negroes whose habits you know, whose fidelity and love you have tested in days when to have proved treacherous meant the ruin of your firesides. Cast down your bucket among these people who have, without strikes and labour wars, tilled your fields, cleared your forests, builded your railroads and cities, and brought forth treasures from the bowels of the earth, and helped make possible this magnificent representation of the progress of the South. Casting down your bucket among my people, helping and encouraging them as you are doing on these grounds, and to education of head, hand, and heart, you will find that they will buy your surplus land, make blossom the waste places in your fields, and run your factories. While doing this, you can be sure in the future, as in the past, that you and your families will be surrounded by the most patient, faithful, law-abiding, and unresentful people that the world has seen. As we have proved our loyalty to you in the past, in nursing your children, watching by the sickbed of your mothers and fathers, and often following them with tear-rimmed eyes to their graves, so in the future, in our humble way, we shall stand by you with a devotion that no foreigner can approach, ready to lay down our lives, if need be, in defence of yours, interlacing our industrial, commercial, civil, and religious life with yours in a way that shall make the interests of both races one. In all things that are purely social we can be as separate as the fingers, yet one as the hand in all things essential to mutual progress.

There is no defence or security for any of us except in the highest intelligence and development of all. If anywhere there are efforts tending to curtail the fullest growth of the Negro, let these efforts be turned into stimulating, encouraging, and making him the most useful and intelligent citizen. Effort or means so invested will pay a thousand per cent interest. These efforts will be twice blessed—blessing him that gives and him that takes.

Nearly sixteen millions of hands will aid you in pulling the load upward, or they will pull against you the load downward. We shall constitute one-third and more of the ignorance and crime of the South, or one-third to the business and industrial prosperity of the South, or we shall prove a veritable body or death, stagnating, depressing, retarding every effort to advance the body politic.

Gentlemen of the Exposition, as we present to you our humble effort at an exhibition of our progress, you must not expect over much. Starting thirty years ago with ownership here and there in a few quilts and pumpkins and chickens (gathered from miscellaneous sources), remember the path that has led from these to the inventions and production of agricultural implements, buggies, steam-engines, newspapers, books, statuary, carving, paintings, the management of drug-stores and banks, has not been trodden without contact with thorns and thistles. While we take pride in what we exhibit as a result of our independent efforts, we do not for a moment forget that our part in this exhibition would fall far short of your expectations but for the constant help that has come to our educational life, not only from the Southern states, but especially from Northern philanthropists, who have made their gifts a constant stream of blessing and encouragement.

The wisest among my race understand that the agitation of questions of social equality is the extremist folly, and that progress in the enjoyment of all the privileges that will come to us must be the result of severe and constant struggle rather than of artificial forcing. No race that had anything to contribute to the markets of the world is long in any degree ostracized. It is important and right all privileges of the law be ours, but it is vastly more important that we be prepared for the exercises of these privileges. The opportunity to earn a dollar in a factory just now is worth infinitely more than the opportunity to spend a dollar in an opera house.

In conclusion, may I repeat that nothing in thirty years has given us more hope and encouragement, and drawn us so near to you of the white race, as this opportunity offered by the Exposition; and here bending, as it were, over the altar that represents the results of the struggles of your race and mine, both starting practically empty-handed three decades ago, I pledge that in your effort to work out the great and intricate problem which God has laid at the doors of the South, you shall have at all times the patient, sympathetic help of my race; only let this be constantly in mind, that, while from representations in these buildings of the product of field, of forest, of mine, of factory, letters, and art, much good will come, yet far above and beyond material benefits will be that higher good, that, let us pray God, will come, in a blotting out of sectional differences and racial animosities and suspicions, in a determination to administer absolute justice, in a willing obedience among all classes to the mandates of law. This, this, coupled with our material prosperity, will bring into our beloved South a new heaven and a new earth.

[1895]

XV

A singularly unique and powerful voice advocating Black Nationalism in the years following the Civil War and into the twentieth century was that of Henry McNeal Turner (1834–1915). A minister of the African Methodist Episcopal Church during the Civil War, Turner was the first black appointed as chaplain to U.S. colored soldiers. Elected to political office in the State of Georgia in 1868 during Reconstruction, his political stay was short lived with the rise of white power and the Jim Crow disfranchisement of blacks that defined the South in the late 19th and early 20th centuries. Turner was further incensed when the U.S. Supreme Court declared the Civil Rights Act of 1875 as unconstitutional. He devoted an increasing amount of his time professing from the pulpit the need for blacks to empower themselves, become economically independent, and to develop their own institutions. He rose to the ranks of Bishop of the AME church and was known for his fiery oratory and his demand that blacks rethink religious teachings and dogma to the benefit and elevation of the race. In one of his most noted speeches, Bishop Turner proclaimed: "God is a Negro." He personified independent thinking. Turner believed that any race that failed to see itself in the image of God was a race that was doomed to inferiority. Was Turner correct? Can we benefit today from what he had to say back then? Do African Americans continue to worship a "white" God?

"God Is A Negro"

Henry McNeal Turner

We have as much right biblically and otherwise to believe that God is a Negro, as you buckra, or white, people have to believe that God is a fine looking, symmetrical and ornamented white man. For the bulk of you, and all the fool Negroes of the country, believe that God is white-skinned, blue-eyed, straight-haired, projecting-nosed, compressed-lipped and finely-robed white gentleman, sitting upon a throne somewhere in the heavens. Every race of people since time began who have attempted to describe their God by words, or by paintings, or by carvings, or by any other form or figure, have conveyed the idea that the God who made them and shaped their destinies was symbolized in themselves, and why should not the Negro believe that he resembles God as much so as other people? We do not believe that there is any hope for a race of people who do not believe that they look like God.

Demented though we be, whenever we reach the conclusion that God or even that Jesus Christ, while in the flesh, was a white man, we shall hang our gospel trumpet upon the willow and cease to preach.

We had rather be an atheist and believe in no God, or a pantheist and believe that all nature is God, than to believe in the personality of a God and not to believe that He is a Negro. Blackness is much older than whiteness, for black was here before white, if the Hebrew word, coshach, or chasack, has any meaning. We do not believe in the eternity of matter, but we do believe that chaos floated in infinite darkness or blackness, millions, billions, quintillions and eons of years before God said, "Let there be light," and that during that time God had no material light Himself and was shrouded in darkness, so far as human comprehension is able to grasp the situation.

Yet we are no stickler as to God's color, anyway, but if He has any we would prefer to believe that it is nearer symbolized in the blue sky above us and the blue water of the seas and oceans: but we certainly protest against God being a white man or against God being white at all; abstract as this theme must forever remain while we are in the flesh. This is one of the reasons we favor African emigration, or Negro nationalization, wherever we can find a domain, for as long as we remain among the whites, the Negro will believe that the devil is black and that he (the Negro) favors the devil, and that God is white and that he (the Negro) bears no resemblance to Him, and the effect of such a sentiment is contemptuous and degrading, and one-half of the Negro race will be trying to get white and the other half will spend their days trying to be white men's scullions in order to please the whites; and the time they should be giving to the study of such things as will dignify and make our race great will be devoted to studying about how unfortunate they are in not being white.

We conclude these remarks by repeating for the information of the Observer what it adjudged us demented for—God is a Negro.

[1898]

XVI

The intensifying of Jim Crow and the color line in the late 1800s placed African Americans in an ever more precarious situation of hardship, obstacles, and declining opportunities. As professional sports became more lucrative during the late nineteenth century, black athletes were effectively banned from sports such as jockeying, boxing, bicycling, and professional baseball. Moses Fleetwood Walker (1857–1924), who in 1884 became the first African American to play Major League Baseball, was a few years later pushed out of professional ball. Walker was a spirited competitor and, even more, a proud black man who stood up for himself at all times. He almost always carried a weapon to defend himself and was forced to do exactly that when he killed a white man in self-defense in Syracuse, New York. Charged with second-degree murder, Fleetwood Walker was found innocent of all charges, by an all-white jury no less. This did not dissuade him in his condemnation of America as a racist society where a black man would never be treated as an equal. Fleetwood Walker returned to his hometown in Ohio where he continued battling the color line. Educated at Oberlin and the University of Michigan, he put his schooling to good use as he developed into an astute social critic. His race pride escalated to rage against the entire American system and the limited opportunities for black folk. Fleetwood Walker channeled his energy into an examination of integration, accommodation, separation of the races, and repatriation back to Africa. In 1908 he published, *Our Home Colony: A Treatise on the Past, Present and Future of the Negro Race in America.* An excerpt from that treatise is presented here. Do you find Fleetwood Walker's take on American society enlightening? Is he speaking as "an angry black," as some dubbed him, or is he making sense of the situation and offering a viable course of action?

"The Destined Period"

Moses Fleetwood Walker

We shall conclude our Treatise by a brief consideration of the several plans which have been suggested for the cure of the Negro Problem as it exists in the United States. That there is a problem, and one of momentous concern, no candid, thoughtful man will for an instant attempt to deny.

Whether we call it the Negro Problem, or a white man's Problem is immaterial.

Perhaps it would be more accurate to call it the white man's Problem, for its solution, as we see it, rests almost entirely with him.

We shall eliminate from this consideration the oft heard, but ridiculous idea of miscegenation. No race as numerous as the American Negro race ever lost its identity by intermarriage with an alien people. The Arabs were in Spain as Conquerors for 600 years, but at the time of their forced return to their native land they left the Spaniards practically as they found them, with their distinct type. The Jew in bondage in Egypt is another instance of the refusal of alien people to lose their type by intermarriage. We may expect extermination of the weaker race by the stronger, rather than absorption by mingling of bloods by marriage.

Segregation of the races into separate parts of this country has been proposed as a remedy of the present and future racial troubles. While it is true that if the Negroes could be placed in a State or Territory apart from the whites it would lessen of course the personal friction of the races, yet the difficulties of governing a Colony so placed would be never ending, and worse than the evils sought to be remedied. This solution of the racial difficulties is so visionary and impracticable as to need no further mention.

The only practical and permanent solution of the present and future race troubles in the United States is entire separation by Emigration of the Negro from America. Even forced Emigration would be better for all than the continued present relations of the races; but there would be no necessity for force if the proper measures are taken and the Negroes are offered reasonable help to return to their native land.

The Negro should be taught he is an alien and always will be regarded as such in this country, and that equal social, industrial and political rights can never be given them. It is doubtful whether or not the Negro as a race would ever turn to Emigration as his salvation if left to take the initiative. He is not of a migratory race, and has never been found further than twenty degrees from the torrid zone unless under force. When forced from home he is loath to return, even when free to do so, and under immense oppression.

We do not believe the wholesale deportation of the Negro is desirable at the present time, nor is it necessary. But the time seems to be fast approaching when the Negroes in very large numbers must leave the Southern States. It used to be said that the South did not want the Negro to leave that section. We now see "Immigration Commissions" formed in several Southern States whose object it is to encourage foreign immigrants to settle in the South. Naturally these white immigrants are to supplant Negro laborers, and these latter must seek new homes. They will not find open arms in the North awaiting them. When they reach the Northern States in large numbers the same condition will prevail there as now exists in the South.

We believe that the Negro race can find superior advantages, and better opportunities on the shores of old Africa, among people of their own race, for developing the innate powers of mind and body that anywhere else upon the face of the earth, and the reasons of this belief we shall try to give in the following pages.

In 1822 a Colony of free Negroes from the United States was settled upon the west coast of Africa, mainly through the efforts of the American Colonization Society. There was no difficulty in procuring sufficient land for these people who desired to emigrate; nor was there at that time any disposition among free Negroes to oppose the opportunity of returning to their native land.

In 1827 free Negroes of Baltimore, Md., and Washington, D.C., memorialized Congress to provide financial aid to transport all who might desire to go to Liberia, as the country provided for them in Africa was named.

In 1847 the independence of Liberia was declared, and in 1848 it was recognized by England and most of the continental countries. The United States did likewise a few years later in 1861.

This Colony since 1847 has exercised full sovereignty over a territory embracing nearly 35,000 square miles; as large as Connecticut, New Jersey, Massachusetts, Maryland and Delaware combined, and one and one half larger than the State of West Virginia. It is no longer an experiment, but a fact. Liberia stands today a recognized Sovereign State among the family of Nations. The Liberians are today exercising all the functions of a free and independent government. If they have not shown the advance some would like to see, it can be easily shown they are far in advance of their Negro brethren left behind in the United States. The few thousand American Negroes who have returned to Africa and builded for themselves and posterity a national edifice recognized and respected by all nations, are deserving of praise and honor from every Negro in the world. These people have demonstrated to mankind that the Negro is capable of organizing and maintaining a civilized government in the very midst of intellectual and moral darkness.

In the early day of African Colonization, Negroes were transported to Liberia for the small sum of twenty dollars a head, and vessels made but one or two voyages per year. With the improved ocean steamer of today and the increased facilities for handling traffic there is every reason to believe that this sum of twenty dollars for passage could be materially lessened if the scheme of deportation was undertaken on a large scale. It is objected to any scheme of Colonization that it would not appreciably reduce even the natural increase of the race, and hence would have no effect on the congested Negro population of the Southern States. This objection is urged more strongly by white than by Negro enemies of Emigration.

A few figures from statistics will show the absurdity of this objection and prove conclusively that in a few years the fear of Negro domination even in the States most densely populated by the black race would have no terror for the most timid. If $85,000,000 had been expended during the period from 1820 up to the present time not more than 1,500,000, and probably not 500,000 Negroes would be in the United States today. The census of the United States for 1820 shows 233,530 free Negroes and 7,538,128 slaves, a total of 1,771,658. Now, a fair allowance for natural increase would be three per cent of the total per year, making in round numbers 53,000.

The American Colonization Society was able, as has been stated, to transport Negroes to Liberia for twenty dollars per head, and at this rate could have carried the 3000 increase to Africa each year for $1,000,000. If just that much had been done for eighty-five years we see the outlay would be less than $90,000,000, and the original stock of 1,771,658 lessened by reason of the loss each year of the most prolific of the race.

This plan of deporting the Negroes willing to return to Africa was ably advocated by many true friends of the race, and most notably by those who were advocates of gradual emancipation. The same plan applied to conditions as they exist today would show equally favorable results. By the census of 1900 the population was 8,849,789, an increase during the decade from 1890 to 1900 of 1,352,001, or 12.2 per cent. Now to transport this increase of 1,352,001 at twenty dollars would cost $27,040,020. If this task was undertakened by the General Government the sum would be less by one-half. Who will deny that the great and powerful Government of the United States could not afford to expend even $100,000,000 per year to accomplish an object so fraught with beneficial results to two races, alien and incongruous?

Let this plan of removing to Africa a number of Negroes equal to the natural increase, but selected from the most prolific of the race, and in a few years the Negro will grow scarce in the United States.

The people of this Republic should understand the great danger that confronts them by a delay in putting into practicable operation some plan to relieve this country of the congested Negro population of the Southern States. There is to our mind no other rational plan but Emigration for the Negro. Every principle of the science of social development is opposed to the unnatural relation existing in this country between seventy millions of the white and ten millions of the black race. This condition would never have occurred had the members of the white race pursued the courses dictated by natural laws. The association of the races in this country originated in a crime, and is unnatural. The conditions in the United States are opposed to the development of any spirit of independence, either of thought or action among the members of the subordinate race. High ideals, lofty and noble thoughts can never enter the brains of a people oppressed. There is no instance in all history where a nation of one race has ever permitted a people of an alien race, existing in a considerable number in the same country, to enjoy equal civil, social, and industrial privileges with themselves. There must always be a dominant and subordinate race in such cases form the very nature of man-kind. The effect upon the subordinate people is destructive of energy both of body and mind, and blights and withers every elevating sentiment of the human soul.

Guizot, the eminent French historian, has said: "There are but two sources in the sphere of politics from which greatness of ambition or firmness of thought can arise. It is necessary to have either the feeling of immense importance, of great power exercised upon the destiny of others, and in a vast extent—or else it is necessary to bear within one's self a feeling of complete individual independence, a confidence in one's own liberty a conviction of a destiny foreign to all will but that the man himself. To one or other of these two conditions seem to belong boldness of thought, greatness of ambition, the desire of acting in an enlarged sphere, and of obtaining great results." Again, he says: "A high ambition, independently of social conditions, enlargement and firmness of political thought, the desire to participate in the affairs of the country, the full consciousness of the greatness of man as man, and of the power which belong to him, if he is capable of exercising it, these are in Europe sentiments and dispositions entirely modern, the fruit of modern civilization, the fruit of that glorious and powerful universality which characterizes it, and which cannot fail of insuring to the public an influence and weight in the government of the country, which were always wanting, and necessarily so, to the burghers, our ancestors."

It is a well known fact that the spirit of haughty, individual independence, noble aspiration, and a desire to do great things is never developed in a people occupying a condition of inferiority or subordination. The American Negro realizes on every hand, or is made to feel that he is regarded, and must act as a subordinate people. The whole situation is filled with discouragement: and the great wonder is that the Negro has one spark left in his soul of those God-given sentiments—love of independence, patriotism, and desire of approbation.

The Negro has often been credited with possessing a strong patriotism; yet the treatment given him at the hand of his white fellow citizen is designed ultimately to make of him an enemy to the government, and a menace to peace and order. Let no one be deceived in respect to these patriotic feelings of the Negro. The love of home and country is an original sentiment of the human soul. It lies in the class of affections, and is strengthened by national pride and association. It can be weakened when the government ceases to protect his life, home and welfare.

It is impossible for the American Negro to feel the same warmth of patriotism for the United States that swells the bosom of an Anglo-Saxon, or that makes it pleasant for an Englishman or Frenchman to die for his country. These people are filled with a national pride arising from the achievements of their fathers and the sacred, inherited trust of maintaining them inviolate to their posterity.

The Negro cannot feel a pure and real national pride, nor are his associations calculated to inspire him with the genuine emotion of patriotism. Persecution never rendered a people moral, law-abiding or patriotic.

These conditions are but the result we could expect from a study of the nature of the races. There is absolutely no foundation either in reason or experience for a hope that the lot of the American Negro will grow better. The difficulties of the past few years between the races, and the more recent discharge, without honor, of a battalion of Negro soldiers by President Roosevelt are ominous signs which ought to alarm every son of Africa. Never since the days of slavery has the assertion that "This is a white man's country" been so often and publicly spoken and applauded by thousands as it is today. Just recently this sentiment was spoken in a speech in the Northern city of Chicago by a United States Senator, and it met applause from the assembled multitude. White men of eminence and power by the hundreds are daily preaching this doctrine. And after all it is a "white man's country." The love of adventure and desire for knowledge impelled Columbus to search for America. The desire for religious freedom and independence led the Pilgrim Fathers to Plymouth Rock. The Declaration of Independence was framed and promulgated by white people. The war of Independence was planned and fought under white officers, under a white Commander-in-chief—the "father of his Country." Every obstacle to the onward progress of the Nation has been met and overcome by the indefatigable energy and genius of the Anglo-Saxon. True, the Negro has been here most of the time, but only as any other burden-bearer. He fought in the wars, but dared not fight until told to do so by white officers. He knew not why he went to fight. It is claimed by almost every white officer of the United States army from Commander-in-chief down that the American Negro is not an efficient soldier under Negro officers. I take it that this is true of the American Negro only. In Hayti, Cuba, or his native Africa, the accusation would be false. The American Negro stands before the world as an example of the most helpless and scullionized people of modern times. Everything is being done that must tend to dehumanize him. The protests he is making against the treatment he receives at the hands of the white man are feeble and do not, nor cannot avail in appreciable amelioration of his condition. The time is not far in the future when the constitutional rights given him by the XIV and XV amendments will be taken away. Events are leading in that direction with far more rapid strides than was made towards his liberation and the granting of those rights. If the white man refuses to take the Negro as a citizen of this Republic on perfect social, industrial, and political equality, then the fate of the black man is sealed. He must either leave the United States, be practically reduced to slavery or be exterminated. It will be impossible for the Negro to have industrial or political equality with the white man without social equality; and this, as we have said, he can never get. It is painful to think of the ignorance displayed by "leading Negroes" when they make such assertions as: "We do not ask for social equality: all we want is a 'square deal' as to our civil and industrial rights." How can a people get industrial or political rights in a country where the dominant race regards personal association or contact with that people obnoxious? Any association of the sexes between the races is looked upon with abomination by all good people of the dominant race. When the relation of husband and wife is entered into by a Negro and white person, instead of creating sympathy between the families of the parties, it only drives them further apart with increased hostile feeling, one to the other.

It is contrary to every sense to believe that a man or race of men will grant equal industrial or political rights to an alien man or race from whom he withholds the privilege of free association in his home or society. Even though the written laws of the land make no discrimination, yet they will be ineffectual in procuring for the alien the equality he wants and needs.

The Negro should learn that he need never expect to realize full industrial or political equality in this country, no more so than he is to have full social equality with the white man. Perhaps when he fully learns this he will want to return to his African home. The Negro is attached to this country more by the hope of equality with the white man than by dread of Africa. Let the white people of the North tell the Negro truthfully the position they expect him to forever occupy, and they will soon see how patriotic the black people are. The white Southerner from his situation and environments cannot but be frank in his representations to the Negro. He tells him that if he wishes to remain in his country he must ever remain at the bottom, and the Negro is correspondingly despondent. Thousands of Negroes in the South are ready and willing to leave the United States if cheap means were provided for them to do so. The recent effort, which is meeting with considerable success, to divert part of the great stream of European immigrants to the Southern States will only force the Negro to the North, and make more acute the already troublesome problem. When the "black belt" moves north of "Mason and Dixon's line," the Northern white man may see more clearly the necessity of moving it across the Atlantic Ocean, where of right it belongs. The Italian, German, Swede, and Hungarian immigrants to the South will, in the course of a few generations, assimilate with the white population of that sections and present a strong homogeneous people. They will be treated as equals in every particular in the home, in the factory and in all the rights of citizenship. Intermarriages with the native population will take place as in the other parts of the country, and close-amity relations will arise. All this is necessary in every healthy and prosperous community. Such a community is impossible of alien races. This fact cannot be too forcibly taught. Many people of kind heart, rather than of good reason in the matter believing that the application of Christian principles will right all the difficulties between the races in this country.

We do not believe that the Christian principle—Fatherhood of God and Brotherhood of man, or, even anything in the eclogue—teaches that alien races can unite in the same state to their mutual welfare.

Furthermore we believe it in perfect accord with the Divine teachings that diverse races remain in separate territories. For the Bible says: "God hath made of one blood all nations of men to dwell on all the face of the Earth, and hath determined the time before appointed, and the bounds of their habitation."

Divine Revelation was not given for the purpose of solving problems which arise in the practical affairs of mankind. Moral beings by the exercise of reason and correct judgment have always at hand the means of finding the path of duty in respect to outward action. Many good-meaning men of both races urge upon the Negro to trust his cause to God and all will come out well. There can be no question about this if there was any proof that God would give it immediate consideration. But the whole trouble is that the Creator has endowed His people with every power and means to attend to their own physical needs, and if they fail in the use of these faculties they may sit until the end of time waiting for outside help.

The opponents of Negro Emigration never fail to picture the Republic of Liberia as the "grossest sham"—the mere pretense of a government. They also recount what terrible savagery the emigrant would have to combat. Wild animals, troublesome pests of all sorts infest the whole continent of Africa, and the "Afro-American," as they choose to call the Negro, soon would be devoured if he should set foot on that bated shore. Some of these same objectors say that the American Negro is unfit for self-government, and hence should not think of leaving the "opportunities and advantages of American civilization."

Just a few words as to all this sort of objection to the separation of the races. In the first place a great injustice is done the people of Liberia when their Government is called a "sham." Those people are recognized by every civilized Nation of the world as constituting an independent sovereign State. Their Government has existed over three quarters of a century without a single revolution, or the loss of a single President by assassination. The leaders of the people have on the whole been men actuated by motives which aimed at the general welfare of the people. It is a fine tribute to the statesmanship of the men who have directed the destiny of Liberia that every international dispute has been settled through diplomacy without the deplorable necessity of resort to war. It does seem inexplicable how any person with the ability to read history can charge that Liberia has been a failure, or who cannot see that the Liberian Negro is as far superior to the American Negro in every element of manhood as the Englishman of the Twentieth Century is to his Hindu subject. The Liberian Negro is a full man, moving onward and upward because he feels himself to be independent and the architect of his own destiny.

We often hear from Negro leaders an appeal that the best men of both races come together and consider the best means for elevating the Negro, so that he can take his place in the American civilization with less friction and disturbance to peace and order. This is only a veiled desire on the part of the Negroes to meet the white man. If the general environments of the Negro race in America are opposed to the development of the best traits in the Negro character, it would seem that the combined work of black and white teachers could avail but little. With all the knowledge of horticulture we cannot raise vegetables in cellars. Sunlight and heat are absolutely necessary for vegetable growth. Equally so are certain conditions needed for the full growth of the human soul.

To attempt to raise the Negro race, while living in America, from the point where slavery left him to a position in harmony with a rapidly advancing Anglo-Saxon civilization, is to undertake that which is opposed by all the teachings of Ethnology, and the experience of ages. No work or effort of well-meaning white or black men can bring the desired results, so long as they are opposed to the rigorous and exacting laws of nature. The Negro never can be raised to an equal point in civilization while occupying his isolated position in the United States.

If the American slaves had been of any of the white races of men, in a very few generations after manumission, assimilation by intermarriage with the dominant people would have wiped out all the taint of former degradation and there would be seen, a homogeneous people—one in type, ideals and sympathies. But the Negro will remain a distinct product; alien in everything that meets the approbation of the white man.

All belief that education, industry, thrift, or religion will or can make the black man equal the white to such an extent that they can live in the same country on even terms is opposed to all reason and experience. The Negro shows some progress in education, industry and thrift, but many fail to see that even while he improves in those directions the times are growing doubly hard for him. An educated Negro is thrown from a hotel or theatre just as certainly as an ignorant one. Discriminating laws and customs are blind to internal qualifications. All men with black skin are to be avoided; no questions asked, nor protests allowed.

The President of the University of Virginia, in an address to the Civic Forum, New York, but recently gave among other premises the following regarding the regulations of the Southern Negro:

"The white man must be in control:" "absolute social separation;" "and that it having been settled that the Negro has humanity he shall be trained to citizenship in the best condition and that the South is the place where his training shall be conducted most intelligently."

Those premises express very nearly the accepted belief of all the intelligent white men of this country. Yet in the face of this position Negro teachers and preachers in every part of the Union are asking for a closer union of the races. Booker Washington says in "The Future of the American Negro:" "Whenever you hear a coloured man say that he hates the people of the other race, there, in most instances, you will find a weak, narrow-minded coloured man. And, whenever you find a white man who expresses the same sentiment toward the people of other races, there, too in almost every case, you will find a narrow-minded prejudiced white man. That person is the broadest, strongest, and most useful who sees something to love and admire in all races, no matter what their colour."

We will not presume to say that Washington would call it 'hate' in the President of the Virginia University that caused him to argue for the entire separation of the races. But it is certainly not the sort of love that he thinks makes the "broadest, strongest and most useful" person.

Again the same writer says: "In every community, by means of organized effort, we should seek, in a manly and honorable way, the confidence, the co-operation, the sympathy, of the best white people in the South and in our respective communities. With the best white people and the best black people standing together, in favour of the law and order and justice, I believe that the safety and happiness of both races will be made secure."

Prof. W. E. B. DuBois in "The Souls of Black Folk" deplores the social ostracism of the Negro in these words: "In a world where it means so much to take a man by the hand and sit beside him, to look frankly into his eyes and feel his heart beating with red blood; in a world where a social cigar or a cup of tea together means more than legislative halls and magazine articles and speeches—one can imagine the consequences of the almost utter absence of social amenities between estranged races, whose separation extends even to parks and street cars." We quote these passages to show how much at variance Negro thought and hope it with the opinions and words of the foremost Educators and Statesmen of the white race. The Negroes generally expect the day to come when, through the effect of education and the accumulation of wealth, they will enjoy full social equality with the white people of the United States. Some are so ignorant of the nature of the marriage relation that they argue it is only a step from concubinage between white men and black women to the Divine institution. These persons do not seem to know that concubinage has its motives in the animal desires, and that the marriage relation never should be entered from considerations based on the passions or impulse. There is absolutely no analogy between concubinage and marriage. The motives that lead to the marriage relation are drawn from considerations that do not enter the mind of the illicit lover. We wish to make it clear that persons living in a state of concubinage are not only not approaching the marriage relation, but the very motives under which they act precludes even its proper consideration. As we have before said the temptations to an immoral life are the most deplorable features in the present conditions of the Negro race. The Negro will never get social equality with the white race, hence there is no escape from condition that will ultimately deprive him of all moral sense. There is no use in trying to go contrary to the known laws of human nature.

We wish every thoughtful white father and mother in the United States, and every Negro interested in the Welfare of his race, could fully appreciate the wide prevalence of concubinage between white men and Negro women all over the land, but especially in the Southern States. This crime needs earnest consideration because its continuance and spread will ultimately sap all that is good from the American home. This foil of vice as it exists between the races is nothing less than a grade of prostitution, and of the most dangerous sort.

The concubinal white man is a lecherous being, and the Negro concubine a human without the least trace of moral sense. Offsprings from such unions swarm the Southern States. What is to prevent this progeny from being worse than animal? Such creatures are more dangerous to society than wild beasts; for these last can easily be hunted and shot, while the former go on procreating their lecherous kind without hindrance.

This species of vice is the most common and persistent of the many that always attends the bringing together of alien races. Women of the subordinate race are unable to resist the temptations to an immoral life. The struggle for existence and a disposition to ape after the ideals of the dominant race are too much for her feeble intellect and will. Mankind shall have to become perfect before alien races can inhabit the same country and remain free from this cancerous form of vice. If the danger to social institutions which concubinage surely holds was well and rightly understood there is no doubt but that a sentiment would soon be aroused that would endeavor to cure the conditions under which it invariably thrives.

It seems to us, and the view is supported by all human experience, that the Negro race in the United States can never have its women develop that high and pure morality which is the bulwark and pride of every civilized people.

How long would the Indian maiden last if she were to leave the Reservation? What is the moral tone of the mongoloid women who infest New York City and San Francisco? Can they ever be saved? Far more hopeless is the condition of the Negro woman! For fear some of our readers may think our view of this phase of the Negro Problem is overdrawn we shall quote a few observations made by notable white men. The Montgomery Advertiser reported this statement made by Dr. J. A. Rice, pastor of the Court Street Methodist Church, of Montgomery, Alabama: "I hesitate before I make another statement which is all too true. I hesitate, because I fear that in saying it I shall be charged with sensationalism. But even at the risk of such a charge I will say, for it must be said, that there are in the city of Montgomery, four hundred Negro women supported by white men." The same Dr. Rice also stated that in addition there were thirty-two Negro dives operated for white patronage, and the statement was quoted in the Montgomery Advertiser. The New Orleans Times-Democrat of February 15, 1906, used the following language to describe the prevailing crime: "It is a public scandal that there should be no law of this kind (against miscegenation) on the statute book of Louisiana, and that it should be left to mobs to break up the miscegenatious couples. The failures to pass a law of this kind is attributed to white degenerates, men who denounce social equality yet practice it, men who are more dangerous to their own race than the most inflammatory Negro orator and social equality preacher, and who have succeeded by some sort of Legislative trickery in pigeon-holing or killing the bills intended to protect Louisiana from a possible danger. Such men should be exposed before the people of the State in their true colors."

In January, 1907, District Attorney J. H. Currie in his address to a jury in Judge Cochran's court at Meridian, Mississippi, used these strong words: "The accursed shadow of miscegenation hangs over the South today like a pall of hell. We talk much of the Negro question and all of its possible ramifications and consequences, but, gentlemen, the trouble is not far afield. Our own people, our white men with their black concubines, are destroying the integrity of the Negro race, raising up a menace to the white race, lowering the standard of both races and preparing the way for riot, mob, criminal assaults, and finally a death struggle for racial supremacy. The trouble is at our own door. We have tolerated the crime long enough, and if our country is not run by policy rather than by law, then it is time to rise up and denounce this sin of the Earth."

Ray Stannard Baker in the "American Magazine" for April, 1908, says: "Negro women, and especially the more comely and intelligent of them, are surrounded by temptations difficult indeed to meet. It has been and is a struggle in Negro communities, especially village communities, to get a moral standard established which will make such relationships with white men unpopular. In some places today, the Negro concubines of white men are received in the Negro churches and among the Negroes generally, and honored rather than ostracized. They are often among the most intelligent of the Negro women, they often have the best homes and the most money to contribute to their churches. They are proud of their slight-colored children."

From these statements there can be no doubt as to the wide extent of this degrading evil, and the alarm already aroused in the minds of some thinking men. What is needed is a cure. What shall it be? All ask this question, but few give the answer that ultimately must be given if the homes and firesides of this Republic are to represent all that is best in honor, morality and religion.

The sort of education that is possible for the American Negro woman cannot be relied upon to keep her from becoming the white man's concubine. Experience shows that hundreds of educated Negro girls are living the life of kept women in every Southern State; and the number is increasing notwithstanding the spread of schools. The whole trouble is that the conditions under which the Negro must live are opposed to the development of true moral character. Teach the Negro girl art, music and literature; but without morals, she will become a concubine at the first opportunity!

If there were no other reasons for separating the two races, consideration of the moral conditions of the Negro and the hopeless task of improving it under existing circumstances ought to convince the most reluctant mind that no other remedy will cure the present evils or save the Republic from more terrible calamities. Against the desire and duty to act for the general welfare of both races the money cost or the magnitude of the undertaking ought not to prevail.

There can be given no sound reason against race separation. All experience, and every deduction from the known laws and principles of human nature and human conduct are against the attempt to harmonize two alien races under the same government. When the races are so differentiated in mental and physical characteristics, as the Negro and Anglo-Saxon, the government that undertakes the experiment rests at all times on a volcano.

The subordinate race grows more and more restless under discriminating laws and customs as the people learn to recognize their social, industrial, and political ostracism. Nothing can prevent this unrest except giving to the subordinate race full and equal rights in every particular.

There is absolutely no probability for any such event to occur. The longer the discontent continues the stronger it will grow. Other circumstances will contribute to arouse the resentment of the dominant people against the subordinate because of their obnoxious pretensions. From bad to worse the situation must ever tend.

Every true friend of humanity must hope that some means may be found to avert the dangers that can already be seen gathering over this grand Republic.

Our fear is that the remedy will not be seen until the evils have accumulated to such proportions, and the passions of the people so fired, that calm and dispassionate reason will be impossible.

The American people have met with honor and courage every difficulty which has seemed to threaten the welfare and existence of their government.

There is yet time for them to stand up bravely and say to the Negro: "We have wronged your race by forcing it from the Home where God placed it into an alien land and there imposed the yoke of slavery. We have liberated your race, and wish to see you develop to the fullest the powers which your Creator has bestowed upon you. Nothing but failure and disappointment awaits your efforts towards betterment while in contact with Anglo-Saxon civilization: hence we as a Nation, with the desire to make partial atonement for the wrong done, and the wish to be of service to your race and to mankind everywhere, will undertake to aid you to return to your native land, where we hope to see you build a civilization which shall be the glory and admiration of the World for all times."

[1908]

XVII

The most prominent intellectual in African-American history, and one of the greatest minds of the twentieth or any century, spoke consistently and fervently about America's race problem and the progress of the race. W. E. B. Du Bois (1868–1963), from his birth in Great Barrington, Massachusetts, to his death in Ghana, West Africa, epitomized the notion of the public intellectual in that he was a scholar and activist and saw no contradiction between the two. After his undergraduate education at historically black Fisk University he went on for further study at Harvard, including the PhD with advanced study at the University of Berlin. His doctoral dissertation, *The Suppression of the African Slave Trade*, in 1896 became his first book and one of many major contributions to African-American history. Outside of the classroom, he was a continuous force that demanded change and equality. The driving force behind the Niagara movement, he was a founding member of the NAACP in 1909. Du Bois became editor of *Crisis* magazine and a persistent voice against the wrongs committed in America and the world. As he warned the United States in his classic book, *The Souls of Black Folk*, "the problem of the twentieth century is the problem of the color line." He also had a strong sense of African identification as witnessed by his key roles in the international Pan-African Conferences and in his book, *The World and Africa*, for example. But Du Bois did not stop there. In *Dusk of Dawn: An Autobiography of a Race Concept*, he talks about his life and the struggle and future of the race. He puts into context serious reflection on and questioning of the black condition and what must be done for the race to progress. Du Bois points out certain realities: that whites have more advantages than blacks and hold superior positions in society. He asks us: What will we do to change that and to elevate people of color? His is a powerful analysis of the problem and a stern demand of what must be the course of action to bring about positive change. He is critical of those blacks who identify more with white society than with their own race and with Africa, extolling them that theirs is a false dichotomy and flawed belief paradigm, a challenge of "double consciousness." Is Du Bois correct in advocating a group consensus in the course of action that the race must take for advancement? Is Du Bois's hope for the reign of intelligence more than just a fervent wish? In "The Colored World Within," included here, the reader is invited to wrestle with these powerful questions and suggested remedies.

"The Colored World Within"

W. E. B. Du Bois

Not only do white men but also colored men forget the facts of the Negro's double environment. The Negro American has for his environment not only the white surrounding world, but also, and touching him usually, much more nearly and compellingly, is the environment furnished by his own colored group. There are exceptions, of course, but this is the rule. The American Negro, therefore, is surrounded and conditioned by the concept which he has of white people and he is treated in accordance with the concept they have of him. On the other hand, so far as his own people are concerned, he is in direct contact with individuals and facts. He fits into this environment more or less willingly. It gives him a social world and mental peace. On the other hand and especially if in education and ambition and income he is above the average culture of his group, he is often resentful of its environing power; partly because he does not recognize its power and partly because he is determined to consider himself part of the white group from which, in fact, he is excluded. This weaving of words does not make the situation entirely clear and yet it does point toward its complications.

It is true, as I have argued, that Negroes are not inherently ugly nor congenitally stupid. They are not naturally criminal and their poverty and ignorance today have clear and well-known and remediable causes. All this is true; and yet what every colored man living today knows is that by practical present measurement Negroes today are inferior to whites. The white folk of the world are richer and more intelligent; they live better; have better government; have better legal systems; have built more impressive cities, larger systems of communication and they control a larger part of the earth than all the colored peoples together.

Against this colored folk may certainly bring many countervailing considerations. But putting these aside, there remains the other fact that the mass of the colored peoples in Asia and Africa, in North America and the West Indies and in South America and in the South Sea Islands are in the mass ignorant, diseased, and inefficient: that the governments which they have evolved, even allowing for the interested interference of the white world, have seldom reached the degree of efficiency of modern European governments; and that particularly in the use, increase, and distribution of wealth, in the regulation of human services, they have at best fallen behind the accomplishment of modern England, France and the United States.

It may be said and with very strong probability back of such assertion, there is no reason to doubt, that what ever white folk have accomplished, black, brown and yellow folk might have done possibly in differing ways with different results. Certainly modern civilization is too new and has steered too crooked a course and been too much a matter of chance and fate to make any final judgment as to the abilities of humankind.

All this I strongly believe and yet today we are faced by these uncomforting facts: the ignorance, poverty and inefficiency of the darker peoples; the wealth, power and technical triumph of the whites. It is not enough when the colored people face this situation, that they decry resulting attitudes of the white world. There is a strong suspicion among themselves and a probability often asserted among whites, that were conditions reversed, blacks would have done everything to white people that white people have done to blacks; or going less far afield than this: if yellow folk in the future gain the domination of the world, their program might not be more philanthropic than that of the whites. But here again, this is not the question. Granting its possible truth, it is no answer to the present plight.

The present question is: What is the colored world going to do about the current situations? Present Negro attitudes can be illuminated by turning our attention for a space to colored America, to an average group of Negroes, say, in Harlem, not in their role of agitation and reform, but in their daily human intercourse and play. Imagine a conversation like this, of which I have heard dozens:

"Just like niggers!"
"This is what colored people always do."
"What can you expect of the 'brother'?"
"I wish to God I had been born white!"

This interchange takes place at midnight. There are no white persons present. Four persons have spent an evening playing bridge, and now are waiting until a fifth, the hostess, brings in the supper. The apartment is small but comfortable; perhaps a little too full of conventional furniture, which does not altogether agree in pattern; but evidently the home of fairly well-to-do people who like each other and are enjoying themselves. But, of course they have begun to discuss "the problem" which no group of American colored people can long keep from discussing. It is and must be the central interest of their lives.

There is a young colored teacher from the public schools of New York—well-paid and well-dressed, with a comely form and an arresting personality. She is from the South. Her mother had been servant and housekeeper in a wealthy Southern white family. Her grandmother had been a slave of their own grandfather. This teacher is complaining bitterly of her walk through Harlem that night; of the loud and vulgar talking; of the way in which the sidewalks were blocked; of the familiarity and even insults of dark loafers; of the insistent bad manners and resentful attitude of so many of these Harlem black folk.

The lawyer lights a cigar. "It certainly is a question where to live," he says. He had been educated at Fisk University and brought in contact for eight years with Northern white teachers. Then he had gone West and eventually studied law at the University of Michigan. He is big, dark, good-natured and well-dressed. He complains of the crowded conditions of living in Harlem; of the noise and dirt in any Negro community; of the fact that if you went out to a better class white neighborhood you could not rent, you had to buy; if you did buy, first you could place no mortgage; then the whites made your life hell; if you survived this, the whites became panicky, sold to anyone for anything: pretty soon, in two, three, five years, people of all sorts and kinds came crowding in. Homes were transformed into lodging houses; undesirable elements became your neighbors. "I moved to a nice apartment on Sugar Hill last year. It had just been turned over to colored people. The landlord promised everything. I started out of the apartment last night; there was a pool of blood in front of my door, where there had been a drunken brawl and cutting the night before."

A young, slim, cream-colored physician, native of New York and a graduate of its schools, but compelled to go to Howard in order to finish the clinical work of his medical education, looked uncomfortable. "I don't mind going with colored people; I prefer it, if they are my kind; but if I go out to lunch here in Harlem, I get pork chops and yams which I do not like, served on a table cloth which is not clean, set down negligently by indifferent waiters. In the movies uptown here I find miscellaneous and often ill-smelling neighbors. On my vacation, where shall I—where can I go? The part of Atlantic City open to me, I continue to frequent, because I see so many charming friends of mine from all over the land but always I get sick at heart not only at the discrimination on the boardwalk, in the restaurants, on the beach in the amusements—that is bad enough; but I gag at the kind of colored people always in evidence, against whom I want to discriminate myself. We tried to support a colored section of the beach; see who crowded in; we failed."

"Yes, but that is all pleasure or convenience," says the fourth man. He was an insurance agent, playing a difficult game of chance with people who made weekly payments to him and then tried to beat him by malingering; or with others who paid promptly and had their claims disallowed by the higher-ups. "What I am bothered about," he says, "is this poverty, sickness and crime; the cheating of Negroes not only by whites, but by Negroes themselves: the hold-ups and murders of colored people by colored people. I am afraid to go to some places to make my collections. I don't know what is going to become of the Negro at this rate."

Just then, the fifth member of the party, the wife of the insurance agent, emerges from the kitchen where she has been arranging the lunch. She is pretty and olive, a little inclined to be fat. She was the daughter of dark laborers who had gone to Boston after emancipation. There she had been educated in the public schools ant was a social worker there before she married. She knew how to cook and liked to, and is accompanied through the swinging door by a delicious aroma of coffee, hot biscuits and fried chicken. She has been listening to the conversation from outside and she came in saying, "What's got me worried to death, is where I am going to send Junior to school. Junior is bright and has got nice manners, if I do say it; but I just can't send him to these Harlem schools. I was visiting them yesterday; dirt, noise, bad manners filthy tales, no discipline, overcrowded. The teachers aren't half trying. They purposely send green teachers to Harlem for experience. I just can't send Junior there; but where can I send him?"

This is a fairly characteristic colored group of the better class and they are voicing that bitter inner criticism of Negroes directed in upon themselves, which is widespread.

It tends often to fierce, angry, contemptuous judgment of nearly all that Negroes do, say, and believe. Of course these words are seldom voiced in the presence of white folk. Every one of these persons, in the presence of whites, would eagerly and fiercely defend their "race."

Such complaints are the natural reaction of people toward the low average of culture among American Negroes. There is some exaggeration here, which the critics themselves, if challenged, would readily admit; and yet, there is sound basis for much of this criticism. Similar phenomena may be noticed always among undeveloped or suppressed peoples or groups undergoing extraordinary experience. None have more pitilessly castigated Jews than the Jewish prophets, ancient and modern. It is the Irish themselves who rail at "dirty Irish tricks." Nothing could exceed the self-abasement of the Germans during the *Sturm und Drang*.

Negro self-criticism recognizes a perfectly obvious fact and that fact is that most Negroes in the United States today occupy a low cultural status; both low in itself and low as compared with the national average in the land. There are cultured individuals and groups among them. All Negroes do not fall culturally below all whites. But if one selects any one of the obviously low culture groups in the United States, the proportion of Negroes who belong to it will be larger than the Negro proportion in the total population. Nor is there anything singular about it; the real miracle would be if this were not so. Former slavery, present poverty and ignorance, with the inevitable resulting sickness and crime are adequate social explanation.

This low social condition of the majority of Negroes is not solely a problem of the whites; a question of historic guilt in slavery and labor exploitation and of present discrimination; it is not merely a matter of the social uplifting of an alien group within their midst; a problem of social contact and political power. Howsoever it may be thus rationalized and explained, it must be, at any current moment, primarily an inner problem of the Negro group itself, a condition from which they themselves are prime sufferers, and a problem with which this group is forced itself to grapple. No matter what the true reasons are, or where the blame lies, the fact remains that among twelve million American Negroes, there are today poverty, ignorance, bad manners, disease, and crime.

A determined fight has been made upon Negro ignorance, both within and without the group, and the results have been notable. Nevertheless, this is still an ignorant people. One in every six Negroes ten years of age and over admitted in 1930 that he could not read and write. It is probable that one in every three would have been justified in confessing to practical illiteracy, to inexperience and lack of knowledge of the meaning of the modern world. In the South not one-half the colored children from five to sixteen are regularly in school and the majority of these schools are not good schools. Any poor, ignorant people herded by themselves, filled with more or less articulate resentment, are bound to be bad-mannered, for manners are a matter of social environment; and the mass of American Negroes have retrograded in this respect.

There has been striking improvement in the Negro death rate. It was better than that of most South American countries, of Italy, Japan and Spain even before the war. Nevertheless it is still bad and costly, and the toll in tuberculosis, pneumonia, heart disease, syphilis, and homicide is far too high. It is hard to know just what the criminal tendencies of the American Negroes are, for our crime statistics are woefully inadequate. We do know that in proportion to population three times as many Negroes are arrested as whites, but to what extent this measures prejudice and to what extent antisocial ills, who shall say? Many of these ought never to have been arrested; most of them are innocent of grave crimes; but the transgression of the poor and sick is always manifest among Negroes: disorder of all sorts, theft and burglary, fighting, breaking the gambling and liquor laws and especially fighting with and killing each other.

Above all the Negro is poor: poor by heritage from two hundred forty-four years of chattel slavery, by emancipation without land or capital and by seventy-five years of additional wage exploitation and crime peonage. Sudden industrial changes like the Civil War, the World War and the spree in speculation during the twenties have upset him. The Negro worker has been especially hard hit by the current depression. Of the nearly three million Negro families in the United States today, probably the breadwinners of a million are unemployed and another million on the lower margin of decent subsistence. Assuming a gradual restoration of fairly normal conditions it is probable that not more than two per cent of the Negro families in the United States would have an income of $2,500 a year and over; while fifty-eight per cent would have incomes between $500 and $2,500.

This social degradation is intensified and emphasized by discrimination; inability to get work, discrimination in pay, improbability of promotion, and more fundamentally, spiritual segregation from contact with manners, customs, incentives to effort despite handicaps. By outer pressure in most cases, Negroes must live among themselves; neighbors to their own people in segregated parts of the city, in segregated country districts. The segregation is not complete and most of it is customary rather than legal. Nevertheless, most Negroes live with Negroes, in what are on the whole the least pleasant dwelling places, although not necessarily always bad places in themselves.

This means that Negroes live in districts of low cultural level; that their contacts with their fellow men involve contacts with people largely untrained and ignorant, frequently diseased, dirty, and noisy, and sometimes anti-social. These districts are not usually protected by the police—rather victimized and tyrannized over by them. No one who does not know can realize what tyranny a low-grade white policeman can exercise in a colored neighborhood. In court his unsupported word cannot be disputed and the only defense against him is often mayhem and assassination by black criminals, with resultant hue and cry. City services of water, sewerage, garbage-removal, street-cleaning, lighting, noise and traffic regulation, schools and hospitalization are usually neglected or withheld. Saloons, brothels, and gambling seek these areas with open or tacit consent. No matter in what degree or in what way the action of the white population may increase or decrease these social problems, they remain the present problems which must be faced by colored people themselves and by colored people of widely different status.

It goes without saying that while Negroes are thus manifestly of low average culture, in no place nor at any time do they form a homogeneous group. Even in the country districts of the lower South, Allison Davis likens the group to a steeple with wide base tapering to a high pinnacle. This means that while the poor, ignorant, sick and anti-social form a vast foundation, that upward from that base stretch classes whose highest members, although few in number, reach above the average not only of the Negroes but of the whites and may justly be compared to the better-class white culture. The class structure of the whites, on the other hand, resembles a tower bulging near the center with the lowest classes small in number as compared with the middle and lower middle classes; and the highest classes far more numerous in proportion than those among blacks. This, of course, is what one would naturally expect, but it is easily forgotten. The Negro group is spoken of continually as one undifferentiated low-class mass. The culture of the higher whites is often considered as typical of all the whites.

American Negroes again are of differing descent, from parents with varied education, born in many parts of the land and under all sorts of conditions. In differing degrees these folk have come through periods of great and vital social change; emancipation from slavery, migration from South to North, from country to city; changes in income and intelligence. Above this they have experienced widely different contacts with their own group and with the whites. For instance, during slavery the dark house servant came into close and intimate contact with the master class. This class itself differed in all degrees from cultured aristocrats to brutal tyrants. Many of the Negroes thus received ideals of gracious manners, of swaggering self assertion, of conspicuous consumption. Later cultural contact came to the best of the Negroes through the mission schools in the South succeeding the war: the more simple and austere intellectual life of New England with its plain living and high thinking; its cleanliness and conscience; this was brought into direct contact with educated Negro life. Its influence is still felt among the descendants of those trained at Fisk and Atlanta, Hampton and Talladega and a score of other schools.

These contacts between the white and colored groups in the United States have gradually changed. On the whole the better cultural contacts have lessened in breadth and time, and greater, cultural segregation by race has ensued. The old bonds between servants and masters in the South disappeared. The white New England teachers gradually withdrew from the Southern schools partly by white Southern caste pressure, partly to make place for Negroes whom the Northern teachers had trained. The bonds that replaced these older contacts were less direct, more temporary and casual and yet, these still involve considerable numbers of persons. In Northern public schools and colleges, numbers of white and colored youth come into direct contact, knowledge and sympathy. Various organizations, movements, and meetings bring white and colored people together; in various occupations they work side by side and in large numbers of cases they meet as employers and employed. Deliberate interracial movements have brought some social contacts in the South.

Thus considerable intercourse between white and black folk in America is current today; and yet on the whole, the more or less clearly defined upper layers of educated and ambitious Negroes find themselves for the most part largely segregated and alone. They are unable, or at least unwilling on the terms offered, to share the social institutions of the cultured whites of the nation, and are faced with inner problems of contact with their own lower classes with which they have few or no social institutions capable of dealing.

The Negro of education and income is jammed beside the careless, ignorant and criminal. He recoils from appeal to the white city even for physical protection against his anti-social elements, for this, he feels, is a form of self-accusation, of attack on the Negro race. It invites the smug rejoinder: "Well, if you can't live with niggers, how do you expect us to?" For escape of the Negro cultured to areas of white culture, with the consequent acceleration of acculturation, there is small opportunity. There is little or no chance for a Negro family to remove to a quiet neighborhood, to a protected suburb or a college town. I tried once to buy a home in the Sage Foundation development at Forest Hills, Long Island. The project was designed for the class of white-collar workers to which I belonged. Robert De Forest and his directors hesitated, but finally and definitely refused, simply and solely because of my dark skin.

What now is the practical path for the solution of the problem? Usually it has been assumed in such cases that the culture recruits rising from a submerged group will be received more or less willingly by corresponding classes of neighboring or enveloping groups. Of course it is clear in the case of immigrant groups and other disadvantaged clusters of folk that this process is by no means easy or natural. Much bitter frustration and social upheaval continually arise from the refusal of the upper social layers to receive recruits from below. Nevertheless, in the United States it has been impossible long or entirely to exclude the better classes of the Irish, the Italians, the Southern poor whites. In the case of the Negro, the unwillingness is greater and public opinion supports it to such a degree, that admission of black folk to cultured circles is slow and difficult. It still remains possible in the United States for a white American to be a gentleman and a scholar, a Christian and a man of integrity, and yet flatly and openly refuse to treat as a fellow human being any person who has Negro ancestry.

The inner contradiction and frustration which this involves is curious. The younger educated Negroes show here vastly different interpretations. One avoids every appearance of segregation. He will not sit in a street car beside a Negro; he will not frequent a Negro church; he will join few, if any, Negro organizations. On the other hand, he will take every opportunity to join in the political and cultural life of the whites. But he pays for this and pays dearly. He so often meets actual insult or more or less veiled rebuffs from the whites that he becomes nervous and truculent through expectation of dislike, even when its manifestation does not always appear. And on the other hand, Negroes more or less withdraw from associating with him. They suspect that he is "ashamed of his race."

Another sort of young educated Negro forms and joins Negro organizations; prides himself on living with "his people"; withdraws from contact with whites, unless there is no obvious alternative. He too pays. His cultural contacts sink of necessity to a lower level. He becomes provincial in his outlook. He attributes to whites a dislike and hatred and racial prejudice of which many of them are quite unconscious and guiltless.

Between these two extremes range all sorts of interracial patterns, and all of them theoretically follow the idea that Negroes must only submit to segregation "when forced." In practically all cases the net result is a more or less clear and definite crystallization of the culture elements among colored people into their own groups for social and cultural contact.

The resultant path which commends itself to many whites is deliberate and planned cultural segregation of the upper classes of Negroes not only from the whites of all classes, but from their own masses. It has been said time and time again: if certain classes of Negroes do not like the squalor, filth and crime of Negro slums, instead of trying to escape to better class white neighborhoods, why do they not establish their own exclusive neighborhoods? In other words, why does not the Negro race build up a class structure of its own, parallel to that of the whites, but separate; and including its own social, economic and religious institutions?

The arresting thing about this advice and program is that even when not planned, this is exactly what Negroes are doing and must do even in the case of those who theoretically resent it. The group with whose conversation this chapter started is a case in point. They form a self-segregated culture group. They have come to know each other partly by chance, partly by design, but form a small integrated clique because of similar likes and ideas, because of corresponding culture. This is happening all over the land among these twelve million Negroes. It is not a matter yet of a few broad super-imposed social classes, but rather of smaller cliques and groups gradually integrating and extending out of their neighborhoods into neighboring districts and cities. In this way a distinct social grouping has long been growing among American Negroes and recent studies have emphasized what we all knew, and that is that the education and acculturation of the Negro child is more largely the result of the training through contact with these cultural groups than it is of the caste-conditioned contacts with whites.

The question now comes as to how far this method of acculturation should and could go, and by what conscious planning the uplift of the Negro race can be accomplished through this means. Is cultural separation in the same territory feasible? To force a group of various levels of culture to segregate itself, will certainly retard its advance, since it must put energy not simply into social advance, but in the vast and intricate effort to duplicate, evolve, and contrive new social institutions to maintain their advance and guard against retrogression.

There can be two theories here: one that the rise of a talented tenth within the Negro race, whether or not it succeeds in escaping to the higher cultural classes of the white race, is a threat to the development of the whole Negro group and hurts their chances for salvation. Or it may be said that the rise of classes within the Negro group is precisely a method by which the level of culture in the whole group is going to be raised. But this depends upon the relations that develop between these masses and the cultural aims of the higher classes.

Many assume that an upper social class maintains its status mainly by reason of its superior culture. It may, however, maintain its status because of its wealth and political power and in that case its ranks can be successfully invaded only by the wealthy. In white America, it is in this direction that we have undoubtedly changed the older pattern of social hierarchy. Birth and culture still count, but the main avenue to social power and class domination is wealth: income and oligarchic economic power, the consequent political power and the prestige of those who own and control capital and distribute credit. This makes a less logical social hierarchy and one that can only be penetrated by the will and permission of the ruling oligarchy or the chances of gambling. Education, thrift, hard work and character undoubtedly are influential, but they are implemented with power only as they gain wealth: and as land, natural resources, credit and capital are increasingly monopolized, they gain wealth by permission of the dominating wealthy class.

If now American Negroes plan a vertical parallel of such a structure and such processes, they will find it practically impossible. First of all, they have not the wealth; secondly, they have not the political power which wealth manipulates, and in the realm of their democratic power they are not only already partly disfranchised by law and custom, but they suffer the same general limitation of democratic power in income and industry, in which the white masses are imprisoned.

There would be greater possibility of the Negro imitating the class structure of the white race if those whites who advise and encourage it were ready to help in its accomplishment, ready to furnish the Negro the broadest opportunity for cultural development and in addition to this to open the way for them to accumulate such wealth and receive such income as would make the corresponding structure secure. But, of course, those who most vehemently tell the Negro to develop his own classes and social institutions, have no plan or desire for such help. First of all and often deliberately, they curtail the education and cultural advantage of black folk and they do this because they are not convinced of the cultural ability or gift of Negroes and have no hope nor wish that the mass of Negroes can be raised even as far as the mass of whites have been.

It is this insincere attitude which especially arouses the ire and resentment of the culture groups among American Negroes.

When the Negro despairs of duplicating white development, his despair is not always because the paths to this development are shut in his face, but back of this lurks too often a lack of faith in essential Negro possibilities, parallel to similar attitudes on the part of the whites. Instead of this proving anything concerning the truth, it is simply a natural phenomenon. Negroes, particularly the better class Negroes, are brought up like other Americans despite the various separations and segregations. They share, therefore, average American culture and current American prejudices. It is almost impossible for a Negro boy trained in a white Northern high school and a white college to come out with any high idea of his own people or any abiding faith in what they can do; or for a Negro trained in the segregated schools of the South wholly to escape the deadening environment of insult and caste, even if he happens to have the good teachers and teaching facilities, which poverty almost invariably denies him. He may rationalize his own individual status as exceptional. He can well believe that there are many other exceptions, but he cannot ordinarily believe that the mass of Negro people have possibilities equal to the whites.

It is this sort of thing that leads to the sort of self-criticism that introduces this chapter. My grandfather, Alexander Du Bois, was pushed into the Negro group. He resented it. He wasn't a "Negro," he was a man. He would not attend Negro picnics or join a Negro church, and yet he had to. Now, his situation in 1810 was much different from mine in 1940, because the Negro group today is much more differentiated and has distinct cultural elements. He could go to a Negro picnic today and associate with interesting people of his own level. So much so, indeed, that some Negro thinkers are beginning to be afraid that we will become so enamored of our own internal social contacts, that we will cease to hammer at the doors of the larger group, with all the consequent loss of breadth through lack of the widest cultural contact; and all the danger of ultimate extinction through exacerbated racial repulsions and violence. For any building of a segregated Negro culture in America in those areas where it is by law or custom the rule and where neglect to take positive action would mean a slowing down or stoppage or even retrogression of Negro advance, unusual and difficult and to some extent unprecedented action is called for.

To recapitulate: we cannot follow the class structure of America; we do not have the economic or political power, the ownership of machines and materials, the power to direct the processes of industry, the monopoly of capital and credit. On the other hand, even if we cannot follow this method of structure, nevertheless we must do something. We cannot stand still; we cannot permit ourselves simply to be the victims of exploitation and social exclusion. It is from this paradox that arises the present frustration among American Negroes.

[1940]

XVIII

A critical mover and shaker for the advancement of the race was Carter G. Woodson (1875–1950), an organizational genius and scholar-activist. Woodson, like Du Bois, was a Harvard graduate with a PhD in history. Woodson said that he spent the next thirty years after graduation "unlearning what they had taught me at Harvard." Woodson demonstrated his devotion to racial uplift when he and others founded the Association for the Study of Negro Life and History in 1915 and then shortly thereafter established the *Journal of Negro History*. He created the *Negro History Bulletin* in the 1930s to reach beyond scholarly confines and appeal to the general audience with information about the African-American experience. It was Woodson who became the father of the black history movement when, in 1927, he took an idea initiated at Omega Psi Phi fraternity to have a week designated for celebration of the achievements and contributions of black folk in American society and the world: a week that became known as Negro History Week, and later Black History Month. His efforts to reach the people was premised on a basic belief he had that knowledge is power and that any group would have to know itself before it could know what to do to advance itself. In that advancement, Woodson urged blacks to look within themselves and not count upon others. "Higher Strivings in the Service of the Country," presented here, is taken from Woodson's most powerful and seminal book, *The Mis-Education of the Negro*. The reader is asked to take special note of what Woodson has to say about African Americans in politics and their contribution to society as a whole. Was he correct in his admonition that as a minority element blacks should not wed themselves to any one political party? Is he right in his advice that for those blacks who do make it into political office that they must think for the benefit of the whole and not just one ethnic group? How does that advice strike you in light of the Obama administration and its agenda today?

"Higher Strivings in the Service of the Country"

Carter G. Woodson

Another factor the Negro needs is a new figure in politics, one who will not concern himself so much with what others can do for him as with what be can do for himself. He will know sufficient about the system of government not to carry his trouble to the federal functionaries and thus confess himself a failure in the community in which he lives. He will know that his freedom from peonage and lynching will be determined by the extent that he can develop into a worthy citizen and impress himself upon his community.

The New Negro in politics will not be so unwise as to join the ignorant delegations from conferences and conventions which stage annual pilgrimages to the White House to complain to the President because they have socially and economically failed to measure up to demands of self-preservation. The New Negro in politics will understand clearly that in the final analysis federal functionaries cannot do anything about these matters within the police powers of the states, and he will not put himself in the position of being received with coldness and treated as these ignorant misleaders of the Negro race have been from time immemorial. The New Negro in politics, then, will appeal to his own and to such friends of other races in his locality as believe in social justice. If he does something for himself others will do more for him.

The increasing vigor of the race, then, will not be fritted away in the interest of the oppressors of the race. It ought not to be possible for the political bosses to induce almost any Negro in the community to abandon his permanent employment to assist them and their ilk in carrying out some program for the selfish purposes of the ones engineering the scheme. It ought not to possible for the politicians to distribute funds at the rate of fifty or a hundred dollars a head among the outstanding ministers and use them and their congregations in vicious partisan strife. It is most shameful that some ministers resort to religion as a camouflage to gain influence in the churches only to use such power for selfish political purpose.

The Negro should endeavor to be a figure in politics, not a tool for politicians. This higher role can be played not by parking all of the votes of a race on one side of the fence as both blacks and whites have done in the South, but by independent action. The Negro should not censure the Republican party for forgetting him and he should not blame the Democratic party for opposing him. Neither can the South blame any one but itself for its isolation in national politics. Any people who will vote the same way for three generations without thereby obtaining results ought to be ignored and disfranchised.

As a minority element the Negro should not knock at the door of any particular political party. He should appeal to the Negroes themselves and from them should come harmony and concerted action for a new advance to that larger freedom of men. The Negro should use his vote rather than give it away to reward the dead for some favors done in the distant past. He should clamor not for the few offices earmarked as Negro jobs but for the recognition of these despised persons as men according to the provision of the Constitution of the United States.

The few state and national offices formerly set aside for Negroes have paled into insignificance when compared with the many highly lucrative positions now occupied by Negroes as a result of their development in other spheres. Sometimes a Negro prominent in education, business or processional life can earn more in a few months than the most successful politicians can earn in years. These political jobs, moreover, have diminished in recent years because the increase of race prejudice, which this policy has doubtless aided, supplies the political leaders with an excuse for not granting their Negro coworkers anything additional.

The New Negro in politics must learn something that the old "ward-heelers" have never been able to realize, namely, not only that the few offices allotted Negroes are insignificant but that even if the Negro received a proportionate share of the spoils, the race cannot hope to solve any serious problem by the changing fortunes of politics. Real politics, the science of government, is deeply rooted in the economic foundation of the social order. To figure greatly in politics the Negro must be a great figure in politics. A class of people slightly lifted above poverty, therefore, can never have much influence in political circles. The Negro must develop character and worth to make him a desirable everywhere so that he will not have to knock at the doors of political parties but will have them thrown open to him.

The New Negro in politics must not ask the party for money, he must not hire himself for a pittance to swing voters in line. He must contribute to the campaign of the party pleasing him, rather than draw upon it for an allowance to drive the wolf from the door during the three months of the political canvass. It will be considered a stroke of good fortune that a Negro of such influence and character has aligned himself with a party, and this fact will speak eloquently for the element to which he belongs.

The New Negro in politics, moreover, must not be a politician. He must be a man. He must try to give the world something rather than extract something from it. The world, as be should see it, does not owe him anything, certainly not a political office; and he should not try solely to secure one, and thus waste valuable years which might be devoted to the development of something of an enduring value. If he goes into office, it should be as a sacrifice because his valuable time is required elsewhere. If he is needed by his country in a civil position, he may respond to the call as a matter of duty, for his usefulness is otherwise assured. From such a Negro, then, we may expect sound advice, intelligent guidance, and constructive effort for the good of all elements of our population.

When such Negroes go into office you will not find them specializing in things which peculiarly concern the Negroes, offering merely antilynching bills and measures for pensioning the freedmen. The New Negro in politics will see his opportunity not in thus restricting himself but in visioning the whole social and economic order with his race as a part of it. In thus working for the benefit of all as prompted by his liberal mindedness the New Negro will do much more to bring the elements together for common good than he will be able to do in prating only of the ills of his particular corner and extending his hand for a douceur.

In suggesting herein the rise of the New Negro in politics the author does not have in mind the so-called radical Negroes who have read and misunderstood Karl Marx and his disciples and would solve the political as well as the economic problems of the race by an immediate application of these principles. History shows that although large numbers of people have actually tried to realize such pleasant dreams, they have in the final analysis come back to a social program based on competition. If no one is to enjoy the fruits of his exceptional labor any more than the individual who is not prepared to render such extraordinary service, not one of a thousand will be sufficiently humanitarian to bestir himself to achieve much of importance, and force applied in this case to stimulate such action has always broken down. If the excited whites who are bringing to the Negroes such strange doctrines are insane enough to believe them, the Negroes themselves should learn to think before it is too late.

History shows that it does not matter who is in power or what revolutionary forces take over the government, those who have not learned to do for themselves and have to depend solely on others never obtain any more rights or privileges in the end than they had in the beginning. Even if the expected social upheaval comes, the Negro will be better prepared to take care of himself in the subsequent reconstruction if he develops the power to ascend to a position higher up after the radically democratic people will have recovered from their revelry in an impossible Utopia.

To say that the Negro cannot develop sufficiently in the business world to measure arms with present-day capitalists is to deny actual facts, refute history, and discredit the Negro as a capable competitor in the economic battle of life. No man knows what he can do until he tries. The Negro race has never tried to do very much for itself. The race has great possibilities. Properly awakened, the Negro can do the so-called impossible in the business world and thus help to govern rather than merely be governed.

In the failure to see this and the advocacy of the destruction of the whole economic order to right social wrong we see again the tendency of the Negro to look to some force from without to do for him what be must learn to do for himself. The Negro needs to become radical, and the race will never amount to anything until it does become so, but this radicalism should come from within. The Negro will be very foolish to resort to extreme measures in behalf of foreign movements before he learns to suffer and die to right his own wrongs. There is no movement in the world working especially for the Negro. He must learn to do this for himself or be exterminated just as the American Indian has faced his doom in the setting sun.

Why should the Negro wait for some one from without to urge him to self-assertion when he sees himself robbed by his employer, defrauded by his merchant, and hushed up by government agents of injustice? Why wait for a spur to action when he finds his manhood insulted, his women outraged, and his fellowmen lynched for amusement? The Negroes have always had sufficient reason for being radical, and it looks silly to see them taking up the cause of others who pretend that they are interested in the Negro when they merely mean to use the race as a means to an end. When the desired purpose of these so-called friendly groups will have been served, they will have no further use for the Negro and will drop him just as the Republican machine has done.

The radicals bring forward, too, the argument that the Negro, being of a minority group, will always be overpowered by others. From the point of view of the selfish elements this may be true, and certainly it has worked thus for some time; but things do not always turn out according to mathematical calculations. In fact, the significant developments in history have never been thus determined. Only the temporary and the trivial can be thus forecast.

The human factor is always difficult for the materialist to evaluate and the prophecies of the alarmist are often upset. Why should we expect less in the case of the Negro?

[1933]

XIX

The most powerful voice articulating a class vision and labor solidarity as the best paths to economic equality and social justice was that of A. Philip Randolph (1889–1979). Randolph, along with Chandler Owen, founded the *Messenger* magazine in 1917, which became one of the vital forces in Harlem and the East Coast that carried as its central message the need for black folk to reject the exploitative nature of capitalism and to embrace socialism. Randolph also believed in working within the existing system to change it and strongly disagreed with those who professed separatism and back-to-Africa for the elevation of African Americans. Through his many articles in the *Messenger*, Randolph gained a reputation, as the Attorney General of the United States defined him by 1920, as "The Most Dangerous Negro in America." A tireless worker for labor solidarity, Randolph founded the Brotherhood of Sleeping Car Porters in 1925, and took on the Pullman Company to better the working conditions and pay of its black workers. Most of Randolph's life would be geared to African-American liberation and empowerment such as his threatened march on Washington in 1941 to protest against discrimination in federal employment, which resulted in the establishing of the Fair Employment Practices Commission, and his activist work to transform the AFL-CIO from within as the union's first black vice president. The essay selected here challenges the reader to make her or his own judgment as to whether Randolph was correct in his socialist path and class analysis over a race-based analysis and strategy to achieve ultimate success for the masses. How do these ideas hold true, or fail to hold true, for all Americans regardless of race, gender, or ethnicity? Is figuring out the system, and working within it, what is most needed on the part of African Americans to attain empowerment and to secure a successful future?

"The State of the Race"

A. Philip Randolph

The state of the race, like the state of the world, is chaotic. The former mirrors the latter. They hold the relation of cause and effect. Thus, in order to understand the causes at the bottom of the existing economic, political and social debacle in the life of the Negro, it is necessary to study the causes underlying the breakdown of the economic and political mechanism of Europe, the overthrow of empires and kingdoms; the rise of revolutions and republics.

Naturally, this carries us back to the war, which is beginning to be regarded as a new epoch in human history. The passions of the Great War swept the hopes of all peoples upward. War cries and slogans rang with a promise of a "new day," a warless world; a "world upon which the gibbet's shadow does not fall; where work and worth go hand in hand": a world without oppression of race, or class, creed or nation. Such was the dream of millions. The psychology was the handiwork of a plutocratic press, pulpit and school. It was essential to the successful prosecution of the war. But, meanwhile, ten million men were killed and thirty million wounded. A world torn and shattered by conflict; burdened with billions of debt, turned to Versailles for peace. But the Elder Statesmen of Europe and America failed to achieve peace. Their League of Nations, like the Holy Alliance of Metternich, holds no promise of order or justice. Following peace, in every country, the blight of unemployment, the result of over production, hovered over the lands. The high wage and high price levels of war, slumped. The buying power of millions of workers, black and white, contracted as their income decreased. A world-wide panic ensued. In America, as elsewhere, this financial and industrial depression reflected itself in the general economic, political and social life of the people. In every field of human effort visible signs of spiritual decay are manifest. Society, as a whole, seems utterly and hopelessly bankrupt of any vitalizing and recuperative powers. Not only is there little or no interest in cultural strivings; no power to heal the wounds of a bleeding world; but far worse and far more alarming, is the absence of a "will" to salvage civilization, to re-establish ordered relationships in the affairs of mankind. In very truth, the Brahmins of the magic cult of profits, driven on by inexorable forces of capitalist imperialism, have called forth monsters that now threaten to devour them. Strife and dissension, splits and disharmonies that are bitter and devastating, beset every group.

The former allies, France and England, have reached the parting of the ways over oil in Mosul. The United States is becoming, a la Coué, day by day, in every way, more estranged from her former allies over the issue of debts. Russia is outlawed and despised by those whom she helped to win the war, because of her social philosophy. Turkey, the once "sick man of Europe," is now tattling the saber of a reborn nationalism; while Germany, her former ally, lies prostrate at the foot of a ruthless world imperialism, her very life's blood ebbing away. Thus the united front of capitalism lies in ruin, with another world war hovering in the offing.

The victorious powers can not agree on anything. Both Soviet Russia and Germany have baffled the ruling class in every conference from Versailles to Lausanne. Such is the international muddle.

Moreover, the internal conditions of the respective countries are not any more reassuring. Even the employing classes within the several countries are divided, unable to settle upon any general policy of either exploiting the Workers or of opposing rival national powers. Neither premiers Bonar Law of England, Mussolini of Italy, Poincare of France, Chancellor Cuno of Germany, President Harding of the United States of America, or Lenin of Soviet Russia can boast a united nation behind their governments. Amidst troubled times that augur grave peril to the very life of the régime of the bourgeoisie, capitalist statesmen, distressed and distracted, play at politics. The European and American diplomatists are the Negros of today, fiddling while the world burns.

One has but cursorily to observe politics in the United States to note its obvious chaos. The hardboiled, stand-pat, Lodge faction is at loggerheads with the LaFollette-Brookhart progressives, sometimes styled by the Lusk fraternity as "parlor Bolsheviks." But even the Progressives are without unanimity of thought and action on general policies. In short, the politicians like the capitalists they represent, are in bitter, ravaging feuds, incapable of evolving a common program.

And what is true of the ruling class is equally true of the subject or working class. Though division invites repression, the ranks of the workers everywhere are driven asunder. There are rights and new-rights, centers and near-centers, lefts and near-lefts. Witness the variety of proletarian political efforts, viz., the Socialist Party, the Socialist Labor Party, the Communist, the Communist Labor and the Proletarian Communist Parties. (In New York City the Workers Party is recognized as the legal expression of one wing of the Communist movement.) Then, there are the liberals, such as the Committee of 48, the Non-Partisan League, etc. What power might not be wielded by the workers, with a united front; still these splits serve their purpose. They are the training school of a nobler and mightier movement.

In industry, too, the workers have no less a variety of splits and splitlets. The Labor Movement of America comprises the American Federation of Labor, which constitutes the conservative wing; the I. W. W., or the left wing; and such independent organizations as the Amalgamated Clothing Workers and the Amalgamated Food Industries Unions, each of which possesses numerous wings that are ever locked in a raging war. Even during periods of strikes, the disastrous internal strife of the Labor Movement proceeds apace with redoubled fury. Doubtless such has ever been, in little measure. But this confusion and disunity in the ranks of the workers and employers are intensified and aggravated during periods of economic storm and stress—panics and the aftermath of wars.

This phenomenon of world-wide political and economic disorder was precipitated and accentuated by the world war, which world war was the outgrowth of commercial rivalry between capitalist nations; and this commercial rivalry flowed as an inevitable consequence of the existence of a socio-economic system under which the workers produce more wealth than their wages will enable them to buy back, thereby piling up a huge surplus.

By a careful study of the economic history of the United States, it will be seen that these periodic commercial and industrial crises have their roots in a system which oscillates well-nigh mechanically from overproduction to underproduction, from high wages to low wages, from high prices to low prices. The capitalist countries of the world alternate from violent business inflation to severe and drastic liquidation, expressing themselves in the closing down of factories, mines, lay-offs on railroads and steamships; widespread unemployment, bankruptcies, strikes, etc. These cycles of economic depression reappear around every decade. While wars may intensify their manifestation, wars are not essentially their cause. Our planless system of producing wealth for profits is the fundamental cause. Thus, this is not the first, and doubtless will not be the last period of industrial upheavals and maladjustments which will reflect itself in a social malaise, spiritual dry-rot, political bankruptcy and intellectual sterility. And every group, whether capitalist or worker, black or white, is a replica in microcosm of this all-encompassing world collapse. No group can escape being afflicted by this virulent bacillus of chaos because no group can escape dependence upon the existing economic order for food, clothing and shelter, the primary needs of life. And just as one loses his equilibrium when the platform upon which he stands is shaken, so does a social order reel, its ethical, religious, legal, political and cultural superstructures lose balance, when once the mechanism for producing the wealth of that society is damaged, either through abuse or disuse.

Hence, the Negro race, being an integral part of the present system, will naturally and logically reflect this chaos; but, perhaps, only more acutely because of its weakness.

It is not unnatural that a group which is the last hired and the first fired, a group which works the hardest and receives the lowest pay, would show signs of moral deterioration under the stresses and strains of the present period of readjustment. Well might the race assemble in a parley to discuss its miserable plight, its apparent degeneration and the probable way out.

Our lines, defensive and offensive, have been pushed back on every sector, political, economic and social. Witness how the Dyer Anti-Lynching Bill, it supreme test of the race's virility and instinct to move forward, died because the overwhelming economic paralysis had sapped our will to battle for manhood rights.

Our political policies, the heritage of Civil War days, are barren of achievement. The job-political-policy of the Old Crowed is insolvent, discredited, repudiated; still political statesmanship goes a-begging.

In industry we have lost ground. Wages have dropped below other groups doing similar work because we lack bargaining power, which can only come with organization.

In business, our failures have been numerous and disastrous, including banks and enterprises of all kinds. Here we lack credit power, knowledge, and experience.

In the educational field the sinister monster of segregation rears its menacing head, in many cases securing our acquiescence, in others pressing us to yield through murder and threat.

Meanwhile, lynchings and riots and the indescribable depredations of the Ku Klux Klan are religiously employed to drive us back into the black night of moral slavery.

To the solution of these problems, the race has evolved many and divers schools of thought, working assiduously at cross purposes. A word about them.

The conservative, or right wing, is led, in the field of education and general social policy, by the Tuskegee-Hampton-National Urban League-Howard University group. In this group, the idea of acquiring property, knowledge of trades and professions, and of being law-abiding, thrifty, home-buying, "cast-down-your-bucket-where-you-are" citizens, rather than of the protesting, insurgent variety, is stressed. The Negro leaders of this group are largely satellites of their white benefactors, reflecting the views of conservative, imperial America.

In the center stands the National Association for the Advancement of Colored People, articulating the opinion of liberal Negro America. Through this medium, liberal white America, in alliance with liberal Negro leaders, seek to achieve civil justice for the Negro.

The radical, or left wing, is represented through the MESSENGER and Crusader groups. With this section, political and economic radicalism is the dominant note, treating race as an incident of the larger world problem of class conflict. The radical black and white leaders combine to unite black and white workers.

Finally, there is the Garvey Movement, with its "back-to-Africa" program. The leader of this group has recently come into great disfavor on account of his interview with King Kleagle Clarke and his subsequent defense of the Ku Klux Klan. Such are, in brief, the broad streams of Negro thinking. Like their white correlatives, the Negro schools of thought are torn with dissension, giving birth to many insurgent factions in each. All are engaged in a war of bitter recriminations, tearing each other limb from limb, while the wide, long-suffering Negro masses trudge aimlessly on, victims of the vanities, foibles, indiscretions and vaulting ambitions, ignorance and dishonesty of varying leaderships.

To the foregoing picture of apparent, amazing race insanity the questions arise: whither are we trending? Is there any way out? What can be done to transform this internecine strife into constructive, co-operative effort?

First, may I observe that the Negro, like the capitalists and workers, like Nordics and Mongoloids, like various sects, cults and movements of all types, together with the great "power nations," is passing through a period of severe and relentless race dialectics, each wing, each leadership desperately striving with a sort of Machiavellian "might is right" creed, to establish a supreme mastery in leadership.

Out of this fierce competitive leadership—movement—struggle will be evolved a clearer vision, a firmer and a more rugged morale, an unconquerable will, and a finer and more comprehensive and scientific Race policy and technique of action. The progress of the mass is indifferent to leadership—egoisms. The race will move forward even though movements of well-merited honor and distinction for service fall into the discard. For social, like organic progress, in the main, responds to material imperatives.

I am not distressed, then, as to the ultimate issue of the race in these times of world readjustment, although I am conscious of a definite summons for a orientation in race policy and method, in harmony with the trend of the economic and social forces of the age. Thus a determination of the character and tendency of these socio-economic forces is the chief desideratum, since it is obvious that the march of the Race is advanced or retarded in proportion as it is guided by the most severely tested conclusions of modern science.

In conference after conference we must search for and work out the remedy. There should be specialized conferences whose agenda is economic, political, educational. But specialized parleys do not obviate the need of an All-Race Conference.

There are myriad questions of pressing immediacy which challenge the Race for an answer, an answer which should emanate from some representative body, embodying itself in a broad, reasoned policy.

What, for instance, should be the attitude of the Negro in the United States on "the conflict between labor and capital," "immigration," "a future war," "the relation of Negroes to white leadership within and without the Race," "the problem of Negro business in periods of expansion and panics," "education in white and Negro schools and colleges," "radicalism among Negroes," "unemployment," "the open and closed shops," "the problem of Africa, the West Indies, Central and South America," "Negro Culture," "lynching, race riots," "which should be the Negro's political party?—Republican, Socialist, Democratic, Workers, or a new Party," "Social Equality," "the Negro farmer," "farm tenant," "peonage," "consumers' and producers' co-operatives," "the relation of the Negro worker to the American Federation of Labor, the I. W. W., and independent unions"; "the attitude of the Negro to workers' international, economic, and political, movements."

Such is a brief sketch of problems of which Negro leadership is either ignorant or indifferent to, but which hold a vital life and death relationship to the fortunes of the race.

To this task of grappling with these riddles of the race, the Negro masses must draft their "best minds and hearts"; men and women who possess a consuming passion to build a great monument of achievement, devotion, and service to the cause of a militant, constructive idealism, a free Race, a free world.

[*The Messenger*, April 1923]

XX

Marcus Garvey (1887–1940), arguably the greatest black organization builder of the 20th century, professed a philosophy of black separatism. Garvey contended that the salvation of the race lay outside of the United States and that blacks throughout the world must think in terms of Pan-Africanism and the ultimate goal of repatriation to mother Africa. He called for blacks to abandon the notion of the American dream and to forge a new nation on the continent of Africa. Garvey's maroon heritage in Jamaica gave him from his youth to adulthood a strong sense of blackness and a tradition of separation from whites to build and develop on one's own terms. With his love of books and learning, he fine-tuned his public education during his years in London, England, before embarking on what would become his lifelong mission of "Africa for Africans both at home and abroad." While the slogan may, indeed, have originated with Duse Mohammed Ali in London, it was Garvey who made it a worldwide cry with the founding of his Universal Negro Improvement Association and the establishment of its most successful chapter in the black community of New York's Harlem in 1916. In his publication, *The Negro World*, Garvey conveyed his message to the black masses on a regular basis. In Garvey's "Unemployment Speech," presented here, he offers a strong plea for self-reliance and separatism. What do you think of Garvey's belief that blacks are industrial peons in the United States and destined to continue in that role if the powers that be have their way? He also speaks of the service of African Americans to the war effort; in his time it was World War I but the message he offers is timeless. Garvey asks if it is fair for people who fought and sacrificed for America not to share in its great bounty. Is it fair? Yet he warns that black folk are destined to be relegated as a permanent underclass labor force while others, including previous foes during the war, are treated with respect. What do you think of his analysis and how does it resonate with the current labor situation among African Americans? Is labor solidarity needed?

"Unemployment: And Whom We Should Blame"

Marcus Garvey

I desire to speak to you this evening in a heart-to-heart manner, because just at the time we are facing critical conditions, and it is but right that we should talk to each other, counsel each other, and get to understand each other, so that all of us may be able to work from one common understanding for the good of all.

I desire to appeal to the memory of the members of this association. You will remember that in the years immediately preceding the great war in Europe there was a great industrial stagnation among Negroes in the United States of America, and that we then faced a hard and difficult task industrially, economically, and we saw no hope, and we had none. Then immediately, whilst undergoing our hard and difficult experience, the war broke out in Europe. Germany declared war, and nearly all of the European powers were dragged into the bloody conflict. Immediately the war started in Europe the participants rushed a large number of orders for war supplies and munitions to the United States of America, that was then neutral in the war. By the abnormal demands for the industrials of these United States of America, a great industrial wave swept the country, and untold opportunities were opened up to Negroes everywhere in these United States of America not only to Negroes, but these untold opportunities were opened up to all races, to peoples within the confines of this country. Factories and mills and industrial plants sprang up everywhere in the great industrial centers, and men who never had employment, men who never had any occupations prior to that time, found opportunities then. Men for years who never had the chance of earning a decent wage, found jobs ranging in weekly salaries or wages from $25 to $100, and some $200 a week. Men everywhere were employed, and even the peons and the serfs of the South broke loose from the South and ran North, where these great industrial opportunities had opened up themselves for each and every one. Men came from the West Indies; men came from all parts of the world to America to enjoy the benefits of the new industrial opportunities offered in America. These opportunities opened up larger and larger, and out of the wealth that was poured out of the great war some of the people who enjoyed the distribution of that wealth conserved the portion they got or received, such as the Jews, the Italians, the Irish and the Poles. Their leaders in the pulpits, through periodicals, through magazines, and from platforms and classrooms, taught their respective groups the value of conserving the wealth that was then poured out into their pockets in the form of salaries and wages, to prepare for the rainy day that would come. Negroes, however, in the most loose, the most slack, the most indifferent manner, received their portion of the wealth that was poured out, and they made absolutely no effort to conserve it. They distributed it as quickly as they received it; they paid it out back to the employer, or to his friend, or to his brother, or some of his relatives, as quickly as they received it from him. And just at that time a large number of the leaders of the country said nothing. They had no advice to give. The preachers said nothing, and they gave no advice to the people.

Just about that time the Universal Negro Improvement Association came upon the scene, with an active propaganda. It taught preparedness — industrial preparedness among the Negroes then. It warned them, and told them that they should prepare to start industries of their own, to save their money, and to make every effort to protect themselves; because after the war there would be a great industrial dearth; there would be a great industrial stagnation. We taught that doctrine; we preached it; we wrote it in the newspapers; we scattered it near and far; we sent the doctrine everywhere and everywhere we got the retort that we were crazy; that we were a bunch of lunatics. The man who inspired the movement was a crazy man and a fit subject for the lunatic asylum. They said all manner of things against him, because we dared then, when no others would do so, to teach the doctrine of industrial, economic preparedness. The people, however, could not see, and they believed we were crazy. But we stuck to our doctrine, we adhered to our belief, and we were able to convert four million people scattered all over the world to our doctrine and to our belief. But we did not convert the four million people at one time; it took us four years to convert them. Some became converted immediately, and assumed the burden and responsibility of carrying and conveying the doctrine to others. Hence tonight I am able to look into the faces of some of the people who started with me when we organized the Universal Negro Improvement Association; people who have made the sacrifices I made—sacrifices in money and in time. They bore the brunt of the situation, because on them laid the responsibility to finance and support the propaganda so as to carry the propaganda to others. And they have borne the price of the propaganda for four years reaching the four millions. But it reached the four millions only too late, because the war and the opportunities were over, and when it reached them they could ill afford to support the doctrine to convey it unto others. Hence the present situation that confronts us now.

There are hundreds and thousands, and later on millions of men in this country of Negro blood who will be thrown out—thrown into the cold. We anticipated it; we saw it, and we warned the people against it. We did it with the feelings of our sympathies for our own; we did it with the feelings of conviction that the men with whom we mingled during the war paid us large wages, paid us large salaries with a vengeance, but they were forced, they were compelled to do so, and they did it with a spite and with a vengeance. Some did not see it, and did not appreciate the fact of those who saw it and warned the people against it. The attitude of the employers in this country was to pay the Negro as small a wage as possible on which he could hardly subsist or hardly live, because he desired to keep the Negro as an industrial peon, as an industrial serf, and make it impossible for him to rise in the great industrial, economic ladder of lift. He kept him down, not because the Negro before the war was not worth more than he was paid for his labor, for at all times the Negro is worth more than twenty, thirty or forty dollars a month. Yet that was all that was paid to us prior to the war, and all of you know it. It was paid to the elevator men, to the porter men, and everybody nearly got the maximum of forty dollars or fifty dollars, or sixty dollars a month from his employer prior to the war, not because we were not worth more than that for our labor, but because the other man was prejudiced against paying us more than that. He desired not to give us a chance to rise in the industrial and economic world. But the war came, and we compelled him by conditions, we forced him by conditions to pay us $100 a week, to pay us $50 a week, to pay us $60 a week, and some of us mechanics forced him to pay us $200 a week, and he paid it, but with a bitter anguish; he paid it with great reluctance; he paid it with a vengeance and he said: "I am going to get even with the Negro." He knew the Negro better than the Negro knew himself. He knew the Negro would spend every dollar, every nickel, every penny he earned which he was compelled to pay him. He laid the plan by which the Negro would spend every nickel but the Negro hadn't sense sufficient to see it and know it. Now, what was the object and purpose of it? To take back every nickel that he paid him. When he raised the cost of living, when he raised the cost of bread, when he raised the cost of butter and of eggs, and of meat, and of other necessities of life, what did he mean? He meant that we should return to him every penny of that which we got from him, and the Negro had not sense enough to see it. He raised the price of everything; he raised the price of luxuries, for he knew well that, above all other peoples, Negroes love luxuries, and he taxed us in the districts where Negroes live, for you paid more for the luxuries you received in your district than the white folks paid for the same luxuries in their district. The White people planned to get every nickel that they paid to you; and we fell for it. We bought silk shirts at $10 apiece, and $15 apiece. We bought shoes at $30 and $25 a pair. We bought ladies' dresses at $100 a suit; we bought the most expensive hats, silk socks at $3 a pair, at $2 a pair, and $1.50 a pair, and we took automobile rides and paid $24 for a Sunday afternoon ride, and we did all kinds of things of that sort. Some of us had six girls and gave presents to each of them. Thus we spent every nickel of what we received.

Did anyone else live at the same rate at which the Negro then lived? Did the Italian live at that rate? Did the Jew live at that rate? They did not. The Jews saved at least fifty per cent of what they earned. The Italian saved at least sixty per cent of what he earned. The Irish saved at least fifty per cent of what he earned. And at the end of the war every one of them had a bank account to show. Every one of them had some investment in Irish interests to show. How much did we save? What interest have we to show? Absolutely none. Whose fault is it? It is the fault of the people; it is the fault, more, of the leaders. You cannot so much blame the people, because the bulk of the people do not think, the bulk of the people follow the advice of their leaders, and the people of that Race that has no leaders is a Race that is doomed. Negroes never had any leaders at any time. That is why we have always been doomed. When we preached the doctrine of preparedness, men like Du Bois criticized the U.N.I.A. and its leader. All of you can remember that when we started the propaganda of the U.N.I.A. and the Black Star, every newspaper and magazine in New York tried to down us. "The Amsterdam News" wrote against us; the "New York News" wrote against us; the "Crusader" wrote against us; the "Challenge" wrote against us; the "Emancipator" wrote against us; everyone of them wrote against us, and discouraged the people. Whose fault is it now?

That is the question, and you yourselves must give the answer. They all said, and pointed to us, saying that we were a crazy bunch of people. What did we tell you during the war period? And immediately following the war, when you were still employed? Didn't we tell you that there was a Black Star Line? Did we not tell you that its capital was $10,000,000? Did we not throw away, during the war, $50 and $100 and more at different times for mere pleasure and expensive, fashionable clothing? And had we invested that money which we then spent so lavishly and foolishly, to subscribing to the capital stock of the Black Star Line; what would have happened? With $10,000,000 of its stock subscribed and paid for, we would tonight have twenty ships that would belong to us as ours, each worth half a million dollars. And what kind of ships would they be? They would be ships of a tonnage of five thousand to eight or ten thousand tens. They would be ships each able to accommodate at least 500 to 1,000 passengers. If we had twenty ships, each able to accommodate a thousand passengers across the Atlantic Ocean, what would happen today? Every day in the week, or every other day of the week, a ship of the Black Star Line would sail out of New York port with at least a thousand unemployed men from New York to Liberia, West Africa. That is what we saw. That is what we tried to tell the people and teach the people. How many of us would be unemployed tonight if the capital stock of the Black Star Line had been subscribed for two years ago? I hardly believe that there would be an unemployed Negro here. Because if we have ten thousand unemployed in Harlem tonight, we could call up ten ships of the Black Star Line, and say to the captains of those ships that we have ten thousand Negro men unemployed to send to Liberia. Take them! But you did not subscribe the capital, you paid it out in silk shirts; you paid it out in expensive socks. And who made those factory silk shirts and those fancy silk socks that you purchased and paid for? White men. Who sold them to you? White men. Where is the money you paid for them? Gone back to white men, and you are still the paupers that you were prior to the war in 1914. Whose fault is it? That is the answer you must give yourselves.

It pains me, it grieves me, it brings tears to my eyes when I see a race, not of children, but of matured minds, of full grown men and women, playing with and threatening their lives and the destiny of themselves and of posterity. What more can we do as leaders of the Universal Negro Improvement Association than to open the eyes of the people by talking to them, preaching to them, pleading with them, and writing to them concerning that which we know, that which we see? That is all we can do. Some of you are crazy now, as crazy as you were, some of you, four years ago. And those of you who are old members of the U.N.I.A. can remember Marcus Garvey in the streets of Harlem. When you had your fat jobs downtown, earning $100 a week, and in other parts of the country, I could have done the same. But I saw the threatening disaster. And what did I do? I had as much ability as the average man; I had as much skill as the average man. The average man was going his way, making his pile, and enjoyed himself when he was at leisure. People would walk up and down Lenox avenue and see Marcus Garvey on a stepladder, and would say: "Look at that crazy black fool!" They called me all kinds of names standing up there talking about Africa! Look at his coat! Look at his shoes, and everything he has on! They said all those things about me. But I saw the future collapse. I saw the results that would follow the then period of prosperity that was only transitory. I saw the day when the very big Negro who then got his pay envelope on a Saturday night of $100 and believed he was the biggest thing in Harlem—I foresaw when he would be the smallest thing in Harlem; that he would be the man without a nickel because I knew the war would soon be over, and I knew the white man would then throw him aside as soon as hostilities were over and there was a slackening in the demand for the commodities or munitions he was then making and give the preference to white men; and that has been the white man's policy ever since his contact with the Negro. That has been his program, and that will be his program always, so long as Negroes are foolish enough to allow him to use them for what he wants.

I am sounding this second warning, and I want you to take it from a man who feels the consciousness of what he says. I am not pretending to be a prophet; I am not pretending to be a sage or a philosopher. I am but an ordinary man with ordinary common sense who can see where the wind blows, and the man who is so foolish as not to be able to see and understand where the wind blows, I am sorry for him; his senses are gone. I can feel; and the man who cannot feel now I am sorry for his dead sense. I can see where the wind is blowing, and it is because of what I see that I am talking to you like this. There are some Negroes in Harlem who are working and some who save money. They believe they are always going to have jobs; they believe they are always going to have money. You will always have money if you know how to use it. There are some men who have money and then lose all they have because they never know how to use it. There are some men who never had and they get and always have it. Now, I want you to realize this one truth that I am endeavoring to point out to you. There are a large number of unemployed Negroes in New York and there are hundreds of thousands of unemployed Negroes in different parts of the country. I have been traveling for the last couple of months and in all of the Western states I have been I have seen Negroes out of work by the hundreds in centers like Pittsburgh, Detroit, Cleveland, Columbus, Youngstown and Chicago—all around the Western and mid-Western stares. So that whether we live in New York or somewhere else, conditions are just as bad. So you might as well stay where you are and face the situation. What we want Negroes who are still working and who have money to do, is to decide upon some wise plan to save the situation. Negroes do not like to help Negroes anyhow; but perforce we will have to help each other or otherwise something will happen to surprise us. I told you but recently that when a man is hungry he is the respecter of no person. A hungry man forgets the look of his father. Understand that. There are some Negroes who believe they should not take interest in other Negroes. Now let me tell you that we are going to face a situation, the most critical ever experienced by this race of ours in these United States of America. I told you some time ago that it is a question of dog eating dog. You know how bad a situation that must be. What I mean by it is just that: that there are some Negroes who are too big, who are too aristocratic and too dicty to take interest in other Negroes. I am going to tell you what I believe will happen to such Negroes later on, if they do not get busy now and do something for all Negroes irrespective of what class these Negroes belong to. No community is safe if in its midst there are thousands of hungry men. I do not care where that community is, it is an unsafe community and especially at midnight. Let the big dicty Negroes say, "What do I care for that good-for-nothing Negro; he is nothing." That poor Negro who has never had a square meal for four days goes to that big dicty Negro—I am trying to picture the conditions later on—he goes to that big dicty Negro and asks for a quarter or 50 cents and he drives him away. That Negro after not having a square meal for two, three or four days, turns away and loses heart and nothing in the world is too desperate for him not to do. To find bread a man is driven to the farthest extreme and at midnight or even in the daylight he resorts to violence and cares not what the result be so long as he finds bread to satisfy his hungry heart and soul. I have just come from Chicago and there I heard of a hungry Negro who never had a square meal for two or three days. He had begged everybody around town and everybody drove him away. He said, "Why should I die for hunger when somebody can give me bread? Since they have refused me, I will take it," and he goes to the house of a preacher somewhere in the outskirts of Chicago and he gets into the house where sleeps the lonely preacher and at midnight what did that hungry Negro do? He took a razor or some sharp instrument and severed the head of that sleeping preacher from the body to get two dollars. He got $2, and killed a man for $2 so as to find bread. When he had spent that two dollars and could not get any more bread he called the police and said, "I will confess to you what I did if you give me a square meal." He was given a meal of chicken and something else and confessed that he killed the man. Those are the conditions that hungry men are not responsible for. I do not care how religious a man is or how many Sunday schools he goes to; I do not care how long he can pray, when that man is hungry he is a dangerous character. And that is the practical common-sense issue that you have to face in a practical common-sense way. White folks have stopped looking out for Negroes; they stopped before there was a war.

The war robbed them of all that there was in the world. Now they have nothing because they have used up all that is in the world. It is a question now of every man looking out for himself. That is all. The white man is deaf to your sympathy and to your cries. You may cry and beg for jobs he will not give you except you are the only fellow who can fill that job that he wants done. But the first man of his own race he finds able to fill that same job with the same ability as you have, you are gone. And he does not wait to ask where the white man comes from. He only wants to know he is a white man, and out you go. He does not wait to know where you are from. He says you are a Negro, and out you go.

Now what to do? We are saying to the men of the Universal Negro Improvement Association and to the Negro race. I am speaking only to those who have confidence. If you do not have any confidence in yourselves, if you do not have any confidence in your own race movements, I am sorry for you, and I would ask you to go your way. Men must have confidence in something and in some one. Without confidence the world is lost. Mankind has retrograded and the world has gone back. The world is built upon confidence—confidence in some one, confidence in some institution, confidence in something. We live as rational human beings, social human beings, because we have confidence in people and in God the creator. Let a man lose his confidence in his people and in a God, and chaos is ushered in and anarchy sweeps the world and human society is destroyed. It is only the belief and the confidence that we have in a God why man is able to understand his own social institutions and move and live like rational human beings. Take away the highest ideal—the highest faith and confidence in God, and mankind at large is destroyed. As with your confidence in God, as with your confidence in religion, whether it be Christianity or any other religion, so must you have confidence in your institutions that mean anything to you as individuals and as a community.

Now I am saying to you who have confidence in the Universal Negro Improvement Association—and if you have no confidence you should not be here. I am here because I have confidence that the men and the women who make up the movement will continue and continue until victory be written on the banner of the red, the black and the green. I am here because I have confidence in humanity; I am here because I have confidence in God, and I expect that all those who wear the red, the black and the green are here because they have confidence in the ultimate triumph of this great cause of ours. If you have confidence; if you have faith in it as you have confidence and faith in your religion, therefore it is time for you to support the movement and make it the success that you want to be, make your support not a half-hearted one, but make it a whole-hearted one. You have seen the first practical demonstration of the utility of the Universal Negro Improvement Association. You have seen the first mistake made by this race of ours, as I have tried to preach to you in these few years—the mistake during the war period. I am asking you now not to repeat or not to make the same mistake. I know as I look into the face of many of you that there are hundreds of you members of the Universal Negro Improvement Association who have not done anything yet for the practical carrying out of the program of this organization. I have asked many of you if you have your Liberty bonds, and you say no. I ask why? You say, well, because you are not able just now to buy. You rate your ability to buy on the surplus money you have. When you bought a share or two in the Black Star Line for $5 or $10 two years ago you did it when you were getting a salary of probably $100 or $50 a week, and you said, "I will invest $10 in the Black Star Line because you had your work and so much surplus cash." Now it is not a question of surplus cash; it is a question of duty. It is a question of your own interest. I am saying to the men and women of the Negro race, there is but one salvation for the Negro as I see it now, and that is the building of Liberia, West Africa. The only salvation for Negroes now is opening up industrial and economic opportunities somewhere, and I don't see it around here. You will have to create another war for it, or you will have to get another Kaiser before I will see it around here. I have no objection to seeing another Kaiser, and I feel sure you would have no objection either, whether he comes from Japan or anywhere, but on the second coming I believe you will be better prepared than the first coming. "Once bitten, twice shy." But you have to bite Negroes a hundred times before they get shy. We have been bitten for 300 years and up to now we are not shy yet. What do I mean? I want you members to act as living missionaries to convince others. There are still Negroes here who can help and buy shares in the Black Star Line. Those of you who have done your duty, I am not speaking to you; but there are thousands who can subscribe to the Liberian Construction Loan. There is a hungry man, he has not a nickel in his pocket and he is begging bread. There is another man with a thousand dollars. The one man without money to buy bread can neither help himself nor his fellow men. The man with a thousand dollars cannot only help himself, but he can help dozens of others; but he is too selfish. He, like the other man, has no money, has no job, and he says: "I have a thousand dollars, but I have no job. I am just going to hold on to this thousand dollars." And every day he spends $3, $4, $5 out of it and still has no job. Every day $5 has gone and he is too selfish to think about the other man.

He is too selfish to think about anybody else he meets and every day $5 goes out of his thousand dollars, and at the end of the year he still has no job. His thousand dollars is gone, and he is like the other fellow, without a nickel. Both of them face each other—two hungry men; one cannot help the other; but that man who had the thousand dollars, if he were a wise man, a man of common ordinary sense, what would he have done when he finds himself without a job and with a thousand dollars only left out of his years of earnings? He would say: Is there an organization around that is endeavoring to do some good? Are there any other men around who want to do some good? If so, I will go and link up with them and do some good. Yes, he would say, there is an organization over there. What are they trying to do? They are trying among other things to raise two million dollars or ten million dollars to put a line of steamships on the ocean to carry hundreds of men from these ports of the world to Africa, where they are going to build factories, mills, railroads, etc, and find employment for hundreds of men They are crying for money to put over the scheme. I will find out how far they have gone, and if it is possible that they can carry it through I will put in $500, and if the other fellow who has his thousand will also put in $500 and others will do likewise $10,000,000 will be subscribed to buy ships and $2,000,000 will be subscribed to buy railroad and building materials, and we will be ready to ship men to Africa to work from January to December and open up opportunities immediately. That is what 1 am trying to get you to understand. A thousand dollars in your pocket without a job may find you worse off at the end of six months. A thousand dollars or $200 or $100 invested in an organization in which you have confidence may save yourself, your children and posterity. If you have no confidence I cannot advise you because I will do nothing myself except I have confidence in it. A man's confidence is his guide; a man's faith is his guide. I am only speaking to those who have faith in the Universal Negro Improvement Association. If you have faith, if you respect the success that we have made in three years when we started without anything and have reached where we are now; if you have faith that we can continue where we are to the greater success to be, I am asking you to support the program of the Universal Negro Improvement Association. I want to find out how many of you have confidence and faith in the Universal Negro Improvement Association. Hold your hands up. I thank you for your faith. I thank you for your confidence; but men and women, remember it is not a question of Marcus Garvey or any other man. It is a question of yourselves. What will you do to save yourselves? Marcus Garvey cannot save anybody because Marcus Garvey is but human like every other man. Jesus Christ is the only man who has the power to save. I am but a man. I cannot save you; you must save yourselves. I am only trying to advise you the way how all of us can save ourselves. If you do not heed it will not be my fault. I have stood by; I have listened and I have heard all kinds of people blaming me for what I never said … somebody is crazy. How can Marcus Garvey prevent Negroes from doing anything? What can I do? I have advised you all the time how to get jobs. That is all I did. If you do not have jobs now it is not my fault. I advised you to put the money you saved into a great corporation—into a great corporation of which you are members; not in some strange thing that you did nor know anything about—but in your own organization. Every member of the organization has a right to know everything about the organization, so that when you put your money into it you are putting your money in your own hands. I am but one individual who helped to carry on the work of the organization, and if you do not trust yourselves who is to blame? You did not have confidence in yourselves.

I am giving you a message that you may impart it to others and tell them there is still a chance; because we have not reached the worst yet; but that chance you must grasp in the next sixty days. I have met men coming to the office who have been out of work for three months and two months and one month. It brings tears to my eyes to see them. I saw a fellow whom I believe four years ago was raising "Cain" up in Harlem. He used to look at me on the street and laugh and walk on; but now he has been reduced to dire straits, and he came to the office and would not leave until I gave him 50 cents. That is the way with the majority of Negroes. That fellow earned as much money as any other men around here, and every evening you saw him on the avenue with a new suit and a new girl. The girls are belonging to somebody else now and he is down and out. And that is the situation, not with one man but with hundreds of our men.

I am going to give this one advice. I have been waiting for the last 60 days to see what the politicians would do in making an effort to present the case of the Negro to the proper authorities. I have searched all the papers, and I have not seen anything done—no attempt made, and because they have done nothing I have to start to do something. You will all understand that I am an African citizen and I am not supposed to interfere in domestic politics; but if the other fellow will not start out, before I see the people perish, I will take my chance. I know, that this nation owes a solemn obligation to the Negro, and I could not stand and see the Negro perish without a hearing; and since the politicians have not spoken we shall send a delegation of the Universal Negro Improvement Association to the Governor of New York to find out what he means by allowing Negroes to be closed out of jobs, when Negroes and especially the boys of the New York 15th fought so nobly in France and Flanders for the preservation of American freedom. What does the State mean by allowing the politicians and citizens of the State to close out Negroes and give alien enemies jobs now? We will send a deputation to Albany to ask Albany, will you want us again? And we will expect an answer from Albany. We will ask Albany, "Will you want us in the American-Japanese war? Will you want us in the Anglo-American war?" Because David Lloyd George is scheming now to write off the war debt, and no American citizen is going to stand for it. Therefore it may end somewhere else. "Will you want us then?" And we will listen for the answer from Albany, and from Albany we will send the same deputation to Washington a couple of days after to ask the same question.

This is no time for bowing and scraping and pussy footing. It is time to let the other fellow know that you are alive. Negroes do not want to beg jobs; Negroes must demand jobs; that is all there is about it. But you must demand jobs in the proper way. Let the leaders of the race, if they are leaders, as Du Bois, and men like Moton, go out and let President-elect Harding know that ten or fifteen million Negroes stood behind the country in time of war, and they must now stand behind those ten or fifteen million Negroes. If you have any men posing as leaders who are going about among white people bowing and scraping they will brush you aside. You must have as your leaders and representatives men who will let our high officials and other influential white people know that you are alive, and that you are going to stay alive. I cannot see the philosophy of taking any other stand but this. I cannot see the reason for it—that Negroes should be drafted and sent three thousand miles away to fight and die at the command of their country, to help make conditions and life safe for other people; that Negroes, those whom their Government did not send to war, remained at home and engaged in making munitions and other necessities for carrying on the war, so as to win the victory— I repeat, I cannot see wherein Negroes who have made sacrifices such as these for their country, now that the war is over and a condition of business depression exists through the country, should be discriminated against, and in favor of other men who were their country's foes, and who have no other claim to preferential consideration than that the color of their skin happens to be white. I cannot see the consistency, the right of it. You men must not yield up your jobs so easily. You have a right to them, and it is a question what you must make up you minds to do; and that is, to demand what is yours; that is all. If you are too cowardly you will never get anything. It is better to die demanding what is yours than starve getting nothing. That's how I feel, and since they have done nothing, in another ten or fifteen days we will have a delegation up in Albany, and from Albany the delegation will go to Washington and ask what do they mean. We preserved the nation and the nation must preserve us.

Men, you have the balance of power in America, and we are the balance of power over the world. Do not let the world bluff you. The American writers themselves acknowledge that the only people they could depend on in America for loyalty to the flag are the fifteen million Negroes in America; because they cannot tell the enemy in that he is white; the German is white, and they have had a hard time finding Germans. But they could tell who were Negroes, and the Kaiser was not from the Negro, either. So they knew the Negro was their friend. When the white man came, they had to ask: "Who comes there?"—and he had to answer: "Friend." But they did not have to ask that when they saw the black man coming, they knew before he came that he was a friend. However, we are going to ask them a question, as I told you a while ago, for since the politicians have not done anything we have got to play a little politics now. But, above all, men, I want you to remember that now is the time for you to support the Universal Liberian Construction Loan—you men who have fifty dollars; you men who have a hundred dollars; you men who have three hundred dollars or two hundred dollars. Now is the time for you to invest part of your money so as to enable us in another couple of weeks to secure the ship which we want to go to Africa. The ship is right down at the foot of Eighty-second street now. We can have it under contract this very hour; but the ship has to go for another twenty-six days, because we haven't the money to sign up the contract. The ship costs $500,000. Oh, some of you think a ship can be bought for $500. Ships in these days cost a million, two million dollars, five hundred thousand dollars, two hundred and fifty thousand dollars, and so on; and when you get a ship for $250,000 you have got a cheap ship. We have been negotiating for the ship, the kind of beautiful ship that we want—a ship with everything on it that we want; but we just had to look and wait awhile, because Negroes wouldn't subscribe enough to buy it.

If we had the money with which to buy the ship we could send three hundred men tomorrow morning to Africa. The ship can carry three hundred passengers at one time; and the money for it is right here in Harlem! Some of you say we are crazy. I can not do better than tell you what we are planning, what we are hoping, what we are doing, what lies before us all in the future, and what we should do to attain the destiny that God has mapped out for us. We are hoping that we will realize the money between now and the 19th of March to complete the contract. But God Almighty knows it depends upon the people. If they will not support the Universal Liberian Construction Loan I cannot work miracles; I cannot take blood out of a stone. Therefore, for this reason I have spoken to you tonight, and I am asking you to advise your friends, those of you who have already subscribed, or who have already invested in the Universal Liberian Construction Loan, to appeal to them and urge them to join in the support of this very necessary and much needed and most worthy object, by subscribing to the Loan and investing whatever money they can at this time in the enterprise so that we can put this great program over.

I thank you very much for your attention. Good-night, all!

[Liberty Hall Speech, New York, 11 February 1921]

XXI

The Mississippi-born Ida B. Wells-Barnett (1862–1931) was one of the most dedicated and fearless "race woman" freedom fighters in African-American history. One of eight children, born to parents who had both been slaves, Ida B. Wells-Barnett embodied the new emancipation and determination of freed blacks to achieve justice, equality, and recognition as citizens of the United States of America and as fellow human beings of the world community. Wells-Barnett would settle for nothing less. She made it her life's work to crusade against lynchings, the abominable dread of the South. Her book, *A Red Record* (1892), was both a testimony to the horrors and inhumanity of lynchings in the United States and also her commitment to rid the nation of this plague. Her years in Memphis, Tennessee, and the injustices she witnessed there, including the lynchings of three African-American grocery store owners for defending themselves against white mobs, were precisely the kinds of indignities and acts of violence against blacks that drove her forward. Wells-Barnett was committed to changing the order of things in the United States, which placed black lives in jeopardy because they demanded their rights as human beings. When a conductor on the Chesapeake, Ohio and Southwestern Railroad ordered her to give up her seat, although she paid for first-class passage, she refused and sued the railroad line for discrimination. Wells-Barnett was the quintessential "bad Negro," in the best sense of the term. More than seventy years before Rosa Parks refused to relinquish her seat on a Montgomery bus, Wells-Barnett conducted her one-person demonstration against segregated transportation. She moved to Chicago, and in 1895 married Ferdinand L. Barnett, an accomplished lawyer, newspaper person, and committed freedom fighter. They had a life together of commitment to elevating the race. Wells-Barnett traveled to Great Britain and other parts of Europe spreading the word for equality and speaking out in support of women's rights and the right of suffrage. She did not back down from threats against her humanity and rights of equal citizenship. Wells-Barnett advocated that black Americans, if need be, arm themselves and that a rifle should occupy a place of respect in every African-American household. She typically carried a pistol, given the threats against her life and her outspokenness against racism. Teacher, activist, journalist, Ida B. Wells-Barnett was a champion of black rights. In the piece presented here, "The Equal Rights League," she gives the reader a glimpse into her life of commitment. The reader would do well to take note of the other African-American leaders she worked with and her perspectives on them and others. What does she have to say about Monroe Trotter, Booker T. Washington, and Marcus Garvey? What does her life of commitment to the elevation of the race, and frontal assault to the problem, say to you?

"The Equal Rights League"

Ida B. Wells-Barnett

In the fall of 1915 a committee appointed to wait upon President Wilson in Washington D.C. called his attention to the segregation enforced in the departments of the government, and asked him to use his influence as president of the United States in abolishing discrimination based on the color line. I was a member of the committee, which was led by Mr. William Monroe Trotter of Boston, executive secretary of the National Equal Rights League.

President Wilson received us standing, and seemingly gave careful attention to the appeal delivered by Mr. Trotter. At its conclusion he said he was unaware of such discrimination, although Mr. Trotter left with him an order emanating from one of his heads of the department, which forbade colored and white clerks to use the same restaurants or toilet rooms. The president promised to look into the matter and again expressed doubt as to the situation.

As the only woman on the committee I was asked to make some comment, but I contented myself with saying to the president that there were more things going on in the government than he had dreamed of in his philosophy, and we thought it our duty to bring to his attention that phase of it which directly concerned us.

The year went by and no word was received from the president, nor was any action taken by him on the matter. Again I was asked to be one of the committee to visit him, but it was not convenient for me to do so. However, Mr. Trotter and his committee made their visit. It seems that the president became annoyed over Mr. Trotter's persistent assertion that these discriminations still were practiced and that it was his duty as president of the United States to abolish them. President Wilson became very angry and he told the committee that if they wanted to call on him in the future they would have to leave Mr. Trotter out.

The Associated Press sent the incident throughout the country, and many papers heralded the assertion that "Mr. Trotter had insulted President Wilson." I knew very well that there had been no breach of courtesy, but that President Wilson had simply become annoyed at Mr. Trotter's persistence. Many of our colored newspapers followed the lead of the white ones and condemned Mr. Trotter's action. The Negro Fellowship League extended him an invitation to visit Chicago and deliver our emancipation address.

We thought that the race should back up the man who had had the bravery to contend for the rights of his race, instead of condemning him. Mr. Trotter had never been West; and I thought that he needed to get out in this part of the country and see that the world didn't revolve around Boston as a hub, and we were very glad to give him an opportunity to do this.

We engaged Orchestra Hall and were forced to charge an admission fee to pay that three-hundred-dollar rental. Again I believed that the loyalty of our people would assert itself and that the encouragement we would give to this young leader would be of great service to him and to the race. We did this all the more readily because the city of

New York, which had already engaged him to appear, had recalled its invitation. It so happened that our celebration fell on Saturday night, the first of January being Sunday.

It also happened to be one night in the year in which all our churches have watch night meetings. Some of the ministers urged their congregations not to attend the Orchestra Hall meeting because they were having services in their churches. One of the leading ministers had announced that he too had a national speaker and they would not have to pay anything to hear him.

Still others announced that Mr. Trotter was a Democrat and that they owed him no support. Suffice it to say that the meeting was a failure in attendance. Had I not been able to have a white friend stand for the rent I would have been unable to open the doors of the hall. We held our meeting, however, and both Mr. William Thompson and Chief Justice Olson, tentative candidates for mayor, also made short addresses

Mr. Trotter was my guest for ten days. Through the efforts of friends he was invited to other meetings, and thus we succeeded in giving him the one hundred dollars I had promised. Not only this, but we made engagements for him as far north as Saint Paul, Minnesota; as far west as Omaha, Nebraska; as far south as Saint Louis, Missouri. When Mr. Trotter returned East it was with the assurance that the West had approved his course and upheld his hands.

The National Equal Rights League met in New York City, 20 September 1917, and I was the guest of Madam C. J. Walker when I went on as a delegate. Nothing startling took place in this session except that Madam Walker entertained the entire delegation royally. She was a woman who by hard work and persistent effort had succeeded in establishing herself and her business in New York City. She already had a town house, beautifully furnished, and had established beauty parlors and agents in and around New York City, thus giving demonstration of what a black woman who has vision and ambition can really do.

Madam Walker was even then building herself a home on the Hudson at a cost of many thousands of dollars. We drove out there almost every day, and I asked her on one occasion what on earth she would do with a thirty-room house. She said, "I want plenty of room in which to entertain my friends. I have worked so hard all of my life that I would like to rest."

I was very proud of her success, because I had met Madam Walker when she first started out eleven years before. I was one of the skeptics that paid little heed to her predictions as to what she was going to do. She had little or no education, and was never ashamed of having been a washerwoman earning a dollar and a half a day. To see her phenomenal rise made me take pride anew in Negro womanhood.

She maintained a wonderful home on 136th Street, and she had learned already how to bear herself as if to the manner born. She gave a dinner to the officers of the Equal Rights League and left the meeting a short time before it adjourned, in order to oversee dinner arrangements. When we were ushered into the dining room, Madam sat at the head of her table in her décolleté gown, with her butler serving dinner under her directions.

I was indeed proud to see what a few short years of success had done for a woman who had been without education and training. Her beautiful home on the Hudson was completed the next year, when Madam took possession, surrounded by prominent people from all over the country. It is a great pity to have to remember that she was permitted to enjoy its splendors less than a year after she moved in. Seven months from the day in which its doors were opened, they laid her away in her grave. The life had been too strenuous and the burden had become too heavy.

The next year the Equal Rights League came to Chicago for its annual meeting at my invitation. The trend of events seemed to show that the world war would not last much longer, and a motion prevailed that we call a national meeting to be held in Washington in December to arrange to send delegates to France to attend the Peace Conference which must follow the close of the war.

The idea met with great favor among the people of the country. And delegates were sent to Washington, at which time delegates and alternates were elected to go to Versailles, for the Armistice had already been signed between the close of the National Equal Rights League meeting in Chicago and the meeting of the Democracy Congress in Washington in December. Madam Walker and myself were the two women elected to go, and there were seven other persons. But none of us got to go because President Wilson forbade it.

The committee which was chosen to bring in nominations at first left out Mr. Trotter, on the ground that his presence would he objectionable to President Wilson. I asked the committee if they were going to allow President Wilson to select our delegates, and whom did they think deserved the right to go if not the man whose brain had conceived the idea. When the committee's report was brought in Mr. Trotter's name was included among those whose expenses were to be paid. Madam Walker and myself had been chosen as alternates with the distinct understanding that we would have to pay our own expenses.

I got the floor on a question of personal privilege and thanked the congress for the honor it had done me, but I regretted that the years I had spent in fighting the race's battles had made me financially unable to accept the honor which they had offered me. I therefore declined with thanks. Immediately a clamor arose; the committee's report was halted and an amendment was made by which both of the women named were included on the list of regular delegates.

Only Mr. Trotter got across after all, and he did so by subterfuge. He disguised himself as a cook and went across on a ship after he as well as the rest of us had been refused a passport.

Not only had I been elected by the Democracy Congress as a delegate, but Marcus Garvey's Universal Negro Improvement Association had already elected me in New York nearly a month before the convening of our congress. Mr. Garvey had visited Chicago a few years before, when he had recently come from Jamaica to accept an invitation that had been extended him by Booker T. Washington to visit Tuskegee.

Mr. Washington had passed away before he came; so Mr. Garvey was traveling from place to place to arouse the interest of other West Indians who were living in the United States to assist him in establishing an industrial school in Jamaica. He visited my husband's law office, and Mr. Barnett brought him home to dinner.

In the course of his conversation he said that ninety thousand of the people on the island of Jamaica were colored, and only fifteen thousand of them were white; yet the fifteen thousand white people possessed all the land, ruled the island, and kept the Negroes in subjection. I asked him what those ninety thousand Negroes were thinking about to be dominated in this way, and he said it was because they had no educational facilities outside of grammar-school work. He wanted to return to his native home to see if he could not help to change the situation there.

Instead he went to New York, began to hold street meetings, and got many of his fellow countrymen as well as American Negroes interested in his program of world-wide Negro unity. For a time it seemed as if his program would go through. Undoubtedly Mr. Garvey made an impression on this country as no Negro before him had ever done. He has been able to solidify the masses of our people and endow them with racial consciousness and racial solidarity.

Had Garvey had the support which his wonderful movement deserved, had he not become drunk with power too soon, there is no telling what the result would have been. Already the countries of the world were beginning to worry very much about the influence of his propaganda in Africa, in the West Indies, and in the United States. His month-long conference in New York City every August, bringing the dusky sons and daughters of Ham from all corners of the earth, attracted a great deal of attention.

It was during this time that he sent me an invitation to come to New York to deliver an address. I accepted the invitation and was met by him at the train on the afternoon of the evening on which I was to appear. The Universal Negro Improvement Association no longer met on the streets. It was housed in the Manhattan Casino, and I talked to an audience of nearly three thousand persons that evening.

Before this Mr. Garvey had spent a couple of hours acquainting me with his idea of establishing what he called the Black Star Line. He wanted me to present the matter that night, but I told him that it was too big an idea and would require more thought and preparation before it should be launched. He had shown me the restaurant that had been established, the newspaper which was circulating regularly each week, and one or two smaller ventures. He had complained that none of them were self-sustaining because they had not been able to obtain efficient help.

I knew that the work involved in a shipping business called for a much more complicated program than he had helpers to carry out, and I advised him to defer the matter. This he did not do, but presented it himself after I had finished my talk, with that eloquence for which he was so famous, and it took among the people like wildfire.

Perhaps if Mr. Garvey had listened to my advice he need not have undergone the humiliations which afterward became his. Perhaps all that was necessary in order to broaden and deepen his own outlook on life. It may be that even though he has been banished to Jamaica the seed planted here will yet spring up and bring forth fruit which will mean the deliverance of the black race—that cause which was so dear to his heart.

[1931]

XXII

A doer, a mover and a shaker who believed in the perseverance of African Americans and was one of its most profound race women was Mary McLeod Bethune (1875–1955). Born in South Carolina to parents who had been born into slavery, Bethune used her inestimable drive and strategic thinking to rise against incredible odds. Her lifelong commitment to the betterment of the race, especially black women, took center stage with her founding of the Daytona School for Negro Girls in 1904. That institution grew to become Bethune-Cookman College. Mary McLeod Bethune was president for four years of the National Association of Colored Women, and founder of the National Council of Negro Women in 1935, organizations that still live on today. Advisor to President Franklin Delano Roosevelt, and confidant of First Lady Eleanor Roosevelt, Bethune helped to set national policy and was a singularly powerful role model for black women and men. She was devoted to service to the race and often touted that the key to success for black people was through education. One of Bethune's favorite statements was, "Knowledge Is Power." In 1974 the Bethune Memorial Statue was erected in Washington, DC, making Mary McLeod Bethune the first black woman so honored. Some of her words of wisdom are shared here in her essay, "Clarifying Our Vision with the Facts," an address she gave at the annual meeting of the Association for the Study of Negro Life and History in Washington, DC, in 1937. Bethune was president of the association at the time. What do you find most compelling about her sage advice? Is she convincing in her faith in education as the key to success for the race? How do you as an individual move forward in taking advantage of Bethune's words of wisdom?

"Clarifying Our Vision with the Facts"

Mary McLeod Bethune

John Vandercook's *Black Majesty* tells the dramatic story of Jean Christophe, the black emperor of Haiti, and how he molded his empire with his bare hands out of the rugged cliffs and the unchained slaves of his native land. One night, in the midst of his Herculean struggles, Sir Home, his English Adviser, accused him of building too fast and working his subjects like slaves until they were discontent.... "For a long moment Christophe was silent....When he spoke, his full rich voice seemed suddenly old.

"You do not understand...."

He stopped again, seemed to be struggling for words. Then he went on:

"My race is as old as yours. In Africa, they tell me, there are as many blacks as there are white men in Europe. In Saint Dominique, before we drove the French out, there were a hundred Negroes to every master. But we were your slaves. Except in Haiti, nowhere in the world have we resisted you. We have suffered, we have grown dull, and, like cattle under a whip, we have obeyed. Why? Because we have no pride! And we have no pride because we have nothing to remember. Listen!"

He lifted his hand. From somewhere behind them was coming a faint sound of drumming, a monotonous, weird melody that seemed to be born of the heart of the dark, rearing hills, that rose and fell and ran in pallid echoes under the moon. The King went on.

"It is a drum, Sir Home. Somewhere my people are dancing. It is almost all we have. The drum, laughter, love for one another, and our share of courage. But we have nothing white men can understand. You despise our dreams and kill the snakes and break the little sticks you think are our gods. Perhaps if we had something we could show you, if we had something we could show ourselves, you would respect us and we might respect ourselves.

"If we had even the names of our great men! If we could lay our hands"—he thrust his out—"on things we've made, monuments and towers and palaces, we might find our strength, gentlemen. While I live I shall try to build that pride we need, and build in terms white men as well as black can understand! I am thinking of the future, not of now. I will teach pride if my teaching breaks every back in my kingdom."

Today I would salute in homage that wise old emperor. I bring you again his vibrant message. Our people cry out all around us like children lost in the wilderness. Hemmed in by a careless world, we are losing our homes and our farms and our jobs. We see vast numbers of us on the land sunk into the degradation of peonage and virtual slavery. In the cities, our workers are barred from the unions, forced to "scab" and often to fight with their very lives for work. About us cling the ever-tightening tentacles of poor wages, economic insecurity, sordid homes, labor by women and children, broken homes, ill health, delinquency and crime. Our children are choked by denied opportunity for health, for education, for work, for recreation, and thwarted with their ideals and ambitions still a-borning. We are scorned of men; they spit in our faces and laugh. We cry out in this awesome darkness. Like a clarion call, I invoke today again the booming voice of Jean Christophe—

"If we had something we could show you, if we had something we could show ourselves, you would respect us and we might respect ourselves. If we had even the names of our great men! If we could lay our hands on things we've made, monuments and towers and palaces, we might find our strength, gentlemen...."

If our people are to fight their way up out of bondage we must arm them with the sword and the shield and the buckler of pride—belief in themselves and their possibilities, based upon a sure knowledge of the achievements of the past. That knowledge and that pride we must give them "if it breaks every back in the kingdom."

Through the scientific investigation and objective presentation of the facts of our history and our achievement to ourselves and to all men, our Association for the Study of Negro Life and History serves to tear the veil from our eyes and allow us to see clearly and in true perspective our rightful place among all men. Through accurate research and investigation, we serve so to supplement, correct, re-orient and annotate the story of world progress as to enhance the standing of our group in the eyes of all men. In the one hand, we bring pride to our own; in the other, we bear respect from the others.

We must tell the story with continually accruing detail from the cradle to the grave. From the mother's knee and the fireside of the home, through the nursery, the kindergarten and the grade school, high school, college and university,—through the technical journals, studies and bulletins of the Association,—through newspaper, storybook and pictures, we must tell the thrilling story. When they learn the fairy tales of mythical king and queen and princess, we must let them hear, too, of the Pharaohs and African kings and the brilliant pageantry of the Valley of the Nile; when they learn of Caesar and his legions, we must teach them of Hannibal and his Africans; when they learn of Shakespeare and Goethe, we must teach them of Pushkin and Dumas. When they read of Columbus, we must introduce the Africans who touched the shores of America before Europeans emerged from savagery; when they are thrilled by Nathan Hale, baring his breast and crying: "I have but one life to give for my country," we must make their hearts leap to see Crispus Attucks stand and fall for liberty on Boston Common with the red blood of freedom streaming down his breast. With the Tragic Era we give them Black Reconstruction; with Edison, we give them Jan Matzeliger; with John Dewey, we place Booker T. Washington; above the folk-music of the cowboy and the hill-billy, we place the spiritual and the "blues"; when they boast of Maxfield Parrish, we show them E. Simms Campbell. Whatever man has done, we have done—and often, better. As we tell this story, as we present to the world the facts, our pride in racial achievement grows, and our respect in the eyes of all men heightens.

Certainly, too, it is our task to make plain to ourselves the great story of our rise in America from "less than the dust" to the heights of sound achievement. We must recount in accurate detail the story of how the Negro population has grown from a million in 1800 to almost 12 million in 1930. The Negro worker is today an indispensable part of American agriculture and industry. His labor has built the economic empires of cotton, sugar cane and tobacco; he furnishes nearly 12 per cent of all American bread-winners, one-third of all servants, one-fifth of all farmers. In 1930, we operated one million farms and owned 750,000 homes. Negroes operate today over 22,000 business establishments with over 27 million dollars in yearly receipts and payrolls of more than five million dollars. Negroes manufacture more than 60 different commodities. They spend annually for groceries over two billion dollars, a billion more for clothes, with total purchasing power in excess of 4 and 1/2 billion dollars. Negro churches have more than five million members in 42,500 organizations, owning 206 million dollars' worth of property and spending 43 million dollars a year. Some 360,000 Negroes served in the World War, with 150,000 of them going to France. Negroes are members of legislatures in 12 states; three or more states have black judges on the bench and a federal judge has recently been appointed to the Virgin Islands. Twenty-three Negroes have sat in Congress, and there is one member of the House at present. Under the "New Deal," a number of well qualified Negroes hold administrative posts.

Illiteracy has decreased from about 95 per cent in 1865 to only 16.3 per cent in 1930. In the very states that during the dark days of Reconstruction prohibited the education of Negroes by law, there are today over 2 million pupils in 25,000 elementary schools, 150,000 high school pupils in 2,000 high schools and 25,000 students in the more than 100 Negro colleges and universities. Some 116 Negroes have been elected to Phi Beta Kappa in white Northern colleges; over 60 have received the degree of Doctor of Philosophy from leading American universities and 97 Negroes are mentioned in Who's Who in America. It is the duty of our Association to tell the glorious story of our past and of our marvelous achievement in American life over almost insuperable obstacles.

From this history, our youth will gain confidence, self-reliance and courage. We shall thereby raise their mental horizon and give them a base from which to reach out higher and higher into the realm of achievement. And as we look about us today, we know that they must have this courage and self-reliance. We are beset on every side with heart-rending and fearsome difficulties.

Recently, in outlining to the President of the United States the position of the Negro in America, I saw fit to put it this way: "The great masses of Negro workers are depressed and unprotected in the lowest levels of agriculture and domestic service while black workers in industry are generally barred from the unions and grossly discriminated against. The housing and living conditions of the Negro masses are sordid and unhealthy; they live in constant terror of the mob, generally shorn of their constitutionally guaranteed right of suffrage, and humiliated by the denial of civil liberties. The great masses of Negro youth are offered only one fifteenth the educational opportunity of the average American child."

These things also we must tell them, accurately, realistically and factually. The situation we face must be defined, reflected and evaluated. Then, armed with the pride and courage of his glorious tradition, conscious of his positive contribution to American life, and enabled to face clear-eyed and unabashed the actual situation before him, the Negro may gird his loins and go forth to battle to return "with their shields or on them." And so today I charge our Association for the Study of Negro Life and History to carry forward its great mission to arm us with the facts so that we may face the future with clear eyes and a sure vision. Our Association may say again with Emperor Jean Christophe: "While I live I shall try to build that pride we need, and build in terms white men as well as black can understand! I am thinking of the future, not of now. I will teach pride if my teaching breaks every back in my Kingdom."

[31 October 1937]

XXIII

Father Divine (c 1883–1965), originally named George Baker, was a dapper dresser, well spoken, and a charismatic leader who developed a cult-like following by the 1930s. Divine used his skillful oratory and philosophy of life to propel him as a religious leader. Although he would later claim to be God, even those who did not accept his declaration of divinity found him powerfully persuasive. Divine urged blacks to become self-sufficient and to develop along the line of what he termed "perfection." He established Peace Missions and Heavens, largely in the Northeast, with his headquarters in Harlem. These cooperatives followed his strict orders and commands. His organization developed its own business establishments, including cleaners, restaurants, a coal company, and other black-run organizations whose earnings went to Father Divine. He provided great banquets and invited the Harlem community to partake of the mountains of food for pennies or nothing if an individual was unable to pay. These gestures, particularly during the Great Depression in the 1930s, made him seem larger than life. It, however, did not convince most skeptics that he was God. Divine would later repudiate color and warned black folk that they must begin to see themselves without any link to color or race. Divine did engage in politics and in the 1940s he and his organization supported the effort for anti-lynching legislation. But for the most part, they pushed home the doctrine of self-sufficiency and economic independence. According to Divine, this would be the only thing that could save black folk from themselves. In the essay presented here, Father Divine gives a glimpse into his philosophy of life in the course of action that he contended would lead blacks to a promised land here on earth. What do you think? Why do you think so many African Americans were moved by him to the point of becoming active members in his organization? Does the Divine philosophy of life and economic advancement make sense for contemporary society?

"We Believe in Individual Independence. We Believe in Serving the Cause of Humanity Through the Cooperative System"

Father Divine

"There is not any such thing as a general organization. Each individual unit is an independent unit. Each individual owning and purchasing a piece of property, after it is purchased, it is then the property of the individual himself. It is an independent unit; it is not in any way obligated to the other connections where I may be represented as FATHER DIVINE'S PEACE MISSION. It is merely known as FATHER DIVINE'S PEACE

MISSION MOVEMENT because of the Spirit and the Teaching of CHRIST as exemplified by ME. Those of MY followers who have selected MY Teaching as the Fundamental and have endeavored to put into practice the Golden Rule according to MY Teaching, it is commonly known among the people as FATHER DIVINE'S PEACE MISSION. But there is no such thing as any surplus coming back to any headquarters, as has been said by people who did not understand the Movement. Not at all! Not on any occasion! Each individual unit is an independent unit. If you yourself, or any other person, would desire to buy property together with one or two or more, that particular unit would be an absolutely independent unit, but it would be your privilege if you wish to, to adhere to MY Teaching as emphasized by ME."

"As a Sample and as an Example for you I stand, that you might recognize GOD'S PRESENCE and be persistent in your ambition—not so much for self gains, but to help others to gain! Do not go into business to see what you can get out of it, but go into it to see how much you can put in it. Now isn't that Wonderful! Do not go into business for the purpose of seeing how much you will gain, but go in it to see how much you can give. Forget about the gaining and receiving and think about the giving instead of the getting. Live it and express it scientifically and perfectly; the reaction of such will give you a desirable result."

"As a Minister of the Gospel as though being One among them, I have not taken up a collection! I have not done any soliciting nor begging, but so freely to the children of men I have given good health, good will, a good appetite, good manners and good behavior! I have given them ALL success and all prosperity! I HAVE given them life, liberty and the reality of happiness in Europe, Asia, Australia and in Africa.

"Then I say, it is a privilege to live in such a conviction and such a recognition, realizing GOD'S Actual Presence as no longer being a supposition but as being the very Essence and Life Substance of all creation!

"I was just thinking about, so many people think we are here for the dollars and cents and some have had the audacity to say, 'FATHER DIVINE takes all of your money!' But oh, how glorious it is to realize, I have taken all of your infirmities! I have taken all of your sickness and affliction without the cost of a penny! I have established your going in the land of the living and I have made the way successful before you and prosperous so that I, as the poorest among men, AM making many rich."

"We usually have a-full and a-plenty to eat. That is the first thought, if you please. Plenty of comfort and convenience! Then the cost of living is cut from forty to seventy-five to eighty percent by MY Cooperative System and by unifying the people together, causing them to love one another.

"When you live in self and selfishness you have to have a house for a person different from you, if you think he is of a different complexion. You have to have a room different from theirs if the other person who does not look like you does not love you, because he does not wish to sleep in the same room.

"I AM talking economics! Living and demonstrating the significance of MY Cooperative System and proving to the world conclusively, you can then able to stand against any outside or inside invasion if you cooperate with MY economic system according to MY Cooperative System. Can you not see the mystery?

"From an economic point of view you should not be in lacks, wants and limitations, and yet I would take the whole nation off the relief completely and give them positions and make them self-supporting and independent, self-respecting and law-abiding citizens; I would bring an end to all graft and greed and bring an end to the system of wasting and being destructive with foodstuffs and other commodities, and I would establish their going in the land of the living. Where there is a land of plenty, I would cause them to have a-plenty and to spare for each and everybody.

"There is a-plenty to do, a-plenty of labor, a-plenty of business and a-plenty of trade. All can be put into expression and be giving active service. If your business, profession, if your labor and your trade will become to be absolutely unselfish and work cooperatively, the very Spirit of MY Presence will lift up a standard so effectively that the spirit of progressiveness will be in evidence among you, even as I have it among ourselves and among MY immediate staff."

"You all have heard ME tell the old familiar story to those of you who have heard ME so long: The old kobold said, 'live not for yourself alone!' When you live for others conscientiously and sincerely, you need not claim anything; you will be blessed! I have experienced it! MOTHER is experiencing it! MOTHER is not claiming anything besides ME! She does not claim houses and land! She does not claim yachts and airplanes! She does not claim anything, as an individual, for Her own self, as a Person; therefore, She refuses even as I do, to have anything from a legalistic, mortal-minded point of view!"

"Of course, I AM not advocating so much charity. I AM and I will establish a standard in the midst of the people and, I will even establish it legally, that will not allow so many charities and so many bread lines to be established, but we will have more work for the people, and give the people work, that they might be self-sustaining! So many charities have caused so many crooks. They are incubators for crooks and for loafers of the different types, and tramps and everything else that is undesirable; but we will eventually establish throughout this country a standard of living, and giving the people a living wage, and see that they have work to that every person that has his health and strength might be employed in some way, in a practical way, that will be useful to GOD and to man. It is indeed Wonderful.

"That is what we will do! — although I may not have said so much, or spoken it so much to the officials, it is an issue we will now put through! We will break up so many bread lines, and so many charitable institutions taking people and feeding them for nothing, causing them to become more impractical and untrue and unreal, and we will make them practical and useful and law-abiding citizens, that they might be self-sustaining, and that they might know that they are independent so long as they have their health and their strength, and I will see that their bodies be well! It is indeed Wonderful.

"This is the next issue on footing! It is indeed Wonderful — and we will put it through! We will have more work, and more jobs opened up than ever before, and all we want you to do is to be willing to work and willing to be profitable.

"Now remember, that does not confine the people collectively to common labor nor hard labor particularly, but whatsoever profession, work, classification, or class of work you can do justifiably in a more profitable way, and be more useful to GOD and to man or to mankind generally than that other — that is the thing for you to do. Every person after his own trade, profession, or classification, according to his qualification, for every man shall receive his reward according as his works may be!"

"The nation must be rescued from the alien powers of graft, greed and division. It must return to the Spirit of Freedom by which Democracy was established.

"It is for this cause that we, the people, are working out the freedom of the whole nation by imbibing the Spirit of it and producing it socially, economically and politically. We cannot be free if we are burdened by such binding laws as the Social Security Act, insurance laws and numerous other laws of economic and moral oppression. We do not believe in putting our trust in laws that deny us our privilege to serve GOD according to the dictates of our own conscience. There is no security in a law that robs the people, not only of more money, but of their faith in the fundamental documents of Americanism.

"We protest all types of insurance laws, and MY followers do not even insure their automobiles and homes, trusting in the Supreme Law of GOD to protect them; for if GOD cannot protect them, money cannot. Now the paying of taxes is an entirely different story. Such is constitutional; in short evangelical, but where laws are instituted through graft and mismanagement, and are detrimental to the morale of the people, we oppose same and refuse to bring ourselves under them.

"Nevertheless, as you see, MY followers are able to express their independence, even on jobs they may not be skilled in, for they are willing to give up such positions they are trained in, and to accept other work for their conscientious religious convictions; and as you see, GOD is with them for they express an independency and a security the average man does not have."

" … Not a true follower of MINE owes any man a dime! Not a true follower of MINE will buy anything on credit or on the installment plan! It is Wonderful! I had a letter today—just recently, whichever—where one is buying a home, and he said he was paying cash for it, because we are putting all mankind on the Cash-and-Carry System!"

"I believe that the subjects of the nation should be equivalently independent, and should stand for their independence even as the country declares and stands for her independence!

"But individually, severally and collectively we refuse to take up a collection; we refuse to do any soliciting, borrowing or begging! … And yet MY followers have unlimited purchasing power! … Our Churches have so much money, they purchase personal and real property into the millions of dollars, through the donations of the immediate followers or church members to the Church! Since they do not have money for a selfish purpose, when they donate to the Church, the Church, in turn, cooperatively purchases personal and real property, such as the Divine Lorraine Hotel up here on North Broad Street! I know you have heard of it since you have been here; and the Tracy Hotel, and other properties, which would belong to the Church directly; but because the followers donated the money to the Church, the Church did not need it directly for a Church, as a Church—the owners who donated the money to the Church derive the benefit of it by the purchase of personal and real property in their own names, who donated the money. They are the owners of these hotels and properties! I do not own anything. And they are independent, as you see here! …

"In Bermuda, Australia and other places MY followers are forbidden to solicit, beg or steal, or buy anything on credit or on the installment plan! …

"They are forbidden to buy a hotel with a mortgage on it, but pay cash as you go and owe no man, and express your individual independence even as our country declared it—her independence—as a nation!"

"We really fulfilled a great part of the Scripture when the Lend-Lease System was instituted into Government, for it is written of you, yea, of those who obey GOD and keep HIS Commandments:

'You shall lend to many nations, but you will not borrow.'"

"Can you not see the Mystery? This country has been lending to many nations, but the time will come when she will not borrow not even from her own subjects, for the way will be made possible through right living and through a just and righteous administration of government and representatives thereof, that all will live exactly according to the Constitution and according to the Declaration of Independence and each subject will be independent even as the country declared it as a nation. And our Government and its representatives will not see scarcity but abundance.

"I need not say more at this instance, but I thought to call your attention to the fact concerning the Mystery of living the abundant life, of paying as you go and of owing no man! You cannot be independent by buying on credit and on the installment plan! You cannot be independent by borrowing and soliciting and always trying to get something. It is more blessed to give than to receive! For this is the Mystery of the Law of the Spirit of Life that CHRIST gave, and those who live it and express it can live thereby."

"I do not believe those who have instituted such laws in government as to destroy foodstuff, to express mass destruction by the wholesale, is the inspiration of true Americanism, for Americanism speaketh on the plan and the method of GOD and according to HIS Word!

"Jesus said on the ground, 'Take up the fragments that nothing be waste!'

"This was an abstract expression of what I AM requesting all creation of every, nation, every language, every tongue and every people, for that which I say to one I AM saying to all creation: 'Take up the fragments that nothing be waste!'

"Even though JESUS had fed the five thousand with two small fishes and five barley loaves, this—I mean five thousand men, besides the women and children, with two small fishes and five barley loaves—there was quite a little left, was there not? Jesus, as an Expresser of mass production, could not produce limitedly. As a great Multiplier, as the Creation's Supplier, HE desired to increase and multiply bountifully because HE was obliged to do it by nature since the abundance of the fullness was in evidence by His increase and by multiplying the supply HE had there! Can you not see the mystery? But yet by this great mass production, having much more than was necessary for the sustenance and supply of those who were there then, HE had the power to mass produce and multiply again and again, but HE said:

'Take up the fragments that nothing
"This was an expression as I say for all creation—
'Take up the fragments that nothing be waste!'

"Do not be wasteful and destructive but express the spirit of mass production. That is what I AM talking about!

"It was through the undermining, no doubt, of some fifth columnists and others who desired to undermine this government in its production, taught them in some way and bewitched them to say, 'Destroy a whole lot of foodstuff and become to be mass destructive representatives instead of mass producers!'...

"By this they caused nation-wide destruction of foodstuff and left hundreds of hungry children and women and men to be suffering all over this land!

"It was the lack of understanding! And I believe, as the Apostle said, 'Who has bewitched you that you would not (or will not) obey the truth?'

"I believe they have been bewitched in some way of expression, or in other words, beguiled by the chicanery-ness or the trickery-ness of others."

"I AM not bothering about what men may think or say. Mass destruction causes scarcity, limitations, lacks and wants: but mass production will cause the abundance of the fullness to be in evidence in each and everyone's experience. Therefore mass production will increase you and multiply you and replenish you of the scarcity of that which you have lost and others through mass destruction. Can you not see the mystery?

"When the famine shall have overwhelmed the land universally and men are in lacks, wants and limitations, this light of this understanding shall have in storehouse for the children of all nations to come and partake of the limitless blessings through this Co-operative System, by instituting for the spirit and system of mass destruction, mass construction and mass production, that we might have a-full and a-plenty for ourselves and for others mentally and spiritually, I say, because we are building up, and also mass construction with mass instruction. Hence, information will be taught in these borders of wisdom, knowledge and understanding and we will have a-full and a-plenty of wisdom, knowledge and understanding by teaching and emphasizing and demonstrating mass instruction."

"I believe in private ownership of enterprise; I believe in the private ownership of personal and real property, but I believe in you acquiring the private ownership of enterprise, of personal and of real property honestly. I do not believe in you taking the advantage of others to acquire your respective aim, but I do believe that a person who is qualified to advance and has the skill and the ability to increase, his holdings and even his ability to acquire more skill and more understanding, more professions and more trades, I believe in mass production from every side! Aren't you glad!

"So I do not believe in curtailing production mentally, spiritually nor physically, but I believe in mass production and in increasing and multiplying!

"The person who has the ability is the person who should have the opportunity. The person who is impractical, unprofitable and good for nothing, why should he acquire the profitable and the practical and good-for-something's enterprises and take charge of them? But let every man have a chance to make his respective advances and GOD will bless them if they are ambitious and courageous!

"I mentioned many years ago, shortly after coming in contact indirectly with Huey Long, that I want not charity, neither do I endorse the sharing of the wealth in the way of taking it from someone else unjustly, but I want a chance! Give ME and all others a chance! If they have the ambition and determination they will make their respective advances, if they have a chance to make the advances! That is what I AM talking about! But some consider because a wealthy man has money, legalistically they should take it away from him. The underground, underworld man, he comes along and considers if you have money he should take it illegally. One may use the law and the other may not use the law.

"I believe in mass production in your respective business, profession and trade. I believe in every person advancing himself and improving himself for the benefit of humanity generally. So these thoughts are well worth considering. Hence, I may not get the endorsement of a good many of the common people, but I know, as the last speaker said, I shall have MY Way! I shall not be discouraged and I shall not be disturbed until I shall have brought all government universally as I have it right here jurisdictionally! Aren't you glad! We all shall live in peaceful and quiet resting places and we all shall live in unison, and yet each and every one shall have a chance to make his respective advances, his respective advance. When this is done you shall know the Truth and Truth shall set you free!"

"That little composition originally composed as 'Count Your Blessings,' but by the transposed version of MY Presence and MY Coming, I bring these thoughts to your consideration: the only hope of your redemption is through sharing your blessings, and sharing them one by one. The blessings of GOD if hoarded, they will become to be stagnant, and if they become to be stagnant, they will also become to be impractical, and if they become to be impractical, they will become to be non-progressive, non-increasable and non-multipliable. It will be a matter of impossibility for your blessings to be increased and multiplied continually. And if they are stagnant, they cease to be increased and multiplied, by the stagnation, that will take place in them as briefly as you allow them to become to be stagnant in expression.

"When you hoard up for yourselves, money, and refuse to put your means of exchange to an exchange, when it is actually an expression for the very same purpose— of which I AM stressing, you are violating the Law of Life, the Law of Progressiveness. But, by putting your means of exchange to work and putting it into circulation, causing it to go around according to the plan and purpose of GOD and man, then and there you are using your means of exchange for the purpose for which it was created. The means of exchange should be put into circulation, to cause you and others to be successful and prosperous. By so doing, you will be using your means of exchange according to the Gospel. Now isn't that Wonderful!

"The average person never stops to think of that, the mystery of putting your means of exchange to an exchange, and into circulation, which it would be ordinarily considered a thrifty person, to get all he can and keep all he gets. But to the extreme reverse, refuse! By sharing your blessings, I mean, sharing them one by one, you will be putting into practice the 'Profit Sharing Plan.' This is not merely a law of the world of commerce, but it is the Law of GOD in man, that they might work in accord with the Profit Sharing Plan by putting their means of exchange into circulation; and by giving MORE apparently than what is due, you will always be receiving the same, for such will be due you."

[1933–1950]

XXIV

Fighting from within the system to affect change was the work and legacy of attorney Charles Hamilton Houston (1895–1950). Born in Washington, DC, he attended Dunbar High School, then on to Amherst College, graduating Phi Beta Kappa in 1915. He taught for a while before going into the US Army during World War I and serving as a lieutenant. Surviving the war, he pledged to devote himself to bringing about change and equality in America. After obtaining his law education at Harvard, he became dean of the Howard University Law School and turned his classroom and the school into a clinic for civil rights litigation. Houston focused on issues that needed to be addressed throughout the United States to bring an end to the color line. Later generations would refer to him affectionately as "the man who killed Jim Crow." He was, indeed, the individual who put together a masterful game plan, a string of Supreme Court victories that would serve as legal precedents, for the frontal assault against the color line and the "separate but equal" doctrine that had ruled supreme since the 1896 rendering of *Plessy versus Ferguson*. Those precedents included successful suits to equalize the pay of black teachers with their white counterparts, and to force educational institutions and state governments to provide equal educational opportunity to its black citizens such as in the case of *Donald Gaines Murray versus Maryland* in 1936. Houston did not live to see the *Brown Decision* of 1954. He did, however, predict the coming success in a personal recording he made just prior to his death. The recording is transcribed here for the reader to imbibe. Do you find Houston's words inspiring? What does he, by example, convey to you about the need for diligent work and persistence in the pursuit of one's goals?

"A Personal Message"

Charles Hamilton Houston

There come times when it is possible [to know] the results of a contest of a battle of a lawsuit or of a struggle long before the final event has taken place. And so far as our struggle for civil rights is concerned, I am not worried about that now. The struggle for civil rights in America is won.

What I am more concerned about is the fact that the Negro shall not be content simply with demanding an equal share in the existing system. It seems to me that his fundamental responsibility and his historical challenge is to use his weight, since he has less to lose in the present system than anybody else or any other group, to make sure that the system which shall survive in the United States of America—I don't care what system you call it—shall be a system which guarantees justice and freedom for everyone.

The way I usually put it is 'sure we are being invited now in to take a front seat, but there is no particular honor in being invited to take a front seat at one's own funeral.' So in the office when I get discouraged, when things go wrong, I look up at this picture [picture of his wife and son] and then realize: one, that we are fighting a system, that we are trying to remove the lid off of the oppressed peoples everywhere.

And also I regard what I am doing, and my work as a lawyer, not as an end in itself but simply as the means of a technician probing in the courts—which are products of the existing system—how far the existing system will permit the exercise of freedom before it clamps down. And I have seen several instances as to the limitations on which the existing system, as represented by its courts, will go.

Beyond that, the appeal must be through the education of the masses themselves to educate them in an intelligent use of their own power. And there again we go to the process of teaching, the process of the open meeting, the process of carrying the message to the masses, of interpreting it to them so that they may recognize the relationship between the particular issue and the whole broad aspect.

Someday as things get worse, and I don't see how they can avoid getting worse because we are in a situation where we have got to have an expanding economy, and our markets are contracting and we are losing our markets, we are losing the power to exploit colonial and other peoples. The struggle for freedom having accomplished itself politically in Asia will soon shift to Africa. So that I say 'I can't see how we can avoid a crisis.' And we have seen enough in the present day to know that the first reaction of the powers that be is going to be silence and oppression, censorship and other things.

They are going to try to cut off the intellectuals from the masses. So that in this day while there is still little time, the primary task is to probe, to struggle, but even more than probing and struggling, to teach, to teach the masses to think for themselves, to teach the masses to know their place and to recognize their power and to apply it intelligently. So this is the significance of the great open air protest meeting.

I hope that you will get the same pleasure out of this picture that I have gotten. And I hope that you will get the same inspiration because I know that you are interested in basically the same things that I have always been interested in. And I hope that you will turn this picture over to Bo when he gets to be a man and tell him that it was one of the great influences in his daddy's life.

[1949]

XXV

Charles Hamilton Houston worked to improve the system using its legal foundation. An individual who significantly upped the ante to improve the condition of African Americans as a lawmaker within the system was Adam Clayton Powell, Jr. (1908–1972). Powell was born to a highly privileged black family headed by his father, Adam Clayton Powell, Sr. Powell, Jr. attended Colgate University in upstate New York and after graduating from there went on to receive a Masters degree in religious studies from Columbia University. He often, during those years at Colgate, passed for white, or as he said, "put on his white face." Powell was a master at beating the system at its own game. He had the temerity to defy his father who was pastor of the Abyssinian Baptist Church, one of the largest congregations in the United States. Powell, Jr. let it be known that he would not succeed his father to the pastorship unless he consented to his intended marriage to Isabel Washington. His father considered Washington to be absolutely inappropriate as a minister's wife because she was an entertainer, a showgirl. Powell, Jr. got his way and married Isabel Washington, his first wife. In later years there would be two more wives, including the famed jazz pianist Hazel Scott. Adam Clayton Powell, Jr. was an activist, feisty, and defiant, and, by the definition of the times, "an uppity Negro" to whites, in particular those of the South. Powell organized and led in the 1930s the "Don't Buy Where You Can't Work" campaign against Harlem white merchants and their practice of not hiring blacks. With that battle won, he took on other employers throughout Harlem to bring an end to their Jim Crow practices. Powell was a consistent force during the era of the Great Depression working for the people and organizing them to better their condition. He became the Democratic representative of New York's Harlem in 1945, and continued in that capacity to 1971. He served on the all-important Committee on Education and Labor; becoming chair of the committee from 1961 through 1967. This vitally important committee dispensed hundreds of millions of dollars annually that were earmarked for education and labor, and made Powell the most powerful African American in the nation. As a legislator he routinely attached what became known as the "Powell Amendment" to every piece of legislation that came out of the House of Representatives. That amendment, which stated that one could not use the funds from all the people to benefit some of the people at the exclusion of others, became a hallmark of his legislative years. Powell would have his disagreements with Martin Luther King, Jr. and his approach to the elevation of the race. Powell considered himself far more practical and believed that real change came from exerting power within the system. In "The First Bad Nigger in Congress," Powell recounts his early years in Congress and challenges to the status quo. What do you think of black legislators today when you compare them to Adam Clayton Powell, Jr.?

"First Bad Nigger in Congress"

Adam Clayton Powell, Jr.

I stood on the Floor of the House of Representatives at the opening of the 79th Congress, on January, 3, 1945, and lifted my hand along with my four hundred and thirty-four colleagues, swearing to uphold the Constitution of the United States. In that Constitution there are certain guarantees based upon the Bill of Rights and the Declaration of Independence: "We hold these Truths to be self-evident...."

Far off in strange lands men were fighting to make this world safe for democracy, yet they fought with complete and rigid segregation in the armed forces, sustained by the Supreme Commander of Allied Forces in Europe, Dwight David Eisenhower: "Negro and white soldiers could not fight together." But in the Battle of the Bulge, Hitler's Panzer divisions, striking with power, began to penetrate and decimate the white fighting man. In desperation, all thought of segregation was lost. Black men, who had hitherto been confined to waging this war in the 310th Quartermaster Corps, the 238th Salvage Collection Company, and the 303rd Rail Head Company, men who had been denied the opportunity to learn the intricacies of modern arms, suddenly had guns thrust into their hands. With the courage that all men are heir to, regardless of color, they fought and they bled and they died, side by side, with whites and the bulge was turned back and victory came closer.

This, then, was our country fighting a war to preserve democracy, but with an undemocratically segregated Navy, Army, and Air Force. Abroad the United States was preaching "the century of the common man" and the "Four Freedoms," yet it was denying any of these freedoms at home, even in the nation's capital. America was talking about the creation of a new world while its conscience was filled with guilt.

In that capital, along the banks of the quiet and muddy Potomac, witness and testimony were given by night and by day to the emasculation of the Bill of Rights and the Constitution that I had sworn to uphold, even when there was no upholding being done by those in high places. The dream of the Founding Fathers was becoming a faint mirage and "these truths" were no longer self-evident because truth had been banished from the land. There was evil there in Washington on January 3, 1945—the evil that comes when one preaches and fails to practice, when one proclaims and does not act, when the outside is clean and the inside is filled with filth. This was Washington, D.C., capital of the "sweet land of liberty."

And in all the "sweet land" there was but one Negro Congressman, William L. Dawson. Arriving from Chicago in 1943, he found not a single hotel that would give him a room. Nor was there a restaurant where he could eat or a lunch counter where he could buy a cup of coffee. Black men were dying for good far afield, for a good they themselves didn't know and that some would never know. High above Washington on the great dome of the Capitol, was the statue of Freedom, and yet below that statue there was no true freedom for people with the "wrong" skin color. For this man who had come from Chicago, a member of the United States Congress, was even discouraged from eating in his own dining room, although the sign read "Reserved for Members of Congress Only." Even the black men and women who toiled for the government could not eat in the government employees' dining room, but stood abjectly in the corridor, waiting for their handouts from a window—even while some received the fateful wire, "We regret to inform you that your son …"

Under the massive, glittering chandelier, reflecting its myriad prismatic lights, with his own polished dome, sat "Mr. Sam." The room was not too large. It had only one large desk and two chairs, but there was a smell of greatness in the air. Through the doorway had come all the men of the centuries whose names little boys sitting in stiff chairs behind plain wooden desks were taught never to forget. I sat there one early January day, thrilled but not awed, nervous but not afraid, excited yet inwardly calm, and the Speaker of the House of Representatives, the Honorable Sam Rayburn of Texas, said, "Adam, everybody down here expects you to come with a bomb in both hands. Now don't do that, Adam. Oh, I know all about you and I know that you can't be quiet very long, but don't throw those bombs. Just see how things operate here. Take your time. Freshmen members of Congress are supposed not to be heard and not even to be seen too much. There are a lot of good men around here. Listen to what they have to say, drink it all in, get reelected a few more times, and then start moving. But for God's sake, Adam, don't throw those bombs."

I said, "Mr. Speaker, I've got a bomb in each hand, and I'm going to throw them right away." He almost died laughing. Meanwhile he was chewing tobacco—and how he could spit: it was said that he could hit a spittoon six to eight feet away without missing.

After that first exchange Mr. Sam and I became close friends. Over the years we had many chats about religion and finally I talked him into joining the church. He was baptized about a year or two before he died.

The New York Herald Tribune reported that on December 17, 1944, over four thousand people packed the Golden Gate Auditorium in New York City to send me off to Congress. In my platform I outlined that I would push for fair racial practices, fight to do away with restrictive covenants and discrimination in housing, fight for the passage of a national Fair Employment Practices Commission and for the abolition of the poll tax, fight to make lynching a Federal crime, do away with segregated transportation, undergird the Thirteenth, Fourteenth, and Fifteenth Amendments to the Constitution, protest the defamation of any group—Protestant, Catholic, Jew, or Negro, fight every form of imperialism and colonialism, and support "all legislation, one hundred percent, to win the war, to win the peace, pro-labor and pro-minority."

The two symbols of the fight against this program were both from Mississippi: Bilbo in the Senate and Rankin in the House. I said, finally, that I was going to Washington to "baptize Rankin or drown him." John E. Rankin was the smartest parliamentarian in the House of Representatives, except for Vito Marcantonio. Just a little taller than Marcantonio, he had a shock of very curly gray hair and a swarthy complexion. Because of the texture of his hair and his color, I always felt he fought Negroes so much because he might have had Negro blood in his veins. Many a time when Rankin was waving his arms and giving vent to one of his tirades against "nigras," Marcantonio would walk down the middle aisle, pass in front of the well in which Rankin was speaking and whisper out of the corner of his mouth, "You look more like a Negro than Powell." Invariably this caused the old man to turn even darker with rage.

Rankin was against everything progressive. Moreover, he had missed killing the Draft Bill by just one vote. He believed more in Hitlerism than he did in Abraham Lincoln and Franklin Delano Roosevelt. On January 8, 1945, he issued a statement saying my election was a "disgrace" and that he would not "let Adam C. Powell sit by me."

The aisle down the center of the House divides the Republicans from the Democrats, although House members cross this aisle whenever they want to and sit wherever they desire. But unlike the Senate, no one seat is assigned to anyone. On hearing Rankin's remarks, I immediately stated that his presence was "distasteful" to me and that the only people "fit for him to sit by are Hitler and Mussolini." On January 10 The Philadelphia Record editorially agreed with me and concluded: "Let's put Rankin in a section by himself and mark it 'Contagious Disease.'"

Whenever Rankin entered the Chamber, I followed after him, sitting next to him or as close as I could. One day the press reported that he moved five times. Finally, on January 15 after a Party caucus, he had to shut up. The newspaper P.M., now defunct, reported: "In order to inherit the un-American power that Martin Dies had previously, Rankin would have to accept Powell and his appointment to the Committee on Education and the Committee on Labor."

One day early in my first term, as I rolled down to Washington on the Congressional Limited, the incessant click-clacking of the wheels seemed to be drumming out the thought in my mind: "What should I do? What could I do? What would I do?" ... over and over. I faced the knowledge that I was only one of four hundred and thirty-five members in the House and ninety-six in the Senate. Yet millions were depending on me to do a task for them, and not just the people in my District.

As soon as I was elected to Congress my mail, involving cases for me to handle, people for me to see, came in such large quantities from behind the color curtain of America that the work of my own constituents had to suffer. Millions of Negro people in the South had no Congressman to speak for them, no one to whom they could turn with their basic problems of discrimination and segregation, no one who would even handle their simple cases. They were the disenfranchised, the ostracized, the exploited, and when they pressed upon me their many problems of many years, I could not refuse them because I love all people.

Then there were the problems of the people of the District of Columbia, with a population which was then close to being half Negro. They too had no vote and no one to speak for them. The District of Columbia Committee was then ruled by men who came from areas that were against the Negroes' dreams and hopes. They too I had to serve.

So there I was, minister of one of the largest Protestant churches in our country, elected Congressman from one of the largest ghettos in the world, and drafted as the Congressman-at-Large for half of the District of Columbia and millions of people across the Mason-Dixon Line... "What should I do? What could I do? What would I do?"

When Clarence Darrow was a member of the Illinois Legislature, he said, "I soon discovered that no independent man who fights for what he thinks is right can succeed in passing legislation. He can kill bad bills by a vigorous fight and publicity, but he can get nothing passed." There was only one thing I could do—hammer relentlessly, continually crying aloud even if in a wilderness, and force open, by sheer muscle power, every closed door. Once inside, I had to pierce the consciences of men so that somewhere someone would have to answer; somewhere something would have to be done ...

for there is no way for an independent man who fights for what he thinks is right to succeed in passing legislation.

The mechanism of legislation in the United States Congress is a wondrous labyrinth of frustration. Numerous devices, each hallowed by tradition, enable a willful minority to frustrate the majority's program. The filibuster in the Senate, the gag rule in the House; the tremendous powers of committee chairmen; the enormous influence of such key committees as Rules, Ways and Means, and Appropriations; the ability of committee conferees to "sell out" the positions of their respective Houses—all these and more are powers for good or for evil. In either case, however, Congressmen without extreme seniority are seldom able to accomplish much of their legislative program.

There are many annoyances and abuses of the rules. For example, when one rises to make a speech after receiving a special order to do so, no one is there to listen, for the special orders come at the close of all business when weary men are returning to their homes and offices, and only the Speaker or his appointed Temporary Speaker is present. The galleries have emptied. You stand there with a document on which you have labored and you look around and no one is there to hear you except two or three members of the press. This is usual at all times for all members. So, when you read about an important speech on foreign policy or some other earth-shaking matter of grave concern to the nation, frequently no one has heard it. Often times it is not even delivered. Under the rules of Congress, by a curious device called "extension of remarks," one needs only to read two or three words of his opening remarks and can insert the rest into the Congressional Record as if the full text had actually been delivered orally.

In the course of debate men can say vile and ridiculous things, and when the copy is sent from the Official Reporters of Debates to a member's office that evening to be corrected, he can delete every single word he has said and substitute the Bible if he desires—and only this will appear in the Congressional Record. In short, what men have actually said in Congress need never be a matter of public record.

In the majority of cases the many quorum calls that abruptly summon one across Independence Avenue to answer on the Floor are instituted by the whims and caprices of a single member. When the bell rings once, it signifies that a teller vote is being taken. Two men stand in the middle aisle—the opponent and the proponent. The members pass up the aisle and are counted one by one: first those who are in favor of the amendments, then those opposed. It is impossible for a man in his office to rush over to the Floor and be there in time to be counted. So the first bell, the teller bell, is of no value. When two bells are rung, it means that a record vote is taking place.

Three bells are often the bells of caprice and whim. There are men in Congress who have never contributed anything to the advancement of our nation, but sit all day on the Floor of Congress, just to look around and see whether two hundred and eighteen members are present. If not, they question the presence of a quorum. Then the Speaker makes a count, finds there is no quorum, and three bells are rung. One must then scurry over to answer the roll call. This I refused to do. What is needed is an electrical system similar to that now in operation in many state legislatures: by pressing a button in his office, each legislator could let the Speaker know that he is in his office and available in the event a vote is taken. Sometimes three bells is an automatic vote when a member objects to the passage of a bill on the grounds of "no quorum."

When the bells ring four times, it's the end of the day.

In order to answer roll calls on present or not-present, to vote on various bills, and now with the new rule that requires recording of voting on amendments—which used to be unrecorded—all a legislator's time could be consumed going back and forth. When there is a roll call it takes twenty-two minutes to go from an office in the Rayburn Building, where my office was; and voting and coming back would consume—unless one has a car and chauffeur ready—almost an hour. This is absolutely antediluvian and I am against it. Thus I always picked only those votes that were important. Proof of this is that the AFL-CIO always rated me as one of the best Congressmen on voting, as did the NAACP and the ADA.

Half the people who are in Congress think that Washington is the biggest city in the world, and of course their wives have never been exposed to the kind of social life you get there—embassy parties, White House invitations, and so on. They're just so happy to come to the big town of Washington that they're carried away with it. They love to live there. To those from urban areas, Washington is nothing but a hick town, and it means nothing for them to parade up and down aisles to vote. Urban legislators frequently feel that they have more serious work to do in their offices. My casework, for example, was often more important to me than casting a vote. That casework load usually averaged five to seven thousand a year, often even involving people whose lives were in danger. To my mind it is also vitally important for a Congressman to spend time in his own bailiwick. When Congressmen live within thirty-five or forty minutes by jet from Washington, their constituents demand that they spend considerable time in their home area because they can see them there without any cost. And as I commented in an article that appeared in Smiling Through the Apocalypse, Esquire's History of the Sixties, "The first duty of a Congressman, regardless of how crass it may appear to be, is to get reelected."

Late in January of 1945 the fading man in the White House sent over a message saying that we had to put through a labor-draft bill—men would either have to work or fight. The cause of democracy was suffering bitterly, but vicious men were still playing Hitler's game. They had taken the same oath of office I had, yet they resorted to every possible method to kill President Roosevelt's request. The strong isolationist bloc in the United States Congress always held to the philosophy of "Let the whole world go to hell. America first!" With absolutely no sincerity, this group introduced an amendment to ban discrimination and segregation, the purpose being to kill Roosevelt's "work-or-fight" legislation.

I stood in the well on January 31, 1945, and said, "This is no time for anyone to use any method to stop full mobilization of the manpower of the United States of America. I brand this amendment as a cheap, partisan trick to play upon racial prejudice in order to defeat a bill which should stand or fall on its own merits. This amendment has erroneously been called an FEPC amendment. This it most emphatically is not. Passage of this amendment will not in the slightest help the Negro worker, or the worker of any minority, any more than he is being helped now. Under Executive Order No. 8802, administered by the Fair Employment Practices Commission, there can be no discrimination in industry during wartime. What we are interested in is a permanent FEPC—a permanent act of this Congress which will forever, in wartime and peacetime, rule out discrimination in public and private employment.

"It is the cheapest and lowest form of politics to play upon any subject as delicate as is the subject of race in connection with legislation which is distinctly of a non-racial character. This bill should stand upon its own merits. It should be passed on its own merits or rejected on its own merits."

Then I helped to lead my colleagues down the aisle past the tellers, and the so-called antidiscrimination amendment was defeated and the bill was passed. The Louisville Courier-Journal wrote that I had raised the debate to a "statesmanlike plane." With a note of prophecy, it concluded, "He showed himself a factor to reckon with in the future."

By this time I had introduced or co-authored whatever civil rights bills were before the United States Congress, including legislation for a permanent FEPC. Also, I was beginning to make friends. The bombs Mr. Sam had advised me against were beginning to drop, drop, drop upon the marble of men's conscience. I was able to start disturbing those who had been too long at ease. Thus, during the month of March, when the bill to draft nurses into the armed forces was passed, an amendment outlawing discrimination in the draft process became part of the historic action of the House of Representatives.

Soon the dream of a United Nations began to bear fruit. As the reality came closer, The New York Times reported, on March 11, my demand that a Negro sit at the first United Nations conference, and commented on what his presence would mean for the submerged peoples of Asia and Africa. As time went on the delegation of our government to the United Nations included names like Edith Sampson, Charming Tobias, Archibald Carey, Marian Anderson, Charles "Dawg" Anderson, Ralph Bunche, and Zelma George.

One day I was sitting in my massive old-fashioned offices in the Old House Office Building. Because of seniority I could have moved, as I later did, to the New Office Building, but I loved the old one: the ancient marble corridors that have been hallowed by the tread of the great, the high ceilings, the view ... this was History. And the view was magnificent—the Capitol dome glistening under the spotlights that burn all night, making it a beacon for all to see and to symbolize the dream that one day what it stands for shall be a reality. I sat there in the polished black-leather chair and began to muse: black men were dying all over the world and yet the nation's two principal military academies, West Point and Annapolis, did not favor their admission. A scarce handful had been graduated from the former, but never in the history of the United States had a Negro been allowed to get beyond the first year at Annapolis. Each Congressman is permitted to appoint five young men to the U.S. Naval Academy at Annapolis, Maryland, and four to the U.S. Military Academy at West Point, New York.

I telephoned a Washington educator and asked, "Who is your outstanding Negro graduate this year?"

"Wesley Brown," he told me.

I phoned Wesley Brown and told him I wanted him to go to Annapolis. He was almost speechless. Finally, he said, "I'll go if you'll appoint me." And I did.

After Wesley Brown had been at Annapolis several months, I wrote a letter to the Secretary of the Navy, James V. Forrestal, one of the grandest men who ever breathed. In the letter I complained that there were "forces at work at Annapolis Naval Academy that are about to put Wesley Brown out." Jim Forrestal was so disturbed by my message that in the midst of that war period he personally went to Annapolis and investigated. He then wrote to me that he found no complaints being made by Cadet Midshipman Brown, nor by his family, and that everyone he talked with said Brown was getting along fine. This I knew. I had deliberately fabricated that letter in order to make sure nothing would happen to Wesley Brown. Sometime later at a cocktail party on Embassy Row I bumped into Forrestal and he asked, "Adam, why did you lie to me?"

"Jim," I said, "I had to lie in order to make sure that Wesley Brown would not be touched by anyone." And so Wesley was the first black man to be graduated from Annapolis and he has gone on to become a career man in the United States Navy.

The only concert hall we had in Washington was Constitution Hall—a national hall owned by the Daughters of the American Revolution but operating under a special charter of Congress and with a tax-exempt status. In October, 1945, my wife, Hazel Scott, had been scheduled for a concert there, but the DAR, under the presidency of Mrs. Julius Talmadge of Atlanta, refused to allow the impresario to have my wife perform. This followed upon the heels of their refusal to have the magnificent Marian Anderson perform and rapidly developed into a cause célèbre.

As a member of Congress I recoiled at the idea that a Congressman's wife, an American citizen, and a gifted artist would not be allowed to perform in a hall largely supported by tax-deductible contributions. I asked the President of the United States, Harry S. Truman, to act, because Washington is controlled by Commissioners appointed by the President and subject to removal by him. These Commissioners could have put pressure on the DAR, but they refused. Representative Rankin, of course, immediately told the press, "This is all Communist-inspired." On Columbus Day I received a wire from President Truman agreeing with me. Yet on the same day his wife accepted an invitation to Constitution Hall as a guest of the DAR. Mrs. Eleanor Roosevelt, when she was First Lady, had resigned from the DAR because of the Marian Anderson episode, and I had expected Bess Truman to follow and to support her husband. I was marching up Fifth Avenue in New York City in the Italian's Columbus Day parade when newsmen stopped me and showed me an AP release: "Bess Truman goes to Constitution Hall to grace the DAR tea."

I said, "From now on there is only one First Lady, Mrs. Roosevelt; Mrs. Truman is the last."

The Philadelphia Record, on October 13, commented editorially: "Doesn't the DAR know that the Civil War is over?" The San Francisco Chronicle, on the same date, editorialized in similar vein. A few days later The Christian Science Monitor said, "This entire affair gives us 'cause for regret,'" and found the DAR's action "unwarranted." The Washington Post condemned the DAR with sober, stern words and said, "They were misguided and unreasonable." Wherever Mrs. Talmadge, the DAR's president, went, pickets began to appear.

On October 18 Congresswoman Helen Gahagan Douglas introduced legislation to stop the DAR's tax exemption, and Congresswoman Clare Boothe Luce said she would resign from the DAR. I knew then that I would win my fight. The women in Congress are far superior to the men. Very few men have been more able during my years than Clare Luce or Helen Gahagan Douglas. Ours would be a much better nation if we had more women in Congress or more men with the character, ability, and the insight of the women who are there now.

The last great dean of the Roosevelt Administration, Senator Robert F. Wagner, Sr., and the Junior Senator from New York, James Mead, both supported my fight against the DAR. And on December 4 United States Federal Judge Phillip Forman banned all members of the DAR from his courtroom for their lack of Americanism.

Harry Truman could have ordered the District of Columbia Commissioners to give the DAR a certain period of time in which to join the Union or lose their tax-exempt status. Instead, in February, 1946, the Truman-appointed Commissioners upheld the DAR's lily-white policy. But the cause was not lost. The cries of outrage that the irritant provoked brought results, and on Sunday, February 17, 1952, Dorothy Maynor sang at Constitution Hall. Another fight had been won.

All during 1945 I had been in contact with the Secretary of War, Robert Patterson, stressing that we could not continue to fight wars to make the world safe for democracy while Negroes were being rigidly segregated in the Army, Navy, and Air Force. Most of the men in the Army were confined to the menial tasks of the Quartermaster Corps. In the Navy most Negroes were messmen. In the Air Force Negroes were practically nonexistent except for one Jim Crow squadron. In the Marines no Negroes were allowed, period. The first step toward integrating the armed forces was taken after my continuing conversations with the War Department, when on January 12, 1946, Secretary Patterson announced that studies were now "under way for integration."

Meanwhile, I was also making strides in the field of fair employment practices. New York State had passed an FEPC law and had established the State Commission Against Discrimination. As soon as I arrived in Washington I introduced the first Congressional legislation in this field, copying almost word for word New York's successful, bipartisan legislation. I began to get bipartisan support, and on January 18, when Harry Truman announced that he would support my legislation, five hundred peaceful demonstrators marched on the Capitol. Two months later Joe Martin, Republican Minority Leader in the House of Representatives, told me that when the FEPC legislation came up, he would marshal his forces to help me.

Secretary of State Dean Acheson also issued a statement calling for an FEPC, declaring that FEPC would be an "aid to the United States' foreign policy." In May of that year the Chicago Defender reported that I forced the Committee on Labor to bypass the Rules Committee and start the first FEPC Bill on its way to a vote. That was in 1946. It took four more years before FEPC reached the Floor for an actual vote.

In January of 1945, in an address at Charlotte, North Carolina, I had pleaded for real democracy, saying, "This nation can never return to pre-Pearl Harbor days of pseudo-democracy." What could I do, I wondered, to assure that this would be true. Was there some amendment that could be phrased in simple words which through the years might serve as a point upon which the isolated, backward, and reactionary thinking of men could be turned?

It was then that I decided to create the Powell Amendment, forbidding Federal funds to those who sought to preserve segregation, and wherever I thought there was an opportunity that it could be passed, or wherever the opportunity arose to defeat bad legislation, there I would introduce it. As I thought and as I prayed, the words came: "No funds under this Act shall be made available to or paid to any State or school...."

The first test came with the school lunch program. Under legislation passed by the Congress, free school lunches were available to schoolchildren. This was of no importance to those in my district but of the utmost importance to millions of children living in those barren, benighted areas of the United States that are subcontinents of human misery. With the support of my colleagues, the first civil rights amendment, attached to the school lunch program, was passed. It is Public Law 396, enacted by the 79th Congress, June 4, 1946. From then on I was to use this important weapon with success, to bring about opportunities for the good of man and to stop those efforts that would harm democracy's forward progress. Sometimes I used it only as a deterrent against the undemocratic practices that would have resulted if that amendment had not been offered.

I was not successful when I introduced an amendment to abolish segregation in the District of Columbia. But within less than a decade Washington, by virtue of the light cast by the Supreme Court in 1954, had become a better place for minorities than even New York City.

My pledge to fight colonialism and imperialism began in July, 1946. It was at that time that the then Congressman, later Senator, Everett M. Dirksen moved to grant a recovery loan to Great Britain. I had not been to Britain nor had I yet witnessed the tremendous suffering, sacrifice, and courage of her people. But they were still in the stranglehold of Winston Churchill, the last of the imperialists. Therefore, I opposed that British loan, saying, "We cannot divorce this loan from imperialism. It could be used to show that the United States is supporting the colonialism of Africa and Asia."

When I returned to the 80th Congress in 1947, I reintroduced all my earlier bills and began my fight to give the citizens of the District of Columbia the right to vote. The Washington Evening Star, one of the few fair papers in this nation, reporting on January 10 that I had introduced the bill, noted that in my introduction I said we could not have "sterile hybrid citizens" at the heart of our government.

As I walked away from the well of Congress after introducing that bill, I happened to look up at the press gallery. The faces were all white, and I said to myself, "Where are the reporters of the Negro press—the daily papers from Atlanta, the weeklies from Chicago, the magazines—where are they?"

I began to investigate and found that the members of the press themselves were in charge of who should be admitted to the gallery. The chairman of the standing committee was a New York Herald Tribune reporter. When I pressed for the admission of Negroes to the press gallery, his standing committee voted four to one to continue barring Negroes. The excuse given was that Negroes did not serve on dailies, although the gallery did admit white journalists serving on weeklies. At last I took my fight to Speaker Rayburn, and on March 19, 1947, Louis Lautier of the Afro-American was admitted to the gallery. Today accredited black journalists no longer have problems in gaining admission to the House, the Senate, or the White House.

I determined that it was time to break down the prejudices within the Capitol itself. As soon as I came to Congress I began to take as many Negroes as I could into the hitherto exclusive restaurant of the House of Representatives. Senator Theodore G. Bilbo of Mississippi was moved to comment that a certain Negro Congressman was a good Negro, but that "Mr. Powell is no good because he continues to use our facilities for Negroes." In March I introduced a resolution demanding that Negro employees of the Federal government, serving in the Capitol, be admitted to the Capitol cafeteria. Senator Wayland Brooks, key Republican leader, immediately called a full meeting of the Senate Committee on Rules and Administration. Although my resolution was never passed, it achieved its purpose because the order went down: "Stop Jim Crow in the United States Congressional facilities."

My father taught me that one should never answer his critics; your friends don't need to hear it and your critics won't believe it, he used to say. Nevertheless, I have never been able to understand how people with intelligence could say I have done nothing in Congress and that I have always been opposed to Federal aid to education, using the Powell Amendment to stop it. As early as May 29, 1948, the Pittsburgh Courier reported, "Powell asked the House of Representatives to proceed immediately to pass Federal aid to education."

One of the important days in my Congressional experience occurred in 1950. This was the sixth year of my fight for an FEPC bill. John Lesinski, Sr., of Michigan was the chairman of the Committee on Education and Labor. A great liberal, he appointed me with full power as chairman of the Special Subcommittee on FEPC. I was to select my own members. Rankin continued to rail at the FEPC, calling it Communist-inspired. Some members of the House were beginning to believe that perhaps it was. From California came a self-proclaimed Sir Galahad in the field of anti-Communism, young, pink-faced, fluid, and fluent. His name was Richard Nixon. I immediately went to him at the opening of the 81st Congress and said, "My name is Powell. I would like you to be a member of my five-man subcommittee on FEPC." He readily assented and because he was such a stern and uncompromising anti-Communist, this immediately shut Rankin's mouth, and the committee got down to work.

We held exhaustive hearings for weeks. I will never forget the testimony of Martin Quigley, prominent Roman Catholic layman and publisher of several trade journals in Hollywood, who told us: "Communism only succeeds when democracy fails." The leaders of the Railroad Brotherhood refused to testify, and I gave them notice that if they didn't, I would use the subpoena power and put them under oath. So they came and I castigated them before the committee for their constitution, which forbade membership to "anyone but Caucasians." Yet in that same year they endorsed and supported me for reelection, and I have lived to see them change those bylaws and constitution.

Finally, the FEPC Bill was ready for the Floor of Congress. In the subcommittee only one man voted against it, and that was Richard Nixon. In the full Committee on Education and Labor, Nixon again voted against the bill. At that point the Southerners, who formed the smartest bloc in Congress, used every method they could to stop FEPC from going to the Floor. The Rules Committee refused to give it a rule. But guided by John Lesinski and others, we resorted to what is called Calendar Wednesday. By the rules of the House, the Rules Committee can be bypassed and a bill presented directly to the House on Calendar Wednesday. Since each committee must wait its turn alphabetically, however, the Committees on Agriculture, Appropriations, Armed Services, Banking and Currency, and District of Columbia were in line to be called ahead of Education and Labor. Knowing of our intention to use this means for securing debate on my FEPC bill, the opposition committee chairmen invoked their powers to exhaust the full time of each Calendar Wednesday for their own bills, thereby forestalling the presentation of our bill. However, only one Calendar Wednesday is allotted to each committee and finally our day came. My FEPC bill was called up, and debate began at last. We did not adjourn until close to four o'clock in the morning, when Republican McConnell, with the support of Richard Nixon, killed the Powell FEPC bill. A toothless substitute that killed the FEPC drive prevailed.

[1971]

XXVI

One of the most articulate, powerful, and beautiful voices in African-American history was that of Paul Robeson (1898–1976), the Rutgers Phi Beta Kappa, All-American football player, gifted Shakespearean actor famed for movie roles such as in "Emperor Jones," gifted singer, and, most importantly, dedicated activist for social justice. Robeson was the quintessential Renaissance man excelling in everything in every endeavor. His breathtaking work for social justice extended beyond the race and borders of the United States. He worked tirelessly against imperialism and fascism. He dedicated himself to a liberated Africa through his work in the Council on African affairs. He spoke out against Hitlerism and supported the anti-fascists' efforts in the Spanish Civil War. His consistent cry for equality and social justice in the U.S., Europe, Soviet Union, and Africa, brought him to the attention of the FBI and the CIA. He was a target of the House Un-American Activities Committee and a victim of McCarthyism in the 1950s. In that same period he penned his autobiography, *Here I Stand.* In "The Power of Negro Action," Robeson asks the black community how long it will wait and permit the injustices against it to continue? Robeson believed in the power of African American activism and that black folks needed to assert themselves if they wanted to bring about real change. Do you think blacks are doing enough on their own to obtain social justice and equality and to secure their rightful place in America? Robeson was very critical of African Americans not taking action to defend one another against hostilities. Not that he was advocating violence, but he was advocating action and the need for African Americans as a people to demand a fair share of America in every avenue of American life including economic, political, social, and cultural. What do you think of Robeson's insistence that African Americans organize themselves and refuse to take "no" as an answer to their demands to be treated as equals and for a fair share of America's wealth. What do you say?

"The Power of Negro Action"

Paul Robeson

"How Long, O Lord, How Long?"—that ancient cry of the oppressed is often voiced these days in editorials in the Negro newspapers whose pages are filled with word-and-picture reports of outrages against our people. A photograph of a Negro being kicked by a white mobster brings the vicious blow crashing against the breast of the reader, and there are all the other horrible pictures—burning cross, beaten minister, bombed school, threatened children, mutilated man, imprisoned mother, barricaded family—which show what is going on.

How long? The answer is: As long as we permit it. I say that Negro action can be decisive. I say that we ourselves have the power to end the terror and to win for ourselves peace and security throughout the land. The recognition of this fact will bring new vigor, boldness and determination in planning our program of action and new militancy in winning its goals.

The denials and doubts about this idea—the second part of the challenge which confronts us today—are even more evident than those I noted in regard to the first. The diehard racists who shout "Never!" to equal rights, and the gradualists who mumble "Not now," are quite convinced that the Negro is powerless to bring about a different decision. Unfortunately, it is also true that to a large extent the Negro people do not know their own strength and do not see how they can achieve the goals they so urgently desire. The basis for this widespread view is obvious. We are a minority, a tenth of the population of our country. In all the terms in which power is reckoned in America—economic wealth, political office, social privilege—we are in a weak position; and from this the conclusion is drawn that the Negro can do little or nothing to compel a change.

It must be seen, however, that this is not a case of a minority pitting itself against a majority. If it were, if we wanted to gain something for ourselves by taking it away from the more powerful majority, the effort would plainly be hopeless. But that is not the case with our demand. Affirming that we are indeed created equal, we seek the equal rights to which we are entitled under the law. The granting of our demand would not lessen the democratic rights of the white people: on the contrary, it would enormously strengthen the base of democracy for all Americans. We ask for nothing that is not ours by right, and herein lies the great moral power of our demand. It is the admitted rightness of our claim which has earned for us the moral support of the majority of white Americans.

The granting of our demand for first-class citizenship, on a par with all others, would not in itself put us in a position of equality. Oppression has kept us on the bottom rungs of the ladder, and even with the removal of all barriers we will still have a long way to climb in order to catch up with the general standard of living. But the equal place to which we aspire cannot be reached without the equal rights we demand, and so the winning of those rights is not a maximum fulfillment but a minimum necessity and we cannot settle for less. Our viewpoint on this matter is not a minority opinion in our country. Though the most rabid champions of "white superiority" are unwilling to test their belief by giving the Negro an equal opportunity, I believe that most white Americans are fair-minded enough to concede that we should be given that chance.

The moral support of the American majority is largely passive today, but what must be recognized—and here we see the decisive power of Negro action—is this:

Wherever and whenever we the Negro peoples claim our lawful rights with all of the earnestness, dignity and determination that we can demonstrate, the moral support of the American people will become an active force on our side.

The most important part of the Little Rock story was not what Governor Faubus and the local mobs did, nor was it what President Eisenhower was moved to do: the important thing was that nine Negro youngsters, backed by their parents, the Negro community and its leadership, resolved to claim their right to attend Central High School. The magnificent courage and dignity these young people displayed in making that claim won the admiration of the American public. Their action did more to win the sympathy and support of democratic-minded white people than all the speeches about "tolerance" that have ever been made.

Little Rock was but one of the first skirmishes in the battle to end Jim Crow schools; much greater tests of our determination will soon be at hand. The desegregation of public education is as yet only in the first stages and the hard core of resistance has not been met. But there is no turning back, and the necessity to prepare ourselves for the struggles that lie ahead is urgent.

I have pointed to the sources of strength that exist at home and abroad. What power do we ourselves have?

We have the power of numbers, the power of organization, and the power of spirit. Let me explain what I mean.

Sixteen million people are a force to be reckoned with, and indeed there are many nations in the U.N. whose numbers are less. No longer can it be said that the Negro question is a sectional matter: the continuing exodus from the South has spread the Negro community to all parts of the land and has concentrated large numbers in places which are economically and politically the most important in the nation. In recent years much has been written about the strategic position of Negro voters in such pivotal states as New York, Ohio, Pennsylvania, Michigan, Illinois and California, but generally it can be said that the power of our numbers is not seen or acted upon. Let us consider this concept in connection with something that is apparent to all.

Very often these days we see photographs in the newspapers and magazines of a Negro family—the husband, wife, their children—huddled together in their newly purchased or rented home, while outside hundreds of Negro-haters have gathered to throw stones, to howl filthy abuse, to threaten murder and arson; and there may or may not be some policemen at the scene. But something is missing from this picture that ought to be there, and its absence gives rise to a nagging question that cannot be stilled: Where are the other Negroes? Where are the hundreds and thousands of other Negroes in that town who ought to be there protecting their own? The power of numbers that is missing from the scene would change the whole picture as nothing else could. It is one thing to terrorize a helpless few, but the forces of race hate that brazenly whoop and holler when the odds are a thousand to one are infinitely less bold when the odds are otherwise.

I am not suggesting, of course, that the Negro people should take law enforcement into their own, hands. But we have the right and, above all, we have the duty, to bring the strength and support of our entire community to defend the lives and property of each individual family. Indeed, the law itself will move a hundred times quicker whenever it is apparent that the power of our numbers has been called forth. The time has come for the great Negro communities throughout the land—Chicago, Detroit, New York, Birmingham and all the rest—to demonstrate that they will no longer tolerate mob violence against one of their own. In listing the inalienable rights of man, Thomas Jefferson put life before liberty, and the pursuit of happiness; and it must be clear that for Negro Americans today the issue of personal security must be put first, and resolved first, before all other matters are attended to. When the Negro is told that he must "stay in his place," there is always the implicit threat that unless he does so mob violence will be used against hire. Hence, as I see it, nothing is more important than to establish the fact that we will no longer suffer the use of mobs against us. Let the Negro people of but a single city respond in an all-out manner at the first sign of a mob—in mass demonstrations, by going on strikes, by organizing boycotts—and the lesson will be taught in one bold stroke to people everywhere.

It was an excellent idea to call for a Prayer Pilgrimage for Freedom to assemble in Washington on May 17, 1957, the third anniversary of the Supreme Court decision, and the thousands who gathered there were inspired with a sense of solidarity and were deeply stirred by the speeches that were made. In terms of dignity and discipline the gathering was a matter for great pride. But there was at the same time a sense of disappointment at the size of the rally which did not, as a national mobilization, truly reflect the power of our numbers. Various charges were later made in the press, and heatedly denied, that important elements of leadership had "dragged their feet" in the preparations, but no constructive purpose would be served by going into those arguments here. The point I wish to make is this: When we call for such mobilization again (and it ought to be done before another three years passes), we must go all-out to rally not tens of thousands but hundreds of thousands in a demonstration that will show we really mean business. And we should do more than listen to speeches and then go quietly home. Our spokesmen should go to the White House and to Congress and backed by the massed power of our people, present our demands for action. Then they should come back to the assembled people to tell them what "the man" said, so that the people can decide whether they are satisfied or not and what to do about it.

The time for pussyfooting is long gone. If someone or other fears that some politician might be "embarrassed" by being confronted by such a delegation, or is concerned lest such action seem too bold—well, let that timid soul just step aside, for there are many in our ranks who will readily go in to "talk turkey" with any or all of the top men in government. We must get it into our heads—and into every leader's head—that we are not asking "favors of the Big White Folks" when, for example, we insist that the full power of the Executive he used to protect the right of Negroes to register and vote in the South. And when we really turn out for such a demand the answer can only be yes.

The power of organization, through which the power of numbers is expressed, is another great strength of the Negro people. Few other areas of American life are as intensively organized as is the Negro community. Some people say that we have far too many organizations—too many different churches and denominations, too many fraternal societies, clubs and associations—but that is what we have and there is no use deploring it. What is important is to recognize a meaningful fact which is so often denied: Negroes can and do band together and they have accomplished remarkable works through their collective efforts. "The trouble with our folks"—how often you have heard it (or perhaps said it yourself)—"is that we just won't get together"; but the plain truth is that we just about do more joining and affiliating than anybody else. "Our folks are just not ready to make financial sacrifices for a good cause," we hear, and yet we see that all over the country congregations of a few hundred poor people contribute and collect thousands of dollars year in and year out for the purposes that inspire them.

The Negro communities are organized and that condition is not made less significant by the fact that our people have formed a great number of organizations to meet their needs and desires. Organizations like the N.A.A.C.P., which has won many splendid victories in the courts for our rights and has done much other notable work, deserve a much greater membership and financial support than is now the case. Yet it is clear that to exert fully our power of organization we must bring together, for united action, all of the many organizations which now encompass the masses of our people. The great struggle and victory in Montgomery, Alabama, against Jim Crow buses proved beyond all doubt that the various existing organizations of the Negro community can be effectively united for a common purpose. Of course the factor of leadership, which I shall discuss later in this chapter, is a key point, but what I wish to emphasize here is that the organizational base for successful struggle exists in all, other communities no less than in Montgomery. And who, in the face of the brilliant organization of every practical detail that was devised and carried through by our people in Montgomery, can still assert that Negroes do not have the capacity for effective collective action? What other mass movement in our country was better planned and carried out?

The central role that was played in Montgomery by the churches and their pastors highlights the fact that the Negro church, which has played such a notable part in our history, is still the strongest base of our power of organization. This is true not only because of the large numbers, who comprise the congregations, but because our churches are, in the main, independent Negro organizations. The churches and other groups of similar independent character—fraternal orders, women's clubs, and so forth—will increasingly take the lead because they are closer to the Negro rank-and-file, more responsive to their needs and less subject to control by forces outside the Negro community.

Here let me point to a large group among this rank-and-file which is potentially the most powerful and effective force in our community—the two million Negro men and women who are members of organized labor. We are working people and the pay-envelope of the Negro worker is the measure of our general welfare and progress. Government statistics on average earnings show that for every dollar that the white worker is paid the Negro worker gets only 53 cents; and that the average Negro family has a yearly income of $2,410, compared with an average of $4,339 per year for white families. Here, on the basic bread-and-butter level, is a crucial front in our fight for equality and here the Negro trade unionists are the main force to lead the way.

It must be seen, too, that in relation to our general struggle for civil rights the Negro trade unionists occupy a key position. They comprise a large part of the membership of our community organizations and at the same time they are the largest section of our people belonging to interracial organizations. Hence, the Negro trade union members are a strategic link, a living connection with the great masses of the common people of America who are our natural allies in the struggle for democracy and whose active support must be won for our side in this critical hour.

To our men and women of organized labor I would say: A twofold challenge confronts you. The Negro trade unionists must increasingly exert their influence in every aspect of our people's community life. No church, no fraternal, civic or social organization in our communities must be permitted to continue without the benefit of the knowledge and experience that you have gained through your struggles in the great American labor movement. You are called upon to provide the spirit, the determination, the organizational, skill, the firm steel of unyielding militancy to the age-old strivings of our people for equality and freedom.

Secondly, on your shoulders there is the responsibility to rally the strength of the whole trade union movement, white and black, to the battle for liberation of our people. Though you are still largely unrepresented in the top levels of labor leadership, you must use your power of numbers to see to it that the leadership of the A.F.L.-C.I.O., which has shown much concern for the so-called "crusade for freedom abroad," shall not continue to be silent and unmoving in our crusade for freedom at home. You must rally your white fellow workers to support full equality for Negro workers; for their right to work at any job; to receive equal pay for equal work; for an end to Jim Crow unions; for the election of qualified Negroes to positions of union leadership; for fair employment practices in every industry; for trade union educational programs to eliminate the notions of "white superiority" which the employers use to poison the minds of the white workers in order to pit them against you.

I have watched and participated in your militant struggles everywhere I have been these past years—in Chicago with the packinghouse workers; with the auto workers of Detroit; the seamen and longshoremen of the West Coast; the tobacco workers of North Carolina; the miners of Pittsburgh and West Virginia; the steel workers of Illinois, Pennsylvania, Indiana and Ohio; the furriers, clerks and garment workers of New York and Philadelphia; with workers in numerous other places throughout the land—and I feel sure that you will meet the challenge which confronts you today.

To all groups in Negro life I would say that the key to set into motion our power of organization is the concept of coordinated action, the bringing together of the many organizations which exist in order to plan and to carry out the common struggle. We know full well that it is not easy to do this. We are divided in many ways—in politics, in religious affiliations, in economic and social classes; and in addition to these group rivalries there are the obstacles of personal ambitions and jealousies of various leaders. But as I move among our people these days, from New York to California, I sense a growing impatience with petty ways of thinking and doing things. I see a rising resentment against control of our affairs by white people, regardless of whether that domination expressed by the blunt orders of political bosses or, more discreetly by the "advice" of white liberals which must be heeded or else. There is a rapidly growing awareness that despite all of our differences it is necessary that we become unified, and I think that the force of that idea will overcome all barriers. Coordinated action will not, of course, come all at once: it will develop in the grass-roots and spread from community to community. And the building of that unity is a task which each of us can undertake wherever we are.

A unified people requires a unified leadership, and let me make very clear what I mean by that. Recently the distinguished Negro journalist Carl T. Rowan, who had published in *Ebony* magazine an interview with me, was himself interviewed about that subject on a radio network program where be said: "It's Robeson's contention that the Negro people will never be free in this country until they speak more or loss as one voice, and, very obviously, Robeson feels that that one voice should be something close to his voice."

Actually, that is not how I feel, and I would not want Mr. Rowan or anyone else to misunderstand my view of this matter. The one voice in which we should speak must be the expression of our entire people on the central issue which is all-important to every Negro—our right to be free and equal. On many other issues there are great differences among us, and hence it is not possible for any one person, or any group of people, to presume to speak for us all.

Far from making any such claim for myself, what I am advocating is in fact the opposite idea! I advocate a unity based upon our common viewpoint as Negroes, a nonpartisan unity; a unity in which we subordinate all that divides us, a unity which excludes no one, a unity in which no faction or group is permitted to impose its particular outlook on others. A unified leadership of a unified movement means that people of all political views—conservatives, liberals, and radicals—must be represented therein, Let there be but one requirement made without exception: that Negro leadership, and every man and woman in that leadership, place the interests of our people, and the struggle for those interests, above all else.

There is a need—an urgent need—for a national conference of Negro leadership, not of a handful but a broad representative gathering of leadership from all parts of the country, from all walks of life, from every viewpoint, to work out a common program of action for Negro Americans in the crisis of our times. Such a program does not exist today and without it we are a ship without a rudder; we can only flounder around on a day-to-day basis, trying to meet developments with patchwork solutions. We must chart a course to be followed in the stormy days that are here and in the greater storms that are on the way, a course that heads full square for freedom.

The need for a central fund, not only for legal purposes but for all the purposes of Negro coordinated action, has been expressed in various editorials in the press and elsewhere; and the national conference I speak of could meet this need. A central fund would be a "community chest" to help our struggles everywhere. Nonpartisan and not controlled by any single organization, this fund would be a national institution of our whole people, and a well-organized campaign to build it would meet with a generous response from Negro America. And more: such a fund would undoubtedly receive a great deal of support from white people who sympathize with our struggle.

If we must think boldly in terms of the power of numbers, we must likewise think big in terms of organization. Our cause is the cause of all, and so our methods of reaching our goal must be such that all of our people can play a part. The full potential of the Negro people's power of organization must be achieved in every city and state throughout the land.

The power of spirit that our people have is intangible, but it is a great force that must be unleashed in the struggles of today. A spirit of steadfast determination, exaltation in the face of trials—it is the very soul of our people that has been formed through all the long and weary years of our march toward freedom. It is the deathless spirit of the great ones who have led our people in the past—Douglass, Tubman and all the others—and of the millions who kept "a-inching along." That spirit lives in our people's songs—in the sublime grandeur of "Deep River," in the driving power of "Jacob's Ladder," in the militancy of "Joshua Fit the Battle of Jericho," and in the poignant beauty of all our spirituals.

It lives in every Negro mother who wants her child "to grow up and be somebody," as it lives in our common people everywhere who daily meet insult and outrage with quiet courage and optimism. It is that spirit which gives that "something extra" to our athletes, to our artists, to all who meet the challenge of public performance. It is the spirit of little James Gordon of Clay, Kentucky, who, when asked by a reporter why he wanted to go to school with white children, replied: "Why shouldn't I?"; and it is the spirit of all the other little ones in the South who have walked like mighty heroes through menacing mobs to go to school. It is the spirit of the elderly woman of Montgomery who explained her part in the bus boycott by saying "When I rode in the Jim Crow buses my body was riding but my soul was walking, but now when my body is walking my soul is riding!"

Yes, that power of the spirit is the pride and glory of my people, and there is no human quality in all of America that can surpass it. It is a force only for good: there is no hatefulness about it. It exalts the finest things of life—justice and equality, human dignity and fulfillment. It is of the earth, deeply rooted, and it reaches up to the highest skies and mankind's noblest aspirations. It is time for this spirit to be evoked and exemplified in all we do, for it is a force mightier than all our enemies and will triumph over all their evil ways.

For Negro action to be decisive—given the favorable opportunity which I have outlined in the previous chapter and the sources of strength indicated above—still another factor is needed: effective Negro leadership. In discussing this subject I shall not engage in any personalities, nor is it my intention either to praise or blame the individuals who today occupy top positions in our ranks. Such critical appraisal must, of course, be made of their leaders by the Negro people, and so I would like here to discuss not this or that person but rather the principles of the question, the standards for judgment, the character of leadership that is called for today.

The term "leadership" has been used to express many different concepts, and many of these meanings have nothing to do with what I am concerned with here. Individuals attain prominence for a wide, variety of reasons, and often people who have climbed up higher on the ladder are called leaders though they make it plain that their sole interest is personal advancement and the more elevated they are above all other Negroes the better they like it. Then, too, it has been traditional for the dominant group of whites, in local communities and on a national scale as well, to designate certain individuals as "Negro leaders," regardless of how the Negro people feel about it; and the idea is that Negro leadership is something that white folks can bestow as a favor or take away as punishment.

The concept that I am talking about has nothing to do with matters of headline prominence, personal achievement, or popularity with the powers-that-be. I am concerned, rather, with Negro leadership in the struggle for Negro rights. This includes those who are directly in charge of the organizations established for such purpose, and many others as well—the leaders of Negro churches, fraternal and civic organizations, elected representatives in government, trade union officials, and others whose action or inaction directly affects our common cause.

The primary quality that Negro leadership must possess, as I see it, is a single-minded dedication to their people's welfare. Any individual Negro, like any other person, may have many varied interests in life, but for the true leader all else must be subordinated to the interests of those whom he is leading. If today it can be said that the Negro people of the United States are lagging behind the progress being made by colored peoples in other lands, one basic cause for it has been that all too often Negro leadership here has lacked the selfless passion for their people's welfare that has characterized the leaders of the colonial liberation movements. Among us there is a general recognition—and a grudging acceptance—of the fact that some of our leaders are not only unwilling to make sacrifices but they must see some gain for themselves in whatever they do. A few crumbs for a few is too often bailed as "progress for the race." To live in freedom one must be prepared to die to achieve it, and while few if any of us are ever called upon to make that supreme sacrifice, no one can ignore the fact that in a difficult struggle those who are in the forefront may suffer cruel blows. He who is not prepared to face the trials of battle will never lead to a triumph. This spirit of dedication, as I have indicated, is abundantly present in the ranks of our people but progress will be slow until it is much more manifest in the character of leadership.

Dedication to the Negro people's welfare is one side of a coin: the other side is *independence.* Effective Negro leadership must rely upon and be responsive to no other control than the will of their people. We have allies—important allies—among our white fellow-citizens, and we must ever seek to draw them closer to us and to gain many more. But the Negro people's movement must be led by Negroes, not only in terms of title and position but in reality. Good advice is good no matter what the source and help is needed and appreciated from wherever it comes, but Negro action cannot be decisive if the advisers and helpers hold the guiding reins. For no matter how well-meaning other groups may be, the fact is our interests are secondary at best with them.

Today such outside controls are a factor in reducing the independence and effectiveness of Negro leadership. I do not have in mind the dwindling group of Uncle Toms who shamelessly serve even an Eastland; happily, they are no longer of much significance. I have in mind, rather, those practices of Negro leadership that are based upon the idea that it is white power rather than Negro power that must be relied upon. This concept has been traditional since Booker T. Washington, and it has been adhered to by many who otherwise reject all notions of white supremacy. Even Marcus Garvey who rose to leadership of a nationalist mass movement in the 1920's and who urged that the Negro peoples of the world "go forward to the point of destiny as laid out by themselves," believed that white power was decisive. Indeed, no one has stated the idea more clearly than Garvey did in his essay "The Negro's Place in World Reorganization," in which he said:

"The white man of America has become the natural leader of the world. He, because of his exalted position, is called upon to help in all human efforts. From nations to individuals the appeal is made to him for aid in all things affecting humanity, so, naturally, there can be no great mass movement or change without first acquainting the leader on whose sympathy and advice the world moves?"

Much has changed since those words were written, and I have no doubt that if Garvey were alive today he would recognize that the "white man of America" is no longer all-powerful and that the colored peoples of the world are moving quite independently of that "sympathy and advice."

In Booker Washington's day it was the ruling white man of the South whose sympathy was considered indispensable; today it is the liberal section of the dominant group in the North whose goodwill is said to be the hope for Negro progress. It is clear that many Negro leaders act or desist from acting because they base themselves on this idea. Rejecting the concept that "white is right" they embrace its essence by conceding that "might is right." To the extent that this idea is prevalent in its midst, Negro leadership lacks the quality of independence without which it cannot be effective.

Dedication and independence—these are the urgent needs. Other qualities of leadership exist in abundance: we have many highly trained men and women, experienced in law, in politics, in civic affairs; we have spokesmen of great eloquence, talented organizers, skilled negotiators. If I have stressed those qualities which are most needed on the national level, it is not from any lack of appreciation for much that is admirable. On the local level, especially, there are many examples of dedicated and independent leadership. Indeed, the effective use of Negro power—of numbers, of organization, of spirit—in Montgomery was the result of Negro leadership of the highest caliber. And the whole nation has witnessed the heroic dedication of many other leaders in the South who, at the risk of their lives and all they hold dear, are leading their people's struggles. There are many from our ranks who ought to be elevated to national leadership because by their deeds they have fully demonstrated their right to be there. We should broaden our conception of leadership and see to it that all sections of Negro life are represented on the highest levels. There must be room at the top for people from down below. I'm talking about the majority of our folks who work in factory and field: they bring with them that down-to-earth view which is the highest vision, and they can hammer and plow in more ways than one. Yes, we need more of them in the leadership, and we need them in a hurry.

We need more of our women in the higher ranks, too, and who should know better than the children of Harriet Tubman, Sojourner Truth and Mary Church Terrell that our womenfolk have often led the way. Negro womanhood today is giving us many inspiring examples of steadfast devotion, cool courage under fire, and brilliant generalship in our people's struggles; and here is a major source for new strength and militancy in Negro leadership on every level.

But if there are those who ought to be raised to the top, there are some others already there who should be retired have noted, in another connection, that the Negro people are patient and long-suffering—sometimes to a fault. The fault is often expressed by permitting unworthy leaders to get away with almost anything. It is as if once a man rises to leadership, his responsibility to his people is no longer binding upon him.

But, in these critical days, we ought to become a little less tolerant, a little more demanding that all Negro leaders "do right." I have in mind, for example, the case of an important Negro leader in a large Northern city, who, at the time when mobs were barring the Negro children from high school in Little Rock and beating up Negro newspapermen, got up before his people and said: "We cannot meet this crisis by force against force. Under no circumstances can Federal troops be used. This would be a confession of our moral decadence, it would precipitate a second Civil War—it would open the stopper and send democracy down the drain for at least our generation and maybe forever." These words, so utterly devoid of any concern for his people and lacking all regard for the truth, were hardly spoken before the President sent in Federal troops! No civil war was started, democracy got a new lease on life, the mobs were dispersed, the Negro children were escorted to school, and for the first time since 1876 the lawful force of the Federal government was called out against the lawless force of White Supremacy, in the South.

When, as in this case, a Negro leader vigorously opposes that which be should be fighting for and makes it clear that some other folks' interests are of more concern to him than his own people's—well, the so-called "politically-wise" may say: "Oh, that's just politics—forget it." But the so-called "politically-dumb" just can't see it that way. How can we be led by people who are not going our way?

There are others, honest men beyond all doubt and sincerely concerned with their people's welfare, who seem to feel that it is the duty of a leader to discourage Negro mass action. They think that best results can be achieved by the quiet negotiations they carry on. And so when something happens that arouses the masses of people, and when the people gather in righteous anger to demand that militant actions be started, such men believe it their duty to cool things off.

We saw this happen not long ago when from coast to coast there was a great upsurge of the people caused by the brutal lynching of young Emmett Till. At one of the mass protest meetings that was held, I heard one of our most important leaders address the gathering in words to this effect: "You are angry today, but you are not going to do anything about it. I know that you won't do anything. You clamor for a march on Mississippi but none of you will go. So let's stop talking about marching. Just pay a dollar to our organization and leave the rest to your leaders. If you want to do something yourself, let each of you go to your district Democratic leader and talk to him about it."

Well, what would a congregation think of their pastor if the best he could do was to tell them: "You are all a bunch of sinners, and nothing can make you do right. There is no good in you and I know it. So, brothers and sisters, just put your contributions on the collection plate, go home and leave your salvation to me."

No, a leader should encourage, not discourage; he should rally the people, not disperse them. A wet blanket can never be the banner of freedom.

Of course there must be negotiations made in behalf of our rights, but unless the negotiators are backed by an aroused and militant people, their earnest pleas will be of little avail. For Negro action to be effective—to be decisive, as I think it can be—it must be mass action. The power of the ballot can be useful only if the masses of voters are united on a common program; obviously, if half the Negro people vote one way and the other half the opposite way, not much can be achieved. The individual votes are cast and counted, but the group power is cast away and discounted.

Mass action—in political life and elsewhere—is Negro power in motion; and it is the way to win.

An urgent task which faces us today is an all-out struggle to defeat the efforts of the White Supremacists to suppress the NA.A.C.P. in the South. As in South Africa, where the notorious "Suppression of Communism Act" is used to attack the liberation movement, the enemies of Negro freedom in our country have accused the N.A.A.C.P. of being a "subversive conspiracy" and the organization has been outlawed in Louisiana, Texas and Alabama, and legally restricted in Georgia, Virginia, South Carolina and Mississippi. City ordinances, as in Little Rock, are also used for this purpose.

The indifference with which various other organizations viewed the suppression in 1955 of the Council on African Affairs, which was falsely labeled a "Communist front," should not be repeated now by any group in the case of the N.A.A.C.P. The Red-baiting charges against that organization are utterly untrue, as the makers of such charges know full well; and those elements in Negro leadership who have in the past resorted to Red-baiting as a "smart" tactic should realize that such methods serve no one but our people's worst enemies.

Throughout the South—in Little Rock; in Montgomery and elsewhere—the state and local leaders of the NA.A.C.P. have set a heroic and inspiring example for Negro leadership everywhere. All of us—the Negro people of the entire country—must rally now to sustain and defend them.

In presenting these ideas on the power of Negro action, the sources of that power, and the character of leadership necessary to direct that power most effectively, I offer them for consideration and debate at this time when the challenge of events calls for clarity of vision and unity of action. No one, obviously, has all the answers, and the charting of our course must be done collectively. There must be a spirit of give, and take, and clashing viewpoints must find a common ground. Partisan interests must be subordinated to Negro interests—by each of us. Somehow we must find the way to set aside all that divides us and come together, Negroes all. Our unity will strengthen our friends and win many more to our side; and our unity will weaken our foes who already can see the handwriting on the wall.

To be free—to walk the good American earth as equal citizens, to live without fear, to enjoy the fruits of our toil, to give our children every opportunity in life—that dream which we have held so long in our hearts is today the destiny that we hold in our hands.

[1958]

XXVII

No one symbolized the vigor, tenacity, and commitment to social change during the 1960s more than did Fannie Lou Hamer (1917–1977). A devoutly Christian woman, and a valiant soldier in the struggle for civil rights, the Mississippian stood tall, along with volunteers from SNCC (Student Nonviolent Coordinating Committee) and CORE (Congress of Racial Equality), to register black voters in the deep South and to challenge white supremacy. Hamer and other protestors also took on the ruling Jim Crowism that permeated the Democratic Party and especially the all-white delegation from Mississippi. Hamer suffered incredible abuse at the hands of the racist powers in Mississippi. She had been sterilized without her knowledge in 1961 by white doctors as part of the Mississippi program to limit the number of poor blacks. In 1963 she was jailed and brutally beaten in Mississippi for her efforts to register black voters. At the 1964 Democratic National Convention in Atlantic City, New Jersey, Hamer, one of the founding members of the Mississippi Freedom Democratic Party (MFDP), challenged the validity of seating the all-white delegation from her state. In the selection presented here, from her speech before the 1964 convention, Hamer pleads for fairness in a party that systematically excluded black participation. This was a momentous event that captured national and worldwide attention. What do you think of her passionate account? Do her remarks inspire you to be politically active? Will you become active or remain complacent?

"Speech before the Credentials Committee of the Democratic National Convention"

Fannie Lou Hamer

Mr. Chairman, and to the Credentials Committee, my name is Mrs. Fannie Lou Hamer, and I live at 626 East Lafayette Street, Ruleville, Mississippi, Sunflower County, the home of Senator James O. Eastland, and Senator Stennis.

It was the 31st of August in 1962 that eighteen of us traveled twenty-six miles to the county courthouse in Indianola to try to register to become first-class citizens. We was met in Indianola by policemen, Highway Patrolmen, and they only allowed two of us in to take the literacy test at the time. After we had taken this test and started back to Ruleville, we was held up by the City Police and the State Highway Patrolmen and carried back to Indianola where the bus driver was charged that day with driving a bus the wrong color.

After we paid the fine among us, we continued on to Ruleville, and Reverend Jeff Sunny carried me four miles in the rural area where I had worked as a timekeeper and sharecropper for eighteen years. I was met there by my children, who told me the plantation owner was angry because I had gone down—tried to register.

After they told me, my husband came, and said the plantation owner was raising Cain because I had tried to register. And before he quit talking the plantation owner came and said, "Fannie Lou, do you know—did Pap tell you what I said?"

And I said, "Yes, sir."

He said, "Well I mean that."

Said, "If you don't go down and withdraw your registration, you will have to leave." Said, "Then if you go down and withdraw," said, "you still might have to go because we're not ready for that in Mississippi."

And I addressed him and told him and said, "I didn't try to register for you. I tried to register for myself."

I had to leave that same night.

On the 10th of September 1962, sixteen bullets was fired into the home of Mr. and Mrs. Robert Tucker for me. That same night two girls were shot in Ruleville, Mississippi. Also, Mr. Joe McDonald's house was shot in.

And June the 9th, 1963, I had attended a voter registration workshop; was returning back to Mississippi. Ten of us was traveling by the Continental Trailway bus. When we got to Winona, Mississippi, which is Montgomery County, four of the people got off to use the washroom, and two of the people—to use the restaurant—two of the people wanted to use the washroom.

The four people that had gone in to use the restaurant was ordered out. During this time I was on the bus. But when I looked through the window and saw they had rushed out I got off of the bus to see what had happened. And one of the ladies said, "It was a State Highway Patrolman and a Chief of Police ordered us out."

I got back on the bus and one of the persons had used the washroom got back on the bus, too.

As soon as I was seated on the bus, I saw when they began to get the five people in a highway patrolman's car. I stepped off of the bus to see what was happening and somebody screamed from the car that the five workers was in and said, "Get that one there." And when I went to get in the car, when the man told me I was under arrest, he kicked me.

I was carried to the county jail and put in the booking room. They left some of the people in the booking room and began to place us in cells. I was placed in a cell with a young woman called Miss Ivesta Simpson. After I was placed in the cell I began to hear sounds of licks and screams. I could hear the sounds of licks and horrible screams. And I could hear somebody say, "Can you say, 'yes, sir,' nigger? Can you say 'yes, sir'?"

And they would say other horrible names.

She would say, "Yes, I can say 'yes, sir.'"

"So, well, say it."

She said, "I don't know you well enough."

They beat her, I don't know how long. And after a while she began to pray, and asked God to have mercy on those people.

And it wasn't too long before three white men came to my cell. One of these men was a State Highway Patrolman and he asked me where I was from. And I told him

Ruleville. He said, "We are going to check this." And they left my cell and it wasn't too long before they came back. He said, "You are from Ruleville all right," and he used a curse word. And he said, "We're going to make you wish you was dead."

I was carried out of that cell into another cell where they had two Negro prisoners. The State Highway Patrolmen ordered the first Negro to take the blackjack. The first Negro prisoner ordered me, by orders from the State Highway Patrolman, for me to lay down on a bunk bed on my face. And I laid on my face, the first Negro began to beat me.

And I was beat by the first Negro until he was exhausted. I was holding my hands behind me at that time on my left side, because I suffered from polio when I was six years old.

After the first Negro had beat until he was exhausted, the State Highway Patrolman ordered the second Negro to take the blackjack.

The second Negro began to beat and I began to work my feet, and the State Highway Patrolman ordered the first Negro who had beat to sit on my feet—to keep me from working my feet. I began to scream and one white man got up and began to beat me in my head and tell me to hush.

One white man—my dress had worked up high—he walked over and pulled my dress—I pulled my dress down and he pulled my dress back up.

I was in jail when Medgar Evers was murdered.

All of this is on account of we want to register, to become first-class citizens. And if the Freedom Democratic Party is not seated now, I question America. Is this America, the land of the free and the home of the brave, where we have to sleep with our telephones off of the hooks because our lives be threatened daily, because we want to live as decent human beings, in America?

Thank you.

[22 August 1964]

XXVIII

Lyndon Baines Johnson (1908–1973) believed that the nation was moving toward chaos during much of his Presidency from 1963 to 1968. The Texan, a former schoolteacher, veteran of World War II in the South Pacific, was elected to the Senate in 1948, became the eventual Majority Leader of the Senate and Vice President of the United States, and was always a master tactician and political insider. Upon assuming the Office of President after the assassination of John F. Kennedy in November 1963, he pledged to make America work for all of its citizens. By election to the Presidency in his own right in 1964, Johnson, in his "Great Society" vision, put forth more progressive legislation to the benefit of African Americans than any president in history, with the exception of Abraham Lincoln. It was Johnson who ushered in Medicare and Medicaid, the Economic Opportunity Act, the Work-Study Program, the Higher Education Act, Head Start, Jobs Corps, and increased the funding to public housing and education to heights never seen before in the history of the country. It was under Lyndon Baines Johnson that the 1964 Civil Rights Act was passed, followed that next year by the Voting Rights Act. His Achilles' heel was unquestionably the war in Vietnam. Beyond that the tumultuous 1960s and the numerous riots in urban centers across the nation belied the social programs of his administration. No president since Franklin D. Roosevelt passed more social legislation. In his special message to Congress, "The American Promise," Johnson embraces the civil rights movement and the fight for social justice. On a personal note, he acknowledged being moved by Fannie Lou Hamer's remarks before the DNC. What do you think of Johnson's message? Has the nation worked together, as he said it must, if "we are to overcome"? Have we overcome?

"Special Message to the Congress: The American Promise"

Lyndon Baines Johnson

[Delivered in person before a joint session at 9:02 p.m., and broadcast live nationally]

Mr. Speaker, Mr. President, Members of the Congress:

I speak tonight for the dignity of man and the destiny of democracy.

I urge every member of both parties, Americans of all religions and of all colors, from every section of this country, to join me in that cause.

At times history and fate meet at a single time in a single place to shape a turning point in man's unending search for freedom. So it was at Lexington and Concord. So it was a century ago at Appomattox. So it was last week in Selma, Alabama.

There, long-suffering men and women peacefully protested the denial of their rights as Americans. Many were brutally assaulted. One good man, a man of God, was killed.

There is no cause for pride in what has happened in Selma. There is no cause for self-satisfaction in the long denial of equal rights of millions of Americans. But there is cause for hope and for faith in our democracy in what is happening here tonight.

For the cries of pain and the hymns and protests of oppressed people have summoned into convocation all the majesty of this great Government—the Government of the greatest Nation on earth.

Our mission is at once the oldest and the most basic of this country: to right wrong, to do justice, to serve man.

In our time we have come to live with moments of great crisis. Our lives have been marked with debate about great issues; issues of war and peace, issues of prosperity and depression. But rarely in any time does an issue lay bare the secret heart of America itself. Rarely are we met with a challenge, not to our growth or abundance, our welfare or our security, but rather to the values and the purposes and the meaning of our beloved Nation.

The issue of equal rights for American Negroes is such an issue. And should we defeat every enemy, should we double our wealth and conquer the stars, and still be unequal to this issue, then we will have failed as a people and as a nation.

For with a country as with a person, "What is a man profited, if he shall gain the whole world, and lose his own soul?"

There is no Negro problem. There is no Southern problem. There is no Northern problem. There is only an American problem. And we are met here tonight as Americans— not as Democrats or Republicans—we are met here as Americans to solve that problem.

This was the first nation in the history of the world to be founded with a purpose. The great phrases of that purpose still sound in every American heart, North and South: "All men are created equal"—"government by consent of the governed"—"give me liberty or give me death." Well, those are not just clever words, or those are not just empty theories. In their name Americans have fought and died for two centuries, and tonight around the world they stand there as guardians of our liberty, risking their lives.

Those words are a promise to every citizen that he shall share in the dignity of man. This dignity cannot be found in a man's possessions; it cannot be found in his power, or in his position. It really rests on his right to be treated as a man equal in opportunity to all others. It says that he shall share in freedom, he shall choose his leaders, educate his children, and provide for his family according to his ability and his merits as a human being.

To apply any other test—to deny a man his hopes because of his color or race, his religion or the place of his birth—is not only to do injustice, it is to deny America and to dishonor the dead who gave their lives for American freedom.

THE RIGHT TO VOTE

Our fathers believed that if this noble view of the rights of man was to flourish, it must be rooted in democracy. The most basic right of all was the right to choose your own leaders. The history of this country, in large measure, is the history of the expansion of that right to all of our people.

Many of the issues of civil rights are very complex and most difficult. But about this there can and should be no argument. Every American citizen must have an equal right to vote. There is no reason which can excuse the denial of that right. There is no duty which weighs more heavily on us than the duty we have to ensure that right.

Yet the harsh fact is that in many places in this country men and women are kept from voting simply because they are Negroes.

Every device of which human ingenuity is capable has been used to deny this right. The Negro citizen may go to register only to be told that the day is wrong, or the hour is late, or the official in charge is absent. And if he persists, and if he manages to present himself to the registrar, he may be disqualified because he did not spell out his middle name or because he abbreviated a word on the application.

And if he manages to fill out an application he is given a test. The registrar is the sole judge of whether he passes this test. He may be asked to recite the entire Constitution, or explain the most complex provisions of State law. And even a college degree cannot be used to prove that he can read and write.

For the fact is that the only way to pass these barriers is to show a white skin.

Experience has clearly shown that the existing process of law cannot overcome systematic and ingenious discrimination. No law that we now have on the books—and I have helped to put three of them there—can ensure the right to vote when local officials are determined to deny it.

In such a case our duty must be clear to all of us. The Constitution says that no person shall be kept from voting because of his race or his color. We have all sworn an oath before God to support and to defend that Constitution. We must now act in obedience to that oath.

GUARANTEEING THE RIGHT TO VOTE

Wednesday I will send to Congress a law designed to eliminate illegal barriers to the right to vote.

The broad principles of that bill will be in the hands of the Democratic and Republican leaders tomorrow. After they have reviewed it, it will come here formally as a bill. I am grateful for this opportunity to come here tonight at the invitation of the leadership to reason with my friends, to give them my views, and to visit with my former colleagues.

I have had prepared a more comprehensive analysis of the legislation which I had intended to transmit to the clerk tomorrow but which I will submit to the clerks tonight. But I want to really discuss with you now briefly the main proposals of this legislation.

This bill will strike down restrictions to voting in all elections—Federal, State, and local—which have been used to deny Negroes the right to vote.

This bill will establish a simple, uniform standard which cannot be used, however ingenious the effort, to flout our Constitution.

It will provide for citizens to be registered by officials of the United States Government if the State officials refuse to register them.

It will eliminate tedious, unnecessary lawsuits which delay the right to vote.

Finally, this legislation will ensure that properly registered individuals are not prohibited from voting.

I will welcome the suggestions from all of the Members of Congress — I have no doubt that I will get some — on ways and means to strengthen this law and to make it effective. But experience has plainly shown that this is the only path to carry out the command of the Constitution.

To those who seek to avoid action by their National Government in their own communities; who want to and who seek to maintain purely local control over elections, the answer is simple:

Open your polling places to all your people.

Allow men and women to register and vote whatever the color of their skin.

Extend the rights of citizenship to every citizen of this land.

THE NEED FOR ACTION

There is no constitutional issue here. The command of the Constitution is plain.

There is no moral issue. It is wrong — deadly wrong — to deny any of your fellow Americans the right to vote in this country.

There is no issue of States rights or national rights. There is only the struggle for human rights.

I have not the slightest doubt what will be your answer.

The last time a President sent a civil rights bill to the Congress it contained a provision to protect voting rights in Federal elections. That civil rights bill was passed after 8 long months of debate. And when that bill came to my desk from the Congress for my signature, the heart of the voting provision had been eliminated.

This time, on this issue, there must be no delay, no hesitation and no compromise with our purpose.

We cannot, we must not, refuse to protect the right of every American to vote in every election that he may desire to participate in. And we ought not and we cannot and we must not wait another 8 months before we get a bill. We have already waited a hundred years and more, and the time for waiting is gone.

So I ask you to join me in working long hours — nights and weekends, if necessary — to pass this bill. And I don't make that request lightly. For from the window where I sit with the problems of our country I recognize that outside this chamber is the outraged conscience of a nation, the grave concern of many nations, and the harsh judgment of history on our acts.

WE SHALL OVERCOME

But even if we pass this bill, the battle will not be over. What happened in Selma is part of a far larger movement which reaches into every section and State of America. It is the effort of American Negroes to secure for themselves the full blessings of American life.

Their cause must be our cause too. Because it is not just Negroes, but really it is all of us, who must overcome the crippling legacy of bigotry and injustice.

And we shall overcome.

As a man whose roots go deeply into Southern soil I know how agonizing racial feelings are. I know how difficult it is to reshape the attitudes and the structure of our society.

But a century has passed, more than a hundred years, since the Negro was freed. And he is not fully free tonight.

It was more than a hundred years ago that Abraham Lincoln, a great President of another party, signed the Emancipation Proclamation, but emancipation is a proclamation and not a fact.

A century has passed, more than a hundred years, since equality was promised. And yet the Negro is not equal.

A century has passed since the day of promise. And the promise is unkept.

The time of justice has now come. I tell you that I believe sincerely that no force can hold it back. It is right in the eyes of man and God that it should come. And when it does, I think that day will brighten the lives of every American.

For Negroes are not the only victims. How many white children have gone uneducated, how many white families have lived in stark poverty, how many white lives have been scarred by fear, because we have wasted our energy and our substance to maintain the barriers of hatred and terror?

So I say to all of you here, and to all in the Nation tonight, that those who appeal to you to hold on to the past do so at the cost of denying you your future.

This great, rich, restless country can offer opportunity and education and hope to all: black and white, North and South, sharecropper and city dweller. These are the enemies: poverty, ignorance, disease. They are the enemies and not our fellow man, not our neighbor. And these enemies too, poverty, disease and ignorance, we shall overcome.

AN AMERICAN PROBLEM

Now let none of us in any sections look with prideful righteousness on the troubles in another section, or on the problems of our neighbors. There is really no part of America where the promise of equality has been fully kept. In Buffalo as well as in Birmingham, in Philadelphia as well as in Selma, Americans are struggling for the fruits of freedom.

This is one Nation. What happens in Selma or in Cincinnati is a matter of legitimate concern to every American. But let each of us look within our own hearts and our own communities, and let each of us put our shoulder to the wheel to root out injustice wherever it exists.

As we meet here in this peaceful, historic chamber tonight, men from the South, some of whom were at Iwo Jima, men from the North who have carried Old Glory to far corners of the world and brought it back without a stain on it, men from the East and from the West, are all fighting together without regard to religion, or color, or region, in Vietnam. Men from every region fought for us across the world 20 years ago.

And in these common dangers and these common sacrifices the South made its contribution of honor and gallantry no less than any other region of the great Republic— and in some instances, a great many of them, more.

And I have not the slightest doubt that good men from everywhere in this country, from the Great Lakes to the Gulf of Mexico, from the Golden Gate to the harbors along the Atlantic, will rally together now in this cause to vindicate the freedom of all Americans. For all of us owe this duty; and I believe that all of us will respond to it.

Your President makes that request of every American.

PROGRESS THROUGH THE DEMOCRATIC PROCESS

The real hero of this struggle is the American Negro. His actions and protests, his courage to risk safety and even to risk his life, have awakened the conscience of this

Nation. His demonstrations have been designed to call attention to injustice, designed to provoke change, designed to stir reform.

He has called upon us to make good the promise of America. And who among us can say that we would have made the same progress were it not for his persistent bravery, and his faith in American democracy.

For at the real heart of battle for equality is a deep-seated belief in the democratic process. Equality depends not on the force of arms or tear gas but upon the force of moral right; not on recourse to violence but on respect for law and order.

There have been many pressures upon your President and there will be others as the days come and go. But I pledge you tonight that we intend to fight this battle where it should be fought: in the courts, and in the Congress, and in the hearts of men.

We must preserve the right of free speech and the right of free assembly. But the right of free speech does not carry with it, as has been said, the right to holler fire in a crowded theater. We must preserve the right to free assembly, but free assembly does not carry with it the right to block public thoroughfares to traffic.

We do have a right to protest, and a right to march under conditions that do not infringe the constitutional rights of our neighbors. And I intend to protect all those rights as long as I am permitted to serve in this office.

We will guard against violence, knowing it strikes from our hands the very weapons which we seek—progress, obedience to law, and belief in American values.

In Selma as elsewhere we seek and pray for peace. We seek order. We seek unity. But we will not accept the peace of stifled rights, or the order imposed by fear, or the unity that stifles protest. For peace cannot be purchased at the cost of liberty.

In Selma tonight, as in every—and we had a good day there—as in every city, we are working for just and peaceful settlement. We must all remember that after this speech I am making tonight, after the police and the FBI and the Marshals have all gone, and after you have promptly passed this bill, the people of Selma and the other cities of the Nation must still live and work together. And when the attention of the Nation has gone elsewhere they must try to heal the wounds and to build a new community.

This cannot be easily done on a battleground of violence, as the history of the South itself shows. It is in recognition of this that men of both races have shown such an outstandingly impressive responsibility in recent days—last Tuesday, again today.

RIGHTS MUST BE OPPORTUNITIES

The bill that I am presenting to you will be known as a civil rights bill. But, in a larger sense, most of the program I am recommending is a civil rights program. Its object is to open the city of hope to all people of all races.

Because all Americans just must have the right to vote. And we are going to give them that right.

All Americans must have the privileges of citizenship regardless of race. And they are going to have those privileges of citizenship regardless of race.

But I would like to caution you and remind you that to exercise these privileges takes much more than just legal right. It requires a trained mind and a healthy body. It requires a decent home, and the chance to find a job, and the opportunity to escape from the clutches of poverty.

Of course, people cannot contribute to the Nation if they are never taught to read or write, if their bodies are stunted from hunger, if their sickness goes untended, if their life is spent in hopeless poverty just drawing a welfare check.

So we want to open the gates to opportunity. But we are also going to give all our people, black and white, the help that they need to walk through those gates.

THE PURPOSE OF THIS GOVERNMENT

My first job after college was as a teacher in Cotulla, Tex., in a small Mexican-American school. Few of them could speak English, and I couldn't speak much Spanish. My students were poor and they often came to class without breakfast, hungry. They knew even in their youth the pain of prejudice. They never seemed to know why people disliked them. But they knew it was so, because I saw it in their eyes. I often walked home late in the afternoon, after the classes were finished, wishing there was more that I could do. But all I knew was to teach them the little that I knew, hoping that it might help them against the hardships that lay ahead.

Somehow you never forget what poverty and hatred can do when you see its scars on the hopeful face of a young child.

I never thought then, in 1928, that I would be standing here in 1965. It never even occurred to me in my fondest dreams that I might have the chance to help the sons and daughters of those students and to help people like them all over this country.

But now I do have that chance—and I'll let you in on a secret—I mean to use it. And I hope that you will use it with me.

This is the richest and most powerful country which ever occupied the globe. The might of past empires is little compared to ours. But I do not want to be the President who built empires, or sought grandeur, or extended dominion.

I want to be the President who educated young children to the wonders of their world. I want to be the President who helped to feed the hungry and to prepare them to be taxpayers instead of taxeaters.

I want to be the President who helped the poor to find their own way and who protected the right of every citizen to vote in every election.

I want to be the President who helped to end hatred among his fellow men and who promoted love among the people of all races and all regions and all parties.

I want to be the President who helped to end war among the brothers of this earth.

And so at the request of your beloved Speaker and the Senator from Montana; the majority leader, the Senator from Illinois; the minority leader, Mr. McCulloch, and other Members of both parties, I came here tonight—not as President Roosevelt came down one time in person to veto a bonus bill, not as President Truman came down one time to urge the passage of a railroad bill—but I came down here to ask you to share this task with me and to share it with the people that we both work for. I want this to be the Congress, Republicans and Democrats alike, which did all these things for all these people.

Beyond this great chamber, out yonder in 50 States, are the people that we serve. Who can tell what deep and unspoken hopes are in their hearts tonight as they sit there and listen. We all can guess, from our own lives, how difficult they often find their own pursuit of happiness, how many problems each little family has. They look most of all to themselves for their futures. But I think that they also look to each of us.

Above the pyramid on the great seal of the United States it says—in Latin—"God has favored our undertaking."

God will not favor everything that we do. It is rather our duty to divine His will. But I cannot help believing that He truly understands and that He really favors the undertaking that we begin here tonight.

[15 March 1965]

XXIX

No one was more dedicated to the tenet of "We Shall Overcome" than Martin Luther King, Jr. (1929–1968). King became the master strategist of nonviolent direct action and the agenda of bringing to bear moral outrage on the discriminatory practices of America in the struggle for change. He received his bachelor's degree at Morehouse College in Atlanta in 1948. From there he went on to Crozer Theological Seminary in Pennsylvania and finally worked and received his PhD in religious studies at Boston University in 1955. It was during this same period that he met and married Coretta Scott. He would serve in his father's footsteps in the Ebenezer Baptist Church in Atlanta. Serving later as an assistant pastor at the Dexter Avenue Baptist Church in Montgomery, Alabama, King was thrust into the national limelight when, in 1955, he became head of the Montgomery Improvement Association and the Montgomery bus boycott. With the boycott and the founding of the Southern Christian Leadership Conference, Martin Luther King, Jr., along with African-American leaders Rosa Parks, E. D. Nixon, Fred Shuttlesworth, and others, was at the forefront of what would be defined as the beginning of the civil rights movement in America. Perhaps King's greatest day was in 1963 at the head of the March on Washington. The following year he witnessed President Lyndon Baines Johnson's signing into law the Civil Rights Act of 1964, and the next year the Voting Rights Act of 1965. In "The World House," Martin Luther King, Jr. sees all races in the United States as under the same roof and compelled out of necessity to learn how to live with one another. Is he correct? Are we all in this together? What do you think of King's point that we need a revolution of values, and that this revolution should be worldwide with America taking the lead? Do we have, as he says, a choice between chaos or community?

"The World House"

Martin Luther King, Jr.

Some years ago a famous novelist died. Among his papers was found a list of suggested plots for future stories, the most prominently underscored being this one: "A widely separated family inherits a house in which they have to live together." This is the great new problem of mankind. We have inherited a large home, a great "world house" in which we have to live together — black and white, Easterner and Westerner, Gentile and Jew, Catholic and Protestant, Muslim and Hindu — a family unduly separated in ideas, culture and interest, who, because we can never again live apart, must learn somehow to live with each other in peace.

However deeply American Negroes are caught in the struggle to be at last at home in our homeland of the United States, we cannot ignore the larger world house in which we are also dwellers. Equality with whites will not solve the problems of either whites or Negroes if it means equality in a world society stricken by poverty and in a universe doomed to extinction by war.

All inhabitants of the globe are now neighbors. This worldwide neighborhood has been brought into being largely as a result of the modem scientific and technological revolutions. The world of today is vastly different from the world of just one hundred years ago. A century ago Thomas Edison had not yet invented the incandescent lamp to bring light to many dark places of the earth. The Wright brothers had not yet invented that fascinating mechanical bird that would spread its gigantic wing across the skies and soon dwarf distance and place time in the service of man. Einstein had not yet challenged an axiom and the theory of relativity had not yet been posited.

Human being, searching a century ago as now for better understanding, had no television, no radios, no telephones and no motion pictures through which to communicate. Medical science had not yet discovered the wonder drugs to end many dread plagues and diseases. One hundred years ago military men had not yet developed the terrifying weapons of warfare that we know today—not the bomber, an airborne fortress raining down death; nor napalm, that burner of all things and flesh in its path. A century ago there were no sky-scraping buildings to kiss the stars and no gargantuan bridges to span the waters. Science had not yet peered into the unfathomable ranges of interstellar space, nor had it penetrated oceanic depths. All these new inventions, these new ideas, these sometimes fascinating and sometimes frightening developments, came later. Most of them have come within the past sixty years, sometimes with agonizing slowness, more characteristically with bewildering speed, but always with enormous significance for our future.

The years ahead will see a continuation of the same dramatic developments. Physical science will carve new highways through the stratosphere. In a few years astronauts and cosmonauts will probably walk comfortably across the uncertain pathways of the moon. In two or three years it will be possible, because of the new supersonic jets, to fly from New York to London in two and one-half hours. In the years ahead medical science will greatly prolong the lives of men by finding a cure for cancer and deadly heart ailments. Automation and cybernation will make it possible for working people to have undreamed-of amounts of leisure time. All this is a dazzling picture of the furniture, the workshop, the spacious rooms, the new decorations and the architectural pattern of the large world house in which we are living

Along with the scientific and technological revolution, we have also witnessed a worldwide freedom revolution over the last few decades. The present upsurge of the Negro people of the United States grows out of a deep and passionate determination to make freedom and equality a reality "here" and "now." In one sense the civil rights movement in the United States is a special American phenomenon which must be understood in the light of American history and dealt with in terms of the American situation. But on another and more important level, what is happening in the United States today is a significant part of a world development.

We live in a day, said the philosopher Alfred North Whitehead, "when civilization is shifting its basic outlook: a major turning point in history where the pre-suppositions on which society is structured are being analyzed, sharply challenged, and profoundly changed." What we are seeing now is a freedom explosion, the realization of "an idea whose time has come," to use Victor Hugo's phrase. The deep rumbling of discontent that we hear today is the thunder of disinherited masses, rising from dungeons of oppression to the bright hills of freedom. In one majestic chorus the rising masses are singing, in the words of our freedom song, "Ain't gonna let nobody turn us around." All over the world like a fever, freedom is spreading in the widest liberation movement in history. The great masses of people are determined to end the exploitation of their races and lands. They are awake and moving toward their goal like a tidal wave. You can hear them rumbling in every village street, on the docks, in the houses, among the students, in the churches and at political meetings. For several centuries the direction of history flowed from the nations and societies of Western Europe out into the rest of the world in "conquests" of various sorts. That period, the era of colonialism, is at an end. East is moving West. The earth is being redistributed. Yes, we are "shifting our basic outlooks."

These developments should not surprise any student of history. Oppressed people cannot remain oppressed forever. The yearning for freedom eventually manifests itself. The Bible tells the thrilling story of how Moses stood in Pharaoh's court centuries ago and cried, "Let my people go." This was an opening chapter in a continuing story. The present struggle in the United States is a later chapter in the same story. Something within has reminded the Negro of his birthright of freedom, and something without has reminded him that it can be gained. Consciously or unconsciously, he has been caught up by the spirit of the times, and with his black brothers of Africa and his brown and yellow brothers in Asia, South America and the Caribbean, the United States Negro is moving with a sense of great urgency toward the promised land of racial justice.

Nothing could be more tragic than for men to live in these revolutionary times and fail to achieve the new attitudes and the new mental outlooks that the new situation demands. In Washington Irving's familiar story of Rip Van Winkle, the one thing that we usually remember is that Rip slept twenty years. These is another important point, however, that is almost always overlooked. It was the sign on the inn in the little town on the Hudson from which Rip departed and scaled the mountain for his long sleep. When he went up, the sign had a picture of King George III of England. When he came down, twenty years later, the sign had a picture of George Washington. As he looked at the picture of the first President of the United States, Rip was confused, flustered and lost. He knew not who Washington was. The most striking thing about this story is not that Rip slept twenty years but that he slept through a revolution that would alter the course of human history.

One of the great liabilities of history is that all too many people fail to remain awake through great periods of social change. Every society has its protectors of the status quo and its fraternities of the indifferent who are notorious for sleeping through revolutions. But today our very survival depends on our ability to stay awake, to adjust to new ideas, to remain vigilant and to face the challenge of change. The large house in which we live demands that we transform this neighborhood into a worldwide brotherhood. Together we must learn to live as brothers or together we will be forced to perish as fools.

We must work passionately and indefatigably to bridge the gulf between our scientific progress and our moral progress. One of the great problems of mankind is that we suffer from a poverty of the spirit which stands in glaring contrast to our scientific and technological abundance. The richer we have become materially, the poorer we have become morally and spiritually.

Every man lives in two realms, the internal and the external. The internal is that realm of spiritual ends expressed in art, literature, morals and religion. The external is that complex of devices, techniques, mechanisms and instrumentalities by means of which we live. Our problem today is that we have allowed the internal to become lost in the external. We have allowed the means by which we live to outdistance the ends for which we live. So much of modern life can be summarized in that suggestive phrase of Thoreau: "Improved means to an unimproved end." This is the serious predicament, the deep and haunting problem, confronting modem man. Enlarged material powers spell enlarged peril if there is not proportionate growth of the soul. When the external of man's nature subjugates the internal, dark storm clouds begin to form.

Western civilization is particularly vulnerable at this moment, for our material abundance has brought us neither peace of mind nor serenity of spirit. An Asian writer has portrayed our dilemma in candid terms:

> You call your thousand material devices "labor-saving machinery," yet you are forever "busy." With the multiplying of your machinery you grow increasingly fatigued, anxious, nervous, dissatisfied. Whatever you have, you want more; and wherever you are you want to go somewhere else ... your devices are neither time-saving nor soul-saving machinery. They are so many sharp spurs which urge you on to invent more machinery and to do more business.

This tells us something about our civilization that cannot be cast aside as a prejudiced charge by an Eastern thinker who jealous of Western prosperity. We cannot escape the indictment.

This does not mean that we must turn back the clock of scientific progress. No one can overlook the wonders that science has wrought for our lives. The automobile will not abdicate in favor of the horse and buggy, or the train in favor of the stagecoach, or the tractor in favor of the hand plow, or the scientific method in favor of ignorance and superstition. But our moral and spiritual "lag" must be redeemed. When scientific power outruns moral power, we end up with guided missiles and misguided men. When we foolishly minimize the internal of our lives and maximize the external, we sign the warrant for our own day of doom.

Our hope for creative living in this world house that we have inherited lies in our ability to reestablish the moral ends of our lives in personal character and social justice. Without this spiritual and moral reawakening we shall destroy ourselves in the misuse of our own instruments.

II

Among the moral imperatives of our time, we are challenged to work all over the world with unshakable determination to wipe out the last vestiges racism. As early as 1906 W. E. B. Du Bois prophesied that "the problem of the twentieth century will be the problem of the color line." Now as we stand two-thirds into this exciting period of history we know full well that racism is still that hound of hell which dogs the tracks of our civilization.

Racism is no mere American phenomenon. Its vicious grasp knows no geographical boundaries. in fact, racism and its perennial ally — economic exploitation — provide the key to understanding most of the international complications of this generation.

The classic example of organized and institutionalized racism is the Union of South Africa. Its national policy and practice are the incarnation of the doctrine of white supremacy in the midst of a population which is overwhelmingly black. But the tragedy of South Africa is not simply in its own policy: it is the fact that the racist government of South Africa is virtually made possible by the economic policies of the United States and Great Britain, two countries which profess to be the moral bastions of our Western world.

In country after country we see white men building empires on the sweat and suffering of colored people. Portugal continues its practices of slave labor and subjugation in Angola; the Ian Smith government in Rhodesia continues to enjoy the support of British-based industry and private capital, despite the stated opposition of British government policy. Even in the case of the little country of South West Africa we find the powerful nations of the world incapable of taking a moral position against South Africa, though the smaller country is under the trusteeship of the United Nations. Its policies are controlled by South Africa and its manpower is lured into the mines under slave-labor conditions.

During the Kennedy administration there was some awareness of the problems that breed in the racist and exploitative conditions throughout the colored world, and a temporary concern emerged to free the United States from its complicity though the effort was only on a diplomatic level. Through our ambassador to the United Nations, Adlai Stevenson, there emerged the beginnings of an intelligent approach to the colored peoples of the world. However, there remained little or no attempt to deal with the economic aspects of racist exploitation. We have been notoriously silent about the more than $700 million of American capital which props up the system of apartheid, not to mention the billions of dollars in trade and the military alliances which are maintained under the pretext of fighting Communism in Africa.

Nothing provides the Communists with a better climate for expansion and infiltration than the continued alliance of our nation with racism and exploitation throughout the world. And if we are not diligent in our determination to root out the last vestiges of racism in our dealings with the rest of the world, we may soon see the sins of our fathers visited upon ours and succeeding generations. For the conditions which are so classically represented in Africa are present also in Asia and in our own back yard in Latin America.

Everywhere in Latin America one finds a tremendous resentment of the United States, and that resentment is always strongest among the poorer and darker peoples of the continent. The life and destiny of Latin America are in the hands of United States corporations. The decisions affecting the lives of South Americans are ostensibly made by their government, but there are almost no legitimate democracies alive in the whole continent. The other governments are dominated by huge and exploitative cartels that rob Latin America of her resources while turning over a small rebate to a few members of a corrupt aristocracy, which in turn invests not in its own country for its own people's welfare but in the banks of Switzerland and the playgrounds of the world.

Here we see racism in its more sophisticated form: neocolonialism. The Bible and the annals of history are replete with tragic stories of one brother robbing another of his birthright and thereby insuring generations of strife and enmity. We can hardly escape such a judgment in Latin America, any more than we have been able to escape the harvest of hate sown in Vietnam by a century of French exploitation.

There is the convenient temptation to attribute the current turmoil and bitterness throughout the world to the presence of a Communist conspiracy to undermine Europe and America, but the potential explosiveness of our world situation is much more attributable to disillusionment with the promises of Christianity and technology.

The revolutionary leaders of Africa, Asia and Latin America have virtually all received their education in the capitals of the West. Their earliest training often occurred in Christian missionary schools. Here their sense of dignity was established and they learned that all men were sons of God. In recent years their countries have been invaded by automobiles, Coca-Cola and Hollywood, so that even remote villages have become aware of the wonders and blessings available to God's white children.

Once the aspirations and appetites of the world have been whetted by the marvels of Western technology and the self-image of a people awakened by religion, one cannot hope to keep people locked out of the earthly kingdom of wealth, health and happiness. Either they share in the blessings of the world or they organize to break down and overthrow those structures or governments which stand in the way of their goals.

Former generations could not conceive of such luxury, but their children now take this vision and demand that it become a reality. And when they look around and see that the only people who do not share in the abundance of Western technology are colored people, it is an almost inescapable conclusion that their condition and their exploitation are somehow related to their color and the racism of the white Western world.

This is a treacherous foundation for a world house. Racism can well be that corrosive evil that will bring down the curtain on Western civilization. Arnold Toynbee has said that some twenty-six civilizations have risen upon the face of the earth. Almost all of them have descended into the junk heaps of destruction. The decline and fall of these civilizations, according to Toynbee, was not caused by external invasions but by internal decay. They failed to respond creatively to the challenges impinging upon them. If Western civilization does not now respond constructively to the challenge to banish racism, some future historian will have to say that a great civilization died because it lacked the soul and commitment to make justice a reality for all men.

Another grave problem that must be solved if we are to live creatively in our world house is that of poverty on an international scale. Like a monstrous octopus, it stretches its choking, prehensile tentacles into lands and villages all over the world. Two-thirds of the peoples of the world go to bed hungry at night. They are undernourished, ill-housed and shabbily clad. Many of them have no houses or beds to sleep in. Their only beds are the sidewalks of the cities and the dusty roads of the villages. Most of these poverty-stricken children of God have never seen a physician or a dentist.

There is nothing new about poverty. What is new, however, is that we now have the resources to get rid of it. Not too many years ago, Dr. Kirtley Mather, a Harvard geologist, wrote a book entitled *Enough and to Spare*. He set forth the basic theme that famine is wholly unnecessary in the modern world. Today, therefore, the question on the agenda must read: why should there be hunger and privation in any land, in any city, at any table, when man has the resources and the scientific know-how to provide all mankind with the basic necessities of life? Even deserts can be irrigated and topsoil can be replaced. We cannot complain of a lack of land, for there are 25 million square miles of tillable land on earth, of which we are using less than seven million. We have amazing knowledge of vitamins, nutrition, the chemistry of food and the versatility of atoms. There is no deficit in human resources; the deficit is in human will.

This does not mean that we can overlook the enormous acceleration in the rate of growth of the world's population. The population explosion is very real, and it must be faced squarely if we are to avoid, in centuries ahead, a "standing room only" situation on these earthly shores. Most of the large undeveloped nations in the world today are confronted with the problem of excess population in relation to resources. But even this problem will be greatly diminished by wiping out poverty. When people see more opportunities for better education and greater economic security, they begin to consider whether a smaller family might not be better for themselves and for their children. In other words, I doubt that there can be a stabilization of the population without a prior stabilization of economic resources.

The time has come for an all-out world war against poverty. The rich nations must use their vast resources of wealth to develop the underdeveloped, school the unschooled and feed the unfed. The well-off and the secure have too often become indifferent and oblivious to the poverty and deprivation in their midst. The poor in our countries have been shut out of our minds, and driven from the mainstream of our societies, because we have allowed them to become invisible. Ultimately a great nation is a compassionate nation. No individual or nation can be great if it does not have a concern for "the least of these."

The first step in the worldwide war against poverty is passionate commitment. All the wealthy nations—America, Britain, Russia, Canada, Australia, and those of Western Europe—must see it as a moral obligation to provide capital and technical assistance to the underdeveloped areas. These rich nations have only scratched the surface in their commitment. There is need now for a general strategy of support. Sketchy aid here and there will not suffice, nor will it sustain economic growth. There must be a sustained effort extending through many years. The wealthy nations of the world must promptly initiate a massive, sustained Marshall Plan for Asia, Africa and South America. If they would allocate just a percent of their gross national product annually for a period of ten or twenty years for the development of the underdeveloped nations, mankind would go a long way toward conquering the ancient enemy, poverty.

The aid program that I am suggesting must not be used by the wealthy nations as a surreptitious means to control the poor nations. Such an approach would lead to a new form of paternalism and a neocolonialism which no self-respecting nation could accept. Ultimately, foreign aid programs must be motivated by a compassionate and committed effort to wipe poverty, ignorance and disease from the face of the earth. Money devoid of genuine empathy is like salt devoid of savor, good for nothing except to be trodden under foot of men.

The West must enter into the program with humility and penitence and a sober realization that everything will not always "go our way." It cannot be forgotten that the

Western powers were but yesterday the colonial masters. The house of the West is far from in order, and its hands are far from clean.

We must have patience. We must be willing to understand why many of the young nations will have to pass through the same extremism, revolution and aggression that formed our own history. Every new government confronts overwhelming problems. During the days when they were struggling to remove the yoke of colonialism, there was a kind of preexistent unity of purpose that kept thing moving in one solid direction. But as soon as independence emerges, all the grim problems of life confront them with stark realism: the lack of capital, the strangulating poverty, the uncontrollable birth rates and, above all, the high aspirational level of their own people. The post-colonial period is more difficult and precarious than the colonial struggle itself.

The West must also understand that its economic growth took place under rather pro-pitious circumstances. Most of the Western nations were relatively under-populated when they surged forward economically, and they were greatly endowed with the iron ore and coal that were needed for launching industry. Most of the young governments of the world today have come into being without these advantages, and, above all, they confront staggering problems of overpopulation. There is no possible way for them to make it without aid and assistance.

A genuine program on the part of the wealthy nations to make prosperity a reality for the poor nations will in the final analysis enlarge the prosperity of all. One of the best proofs that reality hinges on moral foundations is the fact that when men and gov-ernments work devotedly for the good of others, they achieve their own enrichment in the process.

From time immemorial men have lived by the principle that "self-preservation is the first law of life." But this is a false assumption, I would say that other-preservation is the first law of life. It is the first law of life precisely because we cannot preserve self with-out being concerned about preserving other selves. The universe is so structured that things go awry if men are not diligent in their cultivation of the other-regarding di-mension. "I" cannot reach fulfillment without "thou." The self cannot be self without other selves. Self-concern without other-concern is like a tributary that has no outward flow to the ocean. Stagnant, still and stale, it lacks both life and freshness. Nothing would be more disastrous and out of harmony with our self-interest than for the de-veloped nations to travel a dead-end road of inordinate selfishness. We are in the for-tunate position of having our deepest sense of morality coalesce with our self-interest.

But the real reason that we must use our resources to outlaw poverty goes beyond material concerns to the quality of our mind and spirit. Deeply woven into the fiber of our religious tradition is the conviction that men are made in the image of God, and that they are souls of infinite metaphysical value. If we accept this as a profound moral fact, we cannot be content to see men hungry, to see men victimized with ill-health, when we have the means to help them. In the final analysis, the rich must not ignore the poor because both rich and poor are tied together. They entered the same mysterious gate-way of human birth, into the same adventure of mortal life.

All men are interdependent. Every nation is an heir of a vast treasury of ideas and labor to which both the living and the dead of all nations have contributed. Whether we realize it or not, each of us lives eternally "in the red." We are everlasting debtors to known and unknown men and women. When we arise in the morning, we go into the bathroom where we reach for a sponge which is provided for us by a Pacific Islander. We reach for soap that is created for us by a European. Then at the table we drink coffee which is provided for us by a South American, or tea by a Chinese or cocoa by a West African. Before we leave for our jobs we are already beholden to more than half of the world.

In a real sense, all life is interrelated. The agony of the poor impoverishes the rich; the betterment of the poor enriches the rich. We are inevitably our brother's keeper because we are our brother's brother. Whatever affects one directly affects all indirectly.

A final problem that mankind must solve in order to survive in the world house that we have inherited is finding an alternative to war and human destruction. Recent events have vividly reminded us that nations are not reducing but rather increasing their arsenals of weapons of mass destruction. The best brains in the highly developed nations of the world are devoted to military technology. The proliferation of nuclear weapons has not been halted, in spite of the limited-test-ban treaty.

In this day of man's highest technical achievement, in this day of dazzling discovery of novel opportunities, loftier dignities and fuller freedoms for all, there is no excuse for the kind of blind craving for power and resources that provoked the wars of previous generations. There is no need to fight for food and land. Science has provided us with adequate means of survival and transportation, which make it possible to enjoy the fullness of this great earth. The question now is do we have the morality and courage required to live together as brothers and not be afraid?

One of the most persistent ambiguities we face is that everybody talks about peace as a goal; but among the wielders of power peace is practically nobody's business. Many men cry "Peace! Peace!" but they refuse to do the things that make for peace.

The large power blocs talk passionately of pursuing peace while expanding defense budgets that already bulge, enlarging already awesome armies and devising ever more devastating weapons. Call the roll of those who sing the glad tidings of peace and one's ears will be surprised by the responding sounds. The heads of all the nations issue clarion calls for peace, yet they come to the peace table accompanied by bands of brigands each bearing unsheathed swords.

The stages of history are replete with the chants and choruses of the conquerors of old who came killing in pursuit of peace. Alexander, Genghis Khan, Julius Caesar, Charlermagne and Napoleon were akin in seeking a peaceful world order, a world fashioned after their selfish conceptions of an ideal existence. Each sought a world at peace which would personify his egotistic dreams. Even within the life span of most of us, another megalomaniac strode across the world stage. He sent his blitzkrieg-bent legions blazing across Europe, bringing havoc and holocaust in his wake. There is grave irony in the fact that Hitler could come forth, following nakedly aggressive expansionist theories, and do it all in the name of peace.

So when in, this day I see the leaden of nations again talking peace while preparing for war, I take fearful pause. When I see our country today intervening in what is basically a civil war, mutilating hundreds of thousands of Vietnamese children with napalm, burning villages and rice fields at random, painting the valleys of that small Asian country red with human blood, leaving broken bodies in countless ditches and sending home half-men, mutilated mentally and physically, when I see the unwillingness of our government to create the atmosphere for a negotiated settlement of this awful conflict by halting bombing in the North and agreeing unequivocally to talk with the Vietcong—and all this in the name of pursuing the goal of peace—I tremble for our world. I do so not only from dire recall of the nightmares wreaked in the wars of yesterday, but also from dreadful realization of today's possible nuclear destructiveness and tomorrow's even more calamitous prospects.

Before it is too late we must narrow the gaping chasm between our proclamations of peace and our lowly deeds which precipitate and perpetuate war. We are called upon to look up from the quagmire of military programs and defense commitments and read the warning on history's signposts.

One day we must come to see that peace is not merely a distant goal that we seek but a means by which we arrive at that goal. We must pursue peaceful ends through peaceful means. How much longer must we play at deadly war games before we heed the plaintive pleas of the unnumbered dead and maimed of past wars?

President John F. Kennedy said on one occasion, "Mankind must put an end to war or war will put an end to mankind." Wisdom born of experience should tell us that war is obsolete. There may have been a time when war served as a negative good by preventing the spread and growth of evil force, but the destructive power of modern weapons eliminates even the possibility that war may serve any good at all. If we assume that life is worth living and that man has a right to survive, then we must find an alternative to war. In a day when vehicles hurtle through outer space and guided ballistic missiles carve highways of death through the stratosphere, no nation can claim victory in war. A so-called limited war will leave little more than a calamitous legacy of human suffering, political turmoil and spiritual disillusionment. A world war will leave only smoldering ashes as mute testimony of a human race whose folly led inexorably to ultimate death. If modern man continues to flirt unhesitatingly with war, he will transform his earthly habitat into an inferno such as even the mind of Dante could not imagine.

Therefore I suggest that the philosophy and strategy of nonviolence become immediately a subject for study and for serious experimentation in every field of human conflict, by no means excluding the relations between nations. It is, after all, nation-states which make war, which have produced the weapons that threaten the survival of mankind and which are both genocidal and suicidal in character.

We have ancient habits to deal with, vast structures of power, indescribably complicated problems to solve. But unless we abdicate our humanity altogether and succumb to fear and impotence in the presence of the weapons we have ourselves created, it is as possible and as urgent to put an end to war and violence between nations as it is to put an end to poverty and racial injustice.

The United Nations is a gesture in the direction of nonviolence on a world scale. There, at least, states that oppose one another have sought to do so with words instead of with weapons. But true nonviolence is more than the absence of violence. It is the persistent and determined application of peaceable power to offenses against the community—in this case the world community. As the United Nations moves ahead with the giant tasks confronting it, I would hope that it would earnestly examine the uses of nonviolent direct action.

I do not minimize the complexity of the problems that need to be faced in achieving disarmament and peace. But I am convinced that we shall not have the will, the courage and the insight to deal with such matters unless in this field we are prepared to undergo a mental and spiritual reevaluation, a change of focus which will enable us to see that the things that seem most real and powerful are indeed now unreal and have come under sentence of death. We need to make a supreme effort to generate the readiness, indeed the eagerness, to enter into the new world which is now possible, "the city which hath foundation, whose Building and Maker is God."

It is not enough to say, "We must not wage war." It is necessary to love peace and sacrifice for it. We must concentrate not merely on the eradication of war but on the affirmation of peace. A fascinating story about Ulysses and the Sirens is preserved for us in Greek literature. The Sirens had the ability to sing so sweetly that sailors could not resist steering toward their island. Many ships were lured upon the rocks, and men forgot home, duty and honor as they flung themselves into the sea to be embraced by arms that drew than down to death. Ulysses, determined not to succumb to the Sirens, first decided to tie himself tightly to the mast of his boat and his crew stuffed their ears with wax. But finally he and his crew learned a better way to save themselves: they took on board the beautiful singer Orpheus, whose melodies were sweeter than the music of the Sirens. When Orpheus sang, who would bother to listen to the Sirens?

So we must see that peace represents a sweeter music, a cosmic melody that is far superior to the discords of war. Somehow we must transform the dynamics of the world power struggle from the nuclear arms race, which no one can win, to a creative contest to harness man's genius for the purpose of making peace and prosperity a reality for all the nations of the world. In short, we must shift the arms race into a "peace race." If we have the will and determination to mount such a peace offensive, we will unlock hitherto tightly sealed doors of hope and bring new light into the dark chambers of pessimism.

III

The stability of the large world house which is ours will involve a revolution of values to accompany the scientific and freedom revolutions engulfing the earth. We must rapidly begin the shift from a "thing"-oriented society to a "person"-oriented society. When machines and computers, profit motives and property rights are considered more important than people, the giant triplets of racism, materialism and militarism are incapable of being conquered. A civilization can flounder as readily in the face of moral and spiritual bankruptcy as it can through financial bankruptcy.

This revolution of values must go beyond traditional capitalism and Communism. We must honestly admit that capitalism has often left a gulf between superfluous wealth and abject poverty, has created conditions permitting necessities to be taken from the many to give luxuries to the few, and has encouraged smallhearted men to become cold and conscienceless so that, like Dives before Lazarus, they are unmoved by suffering, poverty-stricken humanity. The profit motive, when it is the sole basis of an economic system, encourages a cutthroat competition and selfish ambition that inspire men to be more I-centered than thou-centered. Equally, Communism reduces men to a cog in the wheel of the state. The Communist may object, saying that in Marxian theory the state is an "interim reality" that will "wither away" when the classless society emerges. True — in theory; but it is also true that, while the state lasts, it is an end in itself. Man is a means to that end. He has no inalienable nights. His only sights are derived from, and conferred by, the state. Under such a system the fountain of freedom runs dry. Restricted are man's liberties of press and assembly, his freedom to vote and his freedom to listen and to read.

Truth is found neither in traditional capitalism nor in classical Communism. Each represents a partial truth. Capitalism fails to see the truth in collectivism. Communism fails to see the truth in individualism. Capitalism fails to realize that life is social. Communism fails to realize that life is personal. The good and just society is neither the thesis of capitalism nor the antithesis of Communism, but a socially conscious democracy which reconciles the truths of individualism and collectivism.

We have seen some moves in this direction. The Soviet Union has gradually moved away from its rigid Communism and begun to concern itself with consumer products, art and a general increase in benefits to the individual citizen. At the same time, through constant social reforms, we have seen many modifications in laissez-faire capitalism. The problems we now face must take us beyond slogans for their solution. In the final analysis, the right-wing slogans on "government control" and "creeping socialism" are as meaningless and adolescent as the Chinese Red Guard slogans against "bourgeois revisionism." An intelligent approach to the problems of poverty and racism will cause us to see that the words of the Psalmist — "The earth is the Lord's and the fullness thereof" — are still a judgment upon our use and abuse of the wealth and resources with which we have been endowed.

A true revolution of value will soon cause us to question the fairness and justice of many of our past and present policies. We are called to play the Good Samaritan on life's roadside but that will be only an initial act. One day the whole Jericho Road must be transformed so that men and women will not be beaten and robbed as they make their journey through life. True compassion is more than flinging a coin to a beggar; it understands that an edifice which produces beggars needs restructuring.

A true revolution of values will soon look uneasily on the glaring contrast of poverty and wealth. With righteous indignation, it will look at thousands of working people displaced from their jobs with reduced incomes as a result of automation while the profits of the employers remain intact, and say: "This is not just." It will look across the oceans and see individual capitalists of the West investing huge sums of money in Asia, Africa and South America, only to take the profits out with no concern for the social betterment of the countries, and say: "This is not just." It will look at our alliance with the landed gentry of Latin America and say: "This is not just." The Western arrogance of feeling that it has everything to teach others and nothing to learn from them is not just. A true revolution of values will lay hands on the world order and say of war: "This way of settling differences is not just." This business of burning human beings with napalm, of filling our nation's homes with orphans and widows, of injecting poisonous drugs of hate into the veins of peoples normally humane, of sending men home from dark and bloody battlefields physically handicapped and psychologically deranged, cannot be reconciled with wisdom, justice and love. A nation that continues year after year to spend more money on military defense than on programs of social uplift is approaching spiritual death.

America, the richest and most powerful nation in the world, can well lead the way in this revolution of values. There is nothing to prevent us from paying adequate wages to schoolteachers, social workers and other servants of the public to insure that we have the best available personnel in these positions which are charged with the responsibility of guiding our future generations. There is nothing but a lack of social vision to prevent us from paying an adequate wage to every American citizen whether he be a hospital worker, laundry worker, maid or day laborer. There is nothing except shortsightedness to prevent us from guaranteeing an annual minimum — and livable — income for every American family. There is nothing, except a tragic death wish, to prevent us from reordering our priorities, so that the pursuit of peace will take precedence over the pursuit of war, There is nothing to keep us from remolding a recalcitrant status quo with bruised hands until we have fashioned it into a brotherhood.

This kind of positive revolution of values is our best defense against Communism. War is not the answer. Communism will never be defeated by the use of atomic bombs or nuclear weapons. Let us not join those who shout war and who through their misguided passions urge the United States to relinquish its participation in the United Nations. These are days which demand wise restraint and calm reasonableness. We must not call everyone a Communist or an appeaser who advocates the seating of Red China in the United Nations, or who recognizes that hate and hysteria are not the final answers to the problems of these turbulent days. We must not engage in a negative anti-Communism, but rather in a positive thrust for democracy, realizing that our greatest defense against Communism is to take offensive action in behalf of justice. We must with affirmative action seek to remove those conditions of poverty, insecurity and injustice which are the fertile soil in which the seed of Communism grows and develops.

These are revolutionary times. All over the globe men are revolting against old systems of exploitation and oppression, and out of the wombs of a frail world new systems of justice and equality are being born. The shirtless and barefoot people of the earth are rising up as never before. "The people who sat in darkness have seen a great light." We in the West must support these revolutions. It is a sad fact that, because of comfort, complacency, a morbid fear of Communism and our proneness to adjust to injustice, the Western nations that initiated so much of the revolutionary spirit of the modern world have now become the arch anti-revolutionaries. This has driven many to feel that only Marxism has the revolutionary spirit. Communism is a judgment on our failure to make democracy real and to follow through on the revolutions that we initiated. Our only hope today lies in our ability to recapture the revolutionary spirit and go out into a sometimes hostile world declaring eternal opposition to poverty, racism and militarism. With this powerful commitment we shall boldly challenge the status quo and unjust mores and thereby speed the day when "every valley shall be exalted, and every mountain and hill shall be made low; and the crooked shall be made straight and the rough places plain."

A genuine revolution of values means in the final analysis that our loyalties must become ecumenical rather than sectional. Every nation must now develop an overriding loyalty to mankind as a whole in order to preserve the best in their individual societies. This call for a worldwide fellowship that lifts neighborly concern beyond one's tribe, race, class and nation is in reality a call for an all-embracing and unconditional love for all men. This often misunderstood and misinterpreted concept has now become an absolute necessity for the survival of man. When I speak of love, I am speaking of that force which all the great religions have seen as the supreme unifying principle of life. Love is the key that unlocks the door which leads to ultimate reality. This Hindu-Muslim-Christian-Jewish-Buddhist belief about ultimate reality is beautifully summed up in the First Epistle of Saint John:

> Let us love one another: for love is of God:
> and every one that loveth is born of God, and
> knoweth God. He that loveth not knoweth not
> God; for God is love ... If we love one another,
> God dwelleth in us, and his love is perfected in us.

Let us hope that this spirit will become the order of the day. We can no longer afford to worship the God of hate or bow before the altar of retaliation. The oceans of history are made turbulent by the ever-rising tides of hate. History is cluttered with the wreckage of nations and individuals who pursued this self-defeating path of hate. As Arnold Toynbee once said in a speech: "Love is the ultimate force that makes for the saving choice of life and good against the damning choice of death and evil. Therefore the first hope in our inventory must be the hope that love is going to have the last word."

We are now faced with the fact that tomorrow is today. We arc confronted with the fierce urgency of now. In this unfolding conundrum of life and history there is such a thing as being too late. Procrastination is still the thief of time. Life often leaves us standing bare, naked and dejected with a lost opportunity. The "tide in the affairs of men" does not remain at the flood; it ebbs. We may cry out desperately for time to pause in her passage, but time is deaf to every plea and rushes on. Over the bleached bones and jumbled residues of numerous civilizations are written the pathetic words: "Too late." There is an invisible book of life that faithfully records our vigilance or our neglect. "The moving finger writes, and having writ moves on...." We still have a choice today: nonviolent coexistence or violent coannihilation. This may well be mankind's last chance to choose between chaos and community.

[1967]

XXX

Malcolm X (1925–1965) confronted the system with his every breath when he was a minister of the Nation of Islam. Born Malcolm Little in Omaha, Nebraska, in 1925, Malcolm was raised on the memory of a father who was a follower of Marcus Garvey and had been murdered for his activism. His mother broke under the psychological strain and the children were taken away from her. Malcolm was a survivor. Although always possessing a brilliant mind, his early adult years were spent involved in crime, ranging from hustling and gambling to petty larceny and robbery. It was in prison that he discovered the joy of reading and immersed himself in the prison library. It was also while incarcerated that he was converted to Islam and the teachings of Elijah Mohammed. His brilliance and incredible speaking ability made Elijah Mohammed take notice of him. In short order after his release from prison he became Mohammed's national spokesperson for the Nation of Islam, charged with bringing in new members. While in the nation he met and married Betty Shabazz in 1958. They had four children together. His tumultuous split with Elijah Mohammed in the Nation of Islam came in 1964 after his return from Mecca; he established a new organization independent of his former mentor and challenged the unorthodox teachings of the Nation of Islam. Malcolm X was assassinated in 1965 at the age of 39, the same age at which Martin Luther King, Jr. would be killed three years later. Malcolm X left many words of wisdom in his speeches and in writings, including among them the piece presented here, "The Oppressed Masses of the World Cry Out for Action against the Common Oppressor," delivered at the London School of Economics shortly before his death. Was Malcolm correct in advocating that nonviolence made no sense when others were violent to you? Should blacks defend themselves against racist attackers? Is the negative image of blacks a major factor in their oppression and the violence against them? Why did Malcolm see the Bandung Conference as vital to changing the world for people of color? Was he correct in his belief in the necessity of a shared international identity with Africa?

"The Oppressed Masses of the World Cry Out for Action Against the Common Oppressor"

Malcolm X

It is only being a Muslim which keeps me from seeing people by the color of their skin. This religion teaches brotherhood but I have to be a realist—I live in America, a society which does not believe in brotherhood in any sense of the term. Brute force is used by white racists to suppress nonwhites. It is a racist society ruled by segregationists.

We are not for violence in any shape or form but believe that the people who have violence committed against them should be able to defend themselves. By what they are doing to me they arouse me to violence. People should only be nonviolent as long as they are dealing with a nonviolent person. Intelligence demands the return of violence with violence. Every time you let someone stand on your head and you don't do anything about it, you are not acting with intelligence and should not be on this earth— you won't be on this earth very long either.

I have never said that Negroes should initiate acts of aggression against whites, but where the government fails to protect the Negro he is entitled to do it himself. He is within his rights. I have found the only white elements who do not want this advice given to undefensive Blacks are the the racist liberals. They use the press to project us in the image of violence.

There is an element of whites who are nothing but cold, animalistic racists. That element is the one that controls or has strong influence in the power structure. It uses the press skillfully to feed statistics to the public to make it appear that the rate of crime in the Black community, or community of nonwhite people, is at such a high level. It gives the impression or the image that everyone in that community is criminal.

And as soon as the public accepts the fact that the dark-skinned community consists largely of criminals or people who are dirty, then it makes it possible for the power structure to set up a police-state system. Which will make it permissible in the minds of even the well-meaning white public for them to come in and use all kinds of police methods to brutally suppress the struggle on the part of these people against segregation, discrimination, and other acts that are unleashed against them that are absolutely unjust.

They use the press to set up this police state, and they use the press to make the white public accept whatever they do to the dark-skinned public. They do that here in London right now with the constant reference to the West Indian population and the Asian population having a high rate of crime or having a tendency toward dirtiness. They have all kinds of negative characteristics that they project to make the white public draw back, or to make the white public be apathetic when police-state-like methods are used in these areas to suppress the people's honest and just struggle against discrimination and other forms of segregation.

A good example of how they do it in New York: Last summer, when the Blacks were rioting—the riots, actually they weren't riots in the first place; they were reactions against police brutality. And when the Afro-Americans reacted against the brutal measures that were executed against them by the police, the press all over the world projected them as rioters. When the store windows were broken in the Black community, immediately it was made to appear that this was being done not by people who were reacting over civil rights violations, but they gave the impression that these were hoodlums, vagrants, criminals, who wanted nothing other than to get into the stores and take the merchandise.

But this is wrong. In America the Black community in which we live is not owned by us. The landlord is white. The merchant is white. In fact, the entire economy of the Black community in the States is controlled by someone who doesn't even live there. The property that we live in is owned by someone else. The store that we trade with is operated by someone else. And these are the people who suck the economic blood of our community.

And being in a position to suck the economic blood of our community, they control the radio programs that cater to us, they control the newspapers, the advertising, that cater to us. They control our minds. They end up controlling our civic originations. They end up controlling us economically, politically, socially, mentally, and every other kind of way. They suck our blood like vultures.

And when you see the Blacks react, since the people who do this aren't there, they react against their property. The property is the only thing that's there. And they destroy it. And you get the impression over here that because they are destroying the property where they live, that they are destroying their own property. No. They can't get to the man, so they get at what he owns.

This doesn't say it's intelligent. But whoever heard of a sociological explosion that was done intelligently and politely? And this is what you're trying to make the Black man do. You're trying to drive him into a ghetto and make him the victim of every kind of unjust condition imaginable. Then when he explodes, you want him to explode politely! You want him to explode according to somebody's ground rules. Why, you're dealing with the wrong man, and you're dealing with him at the wrong time in the wrong way.

Another example of how this imagery is mastered, at the international level, is the recent situation in the Congo. Here we have an example of planes dropping bombs on defenseless African villages. When a bomb is dropped on an African village, there's no way of defending the people from the bomb. The bomb doesn't make a distinction between men and women. That bomb is dropped on men, women, children, and babies. Now it has not been in any way a disguised fact that planes have been dropping bombs on Congolese villages all during the entire summer. There is no outcry. There is no concern. There is no sympathy. There is no urge on the part of even the so-called progressive element to try and bring a halt to this mass murder. Why?

Because all the press had to do was use that shrewd propaganda word that these villages were in "rebel-held" territory. "Rebel-held," what does that mean? That's an enemy, so anything that they do to those people is all right. You cease to think of the women and the children and the babies in the so-called rebel-held territory as human beings. So that anything that is done to them is done with justification. And the progressives, the liberals don't even make any outcry. They sit twiddling their thumbs, as if they were captivated by this press imagery that has been mastered here in the West also.

They refer to the pilots that are dropping the bombs on these babies as "American-trained, anti-Castro Cuban pilots." As long as they are American-trained, this is supposed to put the stamp of approval on it, because America is your ally. As long as they are anti-Castro Cubans, since Castro is supposed to be a monster and these pilots are against Castro, anybody else they are against is also all right. So the American planes with American bombs being piloted by American-trained pilots, dropping American bombs on Black people, Black babies, Black children, destroying them completely—which is nothing but mass murder—goes absolutely unnoticed..... .

They take this man Tshombe—I guess he's a man—and try and make him acceptable to the public by using the press to refer to him as the only one who can unite the

Congo. Imagine, a murderer—not an ordinary murderer, a murderer of a prime minister, the murderer of the rightful prime minister of the Congo—and yet they want to force him upon the people of the Congo, through Western manipulation and Western pressures. The United States, the country that I come from, pays his salary. They openly admit that they pay his salary. And in saying this, I don't want you to think that I come here to make an anti-American speech. I wouldn't come here for that. I come here to make a speech to tell you the truth. And if the truth is anti-American, then blame the truth, don't blame me.

He's propped up by American dollars. The salaries of the hired killers from South Africa that he uses to kill innocent Congolese are paid by American dollars. Which means that I come from a country that is busily sending the Peace Corps to Nigeria while sending hired killers to the Congo. The government is not consistent; something is not right there. And it starts some of my African brothers and sisters that have been so happy to see the Peace Corps landing on their shores to take another look at that thing, and see what it really is. Exactly what it says: Peace Corps, get a piece of their country.

So what the press does with its skillful ability to create this imagery, it uses its pages to whip up this hysteria in the white public. And as soon as the hysteria of the white public reaches the proper degree, they will begin to work on the sympathy of the white public. And once the sympathy reaches the proper degree, then they put forth their program, knowing that they are going to get the support of the gullible white public in whatever they do. And what they are going to do is criminal. And what they are doing is criminal.

How do they do it? If you recall reading in the paper, they never talked about the Congolese who were being slaughtered. But as soon as a few, whites, the lives of a few whites were at stake, they began to speak of "white hostages," "white missionaries," "white priests," "white nuns"—as if a white life, one white life, was of such greater value than a Black life, than a thousand Black lives. They showed you their open contempt for the lives of the Blacks, and their deep concern for the lives of the whites. This is the press. And after the press had gotten the whites all whipped up, then anything that the Western powers wanted to do against these defenseless, innocent freedom fighters from the eastern provinces of the Congo, the white public went along with it.

So to get towards the end of that, what it has done, just in press manipulation, the Western governments have permitted themselves to get trapped, in a sense, in backing Tshombe, the same as the United States is trapped over there in South Vietnam. If she goes forward she loses, if she backs up she loses. She's getting bogged down in the Congo in the same way.

Because no African troops win victories for Tshombe. They never have. The only war, the only battles won by the African troops, in the African revolution, in the Congo area, were those won by the freedom fighters from the Oriental province. They won battles with spears, stones, twigs. They won battles because their heart was in what they were doing. But Tshombe's men from the central Congo government never won any battles. And it was for this reason that he had to import these white mercenaries, the paid killers, to win some battles for him. Which means that Tshombe's government can only stay in power with white help, with white troops.

Well, there will come a time when he won't be able to recruit any more mercenaries, and the Western powers, who are really behind him, will then have to commit their own troops openly. Which means you will then be bogged down in the Congo the same as you're bogged down over there now in South Vietnam. And you can't win in the Congo. If you can't win in South Vietnam, you know you can't win in the Congo.

Just let me see. You think you can win in South Vietnam? The French were deeply entrenched. The French were deeply entrenched in Vietnam for a hundred years or so. They had the best weapons of warfare, a highly mechanized army, everything that you would need. And the guerrillas come out of the rice paddies with nothing but sneakers on and a rifle and a bowl of rice, nothing but gym shoes—tennis shoes—and a rifle and a bowl of rice. And you know what they did in Dien Bien Phu. They ran the French out of there. And if the French were deeply entrenched and couldn't stay there, then how do you think someone else is going to stay there, who is not even there yet. [From the audience: "You'll have it happen again."] We'll get to you in a minute. [Laughter] I'm going to sit down and you can tell all you want to say. You can even come up here. [From the audience: "Yes, I was just making the point that it was Chinese—"] Make it later on. [Laughter]

Yes, all of them are brothers. They were still—they had a bowl of rice and a rifle and some shoes. I don't care whether they came from China or South Vietnam. And the French aren't there anymore. We don't care how they did it; they're not there anymore. The same thing will happen in the Congo.

See, the African revolution must proceed onward, and one of the reasons that the Western powers are fighting so hard and are trying to cloud the issue in the Congo is that it's not a humanitarian project. It's not a feeling or sense of humanity that makes them want to go in and save some hostages, but there are bigger stakes.

They realize not only that the Congo is a source of mineral wealth, minerals that they need. But the Congo is so situated strategically, geographically, that if it falls into the hands of a genuine African government that has the hopes and aspirations of the African people at heart, then it will be possible for the Africans to put their own soldiers right on the border of Angola and wipe the Portuguese out of there overnight.

So that if the Congo falls, Mozambique and Angola must fall. And when they fall, suddenly you have to deal with Ian Smith. He won't be there overnight once you can put some troops on his borders. Oh yes. Which means it will only be a matter of time before they will be right on the border with South Africa, and then they can talk the type of language that the South Africans understand. And this is the only language that they understand.

I might point out right here and now—and I say it bluntly—that you have had a generation of Africans who actually have believed that they could negotiate, negotiate, negotiate, and eventually get some kind of independence. But you're getting a new generation that is being born right now, and they are beginning to think with their own mind and see that you can't negotiate upon freedom nowadays. If something is yours by right, then you fight for it or shut up. If you can't fight for it, then forget it.

So we in the West have a stake in the African revolution. We have a stake for this reason: as long as the African continent was dominated by enemies, and as long as it was dominated by colonial powers, those colonial powers were enemies of the African people. They were enemies to the African continent. They meant the African people no good, they did the African people no good, they did the African continent no good.

And then in the position that they were, they were the ones who created the image of the African continent and the African people. They created that continent and those people in a negative image. And they projected this negative image abroad. They projected an image of Africa in the people abroad that was very hateful, extremely hateful.

And because it was hateful, there are over a hundred million of us of African heritage in the West who looked at that hateful image and didn't want to be identified with it. We shunned it, and not because it was something to be shunned. But we believed the image that had been created of our own homeland by the enemy of our own homeland. And in hating that image we ended up hating ourselves without even realizing it.

Why? Because once we in the West were made to hate Africa and hate the African, why, the chain-reaction effect was it had to make us end up hating ourselves. You can't hate the roots of the tree without hating the tree, without ending up hating the tree. You can't hate your origin without ending up hating yourself. You can't hate the land, your motherland, the place that you came from, and we can't hate Africa without ending up hating ourselves.

The Black man in the Western Hemisphere—in North America, Central America, South America, and in the Caribbean—is the best example of how one can be made, skillfully, to hate himself that you can find anywhere on this earth.

The reason you're having a problem with the West Indians right now is because they hate their origin. Because they don't want to accept their origin, they have no origin, they have no identity. They are running around here in search of an identity, and instead of trying to be what they are, they want to be Englishmen. Which is not their fault, actually. Because in America our people are trying to be Americans, and in the islands you got them trying to be Englishmen, and nothing sounds more obnoxious than to find somebody from Jamaica running around here trying to outdo the Englishman with his Englishness.

And I say that this is a very serious problem, because all of it stems from what the Western powers do to the image of the African continent and the African people. By making our people in the Western Hemisphere hate Africa, we ended up hating ourselves. We hated our African characteristics. We hated our African identity. We hated our African features. So much so that you would find those of us in the West who would hate the shape of our nose. We would hate the shape of our lips. We would hate the color of our skin and the texture of our hair. This was a reaction, but we didn't realize that it was a reaction.

Imagine now, somebody got nerve enough, some whites have the audacity to refer to me as a hate teacher. If I'm teaching someone to hate, I teach them to hate the Ku Klux Klan. But here in America, they have taught us to hate ourselves. To hate our skin, hate our hair, hate our features, hate our blood, hate what we are. Why, Uncle Sam is a master hate teacher, so much so that he makes somebody think he's teaching love, when he's teaching hate. When you make a man hate himself, why you really got it and gone.

By skillfully making us hate Africa and, in turn, making us hate ourselves, hate our color and our blood, our color became a chain. Our color became to us a chain. It became a prison. It became something that was a shame, something that we felt held us back, us trapped.

So because we felt that our color had trapped us, had imprisoned us, had brought us down, we ended up hating the Black skin, which we felt was holding us back. We ended up hating the Black blood, which we felt was holding us back. This is the problem that the Black man in the West has had.

The African hasn't realized that this was the problem. And it was only as long as the African himself was held in bondage by the colonial powers, was kept from projecting any positive image of himself on our continent, something that we could look at proudly and then identify with—it was only as long as the African himself was kept down that we were kept down.

But to the same degree, during these recent years, that the African people have become independent, and they have gotten in position on that continent to project their own image, their image has shifted from negative to positive. And to the same degree that it has shifted from negative to positive, you'll find that the image of the Black man in the West of himself has also shifted from negative to positive. To the same degree that the African has become uncompromising and militant in knowing what he wants, will find that the Black man in the West has followed the same line.

Why? Because the same beat, the same heart, the same pulse that moves the Black man on the African continent—despite the fact that four hundred years have separated us from that mother continent, and an ocean of water has separated us from that mother continent—still, the same pulse that beats in the Black man on the African continent today is beating in the heart of the Black man in North America, Central America, South America, and in the Caribbean. Many of them don't know it, but it's true.

As long as we hated our African blood, our African skin, our Africanness, we ended up feeling inferior, we felt inadequate, and we felt helpless. And because we felt so inferior and so inadequate and so helpless, instead of trying to stand on our own feet and do something for ourselves, we turned to the white man, thinking was the only one who could do it for us. Because we were taught, we have been taught, that he was the personification of beauty and the personification of success.

At the Bandung Conference in nineteen fifty-five, one of the first and best steps toward real independence for nonwhite people took place. The people of Africa and Asia and Latin America were able to get together. They sat down, they realized that they had differences. They agreed not to place any emphasis any longer upon these differences, but to submerge the areas of differences and place emphasis upon areas where they had something in common.

This agreement that was reached at Bandung produced the spirit of Bandung. So that the people who were oppressed, who had no jet planes, no nuclear weapons, no armies, no navies—and despite the fact that they didn't have this, their unity alone was sufficient to enable them, over a period of years, to maneuver and make it possible for other nations in Asia to become independent, and many more nations in Africa to become independent.

And by 1959, many of you will recall how colonialism on the African continent had already begun to collapse. It began to collapse because the spirit of African nationalism had been fanned from a spark to a roaring flame. And it made it impossible for the colonial powers to stay there by force. Formerly, when the Africans were fearful, the colonial powers could come up with a battleship, or threaten to land an army, or something like that, and the oppressed people would submit and go ahead being colonized for a while longer.

But by 1959 all of the fear had left the African continent and the Asian continent. And because this fear was gone, especially in regards to the colonial powers of Europe, it made it impossible for them to continue to stay in there by the same methods that they had employed up to that time.

So it's just like when a person is playing football. If he has the ball and he gets trapped, he doesn't throw the ball away, he passes it to some of his teammates who are in the clear. And in 1959, when France and Britain and Belgium and some of the others saw they were trapped by the African nationalism on that continent, instead of throwing the ball of colonialism away, they passed it to the only one of their team that was in the clear—and that was Uncle Sam. Uncle Sam grabbed the ball and has been running with it ever since.

The one who picked it up, really, was John F. Kennedy. He was the shrewdest back-field runner that America has produced in a time—oh yes he was. He was very tricky; he was intelligent; he was an intellectual; he surrounded himself with intellectuals who had a lot of foresight and a lot of cunning. The first thing they did was to give a re-analysis of the problem. They realized they were confronted with a new problem.

The newness of the problem was created by the fact that the Africans had lost all fear. There was no fear in them anymore. Therefore the colonial powers couldn't stay there by force, and America, the new colonial power, neocolonial power, neo-imperialist power, also couldn't stay there by force. So they came up a "friendly" approach, a new approach which was friendly. Benevolent colonialism or philanthropic imperialism. They called it humanitarianism, or dollarism. And whereas the Africans could fight against colonialism, they found it difficult to fight against dollarism, or to condemn dollarism. It was all a token friendship, and all of the so-called benefits that were offered to the African countries were nothing but tokens.

But from '54 to '64 was the era of an emerging Africa, an independent Africa. And the impact of those independent African nations upon the civil rights struggle in the United States was tremendous. Number one, one of the first things the African revolution produced was rapid growth in a movement called the Black Muslim movement. The militancy that existed on the African continent was one of the main motivating factors in the rapid growth of the group known as the Black Muslim movement, to which I belonged. And the Black Muslim movement was one of the main ingredients in the entire civil rights struggle, although the movement itself never started it.

They should say thank you for Martin Luther King, because Martin Luther King has held Negroes in check up to recently. But he's losing his grip, he's losing his influence, he's losing his control.

I know you don't want me to say that. But, see, this is why you're in trouble. You want somebody to come and tell you that your house is safe, while you're sitting on a powder keg. This is the mentality, this is the level of Western mentality today. Rather than face up to the facts concerning the danger that you're in, you would rather have someone come along and jive you and tell you that everything is all right and pack you to sleep. Why, the best thing that anybody can tell you is when they let you know how fed up with disillusionment and frustration the man in your house has become.

So to bring my talk to a conclusion, I must point out that just as John F. Kennedy realized the necessity of a new approach on the African problem—and I must say that it was during his administration that the United States gained so much influence on the

African continent. They removed the other colonial powers and stepped in themselves with their benevolent, philanthropic, friendly approach. And they got just as firm a grip on countries on that continent as some of the colonial powers formerly had on that continent. Not only on the African continent but in Asia too. They did it with dollars.

They used a new approach on us in the States, also. Friendly. Whereas formerly they just outright denied us certain rights, they began to use a new, tricky approach. And this approach was to make it appear that they were making moves to solve our problems. They would pass bills, they would come up with Supreme Court decisions. The Supreme Court came up with what they called a desegregation decision in 1954—it hasn't been implemented yet; they can't even implement it in New York City, where I live—outlawing the segregated school system, supposedly to eliminate segregated schooling in Mississippi and Alabama and other places in the South. And they haven't even been able to implement this Supreme Court decision concerning the educational system in New York City and in Boston and some of the so-called liberal cities of the North.

This was all tokenism. They made the world think that they had desegregated the University of Mississippi. This shows you how deceitful they are. They took one Negro, named Meredith, and took all of the world press down to show that they were going to solve the problem by putting Meredith in the University of Mississippi. I think it cost them something like $15 million and they had to use about seven thousand troops—one or the other—to put one Black man in the University of Mississippi.

And then *Look* magazine came out with a story afterwards showing the exposé where the attorney general—at that time Robert Kennedy—had made a deal with Governor Barnett. They were to play a game on the Negro. Barnett was the racist governor of Mississippi. Kennedy was one of these shining liberal progressives—Robert, that is. And they had made a deal, according to *Look* magazine—which all belongs to the same setup, so they must know what they are talking about. *Look* magazine said that Robert Kennedy had told Barnett, "Now, since you want the white votes in the South, what you do is you stand in the doorway and pretend like you're going to keep Meredith out. And when I come, I'm going to come with the marshals, and force Meredith in. So you'll keep all the white votes in the South, and I'll get all the Negro votes in the North."

This is what we face in that country. And Kennedy is supposed to be a liberal. He's supposed to be a friend of the Negro. He's supposed to be the brother of John F. Kennedy—all of them in the one family. You know, he being the attorney general, he couldn't go down with that kind of deal unless he had the permission of his older brother, who was his older brother at that time.

So they come up only with tokenism. And this tokenism that they give us benefits only a few. A few handpicked Negroes gain from this; a few handpicked Negroes get good jobs; a few handpicked Negroes get good homes or go to a decent school. And then they use these handpicked Negroes, they put 'em on television, blow 'em up, and make it look like you got a whole lot of 'em, when you only got one or two.

And this one or two is going to open up his mouth and talk about how the problem is being solved. And the whole world thinks that America's race problem is being solved, when actually the masses of Black people in America are still living in the ghettos and the slums; they still are the victims of inferior housing; they are still the victims of a segregated school system which gives them inferior education. They are still victims, after they get that inferior education, where they can only get the worst form of jobs.

And they do this very skillfully to keep us trapped. They know that as long as they keep us undereducated, or with an inferior education, it's impossible for us to compete with them for job openings. And as long as we can't compete with them and get a decent job, we're trapped. We are low-wage earners. We have to live in a run-down neighborhood, which means our children go to inferior schools. They get inferior education. And when they grow up, they fall right into the same cycle again.

This is the American way. This is the American democracy that she tries to sell to the whole world as being that which will solve the problems of other people too. It's the worst form of hypocrisy that has ever been practiced by any government or society anywhere on this earth, since the beginning of time. And if I'm wrong you can— [Applause].

It is the African revolution that produced the Black Muslim movement. It was the Black Muslim movement that pushed the civil rights movement. And it was the civil rights movement that pushed the liberals out into the open, where today they are exposed as people who have no more concern for the rights of dark-skinned humanity than they do for any other form of humanity.

To bring my talk to a conclusion, all of this created a hot climate, a hot climate. And from 1963, '64 it reached its peak. Nineteen sixty-three was started out in America by all of the politicians talking about this being the hundredth year since the Emancipation Proclamation. They were going to celebrate all over America "a century of progress in race relations." This is the way January and February and March of 1963 started out.

And then Martin Luther King went into Birmingham, Alabama, just trying to get a few Negroes to be able to sit down at a lunch counter and drink an integrated cup of coffee. That's all he wanted. That's all he wanted. They ended up put in jail. They ended up putting thousands of Negroes in jail. And many of you saw on television, in Birmingham, how the police had these big vicious dogs biting Black people. They were crushing the skulls of Black people. They had water hoses turned on our women, stripping off the clothes from our own women, from our children.

And the world saw this. The world saw what the world had thought was going to be a year which would celebrate a hundred years of progress toward good race relations between white and Black in the United States— they saw one of the most inhuman, savage displays there in that country.

Right after that, this was followed by the assassination of John F. Kennedy, all by the same problem, and Medgar Evers, another one by the same problem. And it ended in the bombing of a church in Alabama where four little girls, Christians, sitting in Sunday school, singing about Jesus, were blown apart by people who claim to be Christians. And this happened in the year 1963, the year that they said in that country would mark a hundred years of good relations between the races.

By 1964— 1964 was the year in which three civil rights workers, who were doing nothing other than trying to show Black people in Mississippi how to register and take advantage of their political potential— they were murdered in cold blood. They weren't murdered by some unknown element. They were murdered by an organized group of criminals known as the Ku Klux Klan, which was headed by the sheriff and his deputy and a clergyman. A preacher, a man of the cloth, was responsible for the murder. And when they tell you what was done to the body of that little Black one that they found— all three were murdered, but when they found the three bodies they said that every bone in the body of the black one was broken, as if these brutes had gone insane while they were beating him to death. This was in 1964.

Now 1965 is here, and you got these same old people, jumping up talking about the "Great Society" now is coming into existence. Nineteen sixty-five will be the longest and the hottest and the bloodiest year that has yet been witnessed in the United States. Why? I'm not saying this to advocate violence. I'm saying this after a careful analysis of the ingredients—the sociological, political dynamite that exists in every Black community in that country.

Africa is emerging. It's making the Black man in the Western Hemisphere militant. It's making him shift from negative to positive in his image of himself and in his confidence in himself. He sees himself as a new man. He's beginning to identify himself with new forces. Whereas in the past he thought of his problem as one of civil rights—which made it a domestic issue, which kept it confined to the jurisdiction of the United States, a jurisdiction in which he could only seek the aid of white liberals within continental United States—today the Black man in the Western Hemisphere, especially in the United States, is beginning to see where his problem is not one of civil rights, but it is rather one of human rights. And that in the human rights context it becomes an international issue. It ceases to be a Negro problem, it ceases to be an American problem. It becomes a human problem, a problem of human rights, a problem of humanity, a problem for the world.

And by shifting his entire position from civil rights to human rights, he puts it on the world stage and makes it possible where today he no more has to rely on only the white liberals within continental United States to be his supporters. But he brings it onto the world stage and makes it possible for all of our African brothers, our Asian brothers, our Latin American brothers, and those people in Europe, some of whom claim to mean right, also to step into the picture and do whatever is necessary to help us to see that our rights are guaranteed us—not sometime in the long future, but almost immediately.

So the basic difference between the struggle of the Black man in the Western Hemisphere today from the past: he has a new sense of identity; he has a new sense of dignity; he has a new sense of urgency. And above all else, he sees now that he has allies. He sees that the brothers on the African continent, who have emerged and gotten independent states, can see that they have an obligation to the lost brother who went astray and then found himself today in a foreign land. They are obligated. They are just as obligated to the brother who's gone away as they are to the brother who's still at home.

And just as you see the oppressed people all over the world today getting together, the Black people in the West are also seeing that they are oppressed. Instead of just calling themselves an oppressed minority in the States, they are part of the oppressed masses of people all over the world today who are crying out for action against the common oppressor.

Thank you.

[London School of Economics, 11 February 1965]

XXXI

One who followed closely the teachings of Malcolm X was Stokely Carmichael (1941–1998). Also known as Kwame Ture, the Trinidadian-born activist lived much of his life in Harlem and the Bronx. He attended Howard University and there he began his road to civic activism. Carmichael turned down offers of a graduate fellowship to Harvard University in 1964. Instead he worked with CORE in the freedom rides and became a member of SNCC. He rose to chairman of SNCC in 1966 following John Lewis, who later served in Congress as representative from Georgia. 1966 was also the year that Carmichael gave birth to the slogan "Black Power" in a speech he gave in Jackson, Mississippi, at the conclusion of the march after James Meredith had been shot in his one-man demonstration to get blacks registered to vote in that state. Carmichael's speech launched for many the black power revolution. He was really an advocate of African-American empowerment, political organization, control of the resources of the community, and blacks representing and working for blacks. His activism radicalized further with his involvement in the Black Panther Party for Self-Defense. J. Edgar Hoover and the FBI targeted him as dangerous to America. Carmichael, who in later years was diagnosed with prostate cancer, blamed the U.S. government for infecting him with the disease. Although it was something he could never prove, he believed it and continued to say so until his death. In "Power and Racism," presented here, Carmichael addresses the desperate need for a propertyless people to be politically involved because they have little or no other way to assert themselves for full equality. Was he correct? Is voting still meaningful for blacks today? Was Carmichael correct in his condemnation of America for not sharing its economic prosperity? Do we need, as he argues, a new economic foundation in America? Is, as he proclaims, integration a subterfuge for the maintenance of white supremacy? Finally, must blacks, as Carmichael strongly recommends, organize if they are to have a future and a place in America?

"Power and Racism"

Stokely Carmichael (Kwame Ture)

One of the tragedies of the struggle against racism is that up to now there has been no national organization that could speak to the growing militancy of young black people in the urban ghetto. There has been only a civil rights movement, whose tone of voice was adapted to an audience of liberal whites. It served as a sort of buffer zone between them and angry young blacks. None of its so-called leaders could go into a rioting community and be listened to. In a sense, I blame ourselves—together with the mass media—for what has happened in Watts, Harlem, Chicago, Cleveland, and Omaha. Each time the people in those cities saw Martin Luther King get slapped, they became angry, when they saw four little black girls bombed to death, they were angrier, and when nothing happened, they were steaming. We had nothing to offer that they could see, except to go out and be beaten again. We helped to build their frustration.

For too many years, black Americans marched and had their heads broken and got shot. They were saying to the country, "Look, you guys are supposed to be nice guys and we are only going to do what we are supposed to do — why do you beat us up, why don't you give us what we ask, why don't you straighten yourself out?" After years of this, we are at almost the same point — because we demonstrated from a position of weakness. We cannot be expected any longer to march and have our heads broken in order to say to whites: Come on, you're nice guys. For you are not nice guys. We have found you out.

An organization which claims to speak for the needs of a community — as does the Student Nonviolent Coordinating Committee — must speak in the tone of that community, not as somebody else's buffer zone. This is the significance of Black Power as a slogan. For once, black people are going to use the words they want to use — not just the words whites want to hear. And they will do this no matter how often the press tries to stop the use of the slogan by equating it with racism or separatism.

An organization which claims to be working for the needs of a community — as SNCC does — must work to provide that community with a position of strength from which to make its voice heard. This is the significance of Black Power beyond the slogan.

Black Power can be clearly defined for those who do not attach the fears of white America to their questions about it. We should begin with the basic fact that black Americans have two problems: they are poor and they are black. All other problems arise from this two-sided reality: lack of education, the so-called apathy of black men. Any program to end racism must address itself to that double reality.

Almost from its beginning, SNCC sought to address itself to both conditions with a program aimed at winning political power for impoverished Southern blacks. We had to begin with politics because black Americans are a propertyless people in a country where property is valued above all. We had to work for power, because this country does not function by morality, love, and nonviolence, but by power. Thus we determined to win political power, with the idea of moving on from there into activity that would have economic effects. With power, the masses could make or participate in making the decisions which govern their destinies, and thus create basic change in their day-to-day lives.

But if political power seemed to be the key to self-determination, it was also obvious that the key had been thrown down a deep well many years earlier. Disenfranchisement, maintained by racist terror, made it impossible to talk about organizing for political power in 1960. The right to vote had to be won, and SNCC workers devoted their energies to this from 1961 to 1965. They set up voter registration drives in the Deep South. They created pressure for the vote by holding mock elections in Mississippi in 1963 and by helping to establish the Mississippi Freedom Democratic Party (MFDP) in 1964. That struggle was eased, though not won, with the passage of the 1965 Voting Rights Act. SNCC workers could then address themselves to the question: Who can we vote for, to have our needs met — how do we make our vote meaningful?

SNCC had already gone to Atlantic City for recognition of the Mississippi Freedom Democratic Party by the Democratic convention and been rejected, it had gone with the MFDP to Washington for recognition by Congress and been rejected. In Arkansas, SNCC helped thirty Negroes to run for school board elections; all but one were defeated, and there was evidence of fraud and intimidation, sufficient to cause their defeat. In Atlanta, Julian Bond ran for the state legislature and was elected twice—and unseated—twice. In several states, black farmers ran in elections for agricultural committees which make crucial decisions concerning land use, loans, etc. Although they won places on a number of committees, they never gained the majorities needed to control them.

All of the efforts were attempts to win Black Power. Then, in Alabama, the opportunity came to see how blacks could be organized on an independent party basis. An unusual Alabama law provides that any group of citizens can nominate candidates for county office, and if they win 20 per cent of the vote, may be recognized as a county political party. The same then applies on a state level. SNCC went to organize in several counties, such as Lowndes, where black people—who form 80 per cent of the population and have an average annual income of $943—felt they could accomplish nothing within the framework of the Alabama Democratic Party because of its racism and because the qualifying fee for the 1966 elections was raised from $50 to $500 in order to prevent most Negroes from becoming candidates. On May 3, 1966, five new "freedom organizations" convened and nominated candidates for the offices of sheriff, tax assessor, members of the school boards. Their ballot symbol was the black panther: a bold, beautiful animal, representing the strength and dignity of black demands today. A man needs a black panther on his side when he and his family must endure—as hundreds of Alabamans have endured—loss of job, eviction, starvation, and sometimes death for political activity. He may also need a gun, and SNCC reaffirms the right of black men everywhere to defend themselves when threatened or attacked. As for initiating the use of violence, we hope that such programs as ours will make that unnecessary; but it is not for us to tell black communities whether they can or cannot use any particular form of action to resolve their problems. Responsibility for the use of violence by black men, whether in self-defense or initiated by them, lies with the white community.

This is the specific historical experience from which SNCC's call for Black Power emerged on the Mississippi march in July 1966. But the concept of Black Power is not a recent or isolated phenomenon. It has grown out of the ferment of agitation and activity by different people and organizations in many black communities over the years. Our last year of work in Alabama added a new concrete possibility. In Lowndes County, for example, Black Power will mean that if a Negro is elected sheriff, he can end police brutality. If a black man is elected tax assessor, he can collect and channel funds for the building of better roads and schools serving black people—thus advancing the move from political power into the economic arena. In such areas as Lowndes, where black men have a majority, they will attempt to use it to exercise control. This is what they seek: control. Where Negroes lack a majority, Black Power means proper representation and sharing of control. It means the creation of power bases from which black people can work to change statewide or nationwide patterns of oppression through pressure from strength—instead of weakness. Politically, Black Power means what it has always meant to SNCC: the coming-together of black people to elect representatives and to force those representatives to speak to their needs. It does not mean merely putting black faces into office. A man or woman who is black and from the slums cannot be automatically expected to speak to the needs of black people. Most of the black politicians we see around the country today are not what SNCC means by Black Power. The power must be that of a community, and emanate from there.

SNCC today is working in both North and South on programs of voter registration and independent political organizing. In some places, such as Alabama, Los Angeles, New York, Philadelphia, and New Jersey, independent organizing under the black panther symbol is in progress. The creation of a national "black panther party" must come about; it will take time to build, and it is much too early to predict its success. We have no infallible master plan and we make no claim to exclusive knowledge of how to end racism; different groups will work in their own different ways. SNCC cannot spell out the full logistics of self-determination, but it can address itself to the problem by helping black communities define their needs, realize their strength, and go into action along a variety of lines which they must choose for themselves. Without knowing all the answers, it can address itself to the basic problem of poverty, to the fact that in Lowndes County 86 white families own 90 per cent of the land. What are black people in that county going to do for jobs; where are they going to get money? There must be reallocation of land, of money.

Ultimately, the economic foundations of this country must be shaken if black people are to control their lives. The colonies of the United States—and this includes the black ghettos within its borders, North and South—must be liberated. For a century, this nation has been like an octopus of exploitation, its tentacles stretching from Mississippi and Harlem to South America, the Middle East, southern Africa, and Vietnam; the form of exploitation varies from area to area but the essential result has been the same—a powerful few have been maintained and enriched at the expense of the poor and voiceless colored masses. This pattern must be broken. As its grip loosens here and there around the world, the hopes of black Americans become more realistic. For racism to die, a totally different America must be born.

This is what the white society does not wish to face; this is why that society prefers to talk about integration. But integration speaks not at all to the problem of poverty—only to the problem of blackness. Integration today means the man who "makes it," leaving his black brothers behind in the ghetto. It has no relevance to the Harlem wino or to the cottonpicker making three dollars a day.

Integration, moreover, speaks to the problem of blackness in a despicable way. As a goal, it has been based on complete acceptance of the fact that in order to have a decent house or education, blacks must move into a white neighborhood or send their children to a white school. This reinforces, among both black and white, the idea that "white" is automatically better and "black" is by definition inferior. This is why integration is a subterfuge for the maintenance of white supremacy. It allows the nation to focus on a handful of Southern children who get into white schools, at great price, and to ignore the 94 per cent who are left behind in unimproved all-black schools. Such situations will not change until black people have power—to control their own school boards, in this case. Then Negroes become equal in a way that means something, and integration ceases to be a one-way street. Then integration doesn't mean draining skills and energies from the ghetto into white neighborhoods; then it can mean white people moving from Beverly Hills into Watts, white people joining the Lowndes County Freedom Organization. Then integration becomes relevant.

In April 1966, before the furor over Black Power, Christopher Jencks wrote in a New Republic article on white Mississippi's manipulation of the anti-poverty program:

> The war on poverty has been predicated on the notion that there is such a thing as a community which can be defined geographically and mobilized for a collective effort to help the poor. This theory has no relationship to reality in the Deep South. In every Mississippi county there are two communities. Despite all the pious platitudes of the moderates on both sides, these two communities habitually see their interests in terms of conflict rather than cooperation. Only when the Negro community can muster enough political, economic and professional strength to compete on somewhat equal terms, will Negroes believe in the possibility of true cooperation and whites accept its necessity. En route to integration, the Negro community needs to develop greater independence—a chance to run its own affairs and not cave in whenever "the man" barks...Or so it seems to me, and to most of the knowledgeable people with whom I talked in Mississippi. To OEO, this judgment may sound like black nationalism ...

Mr. Jencks, a white reporter, perceived the reason why America's anti-poverty program has been a sick farce in both North and South. In the South, it is clearly racism which prevents the poor from running their own programs; in the North, it more often seems to be politicking and bureaucracy. But the results are not so different: in the North, non-whites make up 42 per cent of all families in metropolitan "poverty areas" and only 6 per cent of families in areas classified as not poor. SNCC has been working with local residents in Arkansas, Alabama, and Mississippi to achieve control by the poor of the program and its funds; it has also been working with groups in the North, and the struggle is no less difficult. Behind it all is a federal government which cares far more about winning the war on the Vietnamese than the war on poverty; which has put the poverty program in the hands of self-serving politicians and bureaucrats rather than the poor themselves; which is unwilling to curb the misuse of white power but quick to condemn Black Power.

To most whites, Black Power seems to mean that the Mau Mau are coming to the suburbs at night. The Mau Man are coming, and whites must stop them. Articles appear about plots to "get Whitey," creating an atmosphere in which "law and order must be maintained." Once again, responsibility is shifted from the oppressor to the oppressed. Other whites chide, "Don't forget—you're only 10 per cent of the population; if you get too smart, we'll wipe you out." If they are liberals, they complain, "What about me—don't you want my help any more?" These are people supposedly concerned about black Americans, but today they think first of themselves, of their feelings of rejection. Or they admonish, "You can't get anywhere without coalitions," when there is in fact no group at present with whom to form a coalition in which blacks will not be absorbed and betrayed. Or they accuse us of "polarizing the races" by our calls for black unity, when the true responsibility for polarization lies with whites who will not accept their responsibility as the majority power for making the democratic process work.

White America will not face the problem of color, the reality of it. The well-intended say: "We're all human, everybody is really decent, we must forget color." But color cannot be "forgotten" until its weight is recognized and dealt with. White America will not acknowledge that the ways in which this country sees itself are contradicted by being black—and always have been. Whereas most of the people who settled this country came here for freedom or for economic opportunity, blacks were brought here to be slaves. When the Lowndes County Freedom Organization chose the black panther as its symbol, it was christened by the press "the Black Panther Party"—but the Alabama Democratic Party, whose symbol is a rooster, has never been called the White Cock Party. No one ever talked about "white power" because power in this country is white. All this adds up to more than merely identifying a group phenomenon by some catchy name or adjective. The furor over that black panther reveals the problems that white America has with color and sex; the furor over Black Power reveals how deep racism runs and the great fear which is attached to it.

Whites will not see that I, for example, as a person oppressed because of my blackness, have common cause with other blacks who are oppressed because of blackness. This is not to say that there are no white people who see things as I do, but that it is black people I must speak to first. It must be the oppressed to whom SNCC addresses itself primarily, not to friends from the oppressing group.

From birth, black people are told a set of lies about themselves. We are told that we are lazy—yet I drive through the Delta area of Mississippi and watch black people picking cotton in the hot sun for fourteen hours. We are told, "If you work hard, you'll succeed"—but if that were true, black people would own this country. We are oppressed because we are black—not because we are ignorant, not because we are lazy, not because we're stupid (and got good rhythm), but because we're black.

I remember that when I was a boy I used to go to see Tarzan movies on Saturday. White Tarzan used to beat up the black natives. I would sit there yelling, "Kill the beasts, kill the savages, kill 'em!" I was saying: Kill me. It was as if a Jewish boy watched Nazis taking Jews off to concentration camps and cheered them on. Today, I want the chief to beat hell out of Tarzan and send him back to Europe. But it takes time to become free of the lies and their shaming effect on black minds. It takes time to reject the most important lie: that black people inherently can't do the same things white people can do, unless white people help them.

The need for psychological equality is the reason why SNCC today believes that blacks must organize in the black community. Only black people can convey the revolutionary idea that black people are able to do things themselves. Only they can help create in the community an aroused and continuing black consciousness that will provide the basis for political strength. In the past, white allies have furthered white supremacy without the whites involved realizing it—or wanting it, I think. Black people must do things for themselves; they must get poverty money they will control and spend themselves, they must conduct tutorial programs themselves so that black children can identify with black people. This is one reason Africa has such importance: the reality of black men ruling their own nations gives blacks elsewhere a sense of possibility, of power, which they do not now have.

This does not mean we don't welcome help, or friends. But we want the right to decide whether anyone is, in fact, our friend. In the past, black Americans have been almost the only people whom everybody and his momma could jump up and call their friends. We have been tokens, symbols, objects—as I was in high school to many young whites, who liked having "a Negro friend." We want to decide who is our friend, and we will not accept someone who comes to us and says: "If you do X, Y, and Z, then I'll help you." We will not be told whom we should choose as allies. We will not be isolated from any group or nation except by our own choice. We cannot have the oppressors telling the oppressed how to rid themselves of the oppressor.

I have said that most liberal whites react to Black Power with the question, "What about me?" rather than saying: "Tell me what you want me to do and see if I can do it." There are answers to the right question. One of the most disturbing things about almost all white supporters of the movement has been that they are afraid to go into their own communities—which is where the racism exists—and work to get rid of it. They want to run from Berkeley to tell us what to do in Mississippi; let them look instead at Berkeley. They admonish blacks to be nonviolent; let them preach nonviolence in the white community. They come to teach me Negro history; let them, go to the suburbs and open up freedom schools for whites. Let them work to stop America's racist foreign policy; let them press this government to cease supporting the economy of South Africa.

There is a vital job to be done among poor whites. We hope to see, eventually, a coalition between poor blacks and poor whites. That is the only coalition which seems acceptable to us, and we see such a coalition as the major internal instrument of change in American society. SNCC has tried several times to organize poor whites; we are trying again now, with an initial training program in Tennessee. It is purely academic today, to talk about bringing poor blacks and whites together, but the job of creating a poor-white power bloc must be attempted. The main responsibility for it falls upon whites. Black and white can work together in the white community where possible; it is not possible, however, to go into a poor Southern town and talk about integration. Poor whites everywhere are becoming more hostile—not less—partly because they see the nation's attention focused on black poverty and nobody coming to them. Too many young middle-class Americans, like some sort of Pepsi generation, have wanted to come alive through the black community; they've wanted to be where the action is—and the action has been in the black community.

Black people do not want to "take over" this country. They don't want to "get Whitey"; they just want to get him off their backs, as the saying goes. It was, for example, the exploitation by Jewish landlords and merchants which first created black resentment toward Jews—not Judaism. The white man is irrelevant to blacks, except as an oppressive force. Blacks want to be in his place, yes, but not in order to terrorize and lynch and starve him. They want to be in his place because that is where a decent life can be had.

But our vision is not merely of a society in which all black men have enough to buy the good things of life. When we urge that black money go into black pockets, we mean the communal pocket. We want to see money go back into the community and used to benefit it. We want to see the cooperative concept applied in business and banking. We want to see black ghetto residents demand that an exploiting landlord or storekeeper sell them, at minimal cost, a building or a shop that they will own and improve cooperatively; they can back their demand with a rent strike, or a boycott, and a community so unified behind them that no one else will move into the building or buy at the store. The society we seek to build among black people, then, is not a capitalist one. It is a society in which the spirit of community and humanistic love prevail. The word "love" is suspect; black expectations of what it might produce have been betrayed too often. But those were expectations of a response from the white community, which failed us. The love we seek to encourage is within the black community, the only American community where men call each other "brother" when they meet. We can build a community of love only where we have the ability and power to do so: among blacks.

As for white America, perhaps it can stop crying out against "black supremacy," "black nationalism," "racism in reverse," and begin facing reality. The reality is that this nation is racist; that racism is not primarily a problem of "human relations" but of an exploitation maintained—either actively or through silence—by the society as a whole. Can whites, particularly liberal whites, condemn themselves? Can they stop blaming us, and blame their own system? Are they capable of the shame which might become a revolutionary emotion?

We have found that they usually cannot condemn themselves, and so we have done it. But the rebuilding of this society, if at all possible, is basically the responsibility of whites—not blacks. We won't fight to save the present society, in Vietnam or anywhere else. We are just going to work, in the way we see fit, and on goals we define, not for civil rights but for all our human rights.

[1966]

XXXII

Huey P. Newton (1942–1989), who was born in Monroe, Louisiana, would make his mark in Oakland, California, as the cofounder, along with Bobby Seale, of the Black Panther Party for Self-Defense in 1966. Huey P. Newton's life is all about struggle. Although a high school graduate, he was unable to read when he graduated from school and taught himself how to do so in the years that followed. He attended Merritt College in Oakland and supported himself while there through petty theft in Oakland and Berkeley, burglarizing houses. It was later at Merritt College that he became involved in more positive activity and met up with Bobby Seale. Newton, Seale, and other young blacks were tired of the brutality of Oakland police, which had a notorious record for brutality against African Americans, particularly against black males. The Black Panther Party was basically established to defend the community against the police force and to monitor the activities of the Oakland police. Although the organization became best known for its members brandishing firearms, the Panthers also developed social programs in Oakland that included free breakfasts for inner-city youth and the "Ten-Percent Program" supporting housing, jobs, and education in the community. Newton and the Panthers believed in political activism and demonstrated it in 1967 when they showed up armed with rifles at the state legislature in Sacramento to protest against the proposed California Gun Bill. Accused of murder of a police officer and then later a second similar charge, after several trials Newton was never convicted of those charges. Spending several years in Cuba in the 1970s he developed an international appreciation of the struggle of the people. He went on to obtain a PhD from the University of California at Santa Cruz in 1980. Huey P. Newton died nine years later, allegedly shot in a drug transaction gone bad. His piece presented here, "Raising Consciousness," attempts to do what he always professed was the most important first step for any people's salvation: develop their sense of self. Is Newton correct that "raising consciousness" is the key to African-American survival and progress?

"Raising Consciousness"

Huey P. Newton

"The mobilization of the masses, when it arises out of the war of liberation, introduces into each man's consciousness the ideas of a common cause, of a national destiny, and of a collective history. In the same way the second phase, that of the building-up of the nation, is helped on by the existence of this cement which has been mixed with blood and anger."

—Frantz Fanon, *The Wretched of the Earth*

The Black Panthers have always emphasized action over rhetoric. But language, the power of the word, in the philosophical sense, is not underestimated in our ideology. We recognize the significance of words in the struggle for liberation, not only in the media and in conversations with people on the block, but in the important area of raising consciousness. Words are another way of defining phenomena, and the definition of any phenomenon is the first step to controlling it or being controlled by it.

When I read Nietzsche's *The Will to Power*, I learned much from a number of his philosophical insights. This is not to say that I endorse all of Nietzsche, only that many of his ideas have influenced my thinking. Because Nietzsche was writing about concepts fundamental to all men, and particularly about the meaning of power, some of his ideas are pertinent to the way Black people live in the United States; they have had a great impact on the development of the Black Panther philosophy.

Nietzsche believed that beyond good and evil is the will to power. In other words, good and evil are labels for phenomena, or value judgments. Behind these value judgments is the will to power, which causes man to view phenomena as good or evil. It is really the will to power that controls our understanding of something and not an inherent quality of good or evil.

Man attempts to define phenomena in such a way that they reflect the interests of his own class or group. He gives titles or values to phenomena according to what he sees as beneficial; if it is to his advantage, something is called good, and if it is not beneficial, then it is defined as evil. Nietzsche shows how this reasoning was used by the German ruling circle, which always defined phenomena in terms complimentary to the noble class. For example, they used the German word *gut*, which means "godlike" or "good," to refer to themselves; nobles were gut. On the other hand, the word villein, used to describe the poor people and serfs who lived outside the great gates of the noble man's home, suggested the opposite. The poor were said to live in the "village," a word that comes from the same root word (Latin: villa) as the term "villain." So the ruling class, by the power they possessed, defined themselves as "godlike" and called the people "villains" or enemies of the ruling circle. Needless to say, when the poor and common people internalized these ideas, they felt inferior, guilty, and ashamed, while the nobles took their superiority for granted. Thought had been shaped by language.

We have seen the same thing in the United States, where, over a period of time, the adjective "black" became a potent word in the American language, pejorative in every sense. We were made to feel ashamed and guilty because of our biological characteristics, while our oppressors, through their whiteness, felt noble and uplifted. In the past few years, however—and it has been only a few years—the rising level of consciousness within our Black communities has led us to redefine ourselves. People once ashamed to be called Black now gladly accept the label, and our biological characteristics are sources of pride. Today we call ourselves Black people and wear natural hair styles because we have changed the definition of the word "black."

This is an example of Nietzsche's theory that beyond good and evil is the will to power. In the early days of the Black Panthers we tried to find ways to make this theory work in the best interests of Black people. Words could be used not only to make Blacks more proud but to make whites question and even reject concepts they had always unthinkingly accepted. One of our prime needs was a new definition for "policeman." A good descriptive word, one the community would accept and use, would not only advance Black consciousness, but in effect control the police by making them see themselves in a new light.

We thought up new terms for them. At first I figured that the reverse of god — dog — would be a good epithet, but it did not catch on. We tried beast, brute, and animal, but none of them captured the essential quality we were trying to convey. One day, while working on the paper, Eldridge showed us a postcard from Beverly Axelrod. On the front was the slogan "Support Your Local Police"; there was a sheriff's star above the phrase, and in the center of the star a grinning, slobbering pig. It was just what we were looking for. We began to show policemen as pigs in our cartoons, and from time to time used the word. "Pig" caught on; it entered the language.

This was a form of psychological warfare: it raised the consciousness of the people and also inflicted a new consciousness on the ruling circle. If whites and police became caught up in this new awareness, they would soon defect from their own ranks and join us to avoid feelings of guilt and shame.

Nietzsche pointed out that this tactic had been used to good effect by the Christians against the Romans. In the beginning the Christians were weak, but they understood how to make the philosophy of a weak group work for them. By using phrases like "the meek shall inherit the earth," they imposed a new idea on the Romans, one that gave rise to doubt and led to defections to the new sect. Once Christians stated that the meek shall inherit the earth and won over members, they weakened the strength of those in power. They were to be the victors. People like to be on the winning side. We have seen the same principle work on college campuses in this country. Many white youths now identify with Blacks; the identification is manifested in clothes, rhetoric, and life styles.

Thus, even though we came to the term "pig" accidentally, the choice itself was calculated. "Pig" was perfect for several reasons. First of all, words like "swine," "hog," "sow," and "pig" have always had unpleasant connotations. The reason for this probably has theological roots, since the pig is considered an unclean animal in Semitic religions. In the English language well-established "pig" epithets are numerous. We say that someone eats like a hog, is a filthy swine, and so on. In A Portrait of the Artist as a Young Man, James Joyce uses swine as a destructive, devouring image when he describes Ireland as "an old sow that eats her farrow." So the word "pig" is traditionally associated with grotesque qualities.

The pig in reality is an ugly and offensive animal. It likes to root around in the mud; it makes hideous noises; it does not seem to relate to humans as other animals do. Further, anyone in the Black community can relate to the true characteristics of the pig because most of us come from rural backgrounds and have observed the nature of pigs. Many of the police, too, are hired right out of the South and are familiar with the behavior of pigs. They know exactly what the word implies. To call a policeman a pig conveys the idea of someone who is brutal, gross, and uncaring.

"Pig" has another point in its favor: in racial terms "pig" is a neutral word. Many white youths on college campuses began to understand what the police were really like when their heads were broken open during demonstrations against the draft and the Vietnam war. This broadened the use of the term and served to unify the victims against their oppressors. Even though white youths were not victimized in the same way or to the same extent that we were, they nonetheless became our allies against the police. In this case the ruling circle was not able to set victims against each other; as the racists in the South had done by setting poor whites against Blacks.

Our greatest victory, however, lay in the effect on the police themselves. They did not like to be called pigs, and they still do not. Ever since the term came into use, they have conducted a countercampaign by using slogans like "Pigs Are Beautiful" and wearing pig pins; but their effort has failed. Our message, of course, is that if they do not want to be pigs, then they ought to stop their brutalization of the victims of the world. No slogan will change the people's opinion; a change in behavior is the only thing that will do it.

Another expression that helped to raise Black people's consciousness is "All Power to the People." An expression that has meaning on several levels—political, economic, and metaphysical—it was coined by the Black Panther Party around the same time as "pig," and has also gained wide acceptance. When we created it, I had in mind some distinct philosophical goals for the community that many people did not understand. The police and the press wanted everyone to believe that we were nothing more than a bunch of "young toughs" strutting around with guns in order to shock people. But Bobby and I always had a clear understanding of what we wanted to do. We wanted to give the community a wide variety of needed programs, and so we began in a way that would gain the community's support. At the same time we saw the necessity of going beyond these first steps. In developing our newspaper, we were working toward our long-range goals of organizing the community around programs that the people would come to believe in strongly. We hoped these programs would come to mean so much that the people would take up guns for defense against any maneuvers by the oppressor.

All these programs were aimed at one goal: complete control of the institutions in the community. Every ethnic group has particular needs that they know and understand better than anybody else; each group is the best judge of how its institutions ought to affect the lives of its members. Throughout American history ethnic groups like the Irish and Italians have established organizations and institutions within their own communities. When they achieved this political control, they had the power to deal with their problems. Yet there is still another necessary step. In the Black community, mere control of our own institutions will not automatically solve problems. For one thing, it is difficult to get enough places of work in the community to produce full employment for Blacks. The most important element in controlling our own institutions would be to organize them into co-operatives, which would end all forms of exploitation. Then the profits, or surplus, from the co-operatives would be returned to the community, expanding opportunities on all levels, and enriching life. Beyond this, our ultimate aim is to have various ethnic communities co-operating in a spirit of mutual aid, rather than competing. In this way, all communities would be allied in a common purpose through the major social, economic, and political institutions in the country.

This is our long-range objective. Although we are far from realizing it, it is important that the people understand what we want for them and what are, indeed, their natural rights. Therefore, the slogan "All Power to the People" sums up our goals for Black people, as well as our deep love and commitment to them. All power comes from the people, and all power must ultimately be vested in them. Anything else is theft.

Our complete faith in the people is based on our assumptions about what they require and deserve. The first of these is honesty. When it became apparent in the early days that the Black Panthers were a growing force, some people urged us to take either accommodating positions for small gains or a "Black line" based solely on race rather than economic or social strategy. These people were talking a Black game they did not really believe in. But they saw that the people believed and that the Black line could be used to mobilize them. We resisted. To us, it was both wrong and futile to deceive the people; eventually we would have to answer to them.

In the metaphysical sense we based the expression "All Power to the People" on the idea of man as God. I have no other God but man, and I firmly believe that man is the highest or chief good. If you are obligated to be true and honest to anyone, it is to your God, and if each man is God, then you must be true to him. If you believe that man is the ultimate being, then you will act according to your belief. Your attitude and behavior toward man is a kind of religion in itself, with high standards of responsibility.

It was especially important to me that I explore the Judaeo-Christian concept of God, because historically that concept has had an enormous impact on the lives of Black people in America. Their acceptance of the Judaeo-Christian God and religion has always meant submission and an emphasis on the rewards of the life hereafter as relief for the sufferings of the present. Christianity began as a religion for the outcast and oppressed. While the early Christians succeeded in undermining the authority and confidence of their rulers and rising up out of slavery, the Afro-American experience has been just the opposite. Already a people in slavery, when Christianity was imposed upon them, the Blacks only assumed another burden, the tyranny of the future—the hope of heaven and the fear of hell. Christianity increased their sense of hopelessness. It also projected the idea of salvation and happiness into the afterlife, where God would reward them for all their sufferings on this earth. Justice would come later, in the Promised Land.

The phrase "All Power to the People" was meant to turn this around, to convince Black people that their rewards were due in the present, that it was in their power to create a Promised Land here and now. The Black Panthers have never intended to turn Black people away from religion. We want to encourage them to change their consciousness of themselves and to be less accepting of the white man's version of God—the God of the downtrodden, the weak, and the undeserving. We want them to see themselves as the called, the chosen, and the salt of the earth.

Even before we coined the phrase, I had long thought about the idea of God. I could not accept the Biblical version, the Bible is too full of contradictions and irrationality. Either you accept it, and believe, or you do not. I could not believe. I have arrived at my understanding of what is meant by God through other means—through philosophy, logic, and semantics. My opinion is that the term "God" belongs to the realm of concepts, that it is dependent upon man for its existence. If God does not exist unless man exists, then man must be here to produce God. It logically follows, then, that man created God, and if the creator is greater than that which is created, then we must hold that man is the highest good.

I can understand why man feels the need to create God, particularly in earlier periods of history when scientific understanding was limited. The phenomena that man observed around him in the universe sometimes overwhelmed him; he could not explain or account for them. Therefore he created something in his mind that was "greater" than these phenomena, something that was responsible for the mysteries in nature. But I think that when man clings to the idea of a God, whom he has created and placed in the heavens, he actually reduces himself and his own potential. The more he attributes to God, the more inferior he becomes, the less responsible for his own destiny. He says to God, "I am weak but thou art mighty," and therefore accepts things as they are, content to leave the running of the world to a supernatural force greater than himself. This attitude embodies a kind of fatalism, which is inimical to growth and change. On the other hand, the greater man becomes, the less his God will be.

None of this means that I am completely hostile to the many beautiful and admirable things about religion. When I speak of certain aspects of society to Black people, the use of religious phraseology flows naturally; and the audience response is genuine. I also read the Bible frequently, not only for its poetry, but also for its wisdom and insight. Still, much of the Bible is madness. I cannot accept, for example, the notion of divine law and responsibility to "God." As far as I am concerned, if men are responsible beings, they ought to be responsible to each other. And so, when we say "All Power to the People," we mean to convey a sense of deep respect and love for the people, and the idea that the people deserve complete truth and honesty. The judgment of history is the judgment of the people. That is the motivating and controlling idea of our very existence.

[1973]

XXXIII

A contemporary of Stokely Carmichael's and Huey P. Newton's during the 1960s, and a strong symbol of the period in her own right was Angela Davis (1944–). Born in Birmingham, Alabama, she became an activist and educator of international note. Receiving her undergraduate training at Brandeis University in Massachusetts, Davis attended graduate study at the University of California at San Diego in the late 1960s. It was in the '60s that she joined the Black Panther Party. Davis became well known for her work in the Che-Lumumba Club of the Communist Party. The national spotlight focused on her when the University of California at Los Angeles fired her from her teaching post in the philosophy department because of her alleged communist affiliations. This was an act upon which the American Association of University Professors (AAUP) censured UCLA for more than two decades. Davis supported the Soledad Brothers, which included inmate George Jackson. The prison escape attempt in 1970 resulted in several people being killed and Angela Davis was accused of being involved in the escape attempt. She went underground and was quickly placed on the FBI's Ten Most Wanted List. She was charged with murder and complicity to commit murder. After a long battle in the court system, Davis was acquitted in June 1972 after eighteen months in jail. She returned to teaching. And she would never lose her fighting spirit for social justice. Today Angela Davis is Professor Emerita at the University of California at Santa Cruz. She is a world-renowned intellectual and has written numerous books and continues to speak out and to fight for social justice and socialism. What is most striking to you in Davis's piece presented here, "Let Us All Rise Together: Radical Perspectives on Empowerment for African-American Women"? How have African-American women attempted to organize themselves and how effective has it been? Do you agree with Davis that we must create a revolutionary, multiracial women's movement that addresses the issues affecting poor and working-class women? Is employment the key to women's empowerment? Is Davis correct when she says that socialism is what we must have?

"Radical Perspectives on the Empowerment of Afro-American Women: Lessons for the 1980s"

Angela Davis

The concept of empowerment is hardly new to Afro-American women. For almost a century, we have been organized in bodies that have sought collectively to develop strategies that illuminate the way to economic and political power for ourselves and our communities. In the last decade of the nineteenth century, after having been repeatedly shunned by the racially homogeneous women's rights movement, Black women organized their own club movement. In 1895—five years after the founding of the General Federation of Women's Clubs, which consolidated a club movement reflecting concerns of middle-class White women—one hundred Black women from ten states met in the city of Boston, under the leadership of Josephine St. Pierre Ruffin, to discuss the creation of a national organization of Black women's clubs. As compared to their White counterparts, the Afro-American women issuing the call for this national club movement articulated principles that were more openly political in nature. They defined the primary function of their clubs as an ideological as well as an activist defense of Black women and men from the ravages of racism. When the meeting was convened, its participants emphatically declared that, unlike their White sisters, whose organizational policies were seriously tainted by racism, they envisioned their movement as one open to all women:

"Our woman's movement is woman's movement in that it is led and directed by women for the good of women and men, for the benefit of all humanity, which is more than any one branch or section of it. We want, we ask the active interest of our men, and, too, we are not drawing the color line; we are women, American women, as intensely interested in all that pertains to us as such as all other American women; we are not alienating or withdrawing, we are only coming to the front, willing to join any others in the same work and cordially inviting and welcoming any others to join us."

The following year, the formation of the National Association of Colored Women's Clubs was announced. The motto chosen by the Association was "Lifting as We Climb."

The nineteenth-century women's movement was also plagued by classism. Susan B. Anthony wondered why her outreach to working-class women on the issue of the ballot was so frequently met with indifference. She wondered why these women seemed to be much more concerned with improving their economic situation than with achieving the right to vote. As essential as political equality may have been to the larger campaign for women's rights, in the eyes of Afro-American and White working-class women it was not synonymous with emancipation. That the conceptualization of strategies for struggle was based on the peculiar condition of White women of the privileged classes rendered those strategies discordant with working-class women's perceptions of empowerment. It is not surprising that many of them told Ms. Anthony, "Women want bread, not the Ballot!" Eventually, of course, working-class White women, and Afro-American women as well, reconceptualized this struggle, defining the vote not as an end in itself—not as the panacea that would cure all the ills related to gender-based discrimination—but rather as an important weapon in the continuing fight for higher wages, better working conditions, and an end to the omnipresent menace of the lynch mob.

Today, as we reflect on the process of empowering Afro-American women, our most efficacious strategies remain those that are guided by the principle used by Black women in the club movement. We must strive to "lift as we climb." In other words, we must climb in such a way as to guarantee that all of our sisters, regardless of social class, and indeed all of our brothers, climb with us. This must be the essential dynamic of our quest for power—a principle that must not only determine our struggles as Afro-American women, but also govern all authentic struggles of dispossessed people. Indeed, the overall battle for equality can be profoundly enhanced by embracing this principle.

Afro-American women bring to the women's movement a strong tradition of struggle around issues that politically link women to the most crucial progressive causes. This is the meaning of the motto, "Lifting as We Climb." This approach reflects the often unspoken interests and aspirations of masses of women of all racial backgrounds. Millions of women today are concerned about jobs, working conditions, higher wages, and racist violence. They are concerned about plant closings, homelessness, and repressive immigration legislation. Women are concerned about homophobia, ageism, and discrimination against the physically challenged. We are concerned about Nicaragua and South Africa, and we share our children's dreams that tomorrow's world will be delivered from the threat of nuclear homicide. These are some of the issues that should be made a part of the overall struggle for women's rights, if there is to be a serious commitment to the empowerment of women who, throughout history, have been rendered invisible. These are some of the issues we should consider if we wish to lift as we climb.

During this decade we have witnessed an exciting resurgence of the women's movement. If the first wave of the movement appeared in the 1840s, and the second wave in the 1960s, then we are approaching the crest of a third wave in the final days of the 1980s. When the feminist historians of the twenty-first century attempt to recapitulate the third wave, will they ignore the momentous contributions of Afro-American women, who have been leaders and activists in movements often confined to women of color, but whose accomplishments have invariably advanced the cause of White women as well? Will the exclusionary policies of the mainstream women's movement —from its inception to the present—which have often compelled Afro-American women to conduct their struggle for equality outside the ranks of that movement, continue to result in the systematic omission of our names from the roster of prominent leaders and activists of the women's movement? Will there continue to be two distinct continua of the women's movement, one visible and another invisible? One publicly acknowledged and another ignored except by the conscious progeny of the working-class women—Black, Latina, Native American, Asian, and White—who forged that hidden continuum? If this question is answered in the affirmative, it will mean that women's quest for equality will continue to be gravely deficient. The revolutionary potential of the women's movement still will not have been realized. The racist-inspired flaws of the first and second waves of the women's movement will have become the inherited flaws of the third wave.

How can we guarantee that this historical pattern is broken? As advocates of and activists for women's rights in the latter 1980s, we must begin to merge that double legacy and create a single continuum, one that solidly represents the aspirations of all women in our society. We must begin to create a revolutionary, multiracial women's movement that seriously addresses the main issues affecting poor and working-class women. In order to tap the potential for such a movement, we must further develop those sectors of the movement that are addressing seriously issues affecting poor and working-class women, such as jobs, pay equity, paid maternity leave, federally subsidized child care, protection from sterilization abuse, and subsidized abortions. Women of all racial and class backgrounds will benefit greatly from such an approach.

Creating a revolutionary women's movement will not be simple. For decades, White women activists have repeated the complaint that Women of Color frequently fail to respond to their appeals: "We invited them to our meetings, but they didn't come; we asked them to participate in our demonstration, but they didn't show; they just don't seem to be interested in women's studies." The process cannot be initiated merely by intensified efforts to attract Latina or Afro-American or Asian or Native American women into the existing organizations dominated by White women of the more privileged, economic strata. The particular concerns of women of color must be included in the agenda.

An issue of special concern to Afro-American women is unemployment. Indeed, the most fundamental prerequisite for empowerment is the ability to earn an adequate living. The Reagan administration boasts that unemployment has leveled off, leaving only (!) 7.5 million people unemployed. However, Black people in general are twice as likely to be unemployed as White people, and Black teenagers are almost three times as likely to be unemployed as White teenagers. We must remember that these figures do not include the millions who hold part-time jobs, although they want and need full-time employment. A disproportionate number of these underemployed individuals are women. Neither do the figures reflect those who, out of utter frustration, have ceased to search for employment, nor those whose unemployment insurance has run out, nor those who have never had a job. Women on welfare are among those who are not counted as unemployed.

The AFL-CIO estimates that there are 18 million people of working age without jobs. These still critical levels of unemployment, distorted and misrepresented by the Reagan administration, are fundamentally responsible for the impoverished status of Afro-American women, the most glaring evidence of which resides in the fact that women, together with their dependent children, constitute the fastest growing sector of the population of 4 million homeless in the United States. There can be no serious discussion of empowerment today if we do not embrace the plight of the homeless with an enthusiasm as passionate as that with which we embrace issues more immediately related to our own lives.

The United Nations declared 1987 to be the Year of Shelter for the Homeless, although only the developing countries were the initial focus of this resolution. Eventually, it became clear that the United States is an "undeveloping country." Two-thirds of the 4 million homeless in this country are families, and 40 percent of them are Afro-American. In some urban areas, as many as 70 percent of the homeless are Black. In New York City, for example, 60 percent of the homeless population is Black, 20 percent Latino, and 20 percent White. Presently, under New York's Work Incentive Program, homeless women and men are employed to clean toilets, wash graffiti from subway trains, and clean parks at wages of sixty-two cents an hour, a mere fraction of the minimum wage. In other words, the homeless are being compelled to provide slave labor for the government if they wish to receive assistance.

Black women scholars and professionals cannot afford to ignore the straits of those of our sisters who are acquainted with the immediacy of oppression in a way many of us are not. The process of empowerment cannot be simplistically defined in accordance with our own particular class interests. We must learn to lift as we climb.

If we are to elevate the status of our entire community as we scale the heights of empowerment, we must be willing to offer organized resistance to the proliferating manifestations of racist violence across the country. A virtual race riot took place on the campus of one of the most liberal educational institutions in this country some months ago. In the aftermath of the 1986 World Series, White students at the University of Massachusetts, Amherst, who were purportedly fans of the losing Boston Red Sox, vented their wrath on Black students, whom they perceived as surrogates for the winning team, the New York Mets, because of the predominance of Black players on the New York team. When individuals in the crowd yelled "Black bitch" at a Black woman student, a Black man who hastened to defend her was seriously wounded and was rushed, unconscious, to the hospital. Another one of the many dramatic instances of racist harassment to occur on college campuses during this period was the burning of a cross in front of the Black Students Cultural Center at Purdue University. In December 1986, Michael Griffith, a young Black man, lost his life in what amounted to a virtual lynching by a mob of White youths in the Howard Beach, Queens, section of New York City. Not far from Atlanta, civil rights marchers were attacked on Dr. Martin Luther King's birthday by a mob led by the Ku Klux Klan. An especially outrageous instance in which racist violence was officially condoned was the acquittal of Bernhard Goetz, who, on his own admission, attempted to kill four Black youths because he felt threatened by them on a New York subway.

Black women have organized before to oppose racist violence. The birth of the Black Women's Club Movement at the end of the nineteenth century was in large part a response to the epidemic of lynching during that era. Leaders like Ida B. Wells and Mary Church Terrell recognized that Black women could not move toward empowerment if they did not radically challenge the reign of lynch law in the land. Today, in the late 1980s, Afro-American women must actively take the lead in the movement against racist violence, as did our sister-ancestors almost a century ago. We must lift as we climb. As our ancestors organized for the passage of a federal anti-lynch law — and indeed involved themselves in the women's suffrage movement for the purpose of securing that legislation — we must today become activists in the effort to secure legislation declaring racism and anti-Semitism crimes. As extensive as publicized instances of racist violence may be at this time, many more racist-inspired crimes go unnoticed as a consequence of the failure of law enforcement to classify them specifically as such. A person scrawling swastikas or "KKK" on an apartment building may simply be charged — if criminal charges are brought at all — with defacing property or malicious mischief. Recently, a Ku Klux Klansman who burned a cross in front of a Black family's home was charged with "burning without a permit." We need federal and local laws against acts of racist and anti-Semitic violence. We must organize, lobby, march, and demonstrate in order to guarantee their passage.

As we organize, lobby, march, and demonstrate against racist violence, we who are women of color must be willing to appeal for multiracial unity in the spirit of our sister-ancestors. Like them we must proclaim: We do not draw the color line. The only line we draw is one based on our political principles. We know that empowerment for the masses of women in our country will never be achieved as long as we do not succeed in pushing back the tide of racism. It is not a coincidence that sexist-inspired violence —

and, in particular, terrorist attacks on abortion clinics—has reached a peak during the same period in which racist violence has proliferated dramatically. Violent attacks on women's reproductive rights are nourished by these explosions of racism. The vicious anti-lesbian and anti-gay attacks are a part of the same menacing process. The roots of sexism and homophobia are found in the same economic and political institutions that serve as the foundation of racism in this country, and, more often than not, the same extremist circles that inflict violence on people of color are responsible for the eruptions of violence inspired by sexist and homophobic biases. Our political activism must clearly manifest our understanding of these connections.

We must always attempt to lift as we climb. Another urgent point on our political agenda—that of Afro-American as well as all progressive women—must be the repeal of the Simpson-Rodino Act: a racist law that spells repression for vast numbers of women and men who are undocumented immigrants in this country. Camouflaged as an amnesty program, the eligibility restrictions are so numerous that hundreds of thousands of people stand to be prosecuted and deported under its provisions. Amnesty is provided in a restricted way only for those who came to this country before 1982. Thus, vast numbers of Mexicans, who have recently crossed the border in an attempt to flee impoverishment generated by the unrestricted immigration of U.S. corporations into their country, are not eligible for citizenship. Salvadorans and other Central Americans who have escaped political persecution in their respective countries over the last few years will not be offered amnesty. We must organize, lobby, march, and demonstrate for a repeal of the Simpson-Rodino Act. We must lift as we climb.

When we as Afro-American women, when we as Women of Color, proceed to ascend toward empowerment, we lift up with us our brothers of color, our White sisters and brothers in the working class, and indeed all women who experience the effects of sexist oppression. Our activist agenda must encompass a wide range of demands. We must call for jobs and for the unionization of unorganized women workers, and, indeed, unions must be compelled to take on such issues as affirmative action, pay equity, sexual harassment on the job, and paid maternity leave. Black and Latina women are AIDS victims in disproportionately large numbers. We therefore have an urgent need to demand emergency funding for AIDS research. We must also oppose all instances of repressive mandatory AIDS testing and quarantining, as well as homophobic manipulations of the AIDS crisis. Effective strategies for the reduction of teenage pregnancy are needed, but we must beware of succumbing to propagandistic attempts to relegate to young single mothers the responsibility for our community's impoverishment.

In this unfortunate era of Reaganism, it should be clear that there are forces in our society that reap enormous benefits from the persistent, deepening oppression of women. Members of the Reagan administration include advocates for the most racist, sexist, and anti-working-class circles of contemporary monopoly capitalism. These corporations prop up apartheid in South Africa and profit from the spiraling arms race, while they propose the most vulgar and irrational forms of anti-Sovietism—invoking, for example, the "evil empire" image popularized by Ronald Reagan—as justifications for their homicidal ventures. If we are not afraid to adopt a revolutionary stance, if, indeed, we wish to be radical in our quest for change, then we must get to the root of our oppression. After all, "radical" simply means grasping things at the root. Our agenda for women's empowerment must thus be unequivocal in its challenge to monopoly capitalism as a major obstacle to the achievement of equality.

I want to suggest, as I conclude, that we link our grassroots organizing, our essential involvement in electoral politics, and our involvement as activists in mass struggles with the long-range aim of fundamentally transforming the socioeconomic conditions that generate and persistently nourish the various forms of oppression we suffer. Let us learn from the strategies of our sisters in South Africa and Nicaragua. As Afro-American women, as Women of Color in general, as progressive women of all racial backgrounds, let us join our sisters and brothers across the globe who are attempting to forge a new socialist order—an order which will reestablish socioeconomic priorities so that the quest for monetary profit will never be permitted to take precedence over the real interests of human beings. This is not to say that our problems will magically dissipate with the advent of socialism. Rather, such a social order should provide us with the real opportunity to extend further our struggles, with the assurance that one day we will be able to redefine the basic elements of our oppression as useless refuse of the past.

[1988]

XXXIV

Staying clear of socialism, while advocating that blacks participate fully in the existing system to make it work, ably characterizes the political and civil rights agenda of Jesse Jackson (1941–). Born in Greenville, South Carolina, Jackson moved north and came of age in Chicago. He returned south to receive his undergraduate education at an HBCU (Historically Black College or University), North Carolina A & T. He attended Chicago Theological Seminary in 1966, but never finished. Jackson became committed to the civil rights movement and the work of Martin Luther King, Jr. very early on. He was appointed head of Operation Breadbasket in Chicago, which was an initiative of the SCLC. Jackson was in Memphis when King was assassinated in April of 1968, but misspoke about his proximity to King at the time of the shooting. His misstatement and penchant for publicity put him on the outs with the SCLC leadership. Jackson built a base outside of that leadership and used his former position with Operation Breadbasket to expand into what he dubbed the National Rainbow Coalition in 1984, which became Operation Push. He ran for President of the United States of America in 1984, the second black to do so after Shirley Chisholm and her run for the Presidency. Jackson ran again for the office in 1988 and came in second in the Democratic Party vote to the eventual nominee, Governor Michael Dukakis of Massachusetts. At the Democratic convention that year, Jackson was a featured speaker and mesmerized much of the nation with his message of hope. His speech, "Keep Hope Alive," is presented here for your perusal. What do you find to be specific points of engagement in Jackson speech? Why do you think his message evidently transcended racial and ethnic lines for many? Is his a message of hope more than it is a call for action, or is it both?

"Keep Hope Alive"

Jesse Jackson

Tonight, we pause and give praise and honor to God for being good enough to allow us to be at this place at this time. When I look out at this convention, I see the face of America: Red, Yellow, Brown, Black and White. We're all precious in God's sight—the real rainbow coalition.

All of us—All of us who are here think that we are seated. But we're really standing on someone's shoulders. Ladies and gentlemen, Mrs. Rosa Parks—the mother of the civil rights movement.

[Mrs. Rosa Parks is brought to the podium.]

I want to express my deep love and appreciation for the support my family has given me over these past months. They have endured pain, anxiety, threat, and fear. But they have been strengthened and made secure by our faith in God, in America, and in you. Your love has protected us and made us strong. To my wife Jackie, the foundation of our family; to our five children whom you met tonight; to my mother, Mrs. Helen Jackson, who is present tonight; and to our grandmother, Mrs. Matilda Burns; to my brother Chuck and his family; to my mother-in-law, Mrs. Gertrude Brown, who just last month at age 61 graduated from Hampton Institute—a marvelous achievement.

I offer my appreciation to Mayor Andrew Young who has provided such gracious hospitality to all of us this week.

And a special salute to President Jimmy Carter. President Carter restored honor to the White House after Watergate. He gave many of us a special opportunity to grow. For his kind words, for his unwavering commitment to peace in the world, and for the voters that came from his family, every member of his family, led by Billy and Amy, I offer my special thanks to the Carter family.

My right and my privilege to stand here before you has been won, won in my lifetime, by the blood and the sweat of the innocent.

Twenty-four years ago, the late Fannie Lou Hamer and Aaron Henry—who sits here tonight from Mississippi—were locked out onto the streets in Atlantic City; the head of the Mississippi Freedom Democratic Party.

But tonight, a Black and White delegation from Mississippi is headed by Ed Cole, a Black man from Mississippi; twenty-four years later.

Many were lost in the struggle for the right to vote: Jimmy Lee Jackson, a young student, gave his life; Viola Liuzzo, a White mother from Detroit, called "nigger lover," and brains blown out at point blank range; Schwerner, Goodman and Chaney—two Jews and a Black—found in a common grave, bodies riddled with bullets in Mississippi; the four darling little girls in a church in Birmingham, Alabama. They died that we might have a right to live.

Dr. Martin Luther King Jr. lies only a few miles from us tonight. Tonight he must feel good as he looks down upon us. We sit here together, a rainbow, a coalition—the sons and daughters of slavemasters and the sons and daughters of slaves, sitting together around a common table, to decide the direction of our party and our country. His heart would be full tonight.

As a testament to the struggles of those who have gone before; as a legacy for those who will come after; as a tribute to the endurance, the patience, the courage of our forefathers and mothers; as an assurance that their prayers are being answered, that their work has not been in vain, and, that hope is eternal, tomorrow night my name will go into nomination for the Presidency of the United States of America.

We meet tonight at the crossroads, a point of decision. Shall we expand, be inclusive, find unity and power; or suffer division and impotence?

We've come to Atlanta, the cradle of the Old South, the crucible of the New South. Tonight, there is a sense of celebration, because we are moved, fundamentally moved from racial battlegrounds by law, to economic common ground. Tomorrow we'll challenge to move to higher ground.

Common ground. Think of Jerusalem, the intersection where many trails met. A small village that became the birthplace for three great religions—Judaism, Christianity, and Islam. Why was this village so blessed? Because it provided a crossroads where different people met, different cultures, different civilizations could meet and find common ground. When people come together, flowers always flourish—the air is rich with the aroma of a new spring.

Take New York, the dynamic metropolis. What makes New York so special? It's the invitation at the Statue of Liberty, "Give me your tired, your poor, your huddled masses who yearn to breathe free." Not restricted to English only. Many people, many cultures, many languages with one thing in common: They yearn to breathe free. Common ground.

Tonight in Atlanta, for the first time in this century, we convene in the South; a state where Governors once stood in school house doors; where Julian Bond was denied a seat in the State Legislature because of his conscientious objection to the Vietnam War; a city that, through its five Black Universities, has graduated more black students than any city in the world. Atlanta, now a modern intersection of the New South.

Common ground. That's the challenge of our party tonight—left wing, right wing.

Progress will not come through boundless liberalism nor static conservatism, but at the critical mass of mutual survival—not at boundless liberalism nor static conservatism, but at the critical mass of mutual survival. It takes two wings to fly. Whether you're a hawk or a dove, you're just a bird living in the same environment, in the same world.

The Bible teaches that when lions and lambs lie down together, none will be afraid, and there will be peace in the valley. It sounds impossible. Lions eat lambs. Lambs sensibly flee from lions. Yet even lions and lambs find common ground. Why? Because neither lions nor lambs want the forest to catch on fire. Neither lions nor lambs want acid rain to fall. Neither lions nor lambs can survive nuclear war. If lions and lambs can find common ground, surely we can as well—as civilized people.

The only time that we win is when we come together. In 1960, John Kennedy, the late John Kennedy, beat Richard Nixon by only 112,000 votes—less than one vote per precinct. He won by the margin of our hope. He brought us together. He reached out. He had the courage to defy his advisors and inquire about Dr. King's jailing in Albany, Georgia. We won by the margin of our hope, inspired by courageous leadership. In 1964, Lyndon Johnson brought both wings together—the thesis, the antithesis, and the creative synthesis—and together we won. In 1976, Jimmy Carter unified us again, and we won. When do we not come together, we never win. In 1968, the division and despair in July led to our defeat in November. In 1980, rancor in the spring and the summer led to Reagan in the fall. When we divide, we cannot win. We must find common ground as the basis for survival and development and change and growth.

Today when we debated, differed, deliberated, agreed to agree, agreed to disagree, when we had the good judgment to argue a case and then not self-destruct, George Bush was just a little further away from the White House and a little closer to private life.

Tonight, I salute Governor Michael Dukakis. He has run—He has run a well-managed and a dignified campaign. No matter how tired or how tried, he always resisted the temptation to stoop to demagoguery.

I've watched a good mind fast at work, with steel nerves, guiding his campaign out of the crowded field without appeal to the worst in us. I've watched his perspective grow as his environment has expanded. I've seen his toughness and tenacity close up. I know his commitment to public service. Mike Dukakis' parents were a doctor and a teacher; my parents a maid, a beautician, and a janitor. There's a great gap between Brookline, Massachusetts and Haney Street in the Fieldcrest Village housing projects in Greenville, South Carolina.

He studied law; I studied theology. There are differences of religion, region, and race; differences in experiences and perspectives. But the genius of America is that out of the many we become one.

Providence has enabled our paths to intersect. His foreparents came to America on immigrant ships; my foreparents came to America on slave ships. But whatever the original ships, we're in the same boat tonight.

Our ships could pass in the night—if we have a false sense of independence—or they could collide and crash. We would lose our passengers. We can seek a high reality and a greater good. Apart, we can drift on the broken pieces of Reagonomics, satisfy our baser instincts, and exploit the fears of our people. At our highest, we can call upon noble instincts and navigate this vessel to safety. The greater good is the common good.

As Jesus said, "Not My will, but Thine be done." It was his way of saying there's a higher good beyond personal comfort or position.

The good of our Nation is at stake. It's commitment to working men and women, to the poor and the vulnerable, to the many in the world.

With so many guided missiles, and so much misguided leadership, the stakes are exceedingly high. Our choice? Full participation in a democratic government, or more abandonment and neglect. And so this night, we choose not a false sense of independence, not our capacity to survive and endure. Tonight we choose interdependency, and our capacity to act and unite for the greater good.

Common good is finding commitment to new priorities to expansion and inclusion. A commitment to expanded participation in the Democratic Party at every level. A commitment to a shared national campaign strategy and involvement at every level.

A commitment to new priorities that insure that hope will be kept alive. A common ground commitment to a legislative agenda for empowerment, for the John Conyers bill—universal, on-site, same-day registration everywhere. A commitment to D.C. statehood and empowerment—D.C. deserves statehood. A commitment to economic set-asides, commitment to the Dellums bill for comprehensive sanctions against South Africa. A shared commitment to a common direction.

Common ground.

Easier said than done. Where do you find common ground? At the point of challenge. This campaign has shown that politics need not be marketed by politicians, packaged by pollsters and pundits. Politics can be a moral arena where people come together to find common ground.

We find common ground at the plant gate that closes on workers without notice. We find common ground at the farm auction, where a good farmer loses his or her land to bad loans or diminishing markets. Common ground at the school yard where teachers cannot get adequate pay, and students cannot get a scholarship, and can't make a loan. Common ground at the hospital admitting room, where somebody tonight is dying because they cannot afford to go upstairs to a bed that's empty waiting for someone with insurance to get sick. We are a better nation than that. We must do better.

Common ground. What is leadership if not present help in a time of crisis? And so I met you at the point of challenge. In Jay, Maine, where paper workers were striking for fair wages; in Greenville, Iowa, where family farmers struggle for a fair price; in Cleveland, Ohio, where working women seek comparable worth; in McFarland, California, where the children of Hispanic farm workers may be dying from poisoned land, dying in clusters with cancer; in an AIDS hospice in Houston, Texas, where the sick support one another, too often rejected by their own parents and friends.

Common ground. America is not a blanket woven from one thread, one color, one cloth. When I was a child growing up in Greenville, South Carolina and grandmamma could not afford a blanket, she didn't complain and we did not freeze. Instead she took pieces of old cloth—patches, wool, silk, gabardine, crockersack—only patches, barely good enough to wipe off your shoes with. But they didn't stay that way very long. With sturdy hands and a strong cord, she sewed them together into a quilt, a thing of beauty and power and culture. Now, Democrats, we must build such a quilt.

Farmers, you seek fair prices and you are right—but you cannot stand alone. Your patch is not big enough.

Workers, you fight for fair wages, you are right—but your patch of labor is not big enough.

Women, you seek comparable worth and pay equity, you are right—but your patch is not big enough.

Women, mothers, who seek Head Start, and day care and prenatal care on the front side of life, relevant jail care and welfare on the back side of life, you are right—but your patch is not big enough.

Students, you seek scholarships, you are right—but your patch is not big enough.

Blacks and Hispanics, when we fight for civil rights, we are right—but our patch is not big enough.

Gays and lesbians, when you fight against discrimination and a cure for AIDS, you are right—but your patch is not big enough.

Conservatives and progressives, when you fight for what you believe, right wing, left wing, hawk, dove, you are right from your point of view, but your point of view is not enough.

But don't despair. Be as wise as my grandmamma. Pull the patches and the pieces together, bound by a common thread. When we form a great quilt of unity and common ground, we'll have the power to bring about health care and housing and jobs and education and hope to our Nation.

We, the people, can win.

We stand at the end of a long dark night of reaction. We stand tonight united in the commitment to a new direction. For almost eight years we've been led by those who view social good coming from private interest, who view public life as a means to increase private wealth. They have been prepared to sacrifice the common good of the many to satisfy the private interests and the wealth of a few.

We believe in a government that's a tool of our democracy in service to the public, not an instrument of the aristocracy in search of private wealth. We believe in government with the consent of the governed, "of, for and by the people." We must now emerge into a new day with a new direction.

Reaganomics: Based on the belief that the rich had too much money [sic]—too little money and the poor had too much. That's classic Reaganomics. They believe that the poor had too much money and the rich had too little money, so they engaged in reverse Robin Hood—took from the poor, gave to the rich, paid for by the middle class. We cannot stand four more years of Reaganomics in any version, in any disguise.

How do I document that case? Seven years later, the richest 1 percent of our society pays 20 percent less in taxes. The poorest 10 percent pay 20 percent more: Reaganomics.

Reagan gave the rich and the powerful a multibillion-dollar party. Now the party is over. He expects the people to pay for the damage. I take this principal position, convention, let us not raise taxes on the poor and the middle-class, but those who had the party, the rich and the powerful, must pay for the party.

I just want to take common sense to high places. We're spending one hundred and fifty billion dollars a year defending Europe and Japan 43 years after the war is over. We have more troops in Europe tonight than we had seven years ago. Yet the threat of war is ever more remote.

Germany and Japan are now creditor nations; that means they've got a surplus. We are a debtor nation—it means we are in debt. Let them share more of the burden of their own defense. Use some of that money to build decent housing. Use some of that money to educate our children. Use some of that money for long-term health care. Use some of that money to wipe out these slums and put America back to work!

I just want to take common sense to high places. If we can bail out Europe and Japan; if we can bail out Continental Bank and Chrysler—and Mr. Iacocca, make [sic] 8,000 dollars an hour—we can bail out the family farmer.

I just want to make common sense. It does not make sense to close down six hundred and fifty thousand family farms in this country while importing food from abroad subsidized by the U.S. Government. Let's make sense.

It does not make sense to be escorting all our tankers up and down the Persian Gulf paying $2.50 for every one dollar worth of oil we bring out, while oil wells are capped in Texas, Oklahoma, and Louisiana. I just want to make sense.

Leadership must meet the moral challenge of its day. What's the moral challenge of our day? We have public accommodations. We have the right to vote. We have open housing. What's the fundamental challenge of our day? It is to end economic violence. Plant closings without notice—economic violence. Even the greedy do not profit long from greed—economic violence.

Most poor people are not lazy. They are not black. They are not brown. They are mostly White and female and young. But whether White, Black or Brown, a hungry baby's belly turned inside out is the same color—color it pain; color it hurt; color it agony.

Most poor people are not on welfare. Some of them are illiterate and can't read the want-ad sections. And when they can, they can't find a job that matches the address. They work hard every day.

I know. I live amongst them. I'm one of them. I know they work. I'm a witness. They catch the early bus. They work every day.

They raise other people's children. They work every day.

They clean the streets. They work every day. They drive dangerous cabs. They work every day. They change the beds you slept in in these hotels last night and can't get a union contract. They work every day.

No, no, they are not lazy! Someone must defend them because it's right, and they cannot speak for themselves. They work in hospitals. I know they do. They wipe the bodies of those who are sick with fever and pain. They empty their bedpans. They clean out their commodes. No job is beneath them, and yet when they get sick they cannot lie in the bed they made up every day. America, that is not right. We are a better Nation than that. We are a better Nation than that.

We need a real war on drugs. You can't "just say no." It's deeper than that. You can't just get a palm reader or an astrologer. It's more profound than that.

We are spending a hundred and fifty billion dollars on drugs a year. We've gone from ignoring it to focusing on the children. Children cannot buy a hundred and fifty billion dollars worth of drugs a year; a few high-profile athletes — athletes are not laundering a hundred and fifty billion dollars a year — bankers are.

I met the children in Watts, who, unfortunately, in their despair, their grapes of hope have become raisins of despair, and they're turning on each other and they're self-destructing. But I stayed with them all night long. I wanted to hear their case.

They said, "Jesse Jackson, as you challenge us to say no to drugs, you're right; and to not sell them, you're right; and not use these guns, you're right." (And by the way, the promise of CETA [Comprehensive Employment Training Act]; they displaced CETA — they did not replace CETA.)

"We have neither jobs nor houses nor services nor training — no way out. Some of us take drugs as anesthesia for our pain. Some take drugs as a way of pleasure, good short-term pleasure and long-term pain. Some sell drugs to make money. It's wrong, we know, but you need to know that we know. We can go and buy the drugs by the boxes at the port. If we can buy the drugs at the port, don't you believe the Federal government can stop it if they want to?"

They say, "We don't have Saturday night specials anymore." They say, "We buy AK-47's and Uzi's, the latest make of weapons. We buy them across the along these boulevards."

You cannot fight a war on drugs unless and until you're going to challenge the bankers and the gun sellers and those who grow them. Don't just focus on the children; let's stop drugs at the level of supply and demand. We must end the scourge on the American Culture.

Leadership. What difference will we make? Leadership. Cannot just go along to get along. We must do more than change Presidents. We must change direction.

Leadership must face the moral challenge of our day. The nuclear war build-up is irrational. Strong leadership cannot desire to look tough and let that stand in the way of the pursuit of peace. Leadership must reverse the arms race. At least we should pledge no first use. Why? Because first use begets first retaliation. And that's mutual annihilation. That's not a rational way out.

No use at all. Let's think it out and not fight it out because it's an unwinnable fight. Why hold a card that you can never drop? Let's give peace a chance.

Leadership. We now have this marvelous opportunity to have a breakthrough with the Soviets. Last year 200,000 Americans visited the Soviet Union. There's a chance for joint ventures into space — not Star Wars and war arms escalation but a space defense initiative. Let's build in space together and demilitarize the heavens. There's a way out.

America, let us expand. When Mr. Reagan and Mr. Gorbachev met there was a big meeting. They represented together one-eighth of the human race. Seven-eighths of the human race was locked out of that room. Most people in the world tonight—half are Asian, one-half of them are Chinese. There are 22 nations in the Middle East. There's Europe; 40 million Latin Americans next door to us; the Caribbean; Africa—a half-billion people.

Most people in the world today are Yellow or Brown or Black, non-Christian, poor, female, young and don't speak English in the real world.

This generation must offer leadership to the real world. We're losing ground in Latin America, Middle East, South Africa because we're not focusing on the real world. That's the real world. We must use basic principles—support international law. We stand the most to gain from it. Support human rights—we believe in that. Support self-determination—we're built on that. Support economic development—you know it's right. Be consistent and gain our moral authority in the world. I challenge you tonight, my friends, let's be bigger and better as a Nation and as a Party.

We have basic challenges—freedom in South Africa. We've already agreed as Democrats to declare South Africa to be a terrorist state. But don't just stop there. Get South Africa out of Angola; free Namibia; support the front line states. We must have a new humane human rights consistent policy in Africa.

I'm often asked, "Jesse, why do you take on these tough issues? They're not very political. We can't win that way."

If an issue is morally right, it will eventually be political. It may be political and never be right. Fannie Lou Hamer didn't have the most votes in Atlantic City, but her principles have outlasted every delegate who voted to lock her out. Rosa Parks did not have the most votes, but she was morally right. Dr. King didn't have the most votes about the Vietnam War, but he was morally right. If we are principled first, our politics will fall in place.

"Jesse, why do you take these big bold initiatives?" A poem by an unknown author went something like this: "We mastered the air, we conquered the sea, annihilated distance and prolonged life, but we're not wise enough to live on this earth without war and without hate."

As for Jesse Jackson: "I'm tired of sailing my little boat, far inside the harbor bar. I want to go out where the big ships float, out on the deep where the great ones are. And should my frail craft prove too slight for waves that sweep those billows o'er, I'd rather go down in the stirring fight than drowse to death at the sheltered shore."

We've got to go out, my friends, where the big boats are.

And then for our children. Young America, hold your head high now. We can win. We must not lose you to drugs and violence, premature pregnancy, suicide, cynicism, pessimism and despair. We can win. Wherever you are tonight, I challenge you to hope and to dream. Don't submerge your dreams. Exercise above all else, even on drugs, dream of the day you are drug free. Even in the gutter, dream of the day that you will be up on your feet again.

You must never stop dreaming. Face reality, yes, but don't stop with the way things are. Dream of things as they ought to be. Dream. Face pain, but love, hope, faith and dreams will help you rise above the pain. Use hope and imagination as weapons of survival and progress, but you keep on dreaming, young America. Dream of peace. Peace is rational and reasonable. War is irrational in this age, and unwinnable.

Dream of teachers who teach for life and not for a living. Dream of doctors who are concerned more about public health than private wealth. Dream of lawyers more concerned about justice than a judgeship. Dream of preachers who are concerned more about prophecy than profiteering. Dream on the high road with sound values.

And then America, as we go forth to September, October, November and then beyond, America must never surrender to a high moral challenge.

Do not surrender to drugs. The best drug policy is a "no first use." Don't surrender with needles and cynicism. Let's have "no first use" on the one hand, or clinics on the other. Never surrender, young America. Go forward.

America must never surrender to malnutrition. We can feed the hungry and clothe the naked. We must never surrender. We must go forward.

We must never surrender to illiteracy. Invest in our children. Never surrender; and go forward. We must never surrender to inequality. Women cannot compromise ERA or comparable worth. Women are making 60 cents on the dollar to what a man makes. Women cannot buy meat cheaper. Women cannot buy bread cheaper. Women cannot buy milk cheaper. Women deserve to get paid for the work that you do. It's right! And it's fair.

Don't surrender, my friends. Those who have AIDS tonight, you deserve our compassion. Even with AIDS you must not surrender.

In your wheelchairs. I see you sitting here tonight in those wheelchairs. I've stayed with you. I've reached out to you across our Nation. And don't you give up. I know it's tough sometimes. People look down on you. It took you a little more effort to get here tonight. And no one should look down on you, but sometimes mean people do. The only justification we have for looking down on someone is that we're going to stop and pick them up.

But even in your wheelchairs, don't you give up. We cannot forget 50 years ago when our backs were against the wall, Roosevelt was in a wheelchair. I would rather have Roosevelt in a wheelchair than Reagan and Bush on a horse. Don't you surrender and don't you give up. Don't surrender and don't give up!

Why I cannot challenge you this way? "Jesse Jackson, you don't understand my situation. You be on television. You don't understand. I see you with the big people. You don't understand my situation."

I understand. You see me on TV, but you don't know the me that makes me, me. They wonder, "Why does Jesse run?" because they see me running for the White House. They don't see the house I'm running from.

I have a story. I wasn't always on television. Writers were not always outside my door. When I was born late one afternoon, October 8th, in Greenville, South Carolina, no writers asked my mother her name. Nobody chose to write down our address. My mama was not supposed to make it, and I was not supposed to make it. You see, I was born of a teen-age mother, who was born of a teen-age mother.

I understand. I know abandonment, and people being mean to you, and saying you're nothing and nobody and can never be anything.

I understand. Jesse Jackson is my third name. I'm adopted. When I had no name, my grandmother gave me her name. My name was Jesse Burns 'til I was 12. So I wouldn't have a blank space, she gave me a name to hold me over. I understand when nobody knows your name. I understand when you have no name.

I understand. I wasn't born in the hospital. Mama didn't have insurance. I was born in the bed at the house. I really do understand. Born in a three-room house, bathroom in the backyard, slop jar by the bed, no hot and cold running water. I understand. Wallpaper used for decoration? No. For a windbreaker. I understand. I'm a working person's person. That's why I understand you whether you're Black or White. I understand work. I was not born with a silver spoon in my mouth. I had a shovel programmed for my hand.

My mother, a working woman. So many of the days she went to work early, with runs in her stockings. She knew better, but she wore runs in her stockings so that my brother and I could have matching socks and not be laughed at at school. I understand.

At 3 o'clock on Thanksgiving Day, we couldn't eat turkey because momma was preparing somebody else's turkey at 3 o'clock. We had to play football to entertain ourselves. And then around 6 o'clock she would get off the Alta Vista bus and we would bring up the leftovers and eat our turkey—leftovers, the carcass, the cranberries—around 8 o'clock at night. I really do understand.

Every one of these funny labels they put on you, those of you who are watching this broadcast tonight in the projects, on the corners, I understand. Call you outcast, low down, you can't make it, you're nothing, you're from nobody, subclass, underclass; when you see Jesse Jackson, when my name goes in nomination, your name goes in nomination.

I was born in the slum, but the slum was not born in me. And it wasn't born in you, and you can make it.

Wherever you are tonight, you can make it. Hold your head high; stick your chest out. You can make it. It gets dark sometimes, but the morning comes. Don't you surrender!

Suffering breeds character, character breeds faith. In the end faith will not disappoint.

You must not surrender! You may or may not get there but just know that you're qualified! And you hold on, and hold out! We must never surrender!! America will get better and better.

Keep hope alive. Keep hope alive! Keep hope alive! On tomorrow night and beyond, keep hope alive!

I love you very much. I love you very much.

[19 July 1988]

XXXV

No one, including Jesse Jackson, could have believed or predicted what would come true twenty years later. Most African Americans and Americans in general were awed with the 2008 election of Barack H. Obama (1961–) to the Presidency of the United States of America as the Forty-Fourth President. Born in Hawaii of an African father from Kenya and a white American mother from Kansas, his multiracial background and upbringing characterized his life and his "Audacity of Hope," the title of his second book and best-selling memoir. A graduate of Columbia University and Harvard Law School, Obama moved to Chicago, which he adopted as his hometown and worked as a law professor at the University of Chicago teaching constitutional law while being active in the community as an organizer. He was eventually elected to the Illinois State Senate and soon after that elected to the United States Senate in 2004, the only African American in the United States Senate at that time and only the third black senator since the Reconstruction era. Obama's road to the White House was filled with staunch challenges, a hard-fought victory to the end over a determined Hillary Clinton for the nomination of the Democratic Party. With his wife, Michelle Obama, and their two daughters, his spirited call to the nation for "change" was a driving theme that, along with brilliant organizational tactics, intellectual strength, and his personal appeal—and the dire straits of a nation as a result of eight years of the Bush administration—combined to win for him the Presidency of the United States of America on November 4, 2008. During that campaign, Obama addressed the nation on the theme that was always present and that continued to resurface again and again: race in America. Included here is Barack Obama's speech, "A More Perfect Union," perhaps best known as "The Race Speech." Does he clarify the race problem in America for you? Do his words give you hope that race can be overcome in America? Do his words and his election symbolize a post-racial America, as some contend? Does what Barack Obama says about race mean something personally to you and your future in America?

"A More Perfect Union: The Race Speech"

Barack Obama

"We the people, in order to form a more perfect union."

Two hundred and twenty one years ago, in a hall that still stands across the street, a group of men gathered and, with these simple words, launched America's improbable experiment in democracy. Farmers and scholars; statesmen and patriots who had traveled across an ocean to escape tyranny and persecution finally made real their declaration of independence at a Philadelphia convention that lasted through the spring of 1787.

The document they produced was eventually signed but ultimately unfinished. It was stained by this nation's original sin of slavery, a question that divided the colonies and brought the convention to a stalemate until the founders chose to allow the slave trade to continue for at least twenty more years, and to leave any final resolution to future generations.

Of course, the answer to the slavery question was already embedded within our Constitution—a Constitution that had at its very core the ideal of equal citizenship under the law; a Constitution that promised its people liberty, and justice, and a union that could be and should be perfected over time.

And yet words on a parchment would not be enough to deliver slaves from bondage, or provide men and women of every color and creed their full rights and obligations as citizens of the United States. What would be needed were Americans in successive generations who were willing to do their part—through protests and struggle, on the streets and in the courts, through a civil war and civil disobedience and always at great risk— to narrow that gap between the promise of our ideals and the reality of their time.

This was one of the tasks we set forth at the beginning of this campaign—to continue the long march of those who came before us, a march for a more just, more equal, more free, more caring and more prosperous America. I chose to run for the presidency at this moment in history because I believe deeply that we cannot solve the challenges of our time unless we solve them together, unless we perfect our union by understanding that we may have different stories, but we hold common hopes; that we may not look the same and we may not have come from the same place, but we all want to move in the same direction—towards a better future for our children and our grandchildren.

This belief comes from my unyielding faith in the decency and generosity of the American people. But it also comes from my own American story.

I am the son of a black man from Kenya and a white woman from Kansas. I was raised with the help of a white grandfather who survived a Depression to serve in Patton's Army during World War II and a white grandmother who worked on a bomber assembly line at Fort Leavenworth while he was overseas. I've gone to some of the best schools in America and lived in one of the world's poorest nations. I am married to a black American who carries within her the blood of slaves and slaveowners—an inheritance we pass on to our two precious daughters. I have brothers, sisters, nieces, nephews, uncles and cousins, of every race and every hue, scattered across three continents, and for as long as I live, I will never forget that in no other country on Earth is my story even possible.

It's a story that hasn't made me the most conventional candidate. But it is a story that has seared into my genetic makeup the idea that this nation is more than the sum of its parts—that out of many, we are truly one.

Throughout the first year of this campaign, against all predictions to the contrary, we saw how hungry the American people were for this message of unity. Despite the temptation to view my candidacy through a purely racial lens, we won commanding victories in states with some of the whitest populations in the country. In South Carolina, where the Confederate Flag still flies, we built a powerful coalition of African Americans and white Americans.

This is not to say that race has not been an issue in the campaign. At various stages in the campaign, some commentators have deemed me either "too black" or "not black enough." We saw racial tensions bubble to the surface during the week before the South Carolina primary. The press has scoured every exit poll for the latest evidence of racial polarization, not just in terms of white and black, but black and brown as well. And yet, it has only been in the last couple of weeks that the discussion of race in this campaign has taken a particularly divisive turn.

On one end of the spectrum, we've heard the implication that my candidacy is somehow an exercise in affirmative action; that it's based solely on the desire of wide-eyed liberals to purchase racial reconciliation on the cheap. On the other end, we've heard my former pastor, Reverend Jeremiah Wright, use incendiary language to express views that have the potential not only to widen the racial divide, but views that denigrate both the greatness and the goodness of our nation and that rightly offend white and black alike.

I have already condemned, in unequivocal terms, the statements of Reverend Wright that have caused such controversy. For some, nagging questions remain. Did I know him to be an occasionally fierce critic of American domestic and foreign policy? Of course. Did I ever hear him make remarks that could be considered controversial while I sat in church? Yes. Did I strongly disagree with many of his political views? Absolutely—just as I'm sure many of you have heard remarks from your pastors, priests, or rabbis with which you strongly disagreed.

But the remarks that have caused this recent firestorm weren't simply controversial. They weren't simply a religious leader's effort to speak out against perceived injustice. Instead, they expressed a profoundly distorted view of this country—a view that sees white racism as endemic, and that elevates what is wrong with America above all that we know is right with America; a view that sees the conflicts in the Middle East as rooted primarily in the actions of stalwart allies like Israel, instead of emanating from the perverse and hateful ideologies of radical Islam.

As such, Reverend Wright's comments were not only wrong but divisive, divisive at a time when we need unity; racially charged at a time when we need to come together to solve a set of monumental problems—two wars, a terrorist threat, a falling economy, a chronic health care crisis and potentially devastating climate change; problems that are neither black or white or Latino or Asian, but rather problems that confront us all.

Given my background, my politics, and my professed values and ideals, there will no doubt be those for whom my statements of condemnation are not enough. Why associate myself with Reverend Wright in the first place, they may ask? Why not join another church? And I confess that if all that I knew of Reverend Wright were the snippets of those sermons that have run in an endless loop on the television and YouTube, or if Trinity United Church of Christ conformed to the caricatures being peddled by some commentators, there is no doubt that I would react in much the same way.

But the truth is, that isn't all that I know of the man. The man I met more than twenty years ago is a man who helped introduce me to my Christian faith, a man who spoke to me about our obligations to love one another, to care for the sick and lift up the poor. He is a man who served his country as a U.S. Marine, who has studied and lectured at some of the finest universities and seminaries in the country, and who for over thirty years led a church that serves the community by doing God's work here on Earth—by housing the homeless, ministering to the needy, providing day care services and scholarships and prison ministries, and reaching out to those suffering from HIV/AIDS.

In my first book, Dreams From My Father, I described the experience of my first service at Trinity:

> People began to shout, to rise from their seats and clap and cry out, a forceful wind carrying the reverend's voice up into the rafters.... And in that single note—hope!—I heard something else; at the foot of that cross, inside the thousands of churches across the city, I imagined the stories of ordinary black people merging with the stories of David and Goliath, Moses and Pharaoh, the Christians in the lion's den, Ezekiel's field of dry bones. Those stories—of survival, and freedom, and hope—became our story, my story; the blood that had spilled was our blood, the tears our tears; until this black church, on this bright day, seemed once more a vessel carrying the story of a people into future generations and into a larger world. Our trials and triumphs became at once unique and universal, black and more than black; in chronicling our journey, the stories and songs gave us a means to reclaim memories that we didn't need to feel shame about ... memories that all people might study and cherish and with which we could start to rebuild.

That has been my experience at Trinity. Like other predominantly black churches across the country, Trinity embodies the black community in its entirety—the doctor and the welfare mom, the model student and the former gang-banger. Like other black churches, Trinity's services are full of raucous laughter and sometimes bawdy humor. They are full of dancing, clapping, screaming and shouting that may seem jarring to the untrained ear. The church contains in full the kindness and cruelty, the fierce intelligence and the shocking ignorance, the struggles and successes, the love and, yes, the bitterness and bias that make up the black experience in America.

And this helps explain, perhaps, my relationship with Reverend Wright. As imperfect as he may be, he has been like family to me. He strengthened my faith, officiated my wedding, and baptized my children. Not once in my conversations with him have I heard him talk about any ethnic group in derogatory terms, or treat whites with whom he interacted with anything but courtesy and respect. He contains within him the contradictions—the good and the bad—of the community that he has served diligently for so many years.

I can no more disown him than I can disown the black community. I can no more disown him than I can my white grandmother—a woman who helped raise me, a woman who sacrificed again and again for me, a woman who loves me as much as she loves anything in this world, but a woman who once confessed her fear of black men who passed by her on the street, and who on more than one occasion has uttered racial or ethnic stereotypes that made me cringe. These people are a part of me. And they are a part of America, this country that I love.

Some will see this as an attempt to justify or excuse comments that are simply inexcusable. I can assure you it is not. I suppose the politically safe thing would be to move on from this episode and just hope that it fades into the woodwork. We can dismiss Reverend Wright as a crank or a demagogue, just as some have dismissed Geraldine Ferraro, in the aftermath of her recent statements, as harboring some deep-seated racial bias.

But race is an issue that I believe this nation cannot afford to ignore right now. We would be making the same mistake that Reverend Wright made in his offending sermons about America—to simplify and stereotype and amplify the negative to the point that it distorts reality.

The fact is that the comments that have been made and the issues that have surfaced over the last few weeks reflect the complexities of race in this country that we've never really worked through—a part of our union that we have yet to perfect. And if we walk away now, if we simply retreat into our respective corners, we will never be able to come together and solve challenges like health care, or education, or the need to find good jobs for every American.

Understanding this reality requires a reminder of how we arrived at this point. As William Faulkner once wrote, "The past isn't dead and buried. In fact, it isn't even past." We do not need to recite here the history of racial injustice in this country. But we do need to remind ourselves that so many of the disparities that exist in the African-American community today can be directly traced to inequalities passed on from an earlier generation that suffered under the brutal legacy of slavery and Jim Crow.

Segregated schools were, and are, inferior schools; we still haven't fixed them, fifty years after Brown v. Board of Education, and the inferior education they provided, then and now, helps explain the pervasive achievement gap between today's black and white students.

Legalized discrimination—where blacks were prevented, often through violence, from owning property, or loans were not granted to African-American business owners, or black homeowners could not access FHA mortgages, or blacks were excluded from unions, or the police force, or fire departments—meant that black families could not amass any meaningful wealth to bequeath to future generations. That history helps explain the wealth and income gap between black and white, and the concentrated pockets of poverty that persists in so many of today's urban and rural communities.

A lack of economic opportunity among black men, and the shame and frustration that came from not being able to provide for one's family, contributed to the erosion of black families—a problem that welfare policies for many years may have worsened. And the lack of basic services in so many urban black neighborhoods—parks for kids to play in, police walking the beat, regular garbage pick-up and building code enforcement—all helped create a cycle of violence, blight and neglect that continue to haunt us.

This is the reality in which Reverend Wright and other African Americans of his generation grew up. They came of age in the late fifties and early sixties, a time when segregation was still the law of the land and opportunity was systematically constricted. What's remarkable is not how many failed in the face of discrimination, but rather how many men and women overcame the odds; how many were able to make a way out of no way for those like me who would come after them.

But for all those who scratched and clawed their way to get a piece of the American Dream, there were many who didn't make it—those who were ultimately defeated, in one way or another, by discrimination. That legacy of defeat was passed on to future generations—those young men and increasingly young women who we see standing on street corners or languishing in our prisons, without hope or prospects for the future. Even for those blacks who did make it, questions of race, and racism, continue to define their worldview in fundamental ways. For the men and women of Reverend Wright's generation, the memories of humiliation and doubt and fear have not gone away; nor has the anger and the bitterness of those years.

That anger may not get expressed in public, in front of white co-workers or white friends. But it does find voice in the barbershop or around the kitchen table. At times, that anger is exploited by politicians, to gin up votes along racial lines, or to make up for a politician's own failings.

And occasionally it finds voice in the church on Sunday morning, in the pulpit and in the pews. The fact that so many people are surprised to hear that anger in some of Reverend Wright's sermons simply reminds us of the old truism that the most segregated hour in American life occurs on Sunday morning. That anger is not always productive; indeed, all too often it distracts attention from solving real problems; it keeps us from squarely facing our own complicity in our condition, and prevents the African-American community from forging the alliances it needs to bring about real change. But the anger is real; it is powerful; and to simply wish it away, to condemn it without understanding its roots, only serves to widen the chasm of misunderstanding that exists between the races.

In fact, a similar anger exists within segments of the white community. Most working- and middle-class white Americans don't feel that they have been particularly privileged by their race. Their experience is the immigrant experience—as far as they're concerned, no one's handed them anything, they've built it from scratch. They've worked hard all their lives, many times only to see their jobs shipped overseas or their pension dumped after a lifetime of labor.

They are anxious about their futures, and feel their dreams slipping away; in an era of stagnant wages and global competition, opportunity comes to be seen as a zero sum game, in which your dreams come at my expense. So when they are told to bus their children to a school across town; when they hear that an African American is getting an advantage in landing a good job or a spot in a good college because of an injustice that they themselves never committed; when they're told that their fears about crime in urban neighborhoods are somehow prejudiced, resentment builds over time.

Like the anger within the black community, these resentments aren't always expressed in polite company. But they have helped shape the political landscape for at least a generation. Anger over welfare and affirmative action helped forge the Reagan Coalition. Politicians routinely exploited fears of crime for their own electoral ends. Talk show hosts and conservative commentators built entire careers unmasking bogus claims of racism while dismissing legitimate discussions of racial injustice and inequality as mere political correctness or reverse racism.

Just as black anger often proved counterproductive, so have these white resentments distracted attention from the real culprits of the middle class squeeze; a corporate culture rife with inside dealing, questionable accounting practices, and short-term greed; a Washington dominated by lobbyists and special interests; economic policies that favor the few over the many. And yet, to wish away the resentments of white Americans, to label them as misguided or even racist, without recognizing they are grounded in legitimate concerns—this too widens the racial divide, and blocks the path to understanding.

This is where we are right now. It's a racial stalemate we've been stuck in for years. Contrary to the claims of some of my critics, black and white, I have never been so naïve as to believe that we can get beyond our racial divisions in a single election cycle, or with a single candidacy—particularly a candidacy as imperfect as my own.

But I have asserted a firm conviction—a conviction rooted in my faith in God and my faith in the American people—that working together we can move beyond some of our old racial wounds, and that in fact we have no choice if we are to continue on the path of a more perfect union.

For the African-American community, that path means embracing the burdens of our past without becoming victims of our past. It means continuing to insist on a full measure of justice in every aspect of American life. But it also means binding our particular grievances—for better health care, and better schools, and better jobs—to the larger aspirations of all Americans—the white woman struggling to break the glass ceiling, the white man whose been laid off, the immigrant trying to feed his family. And it means taking full responsibility for own lives—by demanding more from our fathers, and spending more time with our children, and reading to them, and teaching them that while they may face challenges and discrimination in their own lives, they must never succumb to despair or cynicism; they must always believe that they can write their own destiny.

Ironically, this quintessentially American—and yes, conservative—notion of self-help found frequent expression in Reverend Wright's sermons. But what my former pastor too often failed to understand is that embarking on a program of self-help also requires a belief that society can change.

The profound mistake of Reverend Wright's sermons is not that he spoke about racism in our society. It's that he spoke as if our society was static; as if no progress has been made; as if this country—a country that has made it possible for one of his own members to run for the highest office in the land and build a coalition of white and black Latino and Asian, rich and poor, young and old—is still irrevocably bound to a tragic past. But what we know—what we have seen—is that America can change. That is true genius of this nation. What we have already achieved gives us hope—the audacity to hope—for what we can and must achieve tomorrow.

In the white community, the path to a more perfect union means acknowledging that what ails the African-American community does not just exist in the minds of black people; that the legacy of discrimination—and current incidents of discrimination, while less overt than in the past—are real and must be addressed. Not just with words, but with deeds—by investing in our schools and our communities; by enforcing our civil rights laws and ensuring fairness in our criminal justice system; by providing this generation with ladders of opportunity that were unavailable for previous generations. It requires all Americans to realize that your dreams do not have to come at the expense of my dreams; that investing in the health, welfare, and education of black and brown and white children will ultimately help all of America prosper.

In the end, then, what is called for is nothing more, and nothing less, than what all the world's great religions demand—that we do unto others as we would have them do unto us. Let us be our brother's keeper, Scripture tells us. Let us be our sister's keeper. Let us find that common stake we all have in one another, and let our politics reflect that spirit as well.

For we have a choice in this country. We can accept a politics that breeds division, and conflict, and cynicism. We can tackle race only as spectacle—as we did in the OJ trial—or in the wake of tragedy, as we did in the aftermath of Katrina—or as fodder for the nightly news.

We can play Reverend Wright's sermons on every channel, every day and talk about them from now until the election, and make the only question in this campaign whether or not the American people think that I somehow believe or sympathize with his most offensive words. We can pounce on some gaffe by a Hillary supporter as evidence that she's playing the race card, or we can speculate on whether white men will all flock to John McCain in the general election regardless of his policies.

We can do that.

But if we do, I can tell you that in the next election, we'll be talking about some other distraction. And then another one. And then another one. And nothing will change.

That is one option. Or, at this moment, in this election, we can come together and say, "Not this time." This time we want to talk about the crumbling schools that are stealing the future of black children and white children and Asian children and Hispanic children and Native American children. This time we want to reject the cynicism that tells us that these kids can't learn; that those kids who don't look like us are somebody else's problem. The children of America are not those kids, they are our kids, and we will not let them fall behind in a 21st-century economy.

Not this time.

This time we want to talk about how the lines in the Emergency Room are filled with whites and blacks and Hispanics who do not have health care; who don't have the power on their own to overcome the special interests in Washington, but who can take them on if we do it together.

This time we want to talk about the shuttered mills that once provided a decent life for men and women of every race, and the homes for sale that once belonged to Americans from every religion, every region, every walk of life. This time we want to talk about the fact that the real problem is not that someone who doesn't look like you might take your job; it's that the corporation you work for will ship it overseas for nothing more than a profit.

This time we want to talk about the men and women of every color and creed who serve together, and fight together, and bleed together under the same proud flag. We want to talk about how to bring them home from a war that never should've been authorized and never should've been waged, and we want to talk about how we'll show our patriotism by caring for them, and their families, and giving them the benefits they have earned.

I would not be running for President if I didn't believe with all my heart that this is what the vast majority of Americans want for this country. This union may never be perfect, but generation after generation has shown that it can always be perfected. And today, whenever I find myself feeling doubtful or cynical about this possibility, what gives me the most hope is the next generation—the young people whose attitudes and beliefs and openness to change have already made history in this election.

There is one story in particularly that I'd like to leave you with today, a story I told when I had the great honor of speaking on Dr. King's birthday at his home church, Ebenezer Baptist, in Atlanta.

There is a young, twenty-three-year-old white woman named Ashley Baia who organized for our campaign in Florence, South Carolina. She had been working to organize a mostly African-American community since the beginning of this campaign, and one day she was at a roundtable discussion where everyone went around telling their story and why they were there. And Ashley said that when she was nine years old, her mother got cancer. And because she had to miss days of work, she was let go and lost her health care. They had to file for bankruptcy, and that's when Ashley decided that she had to do something to help her mom. She knew that food was one of their most expensive costs, and so Ashley convinced her mother that what she really liked and really wanted to eat more than anything else was mustard and relish sandwiches. Because that was the cheapest way to eat.

She did this for a year until her mom got better, and she told everyone at the roundtable that the reason she joined our campaign was so that she could help the millions of other children in the country who want and need to help their parents too.

Now Ashley might have made a different choice. Perhaps somebody told her along the way that the source of her mother's problems were blacks who were on welfare and too lazy to work, or Hispanics who were coming into the country illegally. But she didn't. She sought out allies in her fight against injustice.

Anyway, Ashley finishes her story and then goes around the room and asks everyone else why they're supporting the campaign. They all have different stories and reasons. Many bring up a specific issue. And finally they come to this elderly black man who's been sitting there quietly the entire time. And Ashley asks him why he's there. And he does not bring up a specific issue. He does not say health-care or the economy. He does not say education or the war. He does not say that he was there because of Barack Obama. He simply says to everyone in the room, "I am here because of Ashley."

"I'm here because of Ashley." By itself, that single moment of recognition between that young white girl and that old black man is not enough. It is not enough to give health care to the sick, or jobs to the jobless, or education to our children.

But it is where we start. It is where our union grows stronger. And as so many generations have come to realize over the course of the two hundred and twenty one years since a band of patriots signed that document in Philadelphia, that is where the perfection begins.

[18 March 2008]